The Possibility Machine

MUSIC IN AMERICAN LIFE

A list of books in the series appears at the end of this book.

The Possibility Machine

MUSIC AND MYTH IN LAS VEGAS

Edited by
JAKE JOHNSON

UNIVERSITY OF
ILLINOIS PRESS
Urbana, Chicago, and Springfield

1 2 3 4 5 C P 5 4 3 2 1
♾ This book is printed on acid-free paper.

This book was published with support from the Iberian and Latin American Music Fund and General Fund of the American Musicological Society, supported in part by the National Endowment for the Humanities and the Andrew W. Mellon Foundation.

Library of Congress Cataloging-in-Publication Data
Names: Johnson, Jake, 1984– editor.
Title: The possibility machine : music and myth in Las Vegas / edited by Jake Johnson.
Other titles: Music and myth in Las Vegas | Music in American life.
Description: Urbana : University of Illinois Press, [2023] | Series: Music in American life | Includes bibliographical references and index.
Identifiers: LCCN 2023008522 (print) | LCCN 2023008523 (ebook) | ISBN 9780252045417 (cloth) | ISBN 9780252087530 (paperback) | ISBN 9780252055010 (ebook)
Subjects: LCSH: Performing arts—Nevada—Las Vegas—History—20th century. | Entertainers—Nevada—Las Vegas—History—20th century. | Music trade—Nevada—Las Vegas. | Identity (Psychology)—Nevada—Las Vegas. | Las Vegas (Nev.)—History—20th century.
Classification: LCC F849.L35 P67 2023 (print) | LCC F849.L35 (ebook) | DDC 791/.09793/135—dc23/eng/20230306
LC record available at https://lccn.loc.gov/2023008522
LC ebook record available at https://lccn.loc.gov/2023008523

Contents

Preface

The great risk of a project like this is forgetting that the house always wins. There are far more performers, celebrities, and important musical values intersecting with Las Vegas than any single volume can adequately address. A lot of material was left on the cutting-room floor, and much regrettably.

The Possibility Machine gathers together a collection of chapters that skirts coverage in order to get at what I believe is the heart of how Las Vegas matters in the broader American psyche—its place in the heart of American risk taking, of belief in triumph and winning hands, its metonymic stand-in for fantasy and reinvention, and its ability to overflow into unsuspecting (and sometimes unwilling) places. Ultimately, this volume makes the case that the city's cheeky tagline was itself a fantastical myth. Whatever happens in Vegas has never simply stayed in Vegas.

Which is another way of saying that ideas worth having eventually spill the banks that hold them. This book took hold in part because so little scholarly attention had been given to the place of music in the city of Las Vegas. Our book is poised to remedy that inattention. But *The Possibility Machine* became worth fighting for to me because something about it feels risky, and I have come to admire the risk taker no matter the reason for the gamble.

One of my intellectual gambles is refusing the wet blanket. In my work on American musical theater, I take fantasy and belief on their own terms. This position runs counter to a particular habit of mind prevalent among academics and laypersons alike that snuffs out any spark of fantasy or belief with a cold splash of *there's no such thing*. I've realized that walking through the world needle-poised to burst every bubble you find only leaves you soaked and the world completely bubble free. And besides, I think these bubbles are important—what we believe in, and the fact of belief itself, matters in ways that often have nothing to do with what is real because what is real has never been enough. I wanted in this book to pivot my focus from American musical theater to what just might be the supreme incarnation of America's belief system: Las Vegas, that iconic city of second chances. Las Vegas seems so obvious. It bursts and flashes and surely stands for *something* in the minds of just about every American. Tired of intellectual dismissals and deconstructions of sites of fantasy and untruth, I suspected there was an opportunity to understand this machine of American possibility for what it was rather than what it was not. Truth is a puttering engine. I saw in Las Vegas a chance to figure out music's alchemy in the funny fuel that makes this country run, bubbles and all.

The fact of this book is something of a miracle. Composed and developed entirely during the COVID-19 pandemic and its accompanying shutdowns of archives, research travel, and the numerous resources books require to be made, *The Possibility Machine* came together with remarkable ease. I owe this entirely to the valor of these contributors who, when I came knocking on their doors with a weird message about belief and music in Las Vegas, said yes. Their ingenuity, creativity, adaptability, and willingness to work against the grain upped the ante. They believe in this project. I believe in them.

Outside of the contributors included in this volume, I want to acknowledge a few key players. For their enthusiasm at the start, this project owes a share to Bob Fink, Ray Knapp, and Mitchell Morris—three people who continue to be some of my life's favorite and most vibrant characters. I remain grateful for my editor Laurie Matheson at the University of Illinois Press whose curiosity and creative thinking seem to know no bounds. My colleagues and students at Oklahoma City University stayed in good spirits about my Las Vegas ramblings and helped me keep this project about fantasy honest. My front porch gave me a place to reflect. The baristas and regulars at Stella Nova did their part in keeping the coffee and the ideas flowing. Unnumbered clean windows made everyday moments remarkable again.

And above all a book like this exists because BrieAnn, Cora, and Magnolia make me feel like just about anything is possible. To them and to whomever and whatever steers your life toward possibility: *Viva!*

The Possibility Machine

Introduction

Flash!—Splash

JAKE JOHNSON

This is a book of stories about one of America's most storied places. Las Vegas remains in the minds and hearts of many a machine of possibility: the fantastical realm where magic is real and risks are welcome. It is a place unlike any other, yet also has become so familiar and approachable throughout the years that its power and potency for the not-yet becomes something of a gamble itself. Vegas radiates and explodes outward. It can't help it—as Bruce Bégout puts it, Las Vegas was "born to radiate, to flash, to explode."[1] And with that flash of radiant possibility follows a sonic boom that confirms the power of believing in something all while echoing the dangers of falling for it all.

Which is why in the background of this book is the myth of the flying and falling Icarus. In a flash, the feathered machine built by his father, Daedalus, failed Icarus when he flew too close to the sun. Icarus was warned; his fall was swift and mighty. But he also couldn't help it. The sun's radiant power held him captive. Icarus became an addict—destroyed by the very thing that gave his life possibility.

It's not his failure to escape this world that draws me into Icarus's orbit but rather the machine that made it possible for him to try. Icarus on his sun-obsessed flight, not yet singed or sinking into the sea, is moving toward another world. His flight is about the not-yet. His machine makes the not-yet feel possible. And isn't that the core of Icarus's story? After all, Icarus was never really a bird; he was only pretending, a belief made possible by a machine of feathers and wax that for a moment spun three 7s. Icarus tried. *Flash!* Icarus fell. *Splash.*

Las Vegas is to me America's possibility machine. Pretend and make-believe make up the feathered engine of this city. It is a place where a community of believers gathers under the radiant power of possibility, yes, but Vegas by now is also an *idea* that races outward into the heart of American life and beyond. It would be a great mistake to see in Icarus only a metaphor for how possibility and greed and belief in a different world ahead can lead to disaster. The world as it is is too much with us, as Wordsworth warned. In a moment seemingly poor in possibility, belief in a not-yet world is not nothing. Icarus is an emblem of triumph for me, as is Las Vegas. Both Icarus and Vegas are reminders that just because the house often wins doesn't mean the game isn't worth playing.

But in this book, I'd like to keep an eye on the other shapely figures in the frame. We see Daedalus the father in real time becoming, as Ovid would later describe it, a father no more. He continues to soar as his son falls into the sea. He continues to live as the one who heard the splash that often comes with risking it all. I'm compelled by Bruegel's *Landscape with the Fall of Icarus* that zooms out to take into account the everyday nature of dashed hopes and failure as well as the extraordinary feat its main characters knew it to be. "How everything turns away / Quite leisurely from the disaster," W. H. Auden notes of Bruegel's painting. "The plowman may / Have heard the splash, the forsaken cry, / But for him it was not an important failure."[2] It's the ear indifferent to possibility for me—that's the real myth I want to explore.

I'd like in these pages to follow Bruegel's gaze and foreground the plowman's upturned ear. The sonic consequences of pretend are not always an important failure for us. With all the attention on the dramatic flash of Icarus's fall, not enough has been paid to the boom of its splash. As you'll see, the authors in this book are less interested in readers forming a judgment about deception or flights of fancy common to Icarus and Las Vegas than they are invested in knowing better what happens when we listen to it. A more inclusive world starts to take shape when we do. As you'll see in the chapters ahead, in many ways the sounds splashing out of Las Vegas draw attention to the harsh reality of societal structures in the everyday world that have oppressed and belittled people on the basis of sexual orientation, age, class, race, and more. Vegas offers an alternative for those who can hear it. This book therefore takes the position of the listening Daedalus, bearing sonic witness to the rush of air and crash of wave inherent to the realm of imagination, and calls for the attention of all fellow plowmen that the sound of gamble is worth a glance from our labors.

Flash!

Our story begins with Mormons. They trekked through America's desert middle, fleeing their swampy river town Nauvoo, Illinois, in 1844 only to settle next to an enormous, briny body of water that can never quench your thirst.

With an average depth of only thirteen feet, Utah's Great Salt Lake is a body of surfaces with little mystery beneath—"the liquid lie of the West," as Terry Tempest Williams put it.[3]

Fair enough. But the truth is no less fluid. The journey is what matters so much in Mormonism. Its founder, Joseph Smith, came from a family whose side hustle included searching for hidden treasures.[4] The golden plates that would eventually be translated into the Book of Mormon must have caught in the sun the twinkle of treasure and possibility any Icarus would recognize—and Joseph Smith is as much an American Icarus as there ever has been. Magic and magical worldviews can't help but be part of the Mormon story. The same is true for America itself. Searching for more possible truth in the West, Mormons set out to colonize a broad territory of America's sun-burned valleys ("Power needs solitude," Franco Ferrarotti reminds us, "and feels good only in deserts"), and were the first long-term settlers to try to make Las Vegas home.[5] They may also offer the first recorded example of Vegas entertainment. Their initial optimism for settling this vacant desert meadow was as catchy as this jingle from 1856:

> Our labors are here on the Vegas,
> The Indians are friendly and kind,
> And thus we have nothing to plague us
> As we're all of one heart and one mind.
> 'Tis true our red neighbors are hungry,
> Yet all we can spare them we give.
> And thus they quite seldom are angry
> While here on the Vegas we live.[6]

The cheeriness was premature. The Las Vegas Mormon colony lasted less than two years. *Flash!* Splash.

But Mormons returned and continue to return to Las Vegas, helping establish and sustain it as a mecca of possibility. They are strange bedfellows, Mormons and this city. Yet Mormons seem to have been a part of Las Vegas's every chapter. Mob bosses put Mormons in charge of their casinos, knowing they wouldn't chase their women and wouldn't drink their alcohol. When in 1966 Howard Hughes retreated into the top floor of the Desert Inn, he relied on savvy Mormon lawyers to strategically buy up the entire city. Mormon legal teams continue to aid casino magnates and corporations in finding water and fossil fuels farther and farther away, even at the risk of depleting reservation reservoirs in nearby Arizona. Mormons may seem out of place in a city like Las Vegas, but look askance and Mormonism's thriving there makes as much sense as anything else. Las Vegas may well be the most American city, as Dave Hickey claims, so it is that members of "the American religion," as Harold Bloom dubbed Mormonism, are there too.[7] In this desert town, Mormons, mobsters, and the U.S. military's atomic fantasies all share, in Michael Ventura's words, a "highly developed sense of Anything—a sense of Anything that felt a kinship to the place itself, as though this desert were calling to them."[8] A possibility machine.

Today, one in ten Las Vegans is Mormon, which might make Mormonism the tithe Las Vegas pays for being Las Vegas: fantastical, hopeful, out of touch, evangelist of other worlds. In 1989 the Mormon Church built an eighty-thousand-square-foot temple a dozen miles from the Strip. It is in this temple, like hundreds of others around the world, where devout Mormons perform and enact the great drama of salvation for themselves and their ancestors.

Unsurprisingly, then, Mormon performers have made a cozy home in Las Vegas. The brotherly sensation The Osmonds, their sibling television spinoff, *Donny and Marie*, and Gladys Knight's conversion to Mormonism in 1997 and subsequent relocation to Vegas give the city a weirdly sugary flavor of Mormonism. Newer generations of Mormon performers grew from Las Vegas, including Brandon Flowers of The Killers and Dan Reynolds of Imagine Dragons, and others, like electronic-music sensation Kaskade, have developed a lasting professional relationship with a city caught within Mormonism's orbit that nonetheless seems in a separate universe from whatever Mormonism appears to be. If Vegas was invented by the Mob and the highway, as Dave Hickey liked to say, then Mormons provided the mixtape.[9]

It's a fitting start to Las Vegas, Mormonism is. I want to reflect on these musical fantasies because Mormons have proven themselves really clever in making music work for their world-building enterprises. Mormonism's mystical (and not a little dose of do-it-yourself Americana) variations of godliness—where God was once a ho-hum human and ho-hum humans are simply Gods in waiting—give reality not even a second glance in its pursuit toward the otherworldly.

And Las Vegas is maybe as otherworldly as modern America gets—that "hard white empty core of the world" is how Joan Didion bluntly put it.[10] *It has no memory*, Bruce Bégout writes with his characteristic hard edge.[11] Constantly in the present tense, Las Vegas shows no remorse for the world around it because it lacks the language to even evaluate loss—a "futureless catastrophe" where futures are won and lost nevertheless.[12] Mormonism likewise rushes toward the comedic resolve in both theology and culture. Las Vegas and Mormons can no longer be seen as undiametrical. They are dialectical. As emblems of America, they belong to one another's fantasy of a world unburdened with what is perfectly impossible.

Splash

At least since Mormons sang about their Vegas meadow, music has been a part of Las Vegas's mystique—sometimes in obvious ways, but often not. I'm thinking of *The Twilight Zone*'s 1960 episode "The Fever" where a clergyman visiting Vegas with his wife begins hearing a voice calling from within a slot machine, leading to a maniacal and tragic fall from grace. Or the true crime story of Guy McAfee, head of the Los Angeles Police Department vice squad who alerted Las Vegas crime bosses of police raids by whistling the tune "Listen to the Mockingbird" into the telephone.[13] There's also no lack of commentary on the *noisiness* of Las Vegas: a "unique bombardment of the senses," as Tom Wolfe understood it. "The crowd and band sounds are not very extraordinary, of course. But Las Vegas' Muzak is. Muzak pervades Las Vegas from the time you walk into the airport upon landing to the last time you leave the casinos. It is piped out to the swimming pool. It is in the drugstores. It is as if there were a communal fear that someone, somewhere in Las Vegas, was going to be left with a totally vacant minute on his hands."[14] Or the constant sound of money changing hands, as Pete Earley describes:

> Bells ring, coins tumble into chrome trays, but it is the continuous rhythm made by these slot machines' electronic spinning wheels that permeates the air. *Duh-duh-em-da-a-lop! Duh-duh-em-da-a-lop!* A hundred times each minute. A million times each hour. *Duh-duh-em-da-a-lop! Duh-duh-em-da-a-lop!* . . . Only one noise can challenge it, and that's the metallic snapping that issues from video poker machines dealing their picture-tube cards. *Snap, snap, snap, snap, snap! Duh-duh-em-da-a-lop! Snap, snap, snap, snap, snap! Duh-duh-em-da-a-lop!* Cruise the Strip with your car windows open and the radio switched off early any morning and the ringing of spinning wheels and snapping of electronic cards is all around you. It is the city's unofficial theme song.[15]

Music and sound, as these passages illustrate, make up a busy and loud soundscape for Vegas largely because busyness and loudness have proven useful for making money. Big stars draw crowds into casinos where—*oh why not?*—many then round out the evening with a little gambling. The sonic atmosphere of casinos is carefully calculated, as Naomi Waltham-Smith notes, to keep guests entranced, at the machines, and unaware of passing time.[16] Listening to Vegas means coming to terms with (and then listening past) the flashiness of Vegas—fortunes won and lost in a flash, the belief in something better flowers and dies in a flash, the world itself here and gone in a nearby radiant flash of military might. When The New Frontier labeled Elvis the "Atomic Powered Singer," it was indicative of the sonic boom inside the ears of this city of fantasy, a terrifying reminder that, as Judith Nies points out, "Las Vegas is actually the most sophisticated military border town in the world, a shadow capital for the planet's largest military power."[17]

But listening to Vegas ought to be more than using the ears to deconstruct its fantastical mirage. It has become a scholarly habit of mind to rush toward eliminating untruth and pointing hastily toward the entrapments of late-stage capitalism, the inherent emptiness and ugliness of postmodern this-and-that. While these are fair critiques—and there is plenty left to be said for places like Vegas where deceit runs rampant—such a tact is not what I have planned here. I am interested in holding space for belief. To my mind, Las Vegas is a radiant emblem that America believes in *something*, even if it is that persistent dream of something for nothing. And it is not nothing in an age of disenchantment that people believe in something—anything—at all. Success and fortunes, for better or for worse, are intimately tied to America as a founding religion. What happens, then, whenever we listen to how that religion's engine purrs? What can we say about American possibility whenever we hear it working under the harsh desert sun? How do we think differently about the rises and falls of the American Icarus whenever we stop to listen?

This book therefore hopes not to deconstruct what might seem frivolous about Las Vegas (or America for that matter), but rather to celebrate, take time with, and hold space for the fact of belief. Las Vegas remains a destination of deception; rather than pulling back the curtain to show the machinery making the magic, *The Possibility Machine* hopes instead to illuminate—to *flash*—in wonder the many ways the world builds and is made more possible through its operative fictions. A better world starts with believing in the possibility of a better world, no matter how selfishly that not-yet world is constructed. I'm willing to take a gamble on possibility. That's the risk and the reward that this book puts on the table.

The Landscape of This Book

The Possibility Machine is organized as a collection of essays designed to be read alongside and against one another. Vegas is a big idea. I chose to make this volume about that idea, about how the *idea* of Vegas relies on music and sound in significant ways, rather than a survey of the most important interlocutors of this desert town. As a result, a lot of significant parts of this city and its musical life get short shrift here. While major headliners like Elvis Presley, Frank Sinatra, and Liberace figure into these pages, other equally meteoric stars are notably and regrettably absent. But the balance struck here is not about coverage. The question these pages sort out and toss about is not about Las Vegas. Not really. What *The Possibility Machine* hopes to ask is this: What is music's role in crafting unreality in America? Las Vegas epitomizes so much of American optimism and clarifies the most strident lies about itself. It seems that whatever is happening in Vegas sits right at the heart of whatever it is that keeps America believing in something.

The nineteen chapters in this volume cover a wide range of personalities, ideas, and disciplinary interventions, speaking to the truly far-reaching and intersectional value of Las Vegas in the minds and practices of many scholarly communities. Chapters were streamlined and most kept short. I settled on what I am calling "flash" chapters—short bursts of ideas whose radiant energy speaks both to their brevity as well as to Las Vegas's atomic legacies. Icarus and this city are in many ways birds of a feather. Whatever Vegas is, it happens fast and it can be brutal. *Flash!* Splash.

The book is divided into six parts that might be read atomically (as in, piece by piece) or, as I secretly hope, in the order provided. Each section analyzes Vegas from a particular mythological or fantastical angle. Part One, "The Road to Vegas," gives background on the city's early years and how music and musicians played into its developing image throughout America. In "On the Edge of the Desert," Robert Fink charts a byway between Los Angeles and Las Vegas that reflects on the edges of reality, and how one fantastical desert city seeks refuge from the burdens of its own utopia in the arms of another fantastical desert city. Michael M. Reinhard's chapter on opera diva Helen Traubel's controversial performances in Las Vegas draws a bead on illusions of class and high art in America. And Janis McKay considers the changing and challenging work life of Las Vegas band musicians throughout the twentieth century in her chapter "It Was Better When the Mob Ran the Town."

Part Two, "Overheard," turns up the volume on Vegas magic and mystique, exploring how music often plays an invisible, inaudible role in sustaining the powerful tension between belief and disbelief. In "Music as Misdirection," Jason Leddington builds a connection between Vegas magic shows and musical cues, asking us to consider music as a metric of otherworldliness. In her chapter on Cirque du Soleil performances on the Strip, Lynda Paul shows how unseen live musicians help to enforce the mystery of virtual, unseen worlds crafted on stage. Cassaundra Rodriguez and Celine Ayala then turn our attention to the bonds of musicianship among communities who call Vegas home. Their chapter, "*Pura Alegría*: Young Adult Musicians Learning Mariachi in Schools and Participating in the Las Vegas Mariachi Scene," serves as a reminder of the many forms of music making that happen outside of the Las Vegas Strip and the special place mariachi holds among communities living in a city of second chances.

Part Three, "Second Chances," explores the powerful spirit of reinvention Las Vegas offers aging celebrities, mirroring back to guests the timeless and ageless inoculation Vegas seems to provide against the outside world. Arianne Johnson Quinn's chapter on British entertainer and playwright Noël Coward's four-week residency in Vegas historicizes midcentury American sensibilities toward taste, respectability, and the boundaries of highbrow culture, while Brian F. Wright's chapter on Elvis Presley challenges presumptions that the singer's later years in Vegas were somehow less authentic or less productive than his early career, making the case for the significant role the city played in Elvis's successes by calling out the elitist and classist biases that distorted his contemporary reception.

And finally, Jessica A. Holmes and Michael Kinney take the Vegas residencies of Cher and Céline Dion as opportunities to reconsider the spectacle of women aging and to ask how Las Vegas reframes the narrative of decline so prevalent elsewhere.

Las Vegas's virility and virtuosity are at the heart of Part Four, "Virtuoso Fantastique," which asks how fantasies of sexual prowess, personality, and democracy itself get caught up within musical values inherent to Las Vegas. In "Viva Viagra: Vegas, Elvis, and a 'Little Blue Pill,'" James Deaville and Kirstin Bews explore how pharmaceutical company Pfizer co-opted narratives and emblems of masculinity, power, and virility common to Las Vegas in marketing its erectile-dysfunction medication Viagra. Sam Murray's chapter builds a widened analytical lens to examine how extramusical and unscripted components of Céline Dion's Vegas residency lend themselves to parody and satire in such a way that spills the unreality of Las Vegas into the everyday world. Pheaross Graham then connects Liberace's pianism and musicianship to fantasies of Las Vegas. With a close analysis of one of Liberace's medleys, Graham suggests Liberace and Vegas coconstruct a fantastical world that is accessible and gratifying but ultimately built only of surfaces—an act of inclusion with significant consequence to American values of democracy.

Part Five, "Making Book" shows how various Las Vegas musicians and musical establishments took a gamble with their identity, giving in turn the permission audiences needed (or took as needed) to explore other versions of themselves than what they presented outside of Vegas. Arreanna Rostosky's chapter, "Comedy Tonight: Broadway Musicals on the Las Vegas Strip," sees the growing relationship between Broadway and Vegas casinos as indicative of a shared sensibility toward spectacle, entertainment, and fantasy at the heart of America's musical establishments. Laura Risk then documents the legacy of African American jazz and classical violinist Ginger Smock, whose career in Las Vegas spanned the 1950s to the Musicians' Union strike of 1989, and demonstrates the proactive public archiving required to draw attention to the challenges of gender, race, and age facing musicians like Smock. Louis Niebur's chapter, "'For Adult Audiences Only': A History of LGBTQ Performers on the Las Vegas Stage," then shows how LGBTQ artists on Vegas stages presented alternative sexualities through same-gendered song dedications, costuming, and modes of jazz and popular music performance that contradicted their assumed gender presentation, offering audiences a chance to experience, however vicariously, different kinds of gender and sexuality.

And finally, Part Six, "Leaving Vegas" displaces Vegas itself to show how the *idea* of Vegas travels broadly and widely to other parts of the country. Joanna Dee Das and Maddie House-Tuck compare the tourist destinations of Branson, Missouri, and Las Vegas—two cities often considered vastly different—to argue that they share a reliance on celebrity impersonation to stage visions of the American Dream. Kelly Kessler's chapter then explores how television shows emanating from Las Vegas allowed Vegas to become displaced from its geographical space and erotics and transform into a valued ethos of energy, sparkle, and sex-lite, just right for a developing television industry and a shifting American culture. In "Representation and Value in Michael Daugherty's Las Vegas Works," Laura Dallman analyzes Daugherty's eight contemporary classical works that center on Las Vegas. Dallman suggests that by putting Las Vegas on display in a "classical" setting, Daugherty entangles the essence of Las Vegas with the implied values of the concert hall, thus forcing listeners to reconsider values associated with classical music performance. And in the volume's final chapter, Carlo Lanfossi narrates a 2014 encounter with artist Marta Becket and the opera house she created in the middle of Death Valley. Bookending Robert Fink's opening chapter taking us to Las Vegas, Lanfossi's chapter pulls focus to the journey away from Vegas and asks how the magical surrealism seeps into some of the least suspecting places along the road home. This final section highlights how the migrating idea of Vegas questions how, exactly, Vegas continues to radiate and echo beyond its desert home—to you and you and you.

And that's really the story here. As Bruce Bégout reminds us, "We are all inhabitants of Las Vegas, however far away we are from southern Nevada."[18] This story is about all of us. So take a gamble. Up the ante. Pull the one-armed bandit and see what Fate rewards you. Step into an air-conditioned time machine where aging performers are young again, where belief in possibility is a common vocabulary, and where sound makes the magic work. Be fooled. Believe in more than disbelief. Look up from the plowing. Watch for the flash. Don't forget to listen for the splash.

Notes

1. Bruce Bégout, *Zeropolis: The Experience of Las Vegas* (London: Reaktion, 2004), 18.
2. W. H. Auden, "Musée des Beaux Arts."
3. Terry Tempest Williams, *Refuge: An Unnatural History of Family and Place* (New York: Vintage Books, 1991), 5.
4. See D. Michael Quinn, *Early Mormonism and the Magic World View* (Salt Lake City: Signature Books, 1998).
5. Franco Ferrarotti, "The Destiny of Reason and the Paradox of the Sacred," *Social Research* 46, no. 4 (1979): 654.
6. *Deseret News*, November 27, 1852.
7. Dave Hickey, "A Home in the Neon," in *Air Guitar: Essays on Art and Democracy* (Los Angeles: Art Issues Press, 1997), 24; Harold Bloom, *The American Religion: The Emergence of the Post-Christian Nation* (New York: Simon & Schuster, 1992).

8. Michael Ventura, "Las Vegas: The Odds on Anything," in *Literary Las Vegas: The Best Writing about America's Most Fabulous City*, ed. Mike Tronnes (New York: Henry Holt, 1995), 170.

9. Dave Hickey, "Dialectical Utopias," *Harvard Design Magazine*, no. 4 (1998).

10. Joan Didion, *Play It as It Lays* (New York: Farrar, Straus & Giroux, 1970), 162.

11. Bégout, *Zeropolis*, 21.

12. James Howard Kunstler, *The City in Mind: Meditations on the Urban Condition* (New York: Free Press, 2001), 142–43.

13. Larry Gragg, *Bright Light City: Las Vegas in Popular Culture* (Lawrence: University Press of Kansas, 2013), 61.

14. Tom Wolfe, *The Kandy-Kolored Tangerine-Flake Streamline Baby* (New York: Macmillan, 1965), 7.

15. Pete Earley, *Super Casino: Inside the "New" Las Vegas* (New York: Bantam Books, 2000), 34.

16. Naomi Waltham-Smith, "The Sonic *Habitués* of the Strip: Listening in Las Vegas," *Sound Studies* 3, no. 2 (2017): 115–33.

17. Quoted in Gragg, *Bright Light City*, 142; Judith Nies, *Unreal City: Las Vegas, Black Mesa, and the Fate of the West* (New York: Nation Books, 2014), 8.

18. Bégout, *Zeropolis*, 12.

PART I

The Road to Vegas

In tedious exile now too long detain'd,
Daedalus languish'd for his native land:
The sea foreclos'd his flight; yet thus he said:
Tho' Earth and water in subjection laid,
O cruel Minos, thy dominion be,
We'll go thro' air; for sure the air is free.
Then to new arts his cunning thought applies,
And to improve the work of Nature tries.
A row of quils in gradual order plac'd,
Rise by degrees in length from first to last;
As on a cliff th' ascending thicket grows,
Or, different reeds the rural pipe compose.
Along the middle runs a twine of flax,
The bottom stems are joyn'd by pliant wax.
Thus, well compact, a hollow bending brings
The fine composure into real wings.

1

On the Edge of the Desert

ROBERT FINK

> We were somewhere around Barstow on the edge of the desert when the drugs began to take hold. I remember saying something like "I feel a bit lightheaded; maybe you should drive . . ." And suddenly there was a terrible roar all around us and the sky was full of what looked like huge bats, all swooping and screeching and diving around the car, which was going about a hundred miles an hour with the top down to Las Vegas. And a voice was screaming: "Holy Jesus! What are these goddamn animals?"
>
> —Hunter S. Thompson, *Fear and Loathing in Las Vegas: A Savage Journey to the Heart of the American Dream*

An Island on the Land

Let's begin, not *in* Las Vegas, but on the way there. We're on our way from Los Angeles, and it's shaping up to be a long, strange trip. The date is 1971, in the first days of the new I-15 freeway, successor to Route 91, itself upgraded to an interstate highway in 1926 from the oiled dirt and gravel of the older Arrowhead Trail for motorists, which shadowed the right-of-way of the existing Los Angeles & Salt Lake Railroad, whose turn-of-the-century tracks were laid alongside the wagon ruts of the early-nineteenth-century Mormon Road, a migration route approximating the southern stretch of the original Old Spanish Trail from colonial Nuevo Mexico through Nevada and Alta California to the Pacific.

Adventurers have been sailing restlessly back and forth across this stretch of desert landscape for almost a half a millennium. The influential California journalist Carey McWilliams once attempted to explain the peculiar isolation of midcentury Los Angeles by calling it "an island on the land."[1] An entertainment capital cut off from the rest of California (and indeed the country) by mountains and deserts, it functions as the end point of a resort archipelago, throwing versions of itself far into the arid hinterland. At the other end of the chain is the mythic island of Deseret, a.k.a. Salt Lake City. In between are a series of smaller atolls: Borrego Springs, Palm Desert, Palm Springs, Desert Hot Springs, Joshua Tree, Twentynine Palms, and, of course, Las Vegas.

Strip to Strip

It's arguable that, as he headed east from Barstow toward the Nevada border, "gonzo" journalist Raoul Duke, a.k.a. Hunter S. Thompson, who'd rented his big red convertible from a garage on Hollywood's Sunset Strip, hadn't yet fully left LA and its sprawling auto-driven culture. Consider a classic piece of Southern California car-centered postmodern art like Andrew Holmes's *Golden Hour* (1990), a video installation that consists of twelve simultaneous two-hour streams, each captured by training a camera on a characteristic LA roadside vista. One such monitored the back side of a billboard on the Sunset Strip; another "was made by mounting a camera on the passenger seat of a car which made its way through Death Valley to Las Vegas."[2]

This view, functionally equivalent to the one from Thompson's red convertible, construes the road to Las Vegas, and by extension its famous Strip, as simply an extension of the original Strip, the stretch of Sunset Boulevard that passes through what is now the city of West Hollywood but was for most of the twentieth century an unincorporated section of Los Angeles County. It was thus part of LA's internal desert frontier, its own Wild West, where sheriff's deputies who looked like cowboys selectively patrolled the scrub-covered hills behind a series of gambling dens and nightclubs owned by the Mob. One mobbed-up entertainment Strip bequeathed the other a pack of Hollywood celebrities as both star performers and bit players, but nobody expected the dusty little stretch of unincorporated county land south of Las Vegas to eat the whole LA entertainment scene. Stars like Sinatra and Elvis continued to make movies in LA, but they increasingly preferred to perform and party on the other Strip, as celebrities had always done on the eastern peripheries of Southern California, safely beyond the "thirty-mile zone" where gossip reporters trolled for stories and morals clauses were enforced. By 1971 the party was over in LA, and the Sunset Strip was filled with kids playing at rock 'n' roll, pretending to be hip(pies), and providing the necessary cannon fodder for clubs and cults. All the grown-ups had already left for where the real money was.

Learning from Las Vegas (What It Learned from Los Angeles)

The Sunset Strip also appears to have given Las Vegas its distinctive visual style. In the early 1970s, the postmodern wing of the East Coast architectural establishment, led by Robert Venturi, Denise Scott Brown, and a posse of Yale graduate students, proclaimed they had been "learning from Las Vegas," by which they meant the Las Vegas casino strip as a set of industrial-grade architectural signs on the edge of the desert, big and strong enough to be apprehended from behind the wheel of a speeding car. But, one might ask, where had Las Vegas itself picked up that trick?

Venturi and Scott Brown hint at the answer while twitting architects of public space who pine after the Italian Renaissance while looking down their noses at Bellagio and Caesars Palace: "Architects have been bewitched by a single element of the Italian landscape: the piazza. Its traditional, pedestrian-scaled, and intricately enclosed space is easier to take than the spatial sprawl of Route 66 and Los Angeles."[3] As they note, it was an LA pop artist, Ed Ruscha, who had published the first systematic treatment of strip architecture, a long foldout book of photos from 1966, *Every Building on the Sunset Strip.*[4]

The Vegas Strip is thus the epitome of both stylistic eclecticism and sprawl, the two defining features of midcentury LA as a built environment. Or, at least it *was*. It often comes as a surprise to outsiders to learn that contemporary Los Angeles contains some of the densest urban neighborhoods in the United States. The Vegas Strip has been densifying, too, since real-estate speculation replaced more traditional forms of gambling as the single largest engine of growth in Clark County. In what local historian Eugene Moehring presents as proof that all cities "normalize" as they grow, Las Vegas, once a resort outpost of Los Angeles defined by the anarchic values of the unincorporated Strip, turned its own Strip into a shinier simulacrum of the LA developer's dream: "As the Strip city slowly began to emerge at midcentury, each new resort on the highway and each new expansion of an existing property exerted a multiplier effect on the lands beyond, raising their value and transforming them into sites for residential subdivisions, apartment complexes, office parks, commercial centers, and suburban resorts. The once empty desert now became a canvas where entrepreneurial developers could work their magic."[5]

The other precedent for Las Vegas as a built space is the theme park, also, thanks to Walt Disney, a quintessentially Southern California invention. Sometime in the late 1980s—as more and more visitors chose not to gamble, but to eat, shop, and stroll up and down the Strip, where they could enjoy the kitschy architecture and street-facing shows of water and light—wider sidewalks and a monorail (O, Disneyland!) began to eat away at the frictionless, car-centric mode of circulation that had once so impressed visitors from the East. Normalization theory also holds that as Las Vegas turned into a "regular" postindustrial city, other cities would come to resemble it. The new pedestrianized Strip provided a model of pleasurable, totally controlled urban circulation that, unlike the elaborate "sidewalk ballet" of the traditional city neighborhood described by activist Jane Jacobs, could be prefabricated by top-down coalitions of urban planners and entertainment conglomerates.[6] By the end of the 1990s, Ada Louise Huxtable, doyenne of American architecture critics, could argue at book length that a lucrative fusion of Disneyland and Vegas, underpinned by what she decried as "the architecture of illusion," had become *the* distinctive American contribution to urban architecture: "This remarkable marriage of technologically based and shrewdly programmed artificial experience in a manufactured and managed environment, for a real-life substitute of controlled and pricey pleasures, is a totally American product."[7]

Rumblings in Aztlán

Returning to the desert's edge, outside Barstow: Why was Hunter S. Thompson going to Las Vegas, anyway? The story has multiple layers. Ostensibly, this was a working trip: Thompson, who'd once made a small splash with a scabrous cover story for *Scanlan's Monthly* about, loosely, the grotesque, decadent whiteness of the Kentucky Derby, had been hired by *Sports Illustrated* to cover the Mint 400, a desert road race sponsored by Del Webb's casino of the same name.

Thompson was in range of this dumb little story because he was working on a bigger piece of real journalism set in Chicano Los Angeles. He and his comrade Oscar Acosta were investigating the "accidental" death of journalist Ruben Salazar in the aftermath of a huge antiwar rally in East LA on August 29, 1970. Salazar had been killed when a sheriff's deputy fired a tear-gas projectile into a crowded bar, and, as Thompson's eventual article for *Rolling Stone* makes clear, the level of racial paranoia on both sides of the color line made it unsafe for Acosta, a well-known figure in the Chicano movement, to be seen talking to any kind of journalist, let alone a gringo radical with ties to the hippie counterculture.[8] Suitably enough, the road they took from LA to Vegas wound through the heart of Aztlán, the mythical territory surrendered to settler colonialism under both Spanish and American empires. When the resort archipelago was formed, almost all of its outposts, from Salt Lake City to the Pacific, were white islands in a mestizo sea.

Hunter Thompson was always darkly fascinated by toxic whiteness; a large part of his "gonzo" journalism shtick was to take drug-fueled performances of bullet-headed redneck conservatism so far out that they became both satire and bitter commentary on the twisted mores of Nixon-era white America. Las

Vegas was his perfect foil, filled with the casual racism of a high-roller economy based on service and surveillance:

> "Where's your friend?" they asked, while we waited.
> "What friend?"
> "The big spic."
> "Look," I said, "I'm a Doctor of Journalism. You'd never catch me hanging around this place with a goddamn spic."
> They laughed. "Then what about *this*?" they said. And they confronted me with a big photograph of me and my attorney at a table in the floating bar.
> I shrugged. "That's not me," I said. "That's a guy named Thompson. He works for *Rolling Stone* . . . a really vicious, crazy kind of person. And that guy sitting next to him is a hit man for the Mafia in Hollywood. Shit, have you *studied* this photograph? What kind of a maniac would roam around wearing *one black glove*?"
> "We noticed that," they said. "Where is he *now*?"
> I shrugged. "He moves around pretty fast," I said. "His orders come out of St. Louis."
> They stared at me. "How do *you* know all this stuff?"
> I showed them my gold PBA badge, flashing it quickly with my back to the crowd. "Act natural," I whispered. "Don't put me on the spot."[9]

Richard Nixon was the first U.S. president born in the resort archipelago. He brought with him a paranoid, red-baiting style honed in 1940s Southern California, where the corrupt politics of stolen water and land were acted out in the pages of Norman Chandler's *Times* and William Randolph Hearst's *Herald Examiner*. In Washington he met his match in Nevada's senior senator, Pat McCarran, a nominal Democrat whose support for civil aviation caused Las Vegas to name McCarran Field after him, but who is more well known for sponsoring the notorious Internal Security Act of 1950, which created a Senate committee to fight communism and a string of camps where "subversives" could be isolated and concentrated by emergency order of the president of the United States.

During his second visit to Las Vegas, Thompson's own paranoia was particularly intense: the city was flooded with law enforcement, hundreds of district attorneys and prosecutors in town for a conference on "the drug problem," with the specter of arbitrary detention and incarceration shadowing every bad, drug-addled decision he and his "attorney" made. They had driven out from LA to document a twisted version of the American Dream, to find "Horatio Alger gone mad on drugs in Vegas," but what they found was a desert nightmare of cartel politics and unreconstructed racism.[10] LA, Vegas, all the same shit; the resort archipelago, just another gulag.

Las Vegas Once Happened Here

This chapter is being written fifty years and one month since *Rolling Stone*, a small magazine of the San Francisco hippie counterculture, serialized "Fear and Loathing in Las Vegas" across two November issues in 1971. McCarran International Airport has recently been renamed after the late senator Harry Reid, a very different kind of Democratic power broker from a new, more enlightened Nevada. Both Clark County *and* Los Angeles County are now multicultural urban areas with strong Latino power structures that skew reliably liberal. Neither the Horatio Alger myth nor countercultural drug paranoia seem particularly relevant there today.

One of Thompson's favorite descriptors for Los Angeles and Las Vegas back in 1971 was "atavistic." To a veteran of the San Francisco counterculture, these sprawling cities on the edge of the desert were both a throwback to the worst impulses of America's past and a warning, a foretaste of an alternate future in which the "long fine flash" of the sixties had never happened.[11] So which is it? Is Vegas our future—or our past?

On the one hand, everything that happens in Las Vegas seems already to have happened in Los Angeles, sometimes more than once: a resort town conjured out of the desert; explosive population growth and rampant real-estate speculation; right-wing, racist policing; endemic corruption outside the city limits along an auto-driven entertainment strip; Disneyfication as a model for postmodern urbanism. On the other, as so often happens in postmodern society, the copy seems to have usurped the place of the original in the collective imaginary. The neon-lit sidewalks of Hollywood and the Sunset Strip fade beside the LED glare of a "Strip City" with almost a million inhabitants and a club scene second to none; Disneyland, now aging and riddled by nostalgia, seems pathetic for clinging to yesterday's Tomorrowland, while Vegas renews itself constantly through implosion and reconstruction; Los Angeles, the city that perfected perpetual population growth as economic motor, has been entirely eclipsed by metropolitan Clark County, which has managed to grow 20 percent over the past decade while LA stood still.[12]

New York's governor Mario Cuomo once captured in a characteristically memorable oxymoron its proud history of New Deal liberalism. "The future," he said, "once happened here."[13] Los Angeles might, in a darker mood, say the same of Las Vegas. If Vegas is America's future, it's also LA's flashback, a long bad trip into the darkness that has always been visible here, just out of range of the flashbulbs and the marquee lights.

That's the thing about the desert's edge: to really see it, you've got to leave town.

Notes

1. Carey McWilliams, *Southern California Country: An Island on the Land*, American Folkways (New York: Duell, Sloan & Pearce, 1946).

2. Philip Hughes, "Andrew Holmes: *The Golden Hour*, AA Lecture Hall, 5 June 1990," *AA Files*, no. 21 (Spring 1991): 86.

3. Robert Venturi and Denise Scott Brown, "A Significance for A&P Parking Lots or Learning from Las Vegas," *Architectural Forum* 128 (January–June 1968): 39. It is not well known that the Yale seminar trip to the West that gave rise to this pivotal study first set down in Los Angeles, where the group spent at least a week, before heading out onto Route 66.

4. Ed Ruscha, *Every Building on the Sunset Strip* (self-published, 1966; second printing, 1971).

5. Eugene P. Moehring, *Reno, Las Vegas, and the Strip: A Tale of Three Cities*, Wilbur S. Shepperson Series in Nevada History (Reno: University of Nevada Press, 2014), 129. Moehring's notion of normalization is taken from Mark Gottdiener, Claudia C. Collins, and David R. Dickens, *Las Vegas: The Social Production of an All-American City* (Malden, MA: Blackwell, 1999).

6. Jane Jacobs, *The Death and Life of Great American Cities* (New York: Vintage, 1961), 50–53.

7. Ada Louise Huxtable, *The Unreal America: The Architecture of Illusion* (New York: New Press, 1997), 88.

8. Hunter S. Thompson, "Strange Rumblings in Aztlan," *Rolling Stone*, April 29, 1971.

9. Hunter S. Thompson, *Fear and Loathing: A Savage Journey to the Heart of the American Dream* (New York: Vintage, 1971), 88.

10. Thompson, *Fear and Loathing*, 8.

11. "The mentality of Las Vegas is so grossly atavistic that a really massive crime often slips by unrecognized." Thompson, *Fear and Loathing*, 79.

12. Los Angeles County grew only 1.49 percent in the period 2010–21 and, starting in 2016, has been shrinking (though ever so slightly) for the first time in its entire U.S. history. In the same eleven-year period, Clark County grew by 20.25 percent. Data taken from worldpopulationreview.com, accessed January 4, 2022.

13. Maurice Carroll, "Cuomo Wants to Go beyond Workfare to Work Ethic," *New York Times*, January 26, 1986, https://www.nytimes.com/1986/01/26/weekinreview/cuomo-wants-to-go-beyond-workfare-to-work-ethic.html.

2

Reimagining the Popular on the Vegas Circuit

Helen Traubel, Diva Populism, and the Labor of Publicity

MICHAEL M. REINHARD

When Wagnerian soprano Helen Traubel leaked her correspondence with the Metropolitan Opera's director, Rudolf Bing, she did so in response to Bing's attempts to secure exclusivity over her stage presence in contract-renewal negotiations.[1] Reflecting classed assumptions about music, performance, and popular culture, Bing's stance, as it was represented in their correspondence, seemed to arise from an attempt to protect the cultural capital of the Met by limiting the ability of opera performers to be seen in venues of "low culture" like the nightclubs featured in Vegas. Bing's attempts reflected the challenges of protecting the cultural authority of institutionalized opera during the introduction of television and its ability to coalesce new commercial publics for musicians. In fact, these contract disputes seemed to arise from Traubel's debut at the Chez Paree nightclub in Chicago with accompanying performances in New York, Las Vegas, and Miami. In leaking her correspondence, her comments included: "To assert that art can be found in the Metropolitan Opera House but not in a night club is a rank snobbery that underrates both the taste of the American public and the talent of its composers."[2] By rejecting a notion of opera's cultural elitism to newspaper readerships in the *Los Angeles Times* and the *Washington Post*, Traubel's career decisions offer insight into the changing perceptions of popular culture in the 1950s. This leaked correspondence, moreover, demonstrates how independent stars seized on these new media conditions to leverage new audiences for their creative work through cultural activism and public engagement.

Spanning recorded music to nightclubs, television, and Hollywood film, this emerging transmedia constellation of cultural industries privileged artists who performed what Nancy Baym has referred to as "relational labor" to describe the act of cultivating relationships with the public.[3,4] Emerging in the postwar moment, Las Vegas as a cultural site demonstrates how relational labor—such as Traubel's performative embrace of ideas about popular music against the gatekeeping of operatic elitism—intensified its value for defining artist brands for national circuits. While this history is not radically new, particularly as legal debates over rights of publicity can be traced at least as far back as the late nineteenth century, this chapter seeks to understand how the cultivation of publics for Vegas nightclubs in this media environment drew upon racial, ethnic, and populist discourses about music.[5] Examining Traubel's film, television, and nightclub appearances, this chapter considers Vegas's relationship to the cultivation of artist brands and other forms of media industry. Traubel's populism is significant for its displacement of older forms of cultural authority signaled by urban geographies like New York and the prestige of the Metropolitan Opera. Positioned as a defense of popular culture against the accusation of being lowbrow—an accusation that has long also marked Vegas—Traubel's move into nightclubs is symbolic of the city's significance in a national and complexifying media industry as it intensified the political orientations of public celebrity. Historicizing the emergence of television as national entertainment, I recover media industry debates that dominated the first decade of the medium, as forms of serious culture were transported from radio into television through licensing requirements to satisfy "the public interest." Drawing on these debates, I examine how these transformations in media industry brought with them a reconsideration of popular culture and new promotional platforms for artists like Traubel. One of the effects of this media landscape was to encourage artists to take charge of their own self-promotion by speaking to national debates about race, citizenship, and antielitism, as evidenced by Traubel's declaration that the "St. Louis Blues" represented "the folk song of her people." Positioned against broader histories of the social construction of music genres through race, these remarks help inform how Vegas as a cultural center harnessed the promotional capacities of the television, film, and music industries and the accompanying social politics that served to sustain the development of these national publics.

Opera, Nationalism, and Folk Culture

Trained in her native St. Louis before Chicago, Traubel's midcentury reputation functioned, like many American opera stars before her, as a representation of national pride. The autobiography *St. Louis Woman* (1959) recounts her recruitment to sing Wagner over radio to the German people during World War II, an event that predates U.S. Cold War strategies of making global diplomatic appeals through music performance. The experience aimed to prove that "at the very time Paul Joseph Goebbels was shrieking there was 'no culture' in our 'barbarian' country, that Wagner was doing all right in America."[6] These international performances raise a long history of American and European tensions around opera, wherein increasing distaste for foreign-language renditions of the genre, as Katherine K. Preston has studied, resulted in the popularization of English vernacular traditions by the 1890s.[7] Intersecting with the emergence of recording industries in the United States, this period challenged hierarchies of "serious listening" and the cultural hegemony of opera by leveling jazz, folk, classical, and other genres within the conditions of the consumer marketplace. Traubel stated, "I love the songs of Gershwin, Hang, Kern, Rodgers, and other great American Composers. . . . Since I cannot sing them at the Metropolitan Opera House, I am singing them at night clubs, and I am happy to have found that night club audiences are enthusiastically accepting me on my own terms."[8] Drawing reference to the new sounds of the early twentieth century, Traubel defended the musical value of racially and ethnically coded sounds of Jewish and African American music by popular composers. Defending the melting-pot idea of "American" folk music, Traubel positioned herself as an embodiment of the national voice in contravention to older hierarchies of culture that informed the Met's prestigious status.

Taking place in the first decade of television's emergence as a popular medium, Traubel's leaked correspondence reflected the larger technological and public changes posed by new forms of independent stardom in this environment. Where Rudolf Bing attempted to maintain opera's cultural status, the soprano seized on new economic opportunities for performers in the 1950s, as a declining studio system in Hollywood and the emergence of TV as a national medium joined the music industry to form a broad array of interlocking and convergent media industries. This period is also marked by the growth of talent agencies that saw the ability to earn more money for artists by maximizing multiple revenue streams.[9] This cultural system required new logics of self-promotion and publicity in order to secure and attract public attention. Within this type of self-promotional culture, Traubel's publicity embodies a form of cultural populism in which performative speech attempts to register greater visibility for moral attitudes held by the public.[10] While the diva appealed to the subtext of opera as an elitist genre, her leaked correspondence represented a reentrenchment of publicity as a particular type of public performance as stars forged independent careers outside gatekeeping institutions like the Hollywood studio system or the Metropolitan Opera House.

Early Television Programming, Opera, and the Public Interest

By 1953—the year Traubel captured the national zeitgeist in defense of popular music—the music industry had already started to coalesce around Las Vegas as a burgeoning cultural center. In fact, that summer saw Milton Berle and Red Skelton, two television pioneers, take up residencies at the hotel casinos. Reflecting how the development of the city relied on the music industry, headliners represented a strategic draw for developing and maintaining the tourist market for the city. In fact, as Larry D. Gragg notes, newspaper reports had gained comment from Hershey Martin of William Morris who suggested that Las Vegas's hotel-casinos were among the firm's biggest buyers.[11] To this point, a whole network of nightclub performances concretized not only a system of touring but also a circuit of workshopping shows in advance of Vegas residencies. These performance spaces included many of the same ones that would dot Helen Traubel's performance schedule like Chicago's Chez Paree and New York's Copacabana that rankled Bing's vision for maintaining the Met as a serious institution for opera. Within the organization of this touring network, these artists sought promotion that would elevate their status to the level of headliner in these venues. Here, Vegas represents a crucial site for understanding the longer histories of media convergence in stitching various networks of modern cultural industry together.

Where Benjaminian ideas about art have suggested that mechanized reproduction diminished sacred ideas about art or its "aura," similar ideas of cultural loss pervade accounts of television, postmodernism, and Vegas in the postwar period. Indeed, these tensions between the exclusivity of art by institutional and intellectual gatekeepers and the democratization of art, even if through commodified channels like recorded sound, radio, and television, have long marked critical discussions of new technology and popular music. Such accounts frequently critique the turning over of classical traditions of music and literature to new logics of advertising, mediatization, and public taste, associating technological shifts with the declining quality of art. These critics, however, miss the ways in which new systems of artistic mediation often reframe more traditional ideas about culture, civilization, and artistic progress. Bing's desire to police the stage presence of the Met's stars was reflective of dismissive attitudes of opera's transposition into other media formats, while ignoring its possibilities to provide greater awareness about the art form of opera. By attempting to restrict the public's access to such music, Bing might be said to reflect the attitude of critics who overlooked the value of increased exposure of opera as revitalizing conditions for the art form, as Danielle Ward-Griffin critiques this perspective in her research on televised opera.[12]

Novel in the late 1940s and 1950s, television arrived in the nation's homes often by employing the music celebrity of radio. Indicative of new promotional opportunities, performers like Traubel were able to enter into an emerging national zeitgeist via television through variety-show programming like *All Star Revue* (1950–52). A number of programs on radio, such as *The Red Skelton Show* (1951–70) and *The Jimmy Durante Show* (1954–56), were brought into television as initial lineups of programming. Consequently, Traubel also appeared on these shows to promote her commercial music projects. While television has largely been celebrated as a storytelling medium based on its repopularization of serialized and episodic narrative styles, the intense pressures to fill airtime and attract audiences required substantial new media production to sate these programming demands. This new medium's positioning within logics of advertising and public taste created deep tensions between ideas about popular culture and the federal government's soft and hard power to organize the medium by stressing "public interest" as a core component of broadcast licensing. Such programming showcasing the strengths of classical and Broadway music as *The Bell Telephone Hour* (1959–68), adapted from the earlier radio show, resulted from these bureaucratic demands in shaping the nascent medium's entertainment; yet television's promotional capacities, promised by some as the democratization of high culture, also led to secondary effects of allowing performers in more hierarchical cultural institutions like the Met or the Hollywood studio system to find economic opportunities in media industry as independent artists. Positioned within this landscape, self-promotion intensified its status as part of the labor of not only stardom but particularly television as a venue for selling other performance work in music and film.

In some ways, Helen Traubel's appearance on shows like *The Ed Sullivan Show* (1948–71), *Perry Como's Kraft Music Hall* (1948–67), and *The Milton Berle Show* (1958–62) responds to this history of independent stardom and its strategies of self-promotion. Against this landscape, opera found itself attractive to television entrepreneurs following its inclusion in radio programming. In the first years of the medium, advertisers sponsored televisual productions; one example included *The Voice of Firestone* produced by Firestone Tire and Rubber Company, which debuted on NBC radio in December 1928 before moving to television in 1949. Telecasting the great voices of opera into the nation's homes, the series privileged classical traditions of art against the confines of more controversial performance modes associated with vaudeville or nightclubs, lest more taboo programming generate public backlash that could be associated with commercial sponsors. Helen Traubel is credited as appearing three times throughout the first two years of the series. In 1950, Traubel appeared in her signature Wagnerian role as Brunhilde singing the Valkyrie battle anthem "Ho-Jo-To-Ho," a song that Kirsten Flagstad popularized earlier in Paramount's *The*

Big Broadcast of 1938 (1938). Recalling live theatrical staging by using only three cuts over the two-minute performance, the camera focuses on intimate shots that establish facial close-ups of Traubel singing. In this way, the framing seemed to exploit visual techniques to center the qualities of live performance, vocal perfection, and the individual personality of the performer. This individuating quality, a hallmark of media celebrity, would become commercially valuable as audiences might take interest in the performer's other recording work in *Helen Traubel Sings Wagner* (1950).

While television opera is said to have died in the 1960s, it is important to understand the cultural and political agendas that its status served within the nascent medium. As the chair of the Federal Communications Commission, Newton N. Minow has long been associated with his speech decrying the "vast wasteland" of television to the National Association of Broadcasters in 1961. Few references to this moment accentuate how Minow's castigation of the TV industry reflected extant hierarchies of culture that have long predominated conversations about new media. Characterizing television broadcasters as relying on the "public property" of the nation's airwaves, Minow encouraged networks to fulfill the public interest by, quoting the association's president, Governor LeRoy Collins, building "the character, citizenship, and intellectual stature of the people, as well as to expand the gross national product."[13] Minow's views reflected a reading of television as socially conscious capitalism—however paradoxical it may appear to the academic's eye—that has long characterized American views of media industry and consumption.[14] Examples of Minow's lauded programming included artists from more established mediums like film, as in the case of *The Fred Astaire Show* (1968), or represented news programming, like *The Nation's Future* (1960–61), *CBS Reports* (1959–Present), and *The Valiant Years* (1960–63). His critique of bad television was largely leveraged toward genre programming like game shows, formula comedies, westerns, gangsters, and the general theme of violence. Reminding broadcasters of their licensing requirements, Minow's address, in many ways, reflected a broader network of audiences, governmental representatives, and other editorial voices that exerted public pressures on the commercial dynamics of television. These industry conditions positioned opera—and its associations with the height of the European tradition its sounds conjured—as uniquely valuable for its status as serious art to advance conceptions of the public good by contributing to the cultivation of a musically educated audience. Creating structures of value around programming, Minow's words, thus, built on long-standing consumer and industry activism that aimed to reform the national marketplace to promote the public good; however, within this critique, such hierarchies between formulaic genres and classical works were expressed through cultural debates about the public good and the duties of mediated citizenship.

Debates between popular and classical music, further, go to the very heart of the reformalization of music industry from sheet music to phonographic records. Writing in 1906, John Philip Sousa originally decried what he saw as the erasure of human skill in the growth of the new music market. He editorialized, "Sweeping across the country with the speed of a transient fashion in slang or Panama hats, political war cries or popular novels, comes now the mechanical device to sing for us a song or play for us a piano in substitute for human skill, intelligence, and soul." Sousa's remarks were rooted in the perceived insincerity of this music, going so far as to cite Wagner's declaration, "I will not write even one measure of music that is not thoroughly sincere."[15] His warning typified the type of moral panic that would be observed throughout much of the twentieth century, where new forms of electronic culture would fundamentally reshape the sensations of American life, pairing understandings of technological progress with fears of moral loss and the decline of serious artistry. These fears of artistic loss, in many ways, frequently raised the specter of a shifting ethnic sound away from more white European traditions of classical music. For example, this dynamic arose, in part, through the location of early recorded sound technologies in the nineteenth century as coin-operated phonographs became found in similar urban and public areas as cinema's early kinetoscope. As Karl Hagstrom Miller notes, these urban geographies reflected their status as novelties, further signaled by their mechanized playbacks of popular music in the styles of Tin Pan Alley, Broadway hits, light classical selections, and the ethnic caricatures furnished by vaudeville and racial minstrelsy. The ethnic situation of this music, in both its genre sound and its urban character, would draw out Sousa's suspicion of slang and Panama hats as constitutive of the perversion of music by commercial aims.[16] The Victor Talking Machine Company and the Edison Phonograph Company, responding to similar attitudes about popular music, looked toward ideologies of serious music, gathered by late-nineteenth-century opera, to position the new machine and its market as part of a broader strategy of cultural uplift. Within this landscape, Victor Records had turned to the creation of its Red Seal label by signing contracts with Enrico Caruso and other opera singers backed by the new cultural authority of the Metropolitan Opera House. Edison took a similar tact, as he sought to anthropomorphize the phonograph through promotional tone tests and advertising strategies that directly analogized virtuosities of the human voice, such as the operatic diva's, and that of the fidelity of the sound machine as coequal instruments.

Thus, these debates about the racial character of music as a representation of national folk traditions frequently took place within debates about popular versus serious music. Constructions of taste in music have, as Larry Hamberlin has studied, often produced its own type of color line, wherein genres of sound like ragtime and opera were deeply racialized.[17] In the nineteenth century, these constructions of taste frequently drew upon ideas of race as emblematic of larger ideologies of national identity. For example, previous white opera singers like Jenny Lind were known by names such as The Swedish Nightingale in the press, suggesting how singers served as embodiments of nationalism within the tradition of associating opera divas with songbirds.[18] In ways that reflected a white racial claim on national identity in the United States, nineteenth-century Black opera singers were often referred to by the color of their skin as imitations of other singers, including Black Patti as a reference to the Italian Adelina Patti for singer Sissieretta Jones or Black Swan for Elizabeth Taylor Greenfield as an echo of Lind's celebrity. In this way, ideas about sound, genre, and nationality have historically been framed as embodied through the diva's privileged status in stage and music performance cultures. When ragtime and blues had secured new forms of popularity within the twentieth century, debates roiled about its status as folk music, where defenders pointed to these genres as uniquely American in their evolution and reflected the "folk" music of urban life. Others soured at their commercial character. Professor James Cloyd Bowman once said of ragtime, "if you can pervert the tastes of ten million persons in these United States—no matter how inferior they are as a class—into liking a thing . . . you may then . . . call the thing American."[19]

When Helen Traubel appeared on Jimmy Durante's show in 1951, she had attracted suspicions for violating these standards of class and artistry expected within the more staid environment of opera. These tensions, as Victoria Etnier Villamil has observed, reflected broader struggles between opera singers and their institutional employers, as baritone Robert Merrill was dismissed from the Met after filming *Aaron Slick from Punkin Crick* (1952).[20] While Merrill was reinstated later, Traubel's encounter with Bing underscored the specific issue with nightclub performance and its associations with urban and popular traditions of music. In many ways, the Helen Traubel incident reflects shifting ideas about genre, race, and performance and the expansion of media industry that allowed for new forms of entrepreneurship by opera and other music performers. Not only did Traubel's leaking of her correspondence synthesize these two points of intersection in her defense of "blues music," but this moment also suggests how new forms of publicity could contest imaginations of the U.S. public in ways that were valuable to music performers as independent artists.

Moreover, Traubel's decision to defend popular music and therefore also nonwhite-Anglo traditions of sound took place within larger cultural shifts taking place in music, theater, and film during the 1950s. Nina Sun Eidsheim has observed opera's response to racial questions of casting posed by the civil rights movement during this same period. In fact, Marian Anderson, who became a powerful symbol for challenging the conditions of segregation in her 1939 performance at the Lincoln Memorial, would be the first Black lead actress on the

Met stage the year after Traubel's departure.[21] The decision to bring Anderson into its company in the 1955 season built on previous attempts to integrate the national stage that culminated earlier in the emergence of the Negro Units in the Federal Theatre Project of FDR's New Deal. Administrators employed one strategy of funding projects, among others, by turning toward "Black" adaptations of classical works as *Macbeth*, *Lysistrata*, and *Cinderella*.[22] Importantly, these projects remained in parallel with the emergence of commercial tastes for African American sounds on Broadway with *Shuffle Along* (1921), *Porgy and Bess* (1935), and *Carmen Jones* (1943). While *Show Boat* (1927) earned the credit as the first racially integrated musical on Broadway, themes of racial integration were exported globally through pan-Americanism in Hollywood film musicals in support of the United States' Good Neighbor policy, such as *Down Argentine Way* (1940) and *The Gang's All Here* (1943).[23] Just as the civil rights movement became identified with consumer boycotts in the American South, national media industries recorded similar social shifts in their entertainment products as new models of African American stardom could be observed in Dorothy Dandridge's first lead-actress Oscar nomination in *Carmen Jones* (1954), while Leontyne Price earned the distinction of being the first African American in a leading-title role for NBC Opera Theatre's 1955 rendition of Puccini's *Tosca*.

In her on-screen debut in MGM's *Deep in My Heart* (1954), Helen Traubel's casting traded on her reputation within these broader debates about the changing sounds of the nation. Directed by Stanley Donen, the film musical dramatizes the life of composer Sigmund Romberg (José Ferrer) as he negotiates feeling conflicted between his European classical training and pursuing modern American sounds through ragtime and jazz.[24] The film arrived in an industrial cycle of Hollywood films that chronicled the changing national sound by locating them in great composers like George Gershwin in *Rhapsody in Blue* (1945) and Cole Porter in *Night and Day* (1946). Celebrating Romberg's career for unsettling hierarchies of sound, *Deep in My Heart* frequently takes up the racial subtexts of these debates about popular music. In particular, the film demonstrates the centrality of white fantasies of race and sexuality as pivotal to the loosening of these cultural hierarchies. Referencing the compositions of *Robinson Crusoe, Jr.* (1916), *Sinbad* (1918), and *Bombo* (1921) as star vehicles for Al Jolson, the film gestures to this racialized sound and its modes of performance in a song medley featuring a series of racial caricatures in "Goodbye Girls," "Fat Fat Fatima," and "Jazz-a-Doo." The scene's mobilizing of racialized assumptions about sound and performance are critical for understanding how the film conceives of popular music, particularly through its shifting of sound in these moments to an upbeat tempo, more syncopation, and a more physicalized mode of dance. Ending with a performance in blackface in "Jazz-a-Doo," José Ferrer's performance as Romberg approximates the sound and physicality of Al Jolson as a touch point for these musical debates, thus highlighting the influence of racial minstrelsy and Tin Pan Alley within this emergent conception of American sound as a melting pot. Underscoring this point, Romberg is shown apologizing to a prospective patron for performing "low-class" entertainment while encouraging her to join the twentieth century in enjoying the less classical and more racially accented sounds of an emergent popular culture.

In the penultimate moment before the final stage number, Traubel's character ventriloquizes the film's critical lesson about challenging cultural hierarchies of art, as she implores Romberg to take his popular music to Carnegie Hall. He protests that his music, like that of his Jolson work, was instead meant for the dance hall, a nod to the more physicalized mode of performance found in nightclubs like those featured in Vegas. In doing so, this scene draws on the intertextual qualities of Traubel's celebrity to heighten the film's message about an inclusive national music canon. Recalling Traubel's praise of "St. Louis Blues" as the folk song of her people, her performance as Anna waxes poetic about the virtues of composing music that anyone can sing in ways that privilege a more vernacular sound. Thus, this character argues for a democratic reading of Romberg's music, stating that despite its composition for a hundred men, she, a woman alone, can sing it just as anyone else can sing it, thus challenging the virtues of technical training and classicism as the only barometer for evaluating music. Justifying an inclusion of folk traditions in the national canon, Romberg ends the film in a seeming recognition of Helen Traubel whose voice he claims is not just technical but full of spirit before attacking cultural criticism that suggests certain forms of art are "too lowbrow" or "too highbrow," instead issuing a firm defense of "the middlebrow." Thus, these later scenes draw upon Traubel's public image in ways that underscore Romberg's contributions to unsettling public conceptions of race, class, and popular music, particularly as they intersected with cultural distinctions between various concert spaces like Carnegie Hall and nightclubs.

Positioned within the onset of the civil rights movement, this broader context highlights how political movements shaped casting responses by a number of media industries in the 1950s in ways that underscore the larger debates about race, sound, and class that informed the leaking of Bing's correspondence to the press. At the same time, Traubel's public calculations illustrate the shifting power centers of artistic production, as it moved away from more institutionalized settings like the Met and became subjected to the commercial whims of the U.S. public through recorded music sales, nightclub, television, and other touring opportunities like those featured in Vegas. While these types of performances may appear disconnected from the social firmament of the city's broader place in the music industry, the importing of touring celebrities from television, film, and music, *however*, illustrates the city's broader transmedia environment as intimately connected to new formations of publicity as a valuable form of labor for independent artists to maintain sufficient public interest in their work. Surveying Traubel's transition from operatic to popular celebrity, this media history demonstrates new public conditions for translating social and political activism into the celebrity images of performers seeking to embody a notion of the popular will at an array of national box offices. Read in this way, the emergence of Vegas as an entertainment center for musicians within the 1950s illustrates the deformalization of national music hierarchies that also brought new attempts to represent public ideas about the "people" through shifting sounds, tastes, and genres of popular music.

Conclusion

Reflecting how popular singers have labored to embody the values of the commercial public and new popular sounds, Helen Traubel's transition into a film and television career speaks to these very themes. Her television appearances, in fact, promoted this very image throughout the 1950s to support her touring and music career. As television offered opportunities to trade operatic prestige for the currency of the television audience, Traubel performed a public version of her status as a Metropolitan Opera diva, as evidenced by her appearances on *The Voice of Firestone* and other shows throughout the decade. When she appeared on *What's My Line?* (1950–67) in 1954, the panel's attempts to guess Traubel's identity as the mystery guest relied on her celebrity status from public incidents like her departure from the Met. Promoting her Copacabana residency, Traubel answered confidently that she sang in the popular field before moments later demurring that she had not had a hit record in the past six months. A panelist joked in response that, perhaps, Traubel was not as much in the popular field as she thought. *What's My Line?*—the type of game show perhaps critiqued by Minow's call for television reform—underscored not only how celebrity entrepreneurs approached television for commercial opportunities but also how television sought to organize its own audience by exploiting previous sources of cultural power like opera. As panelists identified Traubel through her publicity narratives following the uproar at the Met, such moments highlighted how networks of popular culture, artistic hierarchy, and forms of promotional entrepreneurship were resettled by television as a connecting point of various U.S. media industries, which also included Vegas's touring circuits.

While television's place in music is often framed through teen culture like *The Ed Sullivan Show*'s hyping of Elvis and the Beatles or teenyboppers on *American Bandstand*, these histories frequently minimize how the new medium's reliance on advertising and exposure also worked to resituate social advocacy within the terms of promotional culture, as evidenced by Traubel's defense of popular music as the originating point of a new public image for her recording and film career. It is this advocacy in generating new forms of social awareness for her career that became valuable for promoting her tour of the nation's nightlife scene on the Vegas Strip. These intersections between publicity, politics, and celebrity illustrate, in part, the longer history of how the national marketplace of culture maintained its status as a core venue for public social debates. This publicity was also economically valuable for similar touring circuits organized by Vegas's music scene. Within this landscape, Traubel's pursuit of televisual publicity spoke to the shifting politics of "Black" sound in the 1950s. Addressing the public through self-promotion reflects the broader interchanges between culture, industry, and politics that shaped not only national media industry but also specifically Vegas's place within the American imaginary. Situated as a place where fantasies of economic transcendence and libidinal energies of excess take up their truly American character, Vegas as a cultural center emerged in the postwar moment as deeply nostalgic in its collecting of big branded artists as headliners across the myriad performance spaces of casinos and hotels that dot the city.

Recognizing Vegas's larger place within national U.S. culture, these performance contracts have significantly intersected with the promotional capacities of television and film to help serve the broader touristic needs of the city as a cultural center for entertainment and hospitality. More modern divas such as Lady Gaga, Céline Dion, and Cher continue to embody how Vegas as a cultural capital marshals socially liberal entertainment brands. The recognition of these national brands, moreover, draws on a much deeper history of media industry convergence that informs Vegas's place in 1950s entertainment, demonstrating strong connections with the promotional logic of television that made Los Angeles so distinct a landscape for cultural entrepreneurs. To achieve such forms of promotion, independent artists have worked to capture the national imagination in ways that positioned themselves as embodiments of moral and national publics. Thus, Traubel's act of publicity dramatized public support for the multiethnic character of American culture, while demonstrating the ways that these social themes connected to Vegas's own reliance on ideas about publicity, self-promotion, and nightclub touring in the postwar moment.

Notes

1. "Helen Traubel Breaks with Met over Night Club Show," *San Bernardino Sun*, September 28, 1953.

2. Associated Press, "Helen Traubel Breaks with the Met over Night Club Contract," *Atlanta Constitution*, September 28, 1953.

3. While concepts of transmedia narratives refer to the expansion of storytelling universes across multiple media platforms, I follow Elizabeth Evans through Jonathan Gray's discussions of transmedia storytelling as built around the array of marketing, publicity, and other paratextual practices that commodify media brands (such as television performances by independent artists like Helen Traubel). See Jonathan Gray, *Show Sold Separately: Promos, Spoilers, and Other Media Paratexts* (New York: New York University Press, 2010), 6; and Elizabeth Evans, *Transmedia Television: Audiences, New Media, and Daily Life* (New York: Routledge, 2011), 19.

4. Nancy Baym, *Playing to the Crowd: Musicians, Audiences, and the Intimate Work of Connection* (New York: New York University Press, 2018), 18.

5. For more discussion of this history, see Jennifer Rothman, *The Right of Publicity: Privacy Reimagined for a Public World* (Cambridge, MA: Harvard University Press, 2018).

6. Helen Traubel, *St. Louis Woman* (New York: Duell, Sloan & Pearce, 1959), 153.

7. Katherine K. Preston, *Opera for the People: English Language Opera and Women Managers in Late 19th-Century America* (New York: Oxford University Press, 2017).

8. Associated Press, "Helen Traubel Breaks with the Met."

9. Denise Mann, *Hollywood Independents: The Postwar Talent Takeover* (Minneapolis: University of Minnesota Press, 2008).

10. My use of this term builds off political theorists, such as Cristóbal Rovira Kaltwasser et al., who refer to the ways in which populism, as a political ideology, represents "the idea that 'the people' can authoritatively recover power from the government to reconstitute institutions, or wrestle power from corrupt or self-serving elites." Here, I refer to cultural populism as a way of showcasing how ideas about culture manifest similarly populist claims about the nature of art in contradistinction to elitist constructions of taste or institutional gatekeeping about the status of art. See Cristóbal Rovira Kaltwasser et al., "Populism: An Overview of the Concept and the State of Art," in *The Oxford Handbook of Populism* (New York: Oxford University Press, 2017), 3.

11. Larry D. Gragg, *Becoming America's Playground: Las Vegas in the 1950s* (Norman: University of Oklahoma, 2019), 51.

12. Danielle Ward-Griffin, "As Seen on TV: Putting the NBC Opera on Stage," *Journal of the American Musicological Society* 71, no. 3 (2018): 597.

13. Newton N. Minow, "Television and the Public Interest," speech before the National Association of Broadcasters, May 9, 1961.

14. For greater discussion of consumption and the national good, see Lizbeth Cohen, *A Consumers' Republic: The Politics of Mass Consumption in Postwar America* (New York: First Vintage Books, 2004).

15. John Philip Sousa, "The Menace of Mechanical Music," *Appleton's Magazine* 8 (1906): 278, 279.

16. Karl Hagstrom Miller, *Segregating Sound: Inventing Folk and Pop Music in the Age of Jim Crow* (Durham, NC: Duke University Press, 2010), 159–60.

17. Larry Hamberlin, *Tin Pan Opera: Operatic Novelty Songs in the Ragtime Era* (New York: Oxford University Press, 2011), 213.

18. Julia J. Chybowski, "Becoming the 'Black Swan' in Mid-Nineteenth-Century America: Elizabeth Taylor Greenfield's Early Life and Debut Concert Tour," *Journal of the American Musicological Society* 67, no. 1 (2014): 143.

19. Quoted in Hamberlin, *Tin Pan Opera*, 223.

20. Victoria Etnier Villamil, *From Johnson's Kids to Lemonade Opera: The American Classical Singer Comes of Age* (Boston: Northeastern University Press, 2004), 240.

21. Nina Sun Eidsheim, "Marian Anderson and 'Sonic Blackness' in American Opera," *American Quarterly* 63, no. 3 (2011): 641.

22. Lauren Rebecca Sklaroff, *Black Culture and the New Deal: The Quest for Civil Rights in the Roosevelt Era* (Chapel Hill: University of North Carolina Press, 2009), 35.

23. See Shari Roberts, "'The Lady in the Tutti-Frutti Hat': Carmen Miranda, a Spectacle of Ethnicity," *Cinema Journal* 32, no. 3 (1993): 5. Roberts writes: "The complicated relationship between the government and the studio industry also resulted in the Fox translations of the government's Good Neighbor policy into the Miranda 'exotic locale' fantasies, which depicted harmonically exploitative relations between the United States and Latin American countries."

24. *Deep in My Heart*, directed by Stanley Donen, DVD (Los Angeles: MGM, 2014).

3

It Was Better When the Mob Ran the Town

JANIS MCKAY

If you speak to those who have lived in Las Vegas for a long time, sooner or later at least one person will lower their voice confidentially and say, "You know, it was much better when the Mob ran the town." Las Vegas began as a railroad stop and then developed into a small western cowboy town with sawdust on the floors. Since that time, the character of Las Vegas has changed many times. By the late '90s, Las Vegas became the place where "What happens in Vegas stays in Vegas." More growth and change followed as the city reinvented itself again and again. But which of these inventions is the true Las Vegas?

Those who say they miss the Mob remember the spectacular entertainment offerings of the 1950s and early 1960s Strip. This era was for adults, who dressed to go out and casino hopped all night long. The Mob owners seemingly knew everyone and took care of their workers like family. And most important, it was a time when many of the best entertainers in the world were all coming to Las Vegas to perform. No expense was spared on entertainment, used to draw tourists into the casinos.

Entertainment, particularly musical entertainment, drove the city's expansion. It was a period of more jobs than musicians, more showrooms than big-name entertainers. Entertainment writer Bill Willard arrived in 1949, filing hard news for both the daily and the weekly versions of *Variety* magazine. He noted that the budgets for entertainment had gone from $8,000 per week in 1950 to $30,000 per week by 1955.[1]

The musicians who were working during this era made more money in Las Vegas than they could have made just about anywhere else. From the late 1940s until 1989, Las Vegas was an important destination for professional musicians of all types. At the peak, there were as many as fourteen to seventeen hundred musicians working in Las Vegas. They followed the work and then stayed, creating an unusual number of additional musical activities in a town that was not large.

Las Vegas is no longer the hub for professional musicians that it once was, though entertainment has once again become a large economic driver for the city. Popular DJs, clubbing, restaurants, shopping, and designed experiences are some of the main types of entertainment on offer now. Yet the Rat Pack and Mob era still seems to dominate popular imagination about Las Vegas. And the myth "it was better when the Mob ran things" persists.

The reality is much more complex. What was good for some people was not so great for others, and there were a number of factors that led to the changes in Las Vegas. Las Vegas went from a small town where most people knew each other to a major metropolitan area of more than 2.3 million people. Musical tastes and styles changed. Entertainment began to cater to younger audiences. The corporations cut entertainment costs—every part of the hotel was expected to make money. These are just some of the things that influenced the cultural shift of Las Vegas; the Mob owners giving way to corporations is only part of the picture. This chapter examines how Las Vegas musical entertainment reached its peak during the Mob era, thus reinforcing the myth.

"The Boys"

Nevada legalized gambling in 1931 specifically to attract both long-term investors and tourists to the state. When the California state government sought to eliminate illegal gambling in the 1930s, many gamblers moved to Nevada where they saw opportunities to run legitimate businesses. Early casinos like the 91 Club, Pioneer Club, Frontier Club, El Cortez, and El Rancho were all owned by men previously connected to gambling in California.[2] According to Nevada historian Hal Rothman, "The purchase of the El Cortez (in 1945) initiated a pattern; in every subsequent purchase or development of a resort, 'connected' illegal gamblers who became legal in Nevada and prominent local citizens joined together. Outside capital and some form of local respectability were closely linked."[3] By the mid-1940s, the eastern Mob began to infiltrate the casino business, starting with Benjamin "Bugsy" Siegel.

These hotel owners were generous and friendly to their staff. They frequently gave money to those who needed help, knew the names of employees and their family members, and were genuinely impressed by the musicians and entertainers they hired. "They were great, great audiences," said comedian Red Buttons. "You'd look forward to working, and the money was enormous. Four weeks in

Las Vegas could buy you a Third World country."[4] The crime syndicate tipped heavily and paid double and triple fees for performers to continue to work during their off-hours.

It was, in some ways, a simpler time. Deals were made by handshakes, and negotiations were easy. E. Parry Thomas, the first banker to regularly loan money to casino owners in Las Vegas, kept no notes, calendars, or appointment books. "We did so many deals, especially in the early years, where you'd made a verbal agreement with someone on a loan or whatnot, and you'd look them in the eye and shake hands on it and that would be that."[5]

By the early 1960s, there were around 850 musicians working in the showrooms of Las Vegas, a town with a population of about 100,000 people. These musicians were a tight-knit community who helped to establish a vibrant and thriving arts presence outside of Strip entertainment. A cursory look at the professional and amateur groups in Las Vegas during the 1960s shows an abundance of musical activity: the Las Vegas Civic Orchestra, Las Vegas Boulevard Hotel Symphonists, Las Vegas Brass Sextet, Las Vegas Jazz Septet, Las Vegas Junior Symphony Orchestra, Las Vegas Percussion Quartet, Las Vegas Philharmonic (a different group than the current Las Vegas Philharmonic launched in 1998), Las Vegas Pops Concert Orchestra, Las Vegas Symphonic Society Orchestra, Las Vegas Wind Symphony, Las Vegas Youth Band, Musical Arts Workshop of Las Vegas, New Jazz Orchestra, Promenade Orchestra Pops, and Southern Nevada Festival Orchestra. The syndicate owners often supported these efforts financially, by providing the venue or by attending as enthusiastic audience members.

However, the connection between Las Vegas and the Mob hotel owners had distinct downsides. In a letter to his bosses at *Variety* in April of 1951, Willard wrote, "The townspeople resent the gangster methods of the resort hotels and casinos. . . . Petitions are being prepared for circulation, in order that an antigambling bill might be introduced in the legislature next session." He also felt that the talent bookers working for the hotels did not understand show business and resented any criticism of their operations.[6]

An anonymous casino insider from the International Hotel (now the Westgate) told a story of how a visiting band was fired on the spot after one of the members insulted a Mob heavyweight from the stage. A call was made, and the president of the hotel showed up in his pajamas and ordered the band to leave not only the hotel, but Las Vegas as well. Then, another call was made to the Musicians' Union, and the band stopped getting work. Once the band members learned who they had been insulting, they felt lucky to be allowed to leave town at all. "That's the kind of clout people like my friend had at the time. They could get top-of-the-line entertainers into their joints by making a phone call, and they could end someone's career the same way," he said.[7]

When customers cheated, the Mob was mainly concerned about recovering the money. However, this did not mean that no one was ever hurt or killed.

Another anonymous source from a downtown casino remarked, "If it was only nickel and dime stuff, we'd just toss them. But if they took us for anything substantial, they'd be in a cast or on crutches for a while." He added, "Before we turned them loose, they understood what would happen if we ever saw them around again." Tru Hawkins, a Las Vegas radio personality whose father was a manager at the Riviera, remembered the two sides of the mobsters. "If they liked you, they could be kind, considerate, and generous. On the other hand, if you crossed them, they were capable of cutting out your liver without thinking twice about it."[8]

Racial and sexual discrimination was rampant. Women were prohibited from most casino jobs, including dealing. There were few if any openings for female musicians unless they were stars. Casting-couch "auditions" and harassment by the headliners were not uncommon. There were a number of "juice jobs," many of those for Mob friends or girlfriends, and those jobs often came with strings attached. An anonymous female worker who worked at the Mob-controlled Stardust in the late 1970s remarked, "In those days, there were no female casino executives in Las Vegas. . . . Women had their place in accounting, secretarial, or food and beverage service, but *never* in a decision-making position in the casino industry. I was the first."[9]

Black entertainers were not allowed to stay in the hotels where they performed but had to go to the Westside. When the Moulin Rouge opened in 1955, it was the first interracial hotel in Las Vegas, featuring a show with Black entertainers and a Black master of ceremonies, Bob Bailey, who was also a coproducer. Bailey recalled, "Our public relations man Martin Black had the brilliant idea to try a third performance . . . at 2:15am for the entertainers and musicians in town who were just getting off work. . . . We tried it for a week, and discovered that was when the casino truly came to life."[10]

The hotel went bankrupt after only seven months, supposedly because the owners were fighting with each other. There were some who said that the failure was due to the Strip hotel owners, who noticed that they were losing gamblers at night and forbade the showgirls and musicians from going to the Moulin Rouge. The Moulin Rouge proved that desegregation in the casinos was possible. This fact, combined with the civil rights movement of the 1960s, helped to eventually end segregation in Las Vegas. Unfortunately, this also led to the demise of the hotels and casinos on the Westside. According to writer James Roman, "Black entertainers and their entourages now stayed at the hotels that hired them; now their contracts even stipulated the number of hours they needed to remain in the hotels after the show."[11]

As more musicians came to town looking for work, contractors could take their pick of players, sometimes firing the original player if they liked the substitute better. Rising star salaries and increased competition among the growing number of entertainment venues also began to price some of the owners out of using headliners. These hotels began to feature large-production shows that were, for the professional musicians, repetitive and difficult.

Howard Hughes and the Arrival of Corporate Investment

Howard Hughes, after a secretive night arrival in 1966, checked into the Desert Inn and settled in for a long stay. Hughes was not a gambler and spent no money in the casinos. When the hotel owners tried to move him out to make space for their high rollers, Hughes bought the hotel. He continued to purchase properties for investment, including the Sands, the Castaways, and the Frontier, as well as some other major businesses, eventually spending $300 million on Las Vegas properties.[12]

County officials and gambling commissioners were delighted to approve Hughes. District Attorney George Franklin remarked, "This is the best way to improve the image of gambling in Nevada by licensing an industrialist of his stature. It will be an asset and a blessing." Las Vegas lawyer and Gaming Commission chairman George Dickerson noted, "I can think of no one who can enhance the image of Nevada gambling more than Howard Hughes. He has been successful in every business venture he has ever conducted."[13]

By this time, some of the Mob owners were happy to sell to Hughes to escape the increased scrutiny of the federal government. "I don't care what other people say, I have never met a better group of people than the so-called old-timers in Las Vegas," Robert Maheu, longtime aide to Howard Hughes, remarked. "They give you their word, you can go to bed with it, and they'll stick to it. . . . They care about the community. They've made some great, great contributions to this city."[14] Nevertheless, Maheu noted that Las Vegas was depressed when Hughes arrived, with the city in need of new money to support the continued growth.

It was Hughes's success that drew other corporations and legitimate businesspeople to build or buy properties, and government officials made sure that these new investors were given quick approvals for licenses. Hughes was in town for four years, leaving in 1970 as secretly as he arrived, but his time in Las Vegas was a major turning point for the Strip. According to Las Vegas historians Thomas Ainlay Jr. and Judy Dixon Gabaldon, "When he [Hughes] left, it had become a corporate town—a newly opened playground for millionaires."[15]

After his purchase of the Sands, Hughes installed management who would no longer look the other way when their star Frank Sinatra suffered gambling losses and refused to pay up. When the casino cut off his credit, Sinatra reacted with fury, eventually getting involved in a brawl with management. *Las Vegas Review-Journal* writer Don Digilio reported, "Singer Tony Bennett left his heart in San Francisco and Frank Sinatra left his teeth—at least two of them—in Las

Vegas." Sinatra left the Sands for Caesars Palace, and many of the Sands workers were glad to see him go. One waiter said, "Sinatra had been going wild at the hotel all morning. I am told he even set fire to his room. . . . Obviously, I can't give my name, but boy, did he [Sinatra] have it coming." A floor man reported that Sinatra had yanked all the telephone jacks out of the hotel switchboard. He continued, "I don't have anything to say about it but if I did, I would have got rid of Sinatra long ago."[16]

Like many of the former owners, Hughes came to Las Vegas with prejudices he did not hesitate to impose. Some of his policies created temporary setbacks in the progress that had been made following the desegregation of the Strip. Many minorities and women found it easier to get work in the showrooms off the Strip. As late as 1971, women were still barred from dealing in most casinos, and there was a glass ceiling that kept them in low-paying jobs such as keno running or waitressing.

The Mob owners had maintained close relations with their unionized employees, even secretly bringing out "food and cold drinks to the strikers in the Downtown Strike of 1967, hiding from their own security." Hughes and the corporate owners who came after him clashed with the various unions many times. Hal Rothman wrote, "The onset of the corporate era altered the tacit labor arrangement. Unionization worked because gaming made the hotels so consistently profitable, and the union's ability to produce labor contributed to their success. The Corporate Gaming Act of 1967 and its amended version in 1969 allowed corporations with pre-existing assumptions about labor-management relationships to own hotels. . . . Quickly the familiarity between management and labor diminished. The handshake contracts soon disappeared. All the documents bore signatures."[17]

Negotiations were no longer friendly or simple, increasingly leading to conflicts between management and Las Vegas unions. In 1976 workers walked out of the casinos for a strike that lasted fifteen months to protest low pay and poor working conditions. Managers were making spending cuts in every area, including entertainment. Mark Tan, writer for the *Hollywood Reporter*, remarked, "In a matter of a year it seems everything was cut to the bone. Restaurants closed, lounges closed, and all of a sudden restaurants became like bus stations up and down the strip."[18] And, as the lounges closed, Las Vegas began to lose more of its former glamour.

The lounges were always more experimental than the showrooms, and their disappearance meant that entertainment directors were less willing or able to take a chance on an untried performer. Tony Bennett, talking of the Mob-connected owners, noted, "They'd put anybody in. I think they had more flexibility, the pressure was less." Liberace recalled, "There was a time when the lounge shows were almost as important as the main room attractions. Many great stars were born in the lounges—people like Shecky Greene and Sarah Vaughan."[19]

Las Vegas began to develop a reputation for tastelessness, a far cry from its previous status as the hip home of the Rat Pack. The hotels became more similar, with six hotels under Howard Hughes's management and other corporate owners sticking to what was tried-and-true. Writers like Willard and Tan felt that the new managers were creating ill will by letting the quality of their entertainment deteriorate. Mark Tan conducted at least ninety interviews of Las Vegas personalities in 1976 and 1977 and asked how they thought Las Vegas had changed. Their responses were consistently and overwhelmingly negative. During this same time period, Bill Willard was gathering material for a book that he planned to call *Alas Vegas*. "Las Vegas reached its peak as an entertainment force in 1965 and has been going downhill erratically since the mid-60s," remarked Willard. "Yet the myth still persists that Las Vegas is the 'Entertainment Capital of the World.'" *Las Vegas Review-Journal* entertainment writer Mike Weatherford felt that "gradually, between 1968 and 1975, Vegas found itself pushed across the generational line that divides cool from laughable."[20]

The target audience was becoming younger, supplanting the established, more mature gamblers of the '50s. This forced entertainment directors to create productions that were more affordable and that suited their younger audience's entertainment tastes. Desert Inn executive Burton Cohen told Willard the following story: "Last New Year, we had the Jimmy Dorsey Orchestra here for a private party, big band, the old standards. When the Jimmy Dorsey Orchestra performed it was me, my girlfriend, and one other couple up dancing. In between, at intermissions, we had a disco. You couldn't get on the dance floor. . . . I said 'ooooo, times have changed.'"[21]

In 1978 the population of the Las Vegas Valley increased to more than four hundred thousand people, and eleven million tourists visited. Despite the growth in population, the construction of new properties decreased.

The Strip seemed stuck in the past. Increasingly, workers went on strikes for better pay, better working conditions, better benefits, and job security. A number of working musicians suffered from extensive hearing loss due the volume level of music in the showroom pits. Conditions were often uncomfortable, cramped, and even unsafe. The air quality in some showrooms was poor, and the rehearsal spaces could be filthy. Yet musicians continued to come to Las Vegas, not realizing that the business had changed. Local musicians complained about the newcomers, and the union began requiring long residencies in town before one could accept work.

By the end of the 1980s, some of the corporate hotel owners were looking to get rid of live music altogether. On June 3, 1989, the Musicians' Union began a strike against five major hotel-casinos that ultimately failed, permanently granting the corporations the right to use taped music and synthesizers in place of musicians.

Ironically, this occurred just as Las Vegas was experiencing a new period of innovation and growth, including a $300 million expansion project for McCarran Airport. Visionary investor Steve Wynn opened the Mirage hotel on November 22, 1989, the first new Strip property in sixteen years. Hal Rothman said, "Calling Steve Wynn a genius and a visionary is a cliché, but his conception and the boldness of his execution still inspire awe. . . . The corporations that owned the hotels were endowed with cash, but lacked imagination."[22] Wynn was responsible for bringing in the first hugely successful Cirque du Soleil shows and gave magicians Siegfried and Roy their own showroom in the Mirage. Other more innovative casino owners followed his lead, and Las Vegas once more became a popular destination with entertainment as a strong draw. In 1996 the Stratosphere and Monte Carlo were completed on the Strip, and the Orleans opened off the Strip. These were followed by New York New York in 1997, Bellagio in 1998, and Mandalay Bay in 1999.

Bill Willard wrote disparagingly about the "new" Las Vegas in a letter: "I'm not so sure that you could abide contentedly in this people/traffic bloated 'destination,' controlled by the corporate mobsters and wacko execs (dig Sheldon Adelson of Venetian supplanting the dear old Sands, plus the ugly billion-dollar Bellagio on the Dunes corner). . . . Lucy and I are stay-at-home, the steamy nights very much out of the loop."[23]

By 2003 all the top "must-see" shows, with the exception of Siegfried and Roy, were using live musicians rather than recordings. But the groups were much smaller than the full-size big bands of the past. Still, the change was welcomed by many. There were new hotels: Palms in 2001, Wynn in 2005, South Point also in 2005, Encore in 2006, and Palazzo in 2008. The 2008 recession hit Las Vegas hard and most construction came to a stop, but one project on the Strip was still completed between 2009 and 2010 when the City Center opened in phases with Aria, Vdara, Mandarin Oriental, and the Cosmopolitan.

Las Vegas Today

Las Vegas still relies on tourism as its main industry, with more than forty-two million people visiting in 2019, according to the Las Vegas Visitors and Convention Authority. Cirque du Soleil has five shows permanently based on the Strip. Clubs and pools host DJ parties that attract huge crowds despite being expensive for patrons when you include table costs, drinks, bottle service, or line privileges. Superstar headliners make appearances using live bands and orchestras. Céline Dion has appeared in the $95 million theater built especially for her in Caesars Palace. When she is not performing, her theater features other big-name stars.

The Culinary Union is strong in Las Vegas, and it continues to fight for fair wages and fair treatment for laborers. By way of comparison, the casino workers in Reno have none of these protections. The Musicians' Union, much smaller than Culinary, still struggles. Employees are generally less satisfied with their jobs under corporate management. Susan Chandler and Jill B. Jones interviewed a number of female casino workers in Reno and Las Vegas, and their subjects expressed frustration and anxiety. In a review of this work, Liz Benston stated:

> The authors discovered a world where workers pop tranquilizers, antidepressants and pain medications to function. A world where financial dependence upon the job fuels paranoia and tension among co-workers competing for shifts. A world where stress, overwork, and embarrassment fuels self-loathing and alienation from family, friends, and other activities outside of work. The stories of this world are gaming industry stories, Nevada stories. But, taken together, they tell a larger tale of deep disenchantment with corporate America.[24]

The question remains: Was Las Vegas really better when the Mob was in charge? The shift from crime syndicate–controlled casinos to corporate-controlled casinos played a large role in temporarily changing the way people viewed Las Vegas. The exceptional growth of Las Vegas over the decades certainly went a long way toward changing its character, though these changes are not unique—any small town that grows into a larger city would likely experience similar issues. Consumer tastes changed with the generations, and at first, Las Vegas did not change quickly enough to satisfy them. Today, it is once again on the cutting edge. Technology advanced significantly, opening the door to using recordings instead of live music, though live music is again dominant. Many musicians left town, but others came in to take their places. Las Vegas is once again known as "the entertainment capital of the world." Las Vegas musical entertainment will continue to change, and people will continue to have opinions about those changes.

Notes

1. Bill Willard, "Vegas' $164,000,000 Question," *Variety*, July 13, 1955, 52.

2. Thomas "Taj" Ainlay Jr. and Judy Dixon Gabaldon, *Las Vegas: The Fabulous First Century* (Charleston, SC: Arcadia, 2003), 61.

3. Hal Rothman, *The Making of Modern Nevada* (Reno: University of Nevada Press, 2010), 108.

4. Susan Berman, *Lady Las Vegas: The Inside Story behind America's Neon Oasis* (New York: A&E Network and TV Books, 1996), 107.

5. Jack Sheehan, *Quiet Kingmaker of Las Vegas: E. Parry Thomas* (Las Vegas: Stephens Press, 2009), 92–93.

6. Box 9, folder 2, Bill Willard Collection, MS 2001-17, Special Collections, UNLV Libraries, University of Nevada, Las Vegas (hereafter cited as Willard Collection).

7. Dennis N. Griffin, *The Battle for Las Vegas: The Law vs. The Mob* (Las Vegas: Huntington Press, 2006), 33.

8. Griffin, *Battle for Las Vegas*, 34, 37.

9. Griffin, *Battle for Las Vegas*, 62.

10. William H. "Bob" Bailey, *Looking Up! Finding My Voice in Las Vegas* (Las Vegas: Stephens Press, 2009), 109.

11. James Roman, *Chronicles of Old Las Vegas: Exposing Sin City's High Stakes History* (New York: Museyon, 2011), 104.

12. Corey Levitan, "Top Ten Scandals," *Las Vegas Review-Journal*, March 2, 2008.

13. "Hughes Takes DI Reins," *Las Vegas Review-Journal*, April 1, 1967.

14. Interview with Bob Maheu, KNPR Vegas I Remember transcripts, box 1, folder 18, MS 063, Nevada State Museum, Las Vegas, Special Collections.

15. Ainlay and Gabaldon, *Las Vegas*, 127.

16. Don Digilio, "Sinatra Loses Teeth in Strip Hotel Brawl," *Las Vegas Review-Journal*, September 12, 1967.

17. Rothman, *Making of Modern Nevada*, 134, 135.

18. Interview with Mark Tan, 1976, box 1, folder 74, Mark Tan Collection, MS 089, Nevada State Museum, Las Vegas, Special Collections (hereafter cited as Tan Collection).

19. Interview with Tony Bennett, Tan Collection; interview with Liberace, Tan Collection.

20. Interview with Bill Willard, Tan Collection; Mike Weatherford, *Cult Vegas: The Weirdest! The Wildest! The Swingin'est Town on Earth* (Las Vegas: Huntington Press, 2001), 6.

21. Interview with Burton Cohen by Bill Willard, Willard Collection.

22. Hal Rothman, *Neon Metropolis: How Las Vegas Started the Twenty-First Century* (New York: Routledge, 2002), 45.

23. Letter to "Joe" written by Bill Willard, Willard Collection.

24. Liz Benston, "The Toll and the Silence," *Seven*, December 22, 2011–January 4, 2012; Susan Chandler and Jill B. Jones, *Casino Women: Courage in Unexpected Places* (Ithaca, NY: Cornell University Press, 2011).

PART II

Overheard

His boy, young Icarus, that near him stood,
Unthinking of his fate, with smiles pursu'd
The floating feathers, which the moving air
Bore loosely from the ground, and wasted here and there.
Or with the wax impertinently play'd,
And with his childish tricks the great design delay'd.

4

Music as Misdirection

JASON LEDDINGTON

Magic and Vegas have a lot in common. Both have a reputation for bad taste and cheap thrills, and they've both generally been ignored—or at best ridiculed—by the art-critical establishment. It's fitting, then, that no city loves magic like Vegas loves magic. Today, more than one-third of its top-selling shows feature magic, and this means that no complete treatment of art and entertainment in Sin City can afford to ignore it.[1] But what's at risk here is more than theoretical completeness. Magic provides a distinctive—and distinctively powerful—form of aesthetic experience whose appeal spans very different cultures, age groups, and historical periods.[2] Recognizing this opens a variety of theoretical doors and raises a host of questions, among them the issue of the relationship between magic and other genres and art forms.[3] Indeed, magic performances are often complex theatrical events that incorporate drama, humor, elements of horror, and—critically for present concern—music. While these are sometimes incidental accretions, mere presentational window dressing for the magic trick itself, they can also be tools in the magician's toolbox. For example, magicians widely appreciate that a joke can be good for more than a laugh: in virtue of how it shapes the audience's attention, it can directly contribute to the success of a trick.[4]

In this brief chapter, I'll argue that the same is true of music and that magicians employ it not only to set the mood and highlight dramatic moments, but also to facilitate the deception that's necessary for the experience of magic itself. As we will see, music can frame, stimulate, and illuminate, but it can simultaneously also block and blind. No wonder, then, that it's everywhere in Vegas, which, like magic, works only if we're receptive to the illusions it openly manufactures.

The Nature and Experience of Magic

Magic tricks are, of course, meant to fool us. But the magician deceives her audience only as a means to an end. Her real aim is to create the illusion as of an impossible event—say, the transformation or vanishing of a playing card, unaided human flight, or an episode of mind reading. At the same time, however, she is open about her deception; she presents her illusions for what they are. This distinguishes the magician from the charlatan who uses the tools of magic performance to mislead his audience about the nature of reality. Both deceive their audiences; only the magician is honest about doing so.

The magician's honesty has ethical import, but it also has aesthetic significance. It's critical to magic's aesthetic goals that the audience have no illusions about the fact that they're witnessing illusions. Why? First, consider that, if the audience doesn't believe that what seems to be happening onstage is *impossible*—and so, something that *cannot* happen—then they will not experience the performance as magical. Second, if something impossible seems to happen, then we know it *must* be an illusion.[5] Thus, the magician presents herself as an entertainer, not as a "real wizard." This theatrical frame not only telegraphs respect for the audience (as if we'd believe she can really fly, or make coins disappear, or . . .), but also sets the stage for a complex game of intellectual cat-and-mouse: the magician promises an illusion of an impossible event; implicitly, in so doing, she invites us to figure it out, to suss out her "method," and her main job is to sustain the illusion by preventing us from doing so. Critically, however, a good performance should leave us not just ignorant of how the illusion was *actually* accomplished, but *entirely at a loss for any plausible explanation* for what we've seen. Only then will we experience it as impossible.[6] In this respect, magic should leave us in the position of being unable to make sense of the experience it provides.[7] We know it's a trick—that is, that it has an explanation—but absent any candidate account, we can't see how it *could* be a trick. *This* is what it means to have the experience of magic.[8]

In normal circumstances, to be unable to make sense of an experience might be quite unpleasant; or, if you're a scientist, it might prompt serious inquiry. However, in a magic show, it's safe to be baffled. You needn't worry about your grip on reality or if the laws of physics need revision. Still, there is a pressing question here: Why does anyone actually *enjoy* magic? Indeed, why do so *many* people love it? Relatedly, why does strong magic elicit such powerful emotional responses? After all, we all know it's just a trick![9] These are among the interesting psychological/philosophical questions that attention to magic raises. For present purposes, however, the central idea is that magic performances centrally involve a good-natured, playful attempt to deprive the audience of any way to explain what they've witnessed.

Understanding magic in this way reveals one reason it's such a good fit with Vegas, where promises of wealth, glamour, and easy sex are ubiquitous. As if it were a magic show, in Vegas, everyone knows it's a trick: the promises are hollow, and the house always wins in the end. At the same time, however, in the lavish setting of a big hotel, in a club filled with beautiful bodies, or on the floor of a casino with hundreds of thousands of dollars literally *right there on the table*, just a few bets away, it can be hard to see how it *could* be a trick. After all, *the opulence is real, those are real bodies*, and *that's real money*. Like a good magic performance, then, Vegas openly presents convincing illusions, and they are powerful enough to get us to play along, even against our better judgment.

Misdirection

In magic, *misdirection* is the generic term for any technique that manipulates the audience's attention to better conceal the method by which a trick is accomplished. Unsurprisingly, misdirection is generally effective only when it's not obvious. For example, to use an explosion on one side of the stage as cover for vanishing a dove on the other side of the stage is the worst sort of misdirection. Rightly or wrongly, the audience will sense that, had they not looked away, they might have seen how the dove was vanished; so, they will hardly experience its disappearance as an impossibility. The key to effective misdirection is therefore that the audience should have the impression that the magician never actually manipulated their attention. The best misdirection is invisible *as* misdirection.

Here is an example. In sleight-of-hand close-up magic, which is generally performed with spectators within normal conversational range (such as standing together in a group or seated together at a table), magicians make sophisticated use of everyday social cues and behaviors as misdirection. Normally, when you look someone in the eye in a conversational setting, they involuntarily return the favor—at least for an instant. This is regular human behavior, and we hardly ever register it. So, when the magician glances at us, we will generally briefly shift our attention to her face, and, so, away from her hands. This alone can make the difference between noticing and failing to notice a piece of sleight of hand. Indeed, her hands may never actually go out of view, and we may later (incorrectly) report that we never took our eyes off of them. The fact is that we are blissfully unaware of how we allocate our attention in normal social interaction, and we are very bad at assessing how blind this makes us to what's going on around us. Just a glance in your direction—which you'd almost never experience as misdirection—can weaken your attentional focus enough to make you effectively blind to the magician's method. In expert sleight-of-hand magic, a performance may include dozens of such moments, some highly choreographed, some improvised according to the situation.[10] The question, then, is how can music be used in this way?

Music as Misdirection

Historically, the dominant form of magic in Las Vegas is "stage magic," in which the performer works from the stage and is widely separated from most of the audience. Volunteers may be called up to participate in the act, but the show is designed to be witnessed from a distance. Stage acts therefore typically involve large-scale illusions or sleight of hand with highly visible objects such as doves, large candles, and bright scarves. Canonical Vegas stage acts of this sort include Lance Burton, Johnny Thompson, Siegfried and Roy, David Copperfield, Mac King, and Penn and Teller. But thanks in part to the rise in popularity of sleight of hand and "street magic" performers such as David Blaine, as well as the refinement of camera and projection technology that allows large audiences to have intimate experiences of tricks performed onstage with small objects, it was only a matter of time before close-up magic would come play an important role in the Vegas magic scene. The key catalyst here was *America's Got Talent*. Two recent winners—Mat Franco (2014) and Shin Lim (2018)—are primarily close-up card magicians, and both now have successful residencies at Vegas hotels. And while almost all Vegas magic acts make some use of music, arguably no contemporary magician makes better use of it than Shin Lim.[11]

Close-up magic is typically conversational and doesn't often feature music. By contrast, Lim's signature close-up sleight-of-hand performances involve minimal conversation and are carefully choreographed to dramatic, mostly instrumental musical tracks. In this respect, Lim's act resembles the otherwise very different Vegas act of the late Siegfried and Roy, which, instead of sleight of hand, featured exotic cats, big-box illusions, and scantily clad assistants. Despite their differences in style, both acts use music their audiences would recognize as contemporary. Lim's musical choices range from sparsely punctuated atmospheric ambient sound to drum-heavy post-rock. By contrast, Siegfried and Roy deployed electronic music with a decidedly twentieth-century character—often using popular tracks—as well as grandiose orchestral pieces of the sort readers might associate with the schmaltzy theatrics of David Copperfield's TV specials. The fact is that Vegas magicians have relied on a wide variety of (mostly) instrumental music. For instance, Lance Burton performed his classically elegant sleight-of-hand dove act to the opening movement of Vivaldi's *The Four Seasons*. And while at least some of what follows applies to any magic act that makes use of music, Lim's act makes especially rich use of music as misdirection.

There are arguably three basic ways in which music can misdirect. First, most innocuously, by its very presence, it would seem that music reduces the amount of attention we have available to parse what we see. Our attentional resources are finite. So, other things being equal, adding another object of attention to the performance—especially one that surreptitiously weakens our visual-attentional capacities—should make it easier for the magician to deceive us. Admittedly, this is an empirical hypothesis, and one that deserves testing. As always, however, everything will depend on how the music is used. Painfully loud music at a critical moment in the show might easily be experienced as a crude diversion. By contrast, the instrumental tracks in Lim's work come across as innocuous emotion-heightening accompaniment. As such, they're perfectly pitched to function as misdirection.

Second, it would seem that music can misdirect precisely by intensifying the emotions we experience during a performance, whether serious (as in Lim's work) or playful (as in, say, Mac King's). When caught up in the sort of emotionally charged atmosphere that only music can create, it would seem to be more difficult to deploy our cognitive and attentional resources to divine the method behind the trick. Critically, once again, this is a subtle sort of misdirection, one we experience merely as part of what makes the performance entertaining. We do not generally experience the music in Lim's show as a tool that facilitates deception by manipulating us emotionally, but there is good reason to think that it is.[12]

Finally, probably the most important form of musical misdirection involves the use of music to direct attention to particular moments in the show. This sort of misdirection comes in two types, and both are instances of what magicians call "temporal misdirection," which involves creating a temporal gap between the magician's execution of the method by which a trick is accomplished and the audience's awareness of the magical effect that method is used to produce.[13]

First, a piece of music can be used to *circumscribe* a performance, and so to direct attention away from moments before or after the music begins. For example, suppose a performer walks onstage to introduce a trick that she will perform to music. First, however, she invites the audience to inspect the props that she will use. Then, she takes her position, the music starts, and the performance officially begins. The audience will tend to look for secrets only in what happens during the musically accompanied "official" performance. In truth, however, important secrets may in large part lie in things the magician does before the music starts. Yet thanks in part to the musical frame, the audience is unlikely to consider (or even remember) anything outside of this frame when reflecting on how the trick might have been done.[14]

Second, in a performance accompanied by a piece of music, musical accents can be used to highlight particular moments within the official performance itself. The most obvious examples involve using musical climaxes to establish "magic moments"—moments when, from the audience's perspective, particular magical effects happen. Lim's carefully choreographed close-up performances make regular and masterful use of this technique. The idea is that audiences will tend to treat the magic moment as the moment the magician "does" the trick. But, as always in magic, appearance and reality may diverge, and the magician often executes the secret method to accomplish her trick long before she presents it theatrically to her audience. For example, Lim may have ditched a playing card in his pocket (method) long before he pretends to make it vanish from his hand (magic moment).[15] If that magic moment is established by, say, a crescendo in the music, then this is a case of musically driven temporal misdirection. Influenced by the music, the audience will tend to think—erroneously—that the secret to the trick must be in action at the moment the magic seems to happen. So misled, they will find it impossible to explain what they have witnessed.

Knowing how music can function as misdirection opens the door to a richer experience of magic performance. Next time you watch a piece of magic accompanied by music, reflect on how the music works on you and ask yourself how the magician might use it as an ingredient in creating her illusions. Notice whether and how the music frames the performance, highlights moments within it, and diffuses your attention, and consider whether all of this contributes to directing your thinking about the methods employed. Finally, attuned to music's misdirective power, look for places where it might be less innocuous, domains where deception aims, not merely at entertainment, but also at exploitation—which brings us full circle right back to Las Vegas.

Conclusion

The core idea in this chapter is that magic performances make distinctive use of music as an object of attention. Of course, theatrical performances of all kinds use music to shape how audiences allocate their attention, foregrounding some elements, backgrounding others. An opera or musical may highlight the entrance of an important character with a change in the music, so directing our attention to the new arrival at the expense of whatever else is happening onstage. However, merely provoking such a shift in the "figure-ground" relationships in a perceived scene does not constitute misdirection. Misdirection aims at *blindness*, not mere backgrounding. This is why misdirection's proper theatrical home is magic, which, unlike other forms of theater, depends constitutively on the fact that some elements relegated to the attentional shadows should *vanish completely from view*. In the world of theater, then, only in magic is there music as misdirection.

One way to resist this claim is to reject the idea that magic is essentially different from conventional theater (or even cinema). You might think that *all* of them typically aim at "illusions" of reality, and so, on one level or another, at deception. This idea is quite common, but I think it's badly mistaken.[16] Unlike magic, neither conventional theater nor cinema standardly aims at (much less achieves) the illusion that the events it depicts are genuinely happening before the audience.[17] And this is precisely why Vegas is more like magic than conventional theater. As I suggested above, we all know—and Vegas itself admits—that its promises of wealth, glamour, and sex are hollow. At the same time, those promises can certainly feel genuine. In this respect, like magic, Vegas openly traffics in illusions. Importantly, however, this doesn't mean that Vegas is just a big magic show. Magic's openness renders it essentially playful and saves it from deteriorating into base charlatanry. But Vegas's openness is insidious. Magic aims at entertainment and perhaps edification (we might learn something about how easily we're hoodwinked), but Vegas wants our money—all of it—and deploys its illusions to this end. In this context, its openness is a ruse: it allows a highly exploitative business model to avoid being caught in a lie ("We never told you you'd get rich!") while, at the same time, posing as an adult playground that offers only harmless—if hardly wholesome—good fun. So, we let our guard down and play along, and the house cashes in.

In conclusion, when illusions are at play, there may be more to music than meets the ear. This leaves us with a pressing question: Beyond the magician's theater, how does music function to sustain the illusions on which Vegas depends, to render invisible the methods by which those illusions work? Of course, similar questions might be asked about consumer culture more generally, though I'm inclined to think that they'll be less interesting in part because, unlike Vegas, consumer culture is hardly open about its illusioneering. Being honest about this allows Vegas, like the magician, to present itself as playful. By contrast, consumer culture, like charlatanry, asks us to take it seriously, and so depends on our not seeing its illusions for what they are.

Notes

1. "Las Vegas Shows," https://www.vegas.com/shows/.

2. See Jason Leddington, "The Experience of Magic," *Journal of Aesthetics and Art Criticism* 74, no. 3 (2016): 253–64; and Jason Leddington, "The Enjoyment of Negative Emotions in the Experience of Magic," *Behavioral and Brain Sciences* 40 (2017): 34–35.

3. For example, see Jason Leddington, "Comic Impossibilities," *Journal of Aesthetics and Art Criticism* 78, no. 4 (2020): 547–58, where I argue that magic performance deserves to be considered a limit case of stand-up comedy.

4. See Gustav Kuhn, *Experiencing the Impossible* (Cambridge, MA: MIT Press, 2019), 41.

5. Compare performing a "mentalism" show (with illusions of mind-reading, telekinesis, and so on) for an audience that believes in psychic phenomena; at best, they will experience it as a series of demonstrations of unusual abilities. But the point of magic is to present the audience with an event that seems to transcend any possible ability. It should seem *entirely* impossible.

6. "No way!" is an exclamation common in the face of good magic. We should take this literally: the spectator sees *no way* for *that* to be done.

7. Another common audience exclamation: "That makes no sense!"

8. In previous writing, I argue that the experience of magic is therefore an *aporetic* experience that is structurally isomorphic to the sort of experience that Socrates produces in his interlocutors in Plato's early "Socratic" dialogues. See Leddington, "The Experience of Magic"; and Jason Leddington, "Magic: The Art of the Impossible," in *Aesthetics: A Reader in Philosophy of the Arts*, edited by David Goldblatt, Lee B. Brown, and Stephanie Patridge, 373–79, 4th ed. (New York : Routledge, 2017).

9. For some examples of strong candid emotional responses to magic, see David Blaine's recent appearances on *The Tonight Show with Jimmy Fallon*, or, even better, his 1997 TV special, *David Blaine: Street Magic*, produced before he was a household name. For one approach to explaining our enjoyment of magic, see Leddington, "Enjoyment of Negative Emotions." Note, however, that my ideas on this have evolved, and I plan to publish a more complete approach to our enjoyment of magic in an essay tentatively titled "Savoring the Impossible."

10. For a rich discussion of misdirection and the psychological mechanisms involved, see Kuhn's *Experiencing the Impossible*. Though Kuhn does not discuss the use of music for misdirection, he does offer some hints as to how auditory stimuli might have unexpected and unconscious effects on visual experience (98). For a deeper and far-ranging discussion of such sensory cross-over effects, see Casey O'Callaghan, *A Multisensory Philosophy of Perception* (New York: Oxford University Press, 2019).

11. Shin Lim's signature close-up performances are widely available on YouTube. I particularly recommend his appearances on *America's Got Talent* and *Penn & Teller: Fool Us*. Many of these same tricks are performed in his Vegas show.

12. Once again, though, this is an empirical hypothesis worth testing.

13. Kuhn, *Experiencing the Impossible*, 41.

14. A classic piece of magic often performed in this way is the "Linking Rings."

15. I'm not saying that this is how he accomplishes *any* of the many playing card vanishes he performs! I'll leave it to you to puzzle over them.

16. See, for example, Bernard Beckerman, *Theatrical Presentation: Performer, Audience, and Act*, edited by Gloria Brim Beckerman and William Coco (New York: Routledge, 1990).

17. For discussion, see Jason Leddington, "Review of 'The Aesthetic Illusion in Literature and the Arts,'" *Notre Dame Philosophical Reviews* (2018), https://ndpr.nd.edu/news/the-aesthetic-illusion-in-literature-and-the-arts/; and Robert Hopkins, "Moving Because Pictures? Illusion and the Emotional Power of Film," *Midwest Studies in Philosophy* 34, no. 1 (2010): 200–218.

5

Presence, Absence, and Live Virtuality

Soundscapes in Cirque du Soleil on the Las Vegas Strip

LYNDA PAUL

Over the past three and a half decades, Cirque du Soleil has grown from a troupe of traveling street performers to one of the foremost performing arts entertainment companies in the world. This success stems not only from founder Guy Laliberté's oft-cited business acumen (although his talent and skill in this area are well documented), nor simply from the creative ingenuity of the shows' individual performers and directors (many of whom have, nonetheless, contributed an important component to the company's continually evolving identity). I would argue, rather, that it lies more fundamentally in the range of techniques that the company has developed in order to make "traditional" circus arts particularly compatible with an ethos of post–Cold War, rapidly digitalizing, late-twentieth- and early-twenty-first-century globalized and virtualizing culture. Specifically, Cirque has cultivated a symbiotic relationship with sites of carnivalesque inversion and simulacrum-esque invention, has nurtured a fixed and permanent presence at vacation spots that indulge the most wide-ranging and provocative of touristic fantasies, and has become the dominant entertainment in locations that make it a point to virtualize their visitors' live experiences. Through its relationship with these special locations—especially Las Vegas—Cirque du Soleil made itself into one of the most prominent and world-renowned vehicles for the reenchantment of a politically and economically fraught contemporary world around the turn of the twenty-first century.

Offering the perfect contemporary entertainment for fantastical escapist sites, Cirque's surrealistic, optimistic, epic shows provide a comforting break from a fragmentary, unstable, and often difficult real world. They do so in part by showcasing the "magic" of human imagination and ability, often depicting heroes who conquer external obstacles or internal fears in the face of unusual situations and challenges, all within a beautiful and whimsical visual framework. Furthermore, such themes are performed through highly disciplined physical bodies—specifically, the stunning, skilled dexterity of world-class gymnasts and acrobats—that emphasize implicitly a sense of human greatness. Perhaps more fundamentally, as this chapter will demonstrate, the shows' seemingly perfect repeatability may offer a counterbalance to the ever-quickening pace of technological and societal change in today's rapidly shifting and increasingly unstable and ephemeral world. Indeed, the company's success may ultimately lie in the way it situates itself within specially marked fantasy sites, combining utopian themes and unprecedented technical-theatrical panache with a mode of transmission that in itself symbolizes human achievement, control, and stability.

This chapter examines how Cirque intersects with, reflects back, influences, and makes visible some of our societies' most hidden ideologies about presence and absence in body and mind. I argue here that both the Las Vegas Strip and its residential Cirque shows are predicated fundamentally upon the fusion of live bodies and real physical objects with immaterially simulated phenomena, capturing at once the feelings of ephemerality, physical escape, and unpredictability associated with live performance, and the sense of safety and security associated with the perfect repeatability of a digital recording. To do this, they offer a part-live, part-technological, part-concrete, part-immaterial construction of simulated space—a physically grounded, materially anchored oxymoronic version of virtual reality that relies in large part upon the creation of a live but technologically mediated soundscape that imperceptibly perfects the live elements in real time. Ultimately, it is through the use of covert musical mediation *and* covert musical liveness that Cirque, and Vegas itself, is able to create experiences that come across, night after night, and for years on end, as both *very* live and *very* perfect—featuring bodies both very present and very absent, and pointing us toward a counterintuitive construction of absence and presence that can help us think more deeply about our own values and beliefs about the absent presences of our world today.

The Las Vegas Strip

The Las Vegas Strip is known famously for its disorienting signals of time and space. The lack of timepieces and natural light is intended to erase the signals of time's passage, encouraging visitors to forget it—to focus, without temporal distractions, on expensive but immediate pleasures. Time is thus compressed and expanded; while in the everyday world, the days and seasons are marked as moments between a past and a future, time's passage is denied on the Strip, the linear flow of days transformed virtually into an eternal present. Spatially, the Strip is known for its thematic hotel experiences. New York, Venice, Monte Carlo, New Orleans—all are replicated in miniature, the entire urban world symbolically crammed into three-and-a-half miles of casino-hotels. Inside the casinos, ceilings are painted to look like skies, and imitation replicas of miniature buildings line the labyrinthine passageways, all in harmony with the given hotel's theme. In a tiny amount of actual geographical span, space, like time, is made virtually infinite.

The Las Vegas Strip's disorienting visual fakery is more commonly acknowledged than its auditory assault, but sounds, both live and computerized, play a crucial role in the spatial and temporal virtualization of this environment, the conflicting signals of presence and absence that shape the site. The sounds of the environment play an essential, if invisible, role in the simulation of other locales and time periods for which the Vegas Strip is known (for example, French music in the vicinity of the Paris hotel), noisily attracting, distracting, and confusing the visitors, forcing them to become more sensually absorbed in the virtual realm, as one cannot close one's ears or avert them. Passersby routinely walk into each other, tripping over curbs and poles; few of the visitors are paying attention to their immediate surroundings, so captivated are they by the virtual world calling to them. Inside the buildings, one finds the same principle of distraction at work—but even louder. Restaurants, bars, lounges, and casinos inside the hotels all share the same basic auditory space, and each transmits its own music (sometimes live, often recorded—and always amplified). The zones at which auditory worlds overlap are more condensed indoors than they are outside—sound, which cannot be contained, becomes a noisy jumble, a roar in which barely coherent snippets, fragments, and screeches from eating areas and clubs bleed into the jangling major thirds of slot machines and beeps of cash registers and elevator doors.

Ultimately, the Las Vegas Strip manifests—and manufactures—fantasies of control over time and space. Virtually, immaterially, technologically, Las Vegas contains and controls all space and all time. Tourists, in complementary fashion, come to the Strip to cede control of the ever-ticking, uncontrollable progression of their lives, to escape the time and space of their everyday realities. They expect, even desire, to be completely immersed in a live playground turned virtual reality, and to interact with their environment in peculiar ways that are not only undesirable but even impossible in the everyday realm. Las Vegas is thus both a very live and a very virtual world, a simulacrum along the lines of Jean Baudrillard that muddies what is real and what is not—an attempt to encompass the whole world and its collective fantasies, making it, as anthropologist Barbara Kirshenblatt-Gimblett might say, the destination of all destinations.[1]

Cirque du Soleil

So what is the role of a Cirque du Soleil show in such a location? Circus, broadly speaking, might be thought of as the epitome of live performance, an art form grounded fundamentally in the co-presence of bodies. It is commonly defined by such elements as "immediacy, danger, . . . sensationalism, the privileging of the bodily . . . [and] its sense of event."[2] Similar descriptions can be found in the works of diverse circus commentators, from academics to critics to hobbyists, and they suggest that circus is often seen as offering a sort of unmediated presence, a sense of uniqueness, and the ultimate experience of ephemerality. Circus historian Antony Hippisley Coxe, for example, argues that because the circus can be seen from all sides (unlike other types of performance, such as plays or magic shows), "the performers *actually* do what they appear to do."[3] In other words, thanks to the structure of a theater "in the round," the audience feels a greater sense of immediacy because it "knows" that the acrobats *really* flip, contortionists *actually* twist, and countless fire-eaters, aerialists, and others perform a variety of stunts that entail real physical risk. Even less dangerous circus acts (for example, juggling) tend to require a high degree of improvisatory flexibility in order to respond to the contingencies inherent in such physical theater. And finally, most circuses throughout history have been accompanied by the sounds of live musicians, whose instruments are traditionally heard via the live, "natural" acoustics of a surrounding tent.[4] Circus is not simply one example of the many performing arts genres that value liveness. The form is, as a whole, so invested in bodily presence, so permeated by variability, and so dependent upon interactivity that we might think of it as virtually *predicated* upon all that is commonly aligned with a sense of liveness.[5]

This traditional circus emphasis on live performance is, in many ways, continued in Cirque du Soleil: the company's shows frequently feature physical stunts, audience-interactive clowns, and risky feats. Live bodies still matter. But even from its earliest days, Cirque du Soleil also moved away from canonic circus aesthetics, entering into the late-twentieth-century subset of circus now known as "Nouveau Cirque," or "New Circus," which is characterized generally by its absence of animals, its linking of separate acts by themes or even loose narratives, and its engagement with multimedia.[6] With the increase of New Circus features throughout the 1980s and 1990s, the status of Cirque's shows as "live performance" became more complicated: elaborate, cinematic visual effects mediated—and, arguably, mitigated—the sense of presence one would expect to feel when watching real human bodies engaged in dangerous stunts. By the same token, Cirque's live musicians were increasingly supplemented—and in some cases supplanted—by recordings, integrating absence into the very fabric of the soundtracks.

This process of "multimediation" became particularly pronounced when the troupe began to produce resident shows for the Las Vegas Strip. In one of their Vegas shows, *Love* (a Beatles-themed show, which premiered in 2006), there is a striking amount of cinematic apparatus. The "real" performers in some scenes are dwarfed by the surrounding special effects: the most salient human images at times might be a gigantic projection on a screen surrounding the audience. One might very well ask whether, in such an oversaturated and multimediated visual sphere, the live human bodies doing the physical stunts have become less aesthetically important. The answer, I will argue, is complex and even counterintuitive. When, in these shows, there appears to be an aesthetic emphasis on the live, there is actually a high degree of concealed mediation at work; however, when technology appears to guide a show's aesthetic, there is in fact a great deal of live intervention concealed behind the scenes. Cirque du Soleil's first permanent Vegas show opened in a custom-built theater at the Treasure Island hotel-casino in 1993. The entire Strip is only about three miles long, and the several Cirque shows being performed at any given time since the turn of the twenty-first century are quite densely packed into the space. And in the nearly three decades since, the company has come virtually to dominate the entertainment sector of the Strip.

Cirque's Vegas shows are unusual for a variety of reasons. For example, because the shows are funded largely by casino moguls, they have at their disposal literally millions of dollars in capital for their development. Much of this budget goes toward the creation of high-tech, cutting-edge theatrical technology, and for this reason the Vegas productions represent the most elaborate and multimediated of all Cirque du Soleil's output to date. So heavily do these shows rely upon technology that they *cannot* be performed or even seen anywhere other than in their custom-built theaters inside the various hotel-casinos. Nineteenth-century specialists will surely be reminded of Wagner and his *Festspielhaus*, and this is not an unreasonable comparison. Like pilgrims to Bayreuth, visitors to Vegas travel from afar to a place marked as extraordinary in order to experience fantastical epic productions housed in theaters specially designed to draw the audience member into an absorptive (some might even say totalizing) world.[7]

But most important for the purposes of this chapter, Cirque's Vegas shows participate in the extremely high-stakes and complex tourist economy of the Strip, which today advertises itself essentially as a safe place for tourists to experience different types of fantasies (or simulations thereof) in a kind of immersive, physically grounded virtual reality. Any official entertainment that does not compellingly present itself as perfect and reliable is a potential liability and could be detrimental to its producers' bank accounts (or to the Strip's reputation as a whole). These days the Strip cannot afford to let things "go wrong" in one of its performances, any more than it can afford for things to "go wrong" inside a casino or on the streets.[8] Therefore, in order to guarantee that high-paying investors and audience members get their money's worth, and in order to participate convincingly in the fantastical simulation that is the Las Vegas Strip, Cirque's elaborate Vegas shows must be not only exciting and live, in the tradition of circus, but also *absolutely reliable and repeatable* night after night. A crucial tension arises here between these two demands, for—as musicians well know—"live" performance always includes the potential for imperfection.[9] And the more variable, physical, and spontaneous a show is, the more extreme its potential contingencies, and the more likely they are to occur.

In order to produce shows that can offer *both* seemingly seamless perfection *and* "live" corporeally based excitement, Cirque du Soleil employs music, and sound more generally, as a kind of secretive mediator, a hidden force that allows the shows to feel at once very perfect and very live. On the one hand, the sounds of Cirque's "live" musicians are discreetly mediated and "perfected"—mixed with prerecorded tracks and transmitted via multidimensional surround-sound speaker systems that alter the output of the musicians onstage as well as the theater's natural acoustics.[10] On the other hand, and perhaps more remarkably, Cirque also sometimes inverts this process, hiding its live musicians from the audience and in such moments making its music seem far *less* live than it actually is. In these cases, Cirque's discreetly live music comes across as so seamless and so integrated with the acts that it could be *mistaken for a digital recording*—yet, as I will show, this very aesthetic of perfected mediatization relies entirely upon hidden live processes for its success. Most important, both processes—in a sense, inversions of each other—are all but indiscernible to audiences. Only by sitting backstage during performances and rehearsals and talking to Cirque's musicians can an outsider discern the concealed elements of presence and absence underpinning the soundscapes of these shows.

As a general rule, the instruments showcased to the audience are not the electronic keyboard synthesizers or computer consoles that are as fundamental to Cirque's musical sound as any other instrument, but, rather, those that signify tradition, authenticity, and liveness. In *Mystère*, for example, the audience watches musicians playing Japanese taiko drums in the center of the stage. The musicians in the show's regular band—that is, the amplified ensemble that accompanies the entire show—are located high on a platform, hidden in the darkness toward the far-right upper corner of the image; they are not nearly as visible as the acrobats featured on the taiko drums. In *O*, a djeli from Senegal performs onstage with his kora. Through the acoustic immediacy and authentic connotations of this djeli's traditional instrument, and the backdrop's visual emphasis on nature, the scene conveys a strong sense of liveness. In *KÀ*, in one notable scene, a character inside a wooden cage plays the flute.

However, what the audience actually *hears* is not entirely as "immediate" or as contingently "live" as it appears. In the scene from *KÀ*, for example, the character is only simulating playing the flute: the sounds are in fact being generated by a flute patch on a synthesizer hidden underneath the stage. And this simulation of live flute playing represents only one of the myriad ways in which Cirque du Soleil makes use of sound technology to discreetly mediate the natural sounds of the live musicians in the physical theater in order to control contingency and give the shows a more perfected polish—while at the same time allowing them to *feel* live, and present.

Cirque's technological intervention in the feeling of liveness extends well beyond the production of instrument sounds. Each of their Vegas shows' theaters features unique and innovative loudspeaker systems, designed to mask the building's natural acoustics, creating what we might call a virtual acoustical effect. For example, the acoustics of *O*'s theater balance the need for subtlety and audience responsiveness. *O*'s sound designers explain, "The audience members must hear each other applaud. . . . But at the same time, the room can't be too live, because the musical score features extremely nuanced sound effects." To artificially create a sense of acoustical liveness, then, the engineers "send certain cues to the loudspeakers [concealed inside the walls in the sides of the theater]." And because no one in the audience can see the speakers, they do not necessarily expect to hear mediated sound coming from that direction. Therefore, when sounds are routed to these speakers, and given extra reverb effects, as well as certain kinds of decay, "it creates the impression that the audience is in a much larger room made of marble."[11] The sound designers thus achieve near total control over the degree of acoustic "liveness" experienced in the hall at every moment, and "liveness" itself becomes the product of sonically "perfecting" the hall's natural acoustics via highly controlled mediatized means.

Love's theater is also designed to perfect its soundscape, and it houses the most sonically complex system of Cirque's shows to date. First and foremost, one must understand that the audience is seated on all sides of the stage. This structure allows an audience member to see other members of the house seated both down below and across the stage from them and on the other sides of the large semitransparent screens that sometimes cross through the stage space. So if the audience in one location hears sound streams coming from its left and right, the audience seated across the stage will naturally hear the inverse—and the audience on each of the other two sides will hear yet a different mix. The 360-degree audience design in *Love*'s theater is further complicated by the vast range of height at which audience members are seated, with some people located right next to the stage's floor, and others dozens of feet higher, in uneven distribution. In order to create a mix that could both fill the auditorium and effectively channel the right balance of sounds to everyone, *Love*'s sound designer moved beyond the standard 5.1 surround-sound setup (speakers at the listener's front left, front right, center, back left, back right, plus a subwoofer) into a multidimensional, extremely complex layout that would best be described as *25.5*, with the sources of the sounds originating in multiple planes around you.[12] (If you want to imagine what this sounds like, think of the sound of the best movie theater you've ever been to, and quintuple it.) This system relies on more than six thousand specially located speakers in all parts of the theater, including the walls, floors, ceiling, and inside the audience's seats, and creates a wash of sound that evokes the sense of attending a live concert, but is even "better": screaming girls, for example, whose loudness at one point contributed to the Beatles' decision to stop touring because they could no longer hear themselves playing, can be turned down. A "live but better than live" effect is thus created here entirely by sonic technology, and in this way digital sound is once again made to be experienced as live, immediate, perfected sound.

In addition to artificial acoustics, Cirque's Vegas shows have made increasing use of playback technology, employing digital tracks as surrogate musicians for a variety of purposes. Prerecorded tracks are often used as substitutes for the show's musicians when someone cannot make a show (a rare but not impossible occurrence).[13] For many of Cirque's shows, it would be difficult to employ a "sub" musician in the way a normal pit orchestra would. In the first place, the musicians' individual parts are not always notated in score form, a method that will be discussed below. Second, using a live sub would be, for some shows, physically dangerous. The twelve musicians of the now-closed show *Viva Elvis*, for example, constantly ran around the stage and needed to avoid falling into one of the large, deep holes that frequently opened up across the ever-shifting floor. Far less risky—and far more likely to yield *perfect musical results*—would clearly have been a digital recording of the absent musician. Prerecorded tracks are also used more generally as a supplement to the live bands, even when a musician is not out. Some of the shows even use "virtual orchestras," digital programs like Sinfonia that can synthetically produce the sounds of multiple acoustic instruments and are able to follow and respond to the tempo, dynamics, and general output of live musicians in real time.[14]

In sum: covert technology, from specialized speaker systems to prerecorded digital tracks, discreetly mediates Cirque du Soleil's music, supplementing the shows' live musicians, and allowing them to sound more "perfect" while still appearing live to the audience.

Not all of Cirque's Vegas shows foreground the live elements of their sound, however. The musicians in *O*, for example, like the musicians in *Mystère*, are not very noticeable; they are hidden in booths one can barely see, in the dark patches in the walls on the sides. Occasionally, the booths are lit up, but in general, if you are in the audience, you simply cannot tell what the source of the sounds is—what is live and what is not. Yet although these shows seem recording-like, they actually depend heavily on covert live elements in order to achieve that very sense of mediatized perfection.

The following analysis discusses two ways in which live elements allow them to do this. The first strategy helps Cirque compensate for problems that might occur in a show. As is suggested by the work of a number of scholars, mistakes are an important part of live performance; aberrations mark the uniqueness of a given event, force the performer to improvise a solution, and can even excite the audience.[15] And although Cirque's shows may *seem* perfect on one level, mistakes can certainly occur, sometimes with dangerous consequences. An aerialist, for example, might get caught in her ropes and be unable to extract herself. This very event happened during a live performance of *KÀ* in 2013. *KÀ* is renowned for its extremely high-tech stage, which features a ninety-thousand-pound platform that rotates on multiple planes, leaving, at times, a gaping abyss where the stage floor would normally be; a system failure of the safety measures in place at that time resulted in the death of the performer. The tragedy, unprecedented until this moment, both coincided with and led to a number of closures and new policies for Cirque du Soleil, and a full discussion of that is beyond the scope of this chapter. But most important for the purposes of our discussion, in Vegas, there is always an overriding need to smooth over such performance problems, to cover up disasters, to hide imperfections—*especially dangerous ones*—from the touristic audience. And although the public did witness this one, when problems occur in a live Cirque performance in Las Vegas in general, methods are in place to prevent the audience from discerning them.

Because *Zumanity* (a burlesque-themed show and Cirque's first production intended for an adult audience) has undergone a number of large revisions since its premiere in 2003, emergency situations are so frequent that the band has in its repertoire two entire numbers whose sole purpose is to help smooth over problems during performance.[16] When an emergency arises, the musicians are notified over their headsets. They then discreetly fade out on the piece they are playing and transition seamlessly into whichever of the backup pieces the music director has called. While the band plays, the situation is resolved. Emergency pieces are made up of vamps that can be repeated as many times as necessary and are finished with a fade, so that the show can resume smoothly once the emergency has been handled. This process allows, in most cases, fluid shifts between show and backup piece—and relies upon musicians who can respond quickly, easily, and precisely to changes in real time. Live musicians are in this way indispensable to hiding the flaws in a Cirque show—and thus, ironically, play a crucial role in making the show seem more like a recording.

The second strategy allows Cirque to control for contingencies more generally. The musical soundtracks for Cirque du Soleil's shows sound basically continuous, similar to a film soundtrack, the music corresponding with absolute precision to events that take place onstage. Therefore, in shows in which the musicians are obscured, an audience member might very well believe that the musical soundtrack to the show has been entirely prerecorded. The actual music for most of these shows is, however, only partially prerecorded, and, most important, is in a constant state of live response to the events onstage—even when there is no emergency. The form of the soundtrack thus changes from performance to performance, as the result of live interaction that is happening on a more constant, covert level.

How is such constant mutability effected in performance? The music for Cirque's Vegas shows consists generally of a "score" that has been segmented into modules corresponding to events onstage.[17] The length of these modules varies; they range from around two to several measures long. They may be repeated, skipped, or reordered at any time during the performance, all at the signal of the music director, who watches a video monitor of the show and cues the musicians accordingly. If an acrobat misses a trick, the music can "rewind." If the stage automation is delayed, the music can be repeated. If an onstage progression happens unusually swiftly, the music can skip easily and directly to the appropriate moment. As the switching of these musical modules can happen very quickly, it is not practical for the musicians to use a notated score, even one marked with "vamps," as is often the strategy in musical theater. Cirque's musicians, therefore, know all of their music by heart and simply respond in real time as necessary. It is thus that the soundtrack comes to the audience perfectly coordinated with the onstage action.

Cirque's musical soundtracks, then, are dynamic, flexible, interactive, and responsive—activated, like a video game, by moves made by metaphorical players (the acrobats and stage mechanics, that is, whose actions cue the modules). As the music director for *KÀ* pointed out to me, this show offers its actors the highly unusual opportunity to hear a fully orchestrated, cinematic musical soundtrack being mixed into their performances *in real time*—to experience the sense that they are calling their very aural environment and mood into being. This effect is augmented for the audience of *KÀ* by the fact that the musicians, located underneath the stage, are completely invisible to observers (with a few exceptions). *KÀ*, created by Robert Lepage, is the most narrative of Cirque's ventures thus far; the show depicts an epic tale about two royal twins who are separated and must battle enemy forces to restore peace to their land. With the modular score allowing seemingly perfect coordination of movement and sound, and the obfuscation of musicians creating the impression that the music has simply "come forth" in the world of the performance, this very live show emerges for the audience as a seamless, perfect whole, calling to mind once again Wagner and the hidden orchestra of the *Festspielhaus* (Lepage himself created a new staging of the Ring Cycle which premiered at the New York Metropolitan Opera a few years after *KÀ* premiered in Las Vegas). These musicians are very present, but their physicality is removed from the audience, lending a sense of ethereal mysticism to the environment of the performance.

Interactive musical modules such as these lie at the heart of Cirque du Soleil's negotiation of the tensions created by the need to be both very live and very perfect in Las Vegas. Because different shows require different kinds of flexibility and stability, certain features of the modules vary widely among the six productions on the Strip. Notwithstanding these differences, however, they are used in every show—even *Love*, which provides the material for my last example in this chapter.

Love began as a collaboration between Cirque's founder, Guy Laliberté, and George Harrison. The show's music is made up entirely of Beatles recordings, which were remixed by Sir George Martin (the Beatles' producer and arranger) and his son Giles Martin, with the help of the remaining Beatles (Paul McCartney and Ringo Starr), as well as Yoko Ono and Olivia Harrison. This show is the most ostentatiously technological in appearance, incorporating a number of video projections and extensive use of media in general. The show's music is entirely prerecorded. But although it does not use live musicians, its soundtrack still needs to be as flexible as if it did. Therefore, the producers have made the digital tracks just as interactive and flexible as the modular scores that are performed in the other shows. *Love*'s digitally remastered Beatles tracks have been divided into loops, which are activated during performance by a live playback engineer, who treats them in essentially the same way that the other shows' live musicians treat their music. This show's modules are characterized by an unusual constraint: they were designed, for both legal and aesthetic reasons, to preserve important musical "units" in Beatles songs; that is, the musical integrity of verses and well-known phrases is prioritized in performance over such things as acrobatic contingencies. So unlike musical modules in many of the other Cirque shows, which are generally capable of being shifted around in nonlinear fashion, *Love*'s musical sequences are not, for the most part, programmed to change order. The playback engineer is instead offered a series of binary choices—usually between following the normal course or extending a section—and these choices typically occur during transition sequences in which ambient fragments of Beatles recordings overlap with one another in a nonteleological, not very aurally parsable way. In the course of my research, I interviewed Gavin Whiteley, the original playback engineer for *Love* and the creator and programmer of *Love*'s digital loops, and he explained it to me thus: "*Mystère* [for example] has tricks, and if the acrobats miss a trick the first time, they'll [metaphorically] rewind the music and play it a second time. Here, if you miss a trick, the music carries on, because Paul isn't going to repeat a verse of 'Yesterday.'"[18]

Love's modules may be more linear than those of other shows, but they nonetheless rely on the actions of a live engineer to operate the tracks in real time; thus, even behind this highly mediatized soundtrack lies a fundamentally live process. What is more, even the sacrosanct recordings of the Beatles must be subjected to Cirque's special method, divided into chunks that are manipulated to allow the soundscape underpinning the entire world of the show to function in perfect harmony with the other media.

Conclusion

Cirque's Vegas shows may be designed to look like stable, repeatable, and perfect entities at every performance, but they are nonetheless quite dynamic and ephemeral under the surface—incredibly interactive during performance, and constantly changing over the period during which they are performed. The sonic modules are, in one sense, fixed and permanent; although their content changes from time to time, it is generally not being "improvised" on the spot, only manipulated. However, the performers onstage operate within a more extremely contingent world; injuries, replacements, and unexpected steps force them to move in a different way or at a different time. And this instability is mitigated by the modular musical score, whose flexibility allows every performance to come across as if such small hiccups, inherent to live performance as a medium, had no effect. Cirque's Vegas shows are thus both more *and* less contingent than they appear, both more *and* less live, more *and* less perfect than they seem, and always hiding something from their audiences. And at the heart of the process that allows them to straddle these divides—perhaps even at the heart of Cirque du Soleil's success itself—lies the company's unusual approach to sound.

Because of the strange relationship in the entire Las Vegas Strip environment between what is "real" and what is artificial, what is "present" and what is "absent," what is "live" and what is "mediated," the ideological, political, and theatrical implications of these shows are quite complex. Cirque's Vegas productions, like the world in which they are performed, are both an escape *from* the real world and fundamentally, integrally tied *to* the real world. They depend upon live, physical, present bodies and interactions—and at the same time they would not function without their ghostly simulations, their absent presences. The shows and Strip do not simply "represent" or "simulate" the real world, do not simply emphasize the present or the absent, the live or the virtual, but, rather, constantly traverse the boundary between the two. Cirque du Soleil's Las Vegas shows, like the rest of the Strip, create a set of overlapping, embedded, Matryoshka-like simulations within simulations, complicating the visitor's sense of reality at every level, using sound as a fundamental tool to absorb present spectators into the realm of the virtual but live spectacular world that is being simulated. On the Las Vegas Strip, concrete buildings and physical tourist bodies are not disavowed (they are, in many ways, emphasized), but they are given new meaning within the framework of virtual sensory signals with which all material things are here infused. *This* live world is also a virtual one; this virtual world is also emphatically live; this physically and emphatically present world is also marked by absence at every turn.

This case presents a significant opportunity for us to continue to think more deeply about the role of the virtual, as physical travel has become increasingly curtailed in a world marked by pandemic. Ultimately, I hope that this examination of the subcutaneous manipulation of presence and absence underlying the experience of the visitor to the Las Vegas Strip and its musical multimedia productions can give us broader insight into our own relationships to presence and absence, particularly as we encounter increasingly high-stakes desires for both liveness and virtuality, across the global twenty-first century. Whatever the future of performance in this age may bring, whatever the developments that will arise out of our physically fraught world, we may from our present vantage point appreciate the degree to which Cirque du Soleil has capitalized upon the creative possibilities offered by the age of increasing virtuality. Yet, ultimately, the many aspects of Cirque's shows that have made them so special—the immersive spaces, touristic experiences, and technological marvels both seen and unseen—have worked successfully in large part because of the unique live, real, physical circumstances in which they are made. The visitor must still travel to Las Vegas in order to experience this perfected fantasy, and the shows must still be experienced "live." No element has been more fundamentally important to Cirque's success than its circushood; it is from this background that Cirque takes its flexibility, the ability that is routinely demanded of circus performance to recognize and seize advantages as they appear. Circus—perhaps more than any other kind of performance—succeeds or fails directly on its adaptability and showmanship, the ability to engage and thrill an audience in the ever-present and ever-changing here and now. Cirque thus teaches us that, in our age, success turns on the ability to adapt to our circumstances, making use of both the virtual and the material technologies at our disposal—and shows us that music, and sound more generally, is an especially potent means of finding our way through the present absences and absent presences of this world.

Notes

1. Jean Baudrillard, *Simulacra and Simulations*, trans. Sheila Faria Glaser (Ann Arbor: University of Michigan Press, 1994); Barbara Kirshenblatt-Gimblett, *Destination Culture: Tourism, Museums, and Heritage* (Berkeley: University of California Press, 1998).

2. See, for example, Helen Stoddart, *Rings of Desire: Circus History and Representation* (Manchester: Manchester University Press, 2000), 106–7; and David Lewis Hammarstrom, *Fall of the Big Top: The Vanishing American Circus* (Jefferson, NC: McFarland Press, 2007), 152.

3. Antony Hippisley Coxe quoted in Stoddart, *Rings of Desire*, 79–80.

4. For one discussion of the importance of live music to circus, see Ernest Albrecht, *The Contemporary Circus: Art of the Spectacular* (Lanham, MD: Scarecrow Press, 2006), 72.

5. We might, of course, take a critical stance toward the idea that circus presents unmitigated, pure actuality. After all, the form has been known at times for its fakery: one need only think of the circus "sideshow," a feature developed by the infamous American impresario and sometime hoax man P. T. Barnum (who once, for example, tried to pass off as a legitimate mermaid a monkey skeleton sewn to the posterior end of a fish). But it is nonetheless true that when one is on a high wire, or in the ring with a wild animal, the danger *is* real—and real-time, "live" interactive responses are vitally necessary.

6. For more detailed information about the general history of Cirque du Soleil up to 2004, see Tony Babinski, *Cirque du Soleil: 20 Years under the Sun* (New York: Harry N. Abrams, 2004).

7. I use the term *absorptive* here in reference to Michael Fried's seminal work, *Absorption and Theatricality: Painting and Beholder in the Age of Diderot* (Chicago: University of Chicago Press, 1980).

8. One need only remember the "Siegfried and Roy" debacle to know that this is the case. Between 1990 and 2003, Siegfried Fischbacher and Roy Horn entertained audiences at Steve Wynn's Mirage hotel-casino with a magic and wild animal show (featuring, most famously, lions and tigers) that was renowned the world over; it was even contracted in 2001 to stay at the Mirage for the duration of the lifetime of its performers. On October 3, 2003, however, Horn was injured by a seven-year-old tiger, Montecore, during a performance. The production closed immediately, and the demolition of the theater began the next year. See Mary Manning, "Horn Still Critical after Attack," *Las Vegas Sun*, October 6, 2003; and Ed Koch and Mary Manning, "Roy Still Critical: Show Is Cancelled Indefinitely," *Las Vegas Sun*, October 7, 2003.

9. We might think, for example, of poor yet courageous Ben Heppner cracking his voice during the "Prize Song" of *Die Meistersinger*, as famously discussed by Carolyn Abbate in "Music—Drastic or Gnostic?" *Critical Inquiry* 30 (2004): 505–36.

10. This process of mediating live performance calls to mind the work of scholars such as Philip Auslander and Louise Meintjes, both of whom have analyzed other cases of performances and recordings in which a sense of "liveness" was constructed with the aid of technological mediation. See Philip Auslander, *Liveness*, 2nd ed. (London: Routledge, 2008); and Louise Meintjes, *Sounds of Africa! Making Music Zulu in an African Studio* (Durham, NC: Duke University Press, 2003).

11. Ellen Lampert-Greaux, "The Wizardry of *O*: Cirque du Soleil Takes the Plunge into an Underwater World," *Live Design* (February 1, 1999).

12. See John Huntington, "Tangerine Trees and Marmalade Skies: Cirque du Soleil Meets the Beatles in the Psychedelic New Spectacle Called Love," *Lighting & Sound America* (September 2006); Adam Rogers, "On Las Vegas States, Daring Feats of Engineering Steal the Show," *Wired Magazine* (May 22, 2007); and Matt Hurwitz, "The Sound of Love," *Live Design* (August 1, 2006).

13. Jean-François Brissette, interview by the author, August 27, 2010.

14. Sinfonia is a virtual orchestra that simulates the sounds of instruments, such as string sections. It takes live sonic input through a keyboard player and then uses that to determine the tempo, dynamics, and so on of its output. As summarized succinctly by Jason Leff in "Rage against the Machine: How the NLRB Used Section 8(e) of the National Labor Relations Act to Kill the Virtual Orchestra," *North Carolina Journal of Law & Technology* 6, no. 1 (2004): "The Sinfonia is part of a new breed of virtual orchestra instruments designed to faithfully recreate the sound of a traditional full-size orchestra from a single computerized console. Thus far, the technology has been used in over thirty productions across the country, including the national tours of *Annie* and *Miss Saigon*, as well as the *Cirque du Soleil*." Sinfonia, which is played by a live score-reading musician at a keyboard, has had a somewhat controversial history, as its critics (including musicians as well as musicians' unions) have been concerned that it is replacing live musicians.

15. Abbate, "Music—Drastic or Gnostic?"; Andy Hamilton, "The Art of Recording and the Aesthetics of Perfection," *British Journal of Aesthetics* 43, no. 4 (2003): 345–62; Eric Lott, "Perfect Is Dead: Karen Carpenter, Theodor Adorno, and the Radio; or, If Hooks Could Kill," *Criticism* 50, no. 2 (2008): 219–34.

16. Nate Kimball, interview with the author, August 23, 2010.

17. Richard Oberacker, interview with the author, January 9, 2009.

18. Gavin Whiteley, interview with the author, September 8, 2010.

6

Pura Alegría

Young Adult Musicians Learning Mariachi in Schools and Participating in the Las Vegas Mariachi Scene

CASSAUNDRA RODRIGUEZ AND CELINE AYALA

Mariachi—a word used for a musical style, musical group, and musicians themselves—has been widely understood as part of a distinctly Mexican tradition. However, unlike in Mexico, mariachi instruction is institutionalized in public schools in the United States. Many may already know that mariachi music instruction in public schools has been thriving in states such as Texas and California, but the mariachi program in Nevada, specifically in Las Vegas in the Clark County School District (CCSD), stands as the largest, with approximately six thousand enrolled mariachi students. Since its inception in 2002, the program has grown, and each year students compete across the country for national recognition, bringing home awards for vocal and musical talent. The mariachi scene was further supported as Las Vegas witnessed the inaugural debut of the city's first college-level mariachi group, Mariachi Plata of the College of Southern Nevada, in December 2019. Perhaps the robust mariachi scene in Las Vegas is not surprising in a city where Latino residents make up about 34 percent of the population, but this mariachi scene may not be as familiar to the general public as it can be to locals of the city.

This chapter examines how and why young adults become drawn to mariachi and how their interest propels them to participate in the Las Vegas mariachi scene. We specifically look at the role of the CCSD mariachi program in youth and young adult lives and center their narratives on what mariachi means to them. Further, we find that mariachi contributes to a process of musical place making and belonging for Latino Las Vegas residents. We examine a Las Vegas musical tradition long ignored and taking place not necessarily in the dazzling settings of the Strip but in school classrooms and auditoriums, national competitive venues, restaurants, and private homes where people live, sing, play, and love.

Data and Methods

We come to this research as both insiders and outsiders. As a Mexican American sociologist, first author Rodriguez shares an ethnic identity with all of the participants thus far, along with an interest in mariachi as a musical and cultural art form. However, Rodriguez is an outsider in the sense that she is not a musician. Ayala, the second author, is an Afro-Latina musician and former participant of the CCSD mariachi program. Ayala is also a sociologist who has studied local Las Vegas scenes. Both authors have research interests on race and Latino communities. Together, we aim to bridge our expertise to provide readers a sense of how and why young adults are drawn to the mariachi scene in Las Vegas.

The present study is part of the first author's preliminary and ongoing sociological investigation into how and why youth participate in the CCSD mariachi program and draws on emergent interview data with nine young adults. Interviewees were between the ages of eighteen and thirty-one during the time of the interview. In this preliminary study, all young adults participated in the CCSD mariachi program, many as early as middle school. All young adults are Mexican origin, although they use different identity labels to describe themselves (for example, Hispanic, Latino, Mexican, Mexican American). The interviewees are part of the immigrant second generation, meaning that they are the children of immigrants. All names for interviewees are pseudonyms.

Interviews were carried out during the years 2020–21. As a result of COVID-19, all interviews were conducted virtually on web-based meeting platforms. However, meeting virtually did not detract from the richness of the data or the rapport experienced between the first author and interviewees. Instead, it sometimes seemed that meeting virtually invited a greater sense of intimacy since all interviewees chose to participate while they were at home. For example, interviewees could point to objects in their home that related to their mariachi experiences. Interviewees were also sometimes able to recall a memory or the name of something relating to their mariachi suit, or *traje*, by briefly inquiring with a family member in another room. Interviews with mariachi graduates focused on a number of topics, including their mariachi experiences, training, family, belonging, and social issues.

Mariachi and Music Scenes

Mariachi music brings together the bombastic sounds of the violin, vihuela, guitar, guitarrón, trumpet, powerful vocals, and sometimes a harp. Mariachi dates back to the 1800s, although modern mariachi as we know it emerged in the early twentieth century and is believed to originate from rural sites in western Mexico. Mariachi was popularized in the early twentieth century when mariachi music moved from rural towns to Mexico City, beginning with a performance for President Porfirio Díaz for Mexican Independence Day in 1905.[1] In these early years, mariachi music began to represent Mexico as a national symbol. Further, with the onset of radio broadcasting and recording technologies, mariachi music was disbursed to diverse Mexican audiences. Still, mariachi music instruction in Mexico was and still largely remains within the domain of the family or household. Traditionally in Mexico, the musical tradition is taught from an elder relative to a younger loved one, typically a grandfather or father to a younger, often male, relative.

In the United States, mariachi became popular as a result of Chicano movements of the 1960s and 1970s, the widespread access to radio, and the marketing of mariachi music to wide audiences.[2] Migration from Mexico to the United States also meant that the influence of mariachi would travel to the United States and be embraced by the children of immigrants and others. For Mexicans and Mexican Americans, mariachi music can be the musical backdrop of life's most precious moments; indeed, mariachi musicians are often hired for important family and religious celebrations, including baptisms, weddings, and birthday parties. For Mexican Americans and other youth in the United States, their mariachi training may take place in school settings. The United States has been the site of what some call an academic mariachi educational movement.[3] As a result, mariachi programs can be found in school districts across the United States. In turn, learning mariachi in schools can help prepare students for participating in larger mariachi scenes.

Scene, in fact, is an operative concept for us in our investigation. In order to understand the importance of the mariachi scene, we must first familiarize ourselves with the scholarly meaning of scene. A scene, according to John Irwin, is an entity that is public, voluntary and expressive. Scenes often are occupied by groups of people with similar skills or interests.[4] Pepper G. Glass notes that scenes are spaces that "participants actively create and maintain . . . through shared activity."[5] These spaces may be physical like a backyard for a mariachi performance, or symbolic through the sharing of norms commonly known among people of a particular scene. Historically, "music scene" was used to highlight the once frowned-upon jazz scene by journalists.[6] Music scenes now encompass a wide range of musical genres, including punk, hip-hop, blues, rock, opera, jazz, and mariachi.[7] Andy Bennett and Richard A. Peterson use a scene frame to look at the negotiation and construction activities to maintain a music scene. The authors demonstrate that music scenes (specifically gothic, punk, jazz, country, and hip-hop) can create place-based identities for cities such as Nashville, which is commonly associated as a hub for country music.[8] Since Las Vegas is a city where culture is assumed to be borrowed or nonexistent, the presence of a music scene in the city is important for members to find a sense of place-based pride and belonging.

Music has had an extensive history in various communities prior to its importance in Las Vegas. Music, historically, has been used as a means of communication for centuries. Dynamic hymns were sung on plantations by enslaved African Americans to pass along messages, and Afro–Puerto Ricans used the rhythms of bomba and plena to tell stories and communicate messages of hope and foster a musical space for shared experiences.[9] An ethnographic study done on the Latino music scene in Houston shows that involvement in the scene allows people to form identities and communal belongingness.[10] Another study in Houston notes that the mariachi music scene, which manifests in Mexican restaurants and private family events, allows both performers and spectators to connect with their roots and travel to "different time[s] and geographical places" through the music.[11] Studying music scenes allows for an understanding of the ways music intersects with "everyday life" as well as the historical legacies of music in contemporary periods.[12] Using scene as a frame for youth participation in mariachi music allows for an in-depth understanding of how music can help create a sense of joy and cultural belonging for these youth in Las Vegas.

Local Mariachi Training and Performing

CCSD's comprehensive Mariachi Education Program was first introduced to high schools and middle schools in the 2002–3 academic school year. Aside from several goals concerning increased student achievement, the program was specifically designed to encourage young people to have "opportunities to represent the CCSD and Las Vegas community as music ambassadors through high-level performances."[13] Consequently, school administrators and other stakeholders helped develop a standards-based program, committed to hiring teachers that already had experience as professional mariachis, and created opportunities for district festivals and summer workshops. Doing this meant that professional mariachis from across the country would be recruited to southern Nevada to help build the program. With this program in place, students receive expert training to develop their musical skills.

The CCSD mariachi program is also a response to what the district knew was a large and growing Latino population in the Vegas area. Informally, the first author would often hear at youth-based mariachi performances that the program was something that the local Latino community wanted. In the school district, Latino students represented 47 percent of the student population in the 2020–21 year.[14] The program helps to increase school involvement for students and their families. It can encourage family participation in the schools by having Latino parents attend campus performances that are of a musical tradition and language they may already know. Moreover, the music can also help connect some students to their culture, as many of them are part of the immigrant second generation, or the American-born children of immigrants.

The CCSD Mariachi Program provides a starting point for youth and their families to engage with the mariachi scene in organic ways. For example, mariachi training in schools can actually extend beyond the classroom or campus. Students have opportunities to perform at community events and with other students at different schools at what is called *Noches de Mariachi* (Mariachi Nights), informally called *Noches*. This is a rotating fund-raising event that brings together students from across the district to perform and raise funds. Typically, these events include heavy family participation and Mexican food for sale. Students who initially learn their musical skills in the program may choose to also become involved in mariachi ensembles outside of school, working or gigging at parties or public events. As a result, these (former) students become further entrenched in the mariachi scene. Their families become part of this scene by nature of attending their public performances. Sometimes siblings join the program because their older siblings had a positive experience learning mariachi in school. It is in this way that the CCSD program helps create and sustain a vibrant musical scene in and outside of schools.

Young people have various reasons for learning how to play mariachi music and taking part in this local scene. Many do not initially become involved in their school's mariachi program with aspirations to become professional musicians. Instead, it is clear that most young musicians are attracted to how this musical form and tradition ties them to their families and Mexican culture. In turn, keeping rooted to one's culture inspires happiness and a sense of family and community connectedness. Greg shared his thoughts on why he participated in mariachi: "It . . . brings you back to like what your roots are. Mariachi was originally from Jalisco, which is where my mom was from. So, like that music is, it's played, you know, growing up all the time. And [mariachi] keeps me grounded to that. And the sense of being close to your culture brings a lot of happiness to me. And it's good. It's nice to hear good music." Greg was able to expand his mariachi training outside of school functions and would share his musical talent at family gatherings. He also remembers that he would play for parishioners at his family church. During his teen years, mariachi was most certainly an important part of Greg's life and something he could share with a broader community outside of school.

Many young adults recall becoming interested in mariachi music because of their families. Young adults often reference a specific family member, usually a father, grandfather, or uncle, who would introduce them to mariachi music either because of their musical backgrounds or because they would fill their homes with the sounds of mariachi music from the radio or stereo system. Yolanda, for example, credited her father as her vehicle to mariachi: "Honestly, I think the reason why I kind of got into mariachi was because of my dad. When I was a kid, I was around mariachi. I was always around music. Eventually I had the opportunity to start doing mariachi in school." Yolanda recalls how her father would passionately respond to mariachi music at family parties. These heartfelt memories made an impression on her. Once she started learning mariachi in her school, she shared with me that she felt like she fell in love. Yolanda now plays professionally all across Las Vegas.

Antonio recalls how growing up he would hear mariachi music pour out of the compact discs his parents would play in the house or in their family car. He became drawn to learning as a result of his uncle and father's interest in playing the music. Antonio also remembers live mariachi music from some of his family parties. "At family parties we would have mariachi and I would watch them and think: *I want to do that.* That's pretty cool." Antonio's father did eventually enroll him in a mariachi elective course in middle school. Although Antonio's father made this choice for him, Antonio was pleased with his father's decision. Antonio would later continue his mariachi education into high school. For him, mariachi music brings together people and happiness in a way that is unique to the mariachi tradition. In a bilingual response, Antonio recalls what it was like to participate in mariachi. "Pure enjoyment, *en Español, alegría* [in Spanish, joy]. You know, *pura alegría, pura fiesta, pura felicidad. Y de eso se trata* [pure joy, pure celebration, pure happiness. And that's what it is about]."

Antonio, who is in his twenties, continues to play mariachi professionally. Having learned musical skills in school, he later started gigging with a group. He also reports that he considers himself a mentor to several youth who are interested in participating in the mariachi scene. Antonio shares that his gigging work is not unusual. He explains, "There is a huge, huge community of students and graduates who have now started their own, you know, their own groups here in Las Vegas." Antonio was first invited to be part of a gigging group in middle school and recalls that the experience was at first challenging because his groupmates were older and much more musically advanced. With intensive training and some patience and dedication, he picked up the repertoire and would join his group in performing at private parties. After several years and with more musical experience, Antonio eventually joined another group as an adult.

As students graduate from high school, mariachi can become part of their stories as adults. Some choose to continue their education by studying music in college while supporting themselves full- or part-time as professional musicians. There is also a newly formed mariachi group at one of the local community colleges that was welcomed by the public with a sold-out debut performance in 2019. Some young adults continue their training informally via gigging work. As they do this, they also continue to develop broad musician networks and hone their skills in the mariachi scene in Las Vegas. This music scene is quite diverse in Las Vegas and extends beyond popular tourist attractions on the Strip. Although there are some mariachi performances on the Strip for special events (in malls, casino lobbies, restaurants, and so on), the scene arguably does not have a strong hold on the Strip. Most performances take place in more intimate or event-based spaces. What makes the mariachi scene so unique in Las Vegas is its ability to reach audiences in parts of the community that manifest outside of the Strip. For example, this scene can be found in backyard parties to large-scale performances in Las Vegas auditoriums. This scene also extends beyond common musical performance locations, as mariachi performances have taken place at political rallies, strip malls, and even the local airport.

It is at these performances that young musicians practice the skills they first learned in the program. Sometimes students are initially anxious about performing, but with practice they develop ways to push beyond their nerves. Kate, for example, remembers how her stage fright would go away after being part of mariachi for several years. Now the stage is a place that inspires more sentimental feelings. Kate elaborates, "It almost feels like it's home . . . that's what playing feels like especially when you play with people you love and cherish. That is a really good feeling." Performing becomes part of a larger process of collective joy with other group members. Aside from the shared experience with peers, mariachi musicians comment on the role of the audience in the music scene.

Mariachi students learn in the program that they have to give their best for any and all performances. Whether it is at a school event or elsewhere, young musicians take this commitment to professional excellence very seriously. Still, there is a sense that participating in the music scene is not just a one-way transaction for the musicians and the audience. Mariachi musicians want the audience to really *feel* the music. This is part of what makes performing music so fulfilling to the young adults in this study. Kate explains what being part of mariachi is like: "The exhilaration and the adrenaline. You are almost addicted to it. You want to keep playing. You want to keep playing for the people. Whether they show it or not, you know that you are reaching them. That is the best feeling." In other words, musicians aim to have the audience truly experience the music. For Kate, this passion for performing continues as she has extended her mariachi participation past high school and works with a professional group while balancing her college classes.

Musicians also hope audience members respond with enthusiasm. Greg shares that the audience is what sets the tone for the performance. The "crowd—that's what makes it or breaks it. And if it's like a really good performance, that's when the crowd is just like, they're singing or dancing, drinking or eating. And, you know, those are the ones that I remember. You know, the good ones." Young mariachi musicians share how they want to see audience members respond to the music with visible emotion or physical reactions such as clapping, swaying, dancing, or singing along. Musicians also want to see audience goers enjoy themselves regardless of whether they are familiar with mariachi music or not. Young musicians share that mariachi music is meant to be enjoyed by people of all backgrounds. Therefore, the subtle contract in this scene for audience participants is to simply have an enjoyable experience. Supporting Irwin's assertion that scenes are open spaces for whoever wants to participate, some young mariachis also suggest that young people from all racial or ethnic backgrounds are welcome to learn the music at school or participate as musicians in the broader Vegas scene.[15] Musicians regularly express that although mariachi music is distinctly Mexican, they also want all people to appreciate and listen to the music at their public performances. In some ways, they see themselves as ambassadors of this musical tradition. Antonio also noted how mariachi musicians can also break away from tradition by doing musical renditions of popular English-language songs or blend genres together as a creative outlet and invite broader interest in the music: "We see nowadays there are so many more arrangements that include mariachi instruments or arrangements for songs completely out of our genre of music . . . written for mariachi instrumentation. I've seen Bob Marley, you know, being played by mariachis. I've seen rock mariachis here in Vegas, actually. There are people who implement rock 'n' roll and mariachi together . . . that is the amazing part about mariachi." The mariachi scene in Las Vegas brings together creative musicians who produce musical performances for all to enjoy.

Conclusion

Young men and women are drawn to mariachi because of its distinct ties to their families and Mexican culture. Relatives—namely, fathers, uncles, and grandfathers—are what spark their initial interest in learning how to play mariachi music. These young adults learn how to play mariachi as an homage or remembrance to these loved ones. Once youth are in the CCSD program, they learn the training necessary to participate in the mariachi scene—from learning how to play music from adopting the norms of how to conduct oneself during a performance. The joy they feel in being mariachi musicians keeps them committed to staying in the program, and it is that very joy that also pushes some young adults to extend their musical participation to the larger mariachi scene in Las Vegas. In doing this, they aspire to reach broad audiences with their music and comment on how much they enjoy seeing audience members respond to their performances.

Most young adults in this study were born or raised in Las Vegas after their families migrated from Mexico. Some families moved from neighboring states, namely, California, to settle in Nevada for work opportunities, for the promise of a relatively low-cost living or to reunite with family. Many parents are working in sectors that help maintain the local tourist economy that Las Vegas is known for. For tourists, Las Vegas is a place of escape and fantasy, but for locals it is a place of waged labor, educational training, and the daily routines of living and loving. The things that most people associate with Las Vegas—gambling and illicit thrills or the bright lights of the Strip—are not necessarily part of young mariachi musicians' daily lives in this desert metropolis. Still, locals make homegrown roots and continuously remake the city in their own vision for belonging. Participating in the mariachi scene is not only a source of cultural joy for young people, but also part of taking pride in their hometown. When asked if young adults have other avenues to express their cultures in Las Vegas, many point to mariachi as being one of the few things they can do regularly with others outside of their family and household traditions. It also brings together their Las Vegas community while at the same time enacting a transnational homage to their family's ancestral home. For young mariachi musicians, mariachi is *pura alegría* (pure joy), just as Las Vegas is home.

Notes

1. Daniel Sheehy, *Mariachi Music in America: Experiencing Music, Expressing Culture* (New York: Oxford University Press, 2006).

2. Sheehy, *Mariachi Music in America.*

3. Lauryn Camille Salazar, "From Fiesta to Festival: Mariachi Music in California and the Southwestern United States" (PhD diss. University of California, Los Angeles, 2011), 17.

4. John Irwin, *Scenes* (Beverly Hills, CA: Sage, 1977).

5. Pepper G. Glass, "Doing Scene: Identity, Space, and the Interactional Accomplishment of Youth Culture," *Journal of Contemporary Ethnography* 41, no. 6 (2012): 712.

6. Andy Bennett and Richard A. Peterson, *Music Scenes: Local, Translocal, and Virtual* (Nashville: Vanderbilt University Press, 2004).

7. See Paul Hodkinson, "The Goth Scene and (Sub)Cultural Substance," in *After Subculture: Critical Studies in Contemporary Youth Culture*, edited by Andy Bennett and Keith Kahn-Harris, 135–47 (New York: Palgrave MacMillan, 2004).

8. Bennett and Peterson, *Music Scenes.*

9. Erin Hurt and Cherise A. Pollard, "The Afro-Latin@ Reader: History and Culture in the United States," in *Multi-ethnic Literature of the United States* 38, no. 1 (2013): 171–73.

10. Joseph A. Kotarba, Jennifer L. Fackler, and Kathryn M. Nowotny, "An Ethnography of Emerging Latino Music Scenes," *Symbolic Interaction* 32, no. 4 (2009): 310–33.

11. Kathryn M. Nowotny et al., "Established Latino Music Scenes: Sense of Place and Challenge of Authenticity," *Studies in Symbolic Interaction* 35 (2010): 29–50.

12. Andy Bennett and Ian Rogers, *Popular Music Scenes and Cultural Memory* (London: Palgrave Macmillan, 2016).

13. Marcia MacCagno Neel, "Mariachi and Spanish Speaking English Learners: District Initiatives, Models, and Education Policy," *Arts Education Policy Review* 118, no. 4 (2017): 211.

14. Nevada Accountability Portal, "Demographic Profile," Nevada Department of Education, 2019–20 school year, Nevadareportcard.nv.gov.

15. Irwin, *Scenes*.

PART III

Second Chances

The final master-stroke at last impos'd,
And now, the neat machine compleatly clos'd;
Fitting his pinions on, a flight he tries,
And hung self-ballanc'd in the beaten skies.
Then thus instructs his child: My boy, take care
To wing your course along the middle air;
If low, the surges wet your flagging plumes;
If high, the sun the melting wax consumes:
Steer between both: nor to the northern skies,
Nor south Orion turn your giddy eyes;
But follow me: let me before you lay
Rules for the flight, and mark the pathless way.
Then teaching, with a fond concern, his son,
He took the untry'd wings, and fix'd 'em on;
But fix'd with trembling hands; and as he speaks,
The tears roul gently down his aged cheeks.
Then kiss'd, and in his arms embrac'd him fast,
But knew not this embrace must be the last.
And mounting upward, as he wings his flight,
Back on his charge he turns his aking sight;
As parent birds, when first their callow care
Leave the high nest to tempt the liquid air.
Then chears him on, and oft, with fatal art,
Reminds the stripling to perform his part.

7

The Master and the Mob

Noël Coward's Musical Identity in the Golden Age of Las Vegas

ARIANNE JOHNSON QUINN

> They've suddenly found that some of my early plays are quite good. . . . There seems to be a sort of Noël Coward renaissance going on. Dear old Dad, you know. . . . I love acting . . . But I'm really more creative than interpretive. I have to make a choice between the two because it's a matter of apportioning my time.
>
> —John S. Wilson, "International Romance: An International Romance Set to Music—Coward's Score," *New York Times*, December 8, 1963

Sir Noël Pierce Coward (1899–1973), British playwright, songwriter, actor, and writer, is widely known in Britain and the United States for his songs, plays, and film appearances. Known early on as a rival of Cole Porter, Jerome Kern, and others, he holds a curious place in the world of American entertainment. Coward was hailed as a star and called by Gilbert Millstein of the *New York Times* "the modern Jenny Lind," in reference to the famed Swedish opera singer who toured the United States in the nineteenth century.[1] As a reflection of his creative renaissance of the 1950s, he returned to the United States for a run in Las Vegas at the legendary Desert Inn at the age of fifty-five.

His brief four-week run as a Vegas cabaret artist—a place known for gambling, excess, and whispers of organized crime—raised questions of taste, respectability, and the limits of highbrow culture in 1950s America. Transported to the desert of Vegas, the British sophisticate who had long represented the style and social politics of another age would require a transformation, and transform he did. Coward strategically capitalized on his penchant for rapid-fire humor and personality with musical numbers that relied on a combination of his most popular numbers with lyrics updated as markers of posh Americana and reworkings of songs by other popular writers.

This chapter explores the intermingled aspects of Coward's performative identity on the Vegas stage, situating his cabaret act within his other late works and the style and aesthetic of 1950s Las Vegas. His arrival in Vegas was anything but conventional, and the question remains as to what drew Coward to Vegas, and how this experience shaped his reception in the United States and beyond. Coward, known affectionately by friends and colleagues as "the Master" because of his aptitude for working in every conceivable field of the theater, displayed a curious divide between the modern Vegas world of glitz and organized crime and his own persona as an English sophisticate. Drawing on the myth of "the Master" himself, as demonstrated through his own words and critical reception, it examines the connections between Coward as entertainer and British cultural icon, the Golden Age Vegas audience, and American music in perhaps the most commercial city in America. Through this examination, we catch a glimpse of Coward's inner creative life and can better understand the significance of his contributions to American musical life.

Coward's cabaret run, which was recorded as "Noël Coward in Vegas," represented the culmination of his musical career, including hit songs "What's Going to Happen to the Tots," "Nina," "Mad Dogs and Englishmen," and, infamously, his own risqué spin on old friend and rival Cole Porter's "Let's Do It," one of many numbers that the experimental environment of Vegas enabled. Critic Gilbert Millstein wrote: "All he did was sing his own songs and a parody of Cole Porter's 'Let's Do It,' the lyrics of which may be described as naughty. . . . The room was drenched with nostalgia, both real and assumed."[2] Coward's musical style underwent a transformation befitting the style of Vegas and was accompanied by new arrangements from Peter Matz, the young orchestrator and pianist who accompanied his Vegas act and provided his American musical sound.

With his combination of wit, charm, and boundary-pushing risqué humor, Coward's presence drew in celebrity audiences to the small but renowned Desert Inn, including performers like Judy Garland. His Vegas period, however brief, sparked a revitalization of his American notoriety, with recordings, engagements in New York, television specials of his works including a ninety-minute CBS broadcast titled *Together with Music* with old friend Mary Martin, and his later trio of Broadway musicals including *Sail Away* (1961), *The Girl Who Came to Supper* (1963), and *High Spirits* (1964). The creative work that Coward produced as a result of his return to America experienced mixed reception. However, through his unconventional musical portraits of distinct upper-class British identity mixed with underpinnings of his own hidden identity as a gay man, Coward captured the heart of the American public and cemented his reputation as the vivid, sparkling personality we remember today. Coward's Vegas period nevertheless proved to be a catalyst for his later works and reveals the superficial yet glamorous aesthetic of Vegas, in which celebrities were able to reinvent themselves as often as Vegas itself was reinvented.

Beginnings

Coward's upbringing and background are an important aspect in the creation of the myth of his life and work, a myth that carried over into his Vegas period. Coward crafted a persona that reflected his love of theater, complete with his iconic choice of accent. The outwardly camp yet sophisticated persona shielded him as a gay man in an unforgiving British culture in which homosexuality was criminalized. His early life was humble and decidedly unglamorous; he was born to a middle-class family on Waldegrave Road, Teddington, on December 16, 1899. Largely self-educated, much of his education was gleaned from personal study. Coward's biggest supporter throughout his life was his mother, Violet, who enrolled him in an arts academy. He made his stage debut in 1911 in a play called *The Goldfish*, and after several early attempts, including *The Rat Trap* (1918), Coward's West End debut as playwright and actor was in 1920 with his own work *I'll Leave It to You*. Coward was a voracious reader, a habit he retained throughout his life, often reading for hours every morning, consuming everything he could find, including plays, political commentaries, English literature, and American biographies. Coward's American agent and friend Geoffrey Johnson recalled that this practice continued every day until his death and that he had a particular fascination with American religious practices.[3]

His varied interests are reflected in the multitude of plays, songs, and other writings. Over the course of his lifetime Coward wrote three hundred individual songs and more than forty stage plays and film scripts. Early works of note include the controversial play *The Vortex* (1924) and the popular operetta-style musical play *Bitter Sweet* (1929), which was also adapted into a film, and the nationalist pageant-style production *Cavalcade* (1931). His distinctive style, conversational, personable, and full of biting wit, as seen in his best-known stage plays, including *Hay Fever* (1924), *Present Laughter* (1939), and *Blithe Spirit* (1941), reflects his knowledge of the world around him. As Coward expert Barry Day notes, Coward was a student of the human condition first and a playwright second.[4] This knowledge of human nature is reflected in Coward's propensity for dialogue and character development above all else.

Coward's decision to appear in Las Vegas was a curious one, motivated not only by financial concerns but possibly by his own sense of ennui. He had a brief appearance in a Royal Command performance at the London Palladium, along with Jack Buchanan and Bob Hope. In the interim period, he spent much of 1955 on various creative projects, including a draft of his novel *Pomp and Circumstance*.[5] During Coward's fourth and final season at the Café de Paris in 1954, which received a lackluster critical response from the press, he was approached by Joe Glaser, a New York entertainment agent who sponsored everything from theater to boxing. Glaser offered Coward around $35,000 a week to appear in Las Vegas, easily making him one of the best-paid stars in Vegas. When Lena Horne was scheduled to appear in Las Vegas, it was noted: "She does not even know what she will be earning there. But her manager unbent to say 'about 10,000 dollars a week south of Noël Coward.'"[6] Coward's fee clearly marked him as the then highest paid cabaret star.

As friend and secretary Cole Lesley recalled of Vegas, "In those days it seemed no more than a name, a far distant mirage in the Nevada Desert, a mythical El Dorado, and even if it really existed wasn't it peopled by gamblers and run by gangsters who could not possibly ever have heard of Noël Coward, much less pay him any attention when he stood up to sing his very sophisticated, very English songs[?]"[7] Coward was skeptical at first, but agreed to meet with Glaser, in part because of his financial woes. His company, Noël Coward, Ltd., was overdrawn, and there was no guarantee of income, despite the hope for incoming royalty payments. Lesley argued that this was the first in a chain of events that led to his decision to work in America, where there seemed to be endless money to be made for everyone. He noted: "It seemed like an offer to appear on another planet. But the money, which Noël needed very badly, was very attractive. In the end he said, 'For that money I don't care if they throw beer-bottles at me—I'll go.'"[8]

Coward's Road to Vegas

Biographer Philip Hoare notes that Coward was promised a three-week season at $15,000 a week with another $60,000 from the Desert Inn, easily enough to make up the financial deficit.[9] "I went on to the Café de Paris to see Noël Coward in his new cabaret act," critic Noël Whitcomb recalled. "Sitting next to us was a pal of mine who kept taking a letter out of his pocket and re-reading it. 'It's from an American I know well—Joe Glaser. . . . Joe is a big agent, and he asks me if I would offer Coward £10,000 a week for two months to appear at Las Vegas. D'you think Coward would be offended?'"[10] He then quipped that it would be both above union rates and better than gambling. Joe Glaser was quoted as saying, "I'm going to offer him 30,000 dollars a week to appear at the gambling centre of Las Vegas—the greatest sum ever offered a guy for such a trick." Glaser recalled when he was introduced: "Noël Coward does some introducing: This is my lawyer, he says. This is my accountant. This is my American adviser. . . . [T]his is my accountant's lawyer."[11] Coward spent three weeks rehearsing in Hollywood before coming to Vegas, reworking his songs for the American cabaret scene with Marlene Dietrich's favorite pianist, Peter Matz.[12]

Coward was characteristically cagey with the press when asked about his fee. On his arrival on the *Queen Elizabeth* and rumors of his Vegas fee, he stated, "Nothing has been settled at all. I keep on getting offers and what I am offered is often trebled by the press, which gives me a lovely false feeling of prosperity."[13] Ever evasive and self-effacing, he chose to highlight his own idiosyncrasies rather than bowing to the press. He continually fueled rumors about himself and possible projects that might keep him in the States, including a project he claimed to have written for Groucho Marx.[14] Coward claimed that Marx was to star in a comedy about former British prime minister Benjamin Disraeli and that he flew Marx to Vegas to discuss it with him. According to the *Stage*, the first act was written, but it never materialized, and this story was likely a humorous plant by Coward himself, exemplifying Coward's approach to his insecurities about his work during this period.[15]

Coward arrived on a day that was more than a hundred degrees. His first impression of Las Vegas was that it was "a fabulous, extraordinary madhouse," and he was captivated by the mobsters who ran it. "Their morals are bizarre in the extreme," he noted. "They are generous, mother-worshippers, sentimental and capable of much kindness. They are also ruthless, cruel, violent and devoid of scruples . . . curious products of a most curious adolescent country."[16] He further recalled: "All around is desert sand with pink and purple mountains on the horizon. All the big hotels are luxe to the last degree. . . . Even now, in the pre-Christmas slump, there are myriads of people tearing away at the fruit machines and gambling, gambling, gambling for twenty-four hours a day."[17] None of this stopped Coward, who was enjoying himself as the consummate host and member of the social elite. He attended various shows with Cole Lesley, including those of Rosemary Clooney, Jane Powell, and Sammy Davis Jr. ("a rich talent and brilliant performer but he goes on too long").[18]

Coward thrived on the press and adulation that called him the "greatest attraction that Las Vegas has ever had," which was likely particularly satisfying given the cold reception of his songs in London. Hollywood elites came, but he was also a big draw for the midwestern tourists, and pianist Peter Matz praised Coward's ability to match his jokes with the mood and personalities in the room.[19] This Vegas period provided an unexpected boon for his creativity, allowing him to perform songs that he would not dare to sing as a gay man in Britain, including "Mad About the Boy"—extracted from his earlier revue *Words and Music* (1932), which declared, "This dream that pains me and enchains me . . . I'm mad about the boy."[20]

Coward's contract for the Desert Inn stipulated that he would perform two shows nightly for the four weeks, including on Sundays. His first concern was that of vocal strain; an accomplished actor and performer to be sure, he had nonetheless experienced bouts of vocal injury on tour. At the suggestion of Mary

Martin and Katharine Hepburn, Coward consulted vocal coach Alfred Dixon in New York, who helped Coward overcome issues of breath control and tone. His second musical difficulty involved that of his standard accompanist, Norman Hackforth, who was unable to obtain a work permit. This led to the quick hiring of Peter Matz, who had worked with Marlene Dietrich on her cabaret performances. Matz disapproved of Hackworth's musical arrangements and reportedly created new arrangements for every musical number in the lush, full style of a Las Vegas cabaret.[21]

Movie cameras captured the June 5 arrival and the opening show, which was attended by Frank Sinatra, Judy Garland, Humphrey Bogart, Lauren Bacall, David Niven, Joan Fontaine, "Swifty" Lazar (his U.S. agent), and Zsa Zsa Gabor, among others. The first evening he sang songs such as "Someday I'll Find You," "I'll See You Again," "Poor Uncle Harry," "A Bar on the Piccola Marina," "World Weary," "Nina," "Mad Dogs and Englishmen," and finally a reworking of Cole Porter's "Let's Do It." He ended the show by saying, "I'm terribly touched with how you've received me." Wilbur Clark, owner of the Desert Inn, turned to Lesley and asked, "Who is this guy? . . . You must tell me more about him."[22] The cabaret was a hit.

As his earlier career demonstrated, Coward was a musical chameleon who incorporated nuanced sounds ranging from American popular music to the British songs of his formative years spent in attendance at operetta and musical comedy productions in London. He credited English operetta and light opera as a significant influence on his musical style, recalling: "I was born into a generation that still took light music seriously. The lyrics and melodies of Gilbert and Sullivan were hummed and strummed into my consciousness at an early age."[23] Although Coward's melodies certainly reflect this training, his understanding of Gilbert and Sullivan's work shaped his dramatic sensibilities, particularly the overall sense that the musical material of a work must support the dramatic construction and comedic elements.

One of the most significant aspects of Coward's creative practice was his status as actor, writer, director, composer, and creative director for his early productions. Up to the point that he worked in the United States in the 1950s, Coward commonly oversaw every aspect of his works, regardless of the producer. Although the lines are unclear between precisely which elements Coward oversaw in the entire production, it is clear that he surrounded himself with creative individuals who supported him personally, and enhanced his creative abilities, including his musical amanuensis Elsie April, actor Gertrude Lawrence, set designer Oliver Messel, and costume designer Gladys Calthrop, all of whom also worked with Charles B. Cochran. This practice earned Coward the nickname of "one-man band." As an anonymous critic for the *Sporting Times* argued in 1929 regarding *Bitter Sweet*: "In these days it usually takes a battalion of authors, composers, lyric-writers and contributors of extra numbers to concoct a musical entertainment. So it was rather a risk that C. B. Cochran took when he allowed Noël Coward to write *Bitter Sweet* all by himself—libretto, lyrics, music, everything, in fact, except those poignant lines in the programme which tell you that the chewing-gum used in Act II is by Chumpley's Ltd."[24] This critic characterizes Coward as an independent figure capable of artistic endeavors that reflected his unique abilities and style and his penchant for taking creative risks.

Las Vegas in the Public Eye

The location of Coward's cabaret, the Desert Inn, was a site of spectacle and excess. Built by former craps dealer Wilbur Clark, it saw Frank Sinatra's debut and was later bought by Howard Hughes, who owned it until his death in 1976. Clark was so overbudget on construction that "he was forced to accept an offer from the noted mob figure Moe Dalitz, who ended up owning 74 percent of the two-hundred-acre, $6.5 million dollar property."[25] Although Nevada's largest casino, the Desert Inn boasted a modest twenty-four hundred square feet of gambling space. Still, the rooms were air-conditioned and inexpensive and the gambling rooms well stocked.[26] As Thomas Clavin notes: "As if gambling weren't enough of a lure, the casino managers (who fronted for their mobster owners) booked entertainers into their main rooms." The illusion of spectacle and danger added to the allure of Vegas; if you were here, you felt as if you were on the playground of the rich and famous.[27]

Both the large spaces and the celebrity entertainers played a vital part in creating the mythos of Las Vegas in the 1950s and '60s. The hotel and casino reflected the large-scale desire and materiality of Golden Age Vegas. Tony Bennett recalled: "Those were the sensational days. Entertainers like myself, Dean Martin, Frank Sinatra, Marlene Dietrich, Harpo Marx, and Louis Prima really made that town happen."[28] Stars including Sophie Tucker, Jimmy Durante, Maurice Chevalier, and more who were past their prime in Hollywood found a home in Vegas.

Vegas was likewise a home to others looking for a new start. Coupled with the star personae of the many Vegas entertainers on offer, rumors of organized crime persisted, despite marketing efforts by hotels.[29] The image of Vegas as a home for mobsters had been whispered about for ages, but reached a peak after the murder of Flamingo Hotel and Casino owner Benjamin "Bugsy" Siegel in 1947, which the press hinted was caused by the Mob. As Larry Gragg notes, "Indeed, periodicals across the nation were reporting that mobsters were taking over the gambling business and that Las Vegas casinos were becoming 'hood-ridden war fronts that might flare into open battle at any moment.'"[30] This image persists to this day, as Americans recall images of the Mafia and the Rat Pack as exotic architects of Las Vegas.

Across the pond, in the eyes of the British public, Vegas symbolized American excess and the upward mobility of the U.S. economy. Journalist Arthur Helliwell recalled the spectacular images of Vegas: "Las Vegas is a phenomenon that astonishes even America. There is no other town in this world quite like it."[31] Particularly after a period of post–World War II British austerity, the British public was continually fascinated by the seemingly endless excess of American cities like Hollywood, New York, and especially Las Vegas. Journalist Jennifer Johns noted:

> Here, in Vegas, are night clubs to end all night clubs. Here are the No. 1 goals for every entertainer who even suspects that Hollywood is about to drop into the doldrums. . . . The names of the night spots, too, are something to remember . . . the "Desert Inn" flings its neon advertisements in defiance towards the "Last Frontier." Apt indeed, for Las Vegas is now about the last frontier, all the all-vital boundary which every film player must cross if he wants to keep the electricity running through his neon by-line.[32]

Johns's account notes the crossover between Hollywood, Vegas, and the music world in the United States, and even a hyperbolic comparison to the "Last Frontier" of space travel. For Britain, the seedy, endless dream of Vegas was a continual fascination and led to increased bewilderment at the prospect of someone of Coward's stature assuming the role of American cabaret performer.

Response to Coward

Coward's persona as the British sophisticate was a complete novelty in a town of continual novelty. Larry Gragg notes, "He was so unlike the headliners performing at the other Las Vegas hotels during his run at the Desert Inn. . . . Yet the celebrity-filled showroom eagerly awaited the performance by this fifty-five-year-old man who had come to symbolize English sophistication."[33] For Coward, the performance was an artistic triumph as he was able to successfully reinvent himself as an American cabaret star, overcome vocal challenges, and relish the adulation of his star-studded circle of acquaintances. *New York Times* critic Gilbert Millstein echoed the praise of audiences who responded to the level of chic sophistication Coward brought to the Vegas stage. He remarked: "When Noël Coward, an international figure of terrifying and purposeful chic, like a jeweled darning egg, made his American night club debut here recently to a furious rataplan of applause, he apparently satisfied two endemic yearnings in the breasts of the local pioneers, a number of them sodbusters from New York and Chicago: he attracted a customer that not only came to see him but remained to gamble, and he imparted to Las Vegas, a rude settlement, a definite aura of what is vaguely known as 'class.'"[34] Not only had Coward taken a gamble on his career, but he also challenged the expectations of American audiences by performing Britishness in a way that no other entertainer of his generation could. The combination of nostalgia for 1930s Britain, heard in songs like "Dance Little Lady" and "Room with a View" and boundary-pushing modernity with open whispers of sexuality in "Let's Do It" shocked and delighted both audience and critic.

Back home in Britain, the press wondered how Coward was able to dominate the press so successfully. Critic Henry Lewis argued:

> Not least among the phenomena of 1955—which includes Churchill's retirement from Premiership and the announcement of modernization plans for British Railways—was that Noël Coward took his urbane English manners, his ludicrous English singing voice and his dated English anthems like "Mad Dogs and Englishmen" to Las Vegas fabulous, roaring gambling capital of the United States, and it was a success." Coward's voice—unlikely to be heard here again except on record now that he has forsaken "this country of ours which we love so much" for lesser-taxed climes—is, he has said "a composer's voice," having "considerable range but no tune, little music but lots of meaning."[35]

The *Manchester Evening News* noted that Americans were equally shocked by the success of Coward's cabaret act and the fact that nightly performances were sold out well in advance, remarking, "With so many triumphs behind him, it looks as if the best, financially anyway, is to come and America is prepared to make him their idol."[36] Coward remarked that he was genuinely surprised by the response and the sudden interest in his work; however, he noted that the performances were exhausting. Early in the run, Coward was taken ill and had to miss several performances. "Noël Coward was still too ill last night to appear in either of his two scheduled performances at the Desert Inn in Las Vegas," the papers read. "The British playwright and entertainer missed two shows the night before when he fell ill with influenza and his temperature rose to 104. He was still in bed last night and his temperature was high."[37] As even his health was commented on by the press, it became clear that Coward was an integral part of the Golden Age boom of Las Vegas.

The responses from Britain were not all positive, however. Critics asked many times exactly how much Coward would earn by jumping ship to America, as the *Daily Herald* noted: "Noël Coward left London airport last night for the Las Vegas Nevada night club where he is to appear twice-nightly for a month. Asked about his 'fabulous' fee, he replied 'I don't know how much it will be.'" Envy and speculation swirled as to why he felt the need to travel to the United States. The *Sketch* stated bitterly: "Talk about money is usually concerned with other people's—or the speaker's lack of it. Noël Coward's recent 14,000 pounds a week in cabaret at Las Vegas sparked off a lot of conversations I hear, but there was a little envy, for always within a moment the word 'Taxation' cropped up." Noël Whitcomb remarked: "At a party the other evening Noël Coward was telling me about his June cabaret date at Las Vegas. There was a pretty blonde beside me—Ilona Adams, star of the Folies Bergère show. . . . 'I've just come back from Las Vegas,' she whispered, 'and if Mr. Coward is getting the sort of fortune for his act that I've heard about—£12,000 a week—he'll have to stay off the gambling." Rumors of tax dodging continued to swirl. According to the *Belfast Telegraph*, "He tackled a barrage of questions. Most of them touched on his income tax troubles which are said to be keeping him out of England. He was charmingly evasive. 'I'd much rather talk art than income tax. I get rather muddled about such things. You should get in touch with my accountant in London,'" and noted that when Coward gave up his English residence he was not abandoning Britain, but rather asserting his freedom to live wherever he chose.[38] The article also noted that he had a £19,000 overdraft in Britain.

Coward attempted to either ignore these assertions or to center attention on his continued work for the British theater, even taking part via telephone from Las Vegas in a "Night of 100 Stars" benefit for the Actors' Orphanage, with British personalities Jimmy Edwards, Diana Dors, and Eric Portman. An anonymous reporter wrote, "The house is practically sold out and the audience, if not too dazzled by the scores of star names on the programme, will have an extra value for their money in spotting additional surprise personalities who will appear on the stage from time to time during the evening. Noël Coward is to speak to the house by telephone from Las Vegas, where he is appearing in a cabaret."[39]

Artistic Transformations

After his Vegas run, Coward flew to Hollywood for a stint at Paramount, was passed around Hollywood, and was offered a great deal of parts. On behalf of Bill Paley at CBS, Russell and Hamilton approached Coward with a proposal for a television broadcast, which was billed as a repeat of the Café de Paris show he had starred in along with Mary Martin.[40] The TV show was far more conservative in style, which was likely a shock to Coward after Vegas. Critics hailed the show as a "landmark," drawing on the inclusion of Mary Martin, who was well known and much loved in Britain for her performance in Coward's *Pacific 1860* (although it was a flop) and Rodgers and Hammerstein's *South Pacific* (1949).

Coward's 1960s American works were created because of the success of his Vegas show and television specials. His diaries and letters illustrate he was undergoing a conscious self-reinvention during this period that reflected not only his own sense of uncertainty but the larger insecurities of British playwrights of the era. On the Coward renaissance of the '60s, his friend and former secretary Cole Lesley wrote, "All of Noël's more predominant straight plays enjoyed successful revivals during these years," noting the renewed interest in all of Coward's works, including songs and plays that arose because of his Vegas period.[41] This period also paved the way for Coward's Hollywood period of the '60s, which included films such as *Paris When It Sizzles* (1964) and *The Italian Job* (1969).

Fueled by his success in Vegas, his later Broadway works showed the many facets of Coward's creativity, including the playwright, the composer, and the different sides to his abilities. American audiences experienced Coward's significant stage presence and unique performance style, brought to life through a new generation of recordings and television specials. His status as a cultural outsider in the United States allowed him to comment on the sharp class and cultural divides found in Vegas and in the United States more broadly. This commentary is seen in his late musical Broadway works, including *Sail Away* (1961), *The Girl Who Came to Supper* (1963), and *High Spirits* (1964), all of which demonstrated Coward's skill as playwright and songwriter of sophisticated wit.

Sail Away in particular demonstrated that Coward was clearly not past his prime yet—he managed to create controversial enough lyrics to receive his own BBC ban. The *New York Times* noted: "Four saucy songs from the Noël Coward Broadway show *Sail Away* have been banned from British radio. They are thought to offend on the ground of general taste," said a spokesman for the British Broadcasting Corporation. The offensive songs in question were "The Passenger's Always Right"; its reprise, "The Customer's Always Right"; "Useful Phrases"; and "Why Do the Wrong People Travel."[42] The latter became a signature tune for Elaine Stritch, who played the perfect cynical American hostess who had become fed up with her own countrymen who "drag their cans to Zanzibah / Instead of staying quietly in Omaha," who "do not recoil from suntan oil and the gurgle of Coca Cola." While perhaps Coward's musical touch was unable to compete, several of his early plays enjoyed successful revivals, including *Present Laughter*, and he continued his Hollywood career until his death in 1973.

• • •

Although brief, Coward's Vegas period was a transformative one, in which he not only confronted the negative assumptions by the British press, but also established himself as a sophisticated American entertainer. The creative freedom of Vegas also allowed Coward to express a different, more open side of himself than he was otherwise able to do in Britain. The Noël Coward that lives in the memories of many Americans is not that of the 1930s and '40s, but that of Vegas and his American period. The sounds, sights, and mannerisms we recall today are those of Coward in his prime. By exploring his Vegas period within the context of his later career, we are better able to understand not only Coward's work but also his lasting place in American entertainment.

Notes

1. Gilbert Millstein, "Mr. Coward Dissects Las Vegas: The Eminent Entertainer Finds It Analogous to a Vast Cruise Ship, Where Enjoyment Is So Organized No One Has to Play for Himself; Coward Dissects Las Vegas," *New York Times*, June 26, 1955.

2. Millstein, "Mr. Coward Dissects Las Vegas."

3. My thanks to the late casting director Geoffrey Johnson, Coward's longtime U.S. agent and friend, for this detail of Coward's working habits.

4. My thanks to Coward scholar Barry Day for this observation.

5. Cole Lesley, *Remembered Laughter* (New York: Alfred A. Knopf, 1976), 336; Philip Hoare, *Noël Coward: A Biography* (Chicago: University of Chicago Press, 1998), 409.

6. "South of Coward," *Bradford Observer*, October 14, 1955. See also Benny Lee, "Talking Off the Record," *Beds and Herts Pictorial*, November 23, 1954; and "£10,000-a-Week Job for Noël Coward?" *Manchester Evening News*, November 13, 1954.

7. Lesley, *Remembered Laughter*, 332–33.

8. Vincent Dowd, "Noel Coward's Encounter with the Mob," BBC, September 7, 2015, https://www.bbc.com/news/entertainment-arts-34167871.

9. Hoare, *Noël Coward: A Biography*, 410.

10. Noël Whitcomb, "The Man Who Lost a Racetrack and a Dozen Fortunes, Too," *Daily Mirror*, October 23, 1954.

11. Noël Whitcomb, "Joe Just Wanted a Poodle . . . but Tried to Slip a Lead on Coward," *Daily Mirror*, November 13, 1954.

12. "Marlene Dietrich Is Here," *Birmingham Daily Gazette*, June 17, 1954.

13. "Noël Coward Here, Las Vegas Beckons," *New York Times*, November 25, 1954.

14. "Groucho Marx in Coward Play?" *Stage*, April 7, 1955.

15. My thanks to Barry Day for these observations.

16. Hoare, *Noël Coward: A Biography*, 411.

17. Noël Coward diaries, December 3, 1954, cited in Mike Tronnes, *Literary Las Vegas: The Best Writing about the Most Fabulous City* (New York: Holt Paperbacks, 1995), 212.

18. Tronnes, *Literary Las Vegas*, 213.

19. Hoare, *Noël Coward: A Biography*, 412.

20. Hoare, *Noël Coward: A Biography*, 417.

21. Lesley, *Remembered Laughter*, 338–40.

22. Lesley, *Remembered Laughter*, 342.

23. Milton Levin, *Noël Coward* (1968; reprint, Boston: Twayne, 1989), 31.

24. "One-Man Show," *Sporting Times*, July 27, 1929.

25. William L. Fox, *In the Desert of Desire: Las Vegas and the Culture of Spectacle* (Reno: University of Nevada Press, 2005), 31.

26. Robert D. McCracken, *Las Vegas: The Great American Playground*, expanded ed. (Reno: University of Nevada Press, 1997), 70.

27. Thomas Clavin, *That Old Black Magic: Louis Prima, Keely Smith and the Golden Age of Las Vegas* (Chicago: Chicago Review Press, 2010), 93, 186.

28. Clavin, *That Old Black Magic*, 94.

29. Eugene P. Moehring, *Reno, Las Vegas, and the Strip: A Tale of Three Cities*, Wilbur S. Shepperson Series in Nevada History (Reno: University of Nevada Press, 2014), 222.

30. Larry Dale Gragg, "From 'Sodom and Gomorrah' to the 'Last Frontier Town': The Changing Perceptions of Las Vegas in American Popular Culture, 1929–1941," *Studies in Popular Culture* 29, no. 2 (2007): 43–62.

31. Arthur Helliwell, "I Gambled in Spiv Town and Bang Went My Dollars and My Dinner!," *People*, April 8, 1951.

32. Jennifer Johns, "Night Club Neon Lights Lure the Stars to Vegas," *Aberdeen Evening Express*, January 30, 1954.

33. Larry Gragg, "Noel Coward Wows 'Em in Café Town: The Impact of Noel Coward's 1955 Performance at the Desert Inn," *Nevada Historical Society Quarterly* 53, no. 2 (2010): 108–26.

34. Millstein, "Mr. Coward Dissects Las Vegas."

35. Henry Lewis, "The Stately Voice of England," *Britannia and Eve*, December 1, 1956.

36. "Hollywood Newsflash: Noël Strikes Desert Gold," *Manchester Evening News*, July 2, 1955.

37. "Noël Coward Misses Show," *Leicester Evening Mail*, June 16, 1955. "Coward Has Flu," *Daily Herald*, June 16, 1955, notes that Coward was "too ill to appear last night at the Desert Inn Hotel, Las Vegas." See also "Noël Coward Ill," *Belfast Telegraph*, June 15, 1955.

38. "Noël Flies into Money," *Daily Herald*, May 12, 1955; "Motley Notes: The Inspector Calls the Tune," *Sketch*, July 13, 1955; Noël Whitcomb, "The Lass from Las Vegas," *Daily Mirror*, May 5, 1955; "Mr. Coward, Cool and Composed, Faces Press: Income Tax, an Overdraft, His Plays," *Belfast Telegraph*, September 26, 1956.

39. "Night of 100 Stars," *Stage*, June 16, 1955, to benefit the Actors' Orphanage, with Jimmy Edwards, Diana Dors, and Eric Portman.

40. Hoare, *Noël Coward: A Biography*, 414, 411.

41. Lesley, *Remembered Laughter*, 469.

42. "British Bar 'Sail Away' Songs," *New York Times*, June 19, 1962.

8

Elvis in Vegas

The King of Rock 'n' Roll and the City of Second Chances

BRIAN F. WRIGHT

Some people like me. There's more people than critics.
—Elvis Presley, 1956[1]

Elvis Presley (1935–77) remains one of the most iconic cultural figures of the twentieth century. Yet not all parts of his career are equally celebrated. To this day, most histories of rock 'n' roll still treat Presley's early career as his best and most "authentic" period, while his later years in Las Vegas are presented as a prolonged, tragic decline. Such depictions, however, often gloss over the singer's long-standing and productive relationship with the city.

This chapter analyzes four key moments in Presley's career: his failed first appearance in Vegas in 1956, the release of his 1964 movie musical *Viva Las Vegas*, his 1969 return to live performance at Vegas's International Hotel, and his later Vegas residencies in the 1970s. As I argue, Presley repeatedly furthered his career by explicitly aligning himself with Las Vegas show business. Despite its prevailing reputation as tacky, gaudy, and overly commercialized, Vegas served as an important source of inspiration and revitalization for Presley, which in turn helped him to retain his mythical position at the forefront of American popular culture. At the same time, in each of these moments Presley was also admonished by professional critics, who repeatedly denounced him for failing to meet their preconceived standards and expectations. By detailing Presley's public relationship with Las Vegas alongside the press's criticisms of him, this chapter explores both the significant role that the city played in his successes and the elitist and classist biases that informed his contemporary reception.

The Early Years and His First Vegas Appearance

Presley's musical tastes, humor, and public persona were all directly influenced by his upbringing as poor, rural, and Southern.[2] Born in Tupelo, Mississippi, he moved with his family to Memphis, Tennessee, in 1948. Throughout his childhood, his father worked a series of low-paying jobs, and, at times, the Presleys survived on government food assistance and lived in public housing. As a teenager, Elvis became obsessed with music and was especially captivated by the various styles that then circulated in the American South: pop, country, western swing, gospel, blues, and R&B.

In August 1953, at the age of eighteen, Presley walked into Sun Studios—home of the Memphis-based independent label Sun Records—and paid to record a demo; according to biographer Peter Guralnick, Presley went there secretly hoping to be discovered.[3] Although nothing came of this first encounter, Sam Phillips, Sun's owner and in-house producer, eventually took a chance and decided to record the young singer. After hours of trial and error, they eventually landed on a distinctive rock 'n' roll style that both combined Presley's wide-ranging influences and met Phillips's commercial sensibilities.[4]

These early Sun singles, in combination with his appearances on the local country circuit, made Presley a regional favorite in the South, where he came to be known as "the Hillbilly Cat." Yet while Presley's early sexualized, hip-shaking style thrilled young Southern audiences, these live performances failed to catapult him into the national mainstream. This changed after his manager, Colonel Tom Parker, secured him a new contract with RCA Records, a major label with the financial and logistical resources to promote Presley's career. When Presley's first RCA single, "Heartbreak Hotel," was released in early 1956, it quickly sold more than one million copies and turned him into a star—though he continued to be branded as a "hillbilly."[5]

Presley's Las Vegas debut came on April 23, 1956, the very same week that "Heartbreak Hotel" became his first number-one hit on the *Billboard* Top 100.[6] Booked at the New Frontier Hotel and Casino for a two-week engagement, Presley performed a short four-song set as an "extra added attraction" to bandleader Freddy Martin's show. But despite his recent commercial success, Presley was poorly received by Vegas audiences. Bill Willard, the entertainment columnist for the *Las Vegas Sun*, infamously panned Presley's performances, writing that "Elvis Presley, arriving here on the wave of tremendous publicity, fails to hit the promised mark in a desert isle surfeited with rock and rollers who play in shifts atop every cocktail lounge on the Strip. . . . For the teenagers, the long, tall Memphis lad is a whiz; for the average Vegas spender or showgoer, a bore."[7] The problem, according to Willard, was not that Presley's brand of rock 'n' roll was too wild, it was that his stage show simply was not polished enough to compete. As Richard Zoglin explains:

> [Comedian] Shecky Greene got friendly with Elvis during the run and could see that the kid was out of his element—unable to relate to the audience and lacking the stage experience to win them over. He didn't even dress right. "He came out in a dirty baseball jacket, just shit," Greene recalled. "I went to Parker and I said, you can't let him come out on the stage like that." The Colonel apparently took Greene's advice; for the rest of the engagement, Elvis and his band wore neat sport jackets, slacks, and bow ties. But after the first night, they no longer closed the show. Shecky Greene did.[8]

Confirming Greene's recollection, a bootleg recording of Presley's final New Frontier appearance preserves both the singer's performance and the audience's lukewarm response to it.[9]

While Willard and Greene attribute the audience's reaction to Presley's inexperience and inadequate visual style, it is difficult to overlook the classism inherent in this disapproval. Within their contrasting depictions of "Vegas spenders" and Presley's "dirty baseball jacket" lies the not so subtle implication that Presley was too low-class to recognize the proper etiquette that was expected of a Vegas performer at that time. In turn, both critics and audiences likely interpreted Presley's musical style and the "corny" jokes he told in between songs as not only unsophisticated but distinctly Southern. To them, he was irrevocably marked as a low-class hillbilly. *Newsweek*'s coverage of these performances confirmed as much: according to the article's unnamed writer, "Elvis was something like a jug of corn liquor at a champagne party."[10]

Although Presley repeatedly failed to meet the expectations of the New Frontier's adult audiences, he found more success when he was allowed to play for his fans. During the first Saturday of his engagement, the casino opened the showroom for a special charity matinee for local teenagers. The show was reportedly a huge success, and the sheer pandemonium it provoked was covered by a local Memphis newspaper:

> The teen-agers . . . can't get in to see him because of the age limit, so they had a special show . . . last Saturday afternoon. The carnage was terrific. They pushed and shoved to get into the 1000-seat room and several hundred thwarted youngsters buzzed like angry hornets outside. After the show, bedlam! A laughing, shouting, idolatrous mob swarmed him; he fled to the insufficient sanctuary of his suite. The door wouldn't hold them out. They got his shirt, and it was shredded. A triumphant girl seized a button, clutched it as tho it were a diamond. A squadron of police had to be called to clear the field.[11]

Unlike the class-conscious Vegas regulars that he had been playing to, Presley's fans were genuinely excited to see him perform. As would become a common trope in Presley's career, his fans enthusiastically accepted and appreciated his music, while the critics could not see past his supposed faults.

Presley's visit to the city was also formative for the young singer, as it allowed him to learn from other performers that more successfully embodied a Vegas aesthetic. At the Riviera, he took in a performance by entertainer Lee Liberace, whose critically acclaimed show featured elaborate costumes and high production values. When they met after the show, Liberace counseled Presley that he needed a glitzier, more spectacular look, a suggestion that made a lasting impression.[12] "The following spring," Zoglin notes, "when Elvis began a ten-day tour of the Midwest and Northeast, he was wearing a new outfit: a $2,500 gold-leaf suit, modeled on the one Liberace had worn in Las Vegas" (fig. 8.1).[13] Likewise, while visiting the Sands, Presley took in a floor show by Freddie Bell and the Bellboys, a lounge act that had recently appeared in the film *Rock Around the Clock* (1956). The Bellboys' routine was as much Vegas as it was rock 'n' roll, as Bell recalled: "In order to sell our show, we had to do a lot of choreography and dancing besides just doing rock 'n' roll. We had the snappy tuxedos, the showbiz look."[14] Watching their performance, Presley was struck both by the group's showmanship and by the audience's enthusiastic reaction to it, especially on their high-energy rendition of Big Mama Thornton's "Hound Dog."

FIGURE 8.1 Cover of the compilation LP *50,000,000 Elvis Fans Can't Be Wrong* (1959), featuring Presley in his Liberace-inspired gold lamé suit.

According to Guralnick, this performance "sparked a determination on Elvis's part to incorporate it into his own show," and, as Presley's guitarist Scotty Moore told the writer, "We stole it straight from them. . . . [Elvis] already knew it, knew the song, but when we seen those guys do it, he said, 'There's a natural.'"[15] After the show, Presley got Bell's permission to record and perform a version of the song that relied heavily on the Bellboys' Vegas-style arrangement. When "Hound Dog" was released as Presley's third RCA single, it became a massive hit—reaching number one on the *Billboard* pop, country, and R&B charts. Drawing on the lessons he had learned in Vegas, Presley had solidified his position as the country's biggest rock 'n' roll star.

The Film Years and *Viva Las Vegas*

Riding high on the success of "Hound Dog," Presley leveraged his newfound celebrity to break into acting, eventually appearing in thirty-one feature films between 1956 and 1969.[16] At first, these movie roles were a supplement to his recordings and concerts. However, in 1958, Presley was drafted and served a two-year stint in the U.S. Army, and after he returned, he and Parker decided that he would abandon live performances and instead focus on his movie career. Presley's films and their soundtracks thus became his primary output in the 1960s. But, by 1964, much had changed in popular music; with the arrival of the British Invasion—specifically the unprecedented success of the Beatles—Presley was no longer the country's premier rock 'n' roller. Even so, the movies remained one arena in which he was still able to compete, and that same year Presley reasserted his claim to pop culture relevance through a musical comedy set in Las Vegas.

Viva Las Vegas (fig. 8.2) is a working-class fantasy. It stars Presley as Lucky Jackson, a mechanic/race car driver who goes to compete in the Las Vegas Grand Prix. His foil is Count Elmo Mancini, a wealthy Italian who tries to pay Jackson to throw the race. Over the course of the film, both men also compete for the affections of Rusty Martin (played by Ann-Margret), a swimming instructor at one of the local hotels. After an accident causes him to lose the money he needs for a new engine, Jackson ends up working for the same hotel, where he flirts and sings his way into Martin's heart.[17] By the end of the movie, Presley has won the race and the girl, whom he is shown marrying in the closing scene.

The film was a box-office smash: *Variety* reported that it had grossed $4,675,000 domestically by the end of 1964—making it the eleventh best-grossing film of the year. Yet despite its popularity, the film received mixed reviews from the critics. The most glowing report came from *Boxoffice*, which stated that "Elvis Presley is in his singing element in this lavishly filmed musical romance laid in that city of gambling and show business glitter, Las Vegas." Other critics were far less generous, with most dismissing the whole project as

FIGURE 8.2 Promotional poster for *Viva Las Vegas* (1964).

trite and formulaic. *Time* claimed, "*Viva Las Vegas* has the wholesome, mindless spontaneity it takes to create a successful Elvis Presley movie." The *New York Times* critic wrote that the film was "as pleasant and unimportant as a banana split." And *Variety* called it a "hackneyed yarn" that was "designed to dazzle the eye, assault the ear and ignore the brain."[18]

Although *Viva Las Vegas* was always intended to be a lightweight, fun summer film, there were other reasons it resonated more with moviegoers than with critics. Elvis's ongoing star power, his on-screen chemistry with Ann-Margret, and the film's soundtrack were all obviously selling points. Beyond that, though, the film also presents an inviting, fictionalized meritocracy in which anyone can rise above their station through skill, hard work, and a bit of luck. Aligning with his earlier, well-publicized hillbilly reputation, Presley plays a working-class mechanic who must take on menial jobs to finance his dream. Using his wits, his singing, and his driving abilities, he ultimately triumphs over the rich Italian count. As Douglas Brode notes, Elvis's character uses hard work and self-reliance to achieve a version of the American dream, a dream that—thanks to Presley's own life story—"finally appeared as open to the lower classes as it always had been to the privileged few."[19]

It is no coincidence that this all plays out in Las Vegas, the so-called city of second chances. In fact, the city is a constant presence in the film. The opening sequence is an overhead trip through the Las Vegas Strip superimposed with shots of the illuminated signs of various casinos—all presented in wide-screen and vibrant color. Soon thereafter, there is an entire four-minute sequence in which Jackson and the count travel to multiple casinos to look for Martin among different teams of dancing showgirls. Both Ann-Margaret and Presley also perform entire songs onstage in a Vegas showroom, with the latter performing the film's iconic title song in a single unedited take.[20] Throughout, Vegas is presented in all its glitzy, glamorous glory, a place of possibility and reinvention where anyone could be just one big win away from changing their lot in life.

With *Viva Las Vegas*, Presley sought commercial success by deliberately associating himself with the trappings of Las Vegas show business—and it worked. Released at the height of Beatlemania, Presley's film outgrossed the Beatles' own movie musical, *A Hard Day's Night*, from that same year.[21] At a time when his singles were no longer topping the pop charts, Presley's working-class Vegas fantasy allowed him to stay relevant.

Return to Live Performances and the First Vegas Residency

As it turned out, *Viva Las Vegas* was the apex of Presley's film career, and while many of his later movies continued to turn a profit, by the late sixties he had developed a new reputation among critics: that of the has-been. In comparison to the psychedelic, countercultural rock acts that were now appearing on the charts, Presley seemed like a relic from a bygone era. With his career beginning to flounder, he set out yet again to reclaim his position in popular culture. In December 1968, he starred in a dedicated NBC-TV special (now known as the "Comeback Special"). Its success energized Presley and convinced him to return to performing live. He tasked Parker to sort out the details, and in search of the most lucrative deal he could arrange, his manager secured Presley $400,000 for a monthlong residency at the International Hotel in Las Vegas—a return to the city that would once again revitalize his career.

When the International opened in July 1969, it was the largest casino in the world, featuring more than fifteen hundred individual rooms and a two-thousand-seat showroom.[22] As the hotel's second headliner, Presley was scheduled to appear from July 31 through August 28, 1969 (fig. 8.3), where he would perform ten sets per week for four weeks. And, thanks to Parker's uncanny knack for promotion, the entire run was nearly sold out before it even started (and was completely sold out not long after).[23] Presley took the residency seriously. He hired a team of first-rate LA session musicians for his band, as well

FIGURE 8.3 Ad in the *Las Vegas Sun* promoting Presley's first Vegas residency.

as two different groups of backup singers, all of which he paid for himself; he also threw himself into rehearsals and had the band learn hundreds of songs that encapsulated his wide-ranging musical interests.[24] They eventually settled on around twenty, a mix of his old material, songs featured in the Comeback Special, covers of contemporary hits, and brand-new songs that he had recently recorded.[25] In total, the set acknowledged his past successes while simultaneously asserting his claim to being a relevant contemporary artist.

Presley's first appearances at the International were an immense success. On opening night—which had been reserved solely for critics, celebrities, and high rollers—rhythm guitarist John Wilkinson recalled that the audience "wouldn't shut up, all through the first song they kept shouting and cheering, they couldn't get enough of him. It was amazing, that thunderous applause coming from one showroom." The owner of the International, Kirk Kerkorian, similarly recalled: "Elvis just tore the place down. . . . His show was fantastic. It was one of the most exciting shows I've ever seen."[26] Kerkorian was so enthusiastic about the opening-night performance that the very next day he retroactively raised Presley's weekly rate to $125,000, secured a second run of performances for January, and signed a contract for Presley to appear at the International for two residencies every year for the next five years. This deal made Presley the highest-earning entertainer in Vegas, beating out the likes of Frank Sinatra and Dean Martin—who were only making $100,000 per week.[27]

After opening night, the audiences were largely composed of Presley's fans, who were equally enthralled. This is evident on the multiple recordings of his 1969 International shows, which capture the energy and excitement that Presley and his band brought to these performances.[28] Based on these recordings, it seems as if the fans hang on every note he sings. Even the jokes he tells in between songs are met with uproarious laughter. By the end of his residency, Presley had drawn a reported total of 101,500 attendees and brought in $1.5 million in gross box-office revenue, making him "the most successful act in Las Vegas history."[29] According to Zoglin, "In a town where showroom entertainment was traditionally a loss leader, Elvis's was reputedly the first Vegas show to actually make money."[30]

Even the new generation of rock critics were impressed, although they nonetheless continued to disparage Presley and his fans. For example, the *Time* magazine reviewer wrote that "[Presley] stepped onstage in front of a gold lamé curtain at Las Vegas' new International Hotel, coordinated his pelvic girdle and his phallic guitar, closed his eyes, tossed his head and sent a solar wind of nostalgia over the 2,000 middle-aged record executives, hotel guests and show folk assembled for the opening night. It was like being back in the innocent '50s. . . . But things weren't quite the same. The audience was too grown up to scream and squeal." In *Rolling Stone*, David Dalton described Presley as "putting himself on. Elvis imitating Elvis . . . he's putting-on a whole era, he's putting-on the Fifties." Dalton then explicitly criticized Presley's audience for having "sold out," broadly characterizing them as "super-straight, mostly middle-aged people with children and affluent old Elvis fans in their late thirties, their ducktails trimmed into neat executive crewcuts, their leather jackets turned in for seersucker suits."[31] Here again, there is an underlying classism to the critics' judgments, although this time it plays out in reverse: because they have grown up and become middle and upper class—in essence, because they appear too comfortable in a place like Las Vegas—Presley and his audience stand in opposition to the critics' conceptions of rock authenticity.[32] As Richard Goldstein described the opening night for the *New York Times*, "It felt like getting hit in the face with a bucket of melted ice. He looked so timeless up there, so constant, and yet you knew he was . . . in it for the money."[33]

Taken at face value, the critics' objections seem to be directed less at Presley's actual performance—which most praised—than at his status as an "oldies" act. Yet the recordings of these shows clearly demonstrate that Presley had very little interest in living in the past. Of his seventeen number-one hits up to that point, he included only five in the show: "All Shook Up," "Love Me Tender," "Jailhouse Rock," "Don't Be Cruel," and "Hound Dog." Moreover, he front-loaded them at the beginning of the set, often in abbreviated arrangements, and performed them at breakneck tempos. There is thus every indication that Presley wanted to get through this material as quickly as possible, paying only the barest lip service to his early career. Further undercutting their significance, Presley often prefaced these songs with self-deprecating jokes; for instance, he introduced the ballad "Love Me Tender" as "one of the first records I recorded back in . . . 1927, I think it was. Just before the stock market crashed."[34]

Most significantly, what the critics seem to have missed is that Presley was once again having bona fide hits. Just prior to the residency, his recording of "In the Ghetto" had reached number three on the pop charts, making it his first Top 10 hit since 1965. During his first Vegas residency, Presley followed "In the Ghetto" with "Suspicious Minds," a new song that alternated between frenzied energy and subdued calm for more than six minutes. Drawing on a Vegas showroom aesthetic, the entire band takes part, providing soaring backup vocals, call-and-response horns, propulsive drumming, and a driving electric bass line. Combined with Presley's vocal performance, the song was the highlight of the set each night. And at least one critic took notice: describing the opening-night performance for the *New Yorker*, Ellen Willis wrote, "If Elvis continues to perform . . . and 'Suspicious Minds' is as big a hit as it should be, he could have a significant impact on pop music in the coming months."[35] Willis's prediction proved correct. In August 1969, Presley released a version of "Suspicious Minds" that closely matched the live performances that were being so enthusiastically received by his Vegas audiences—a connection that RCA made sure to highlight in their promotional material (fig. 8.4). Thanks in

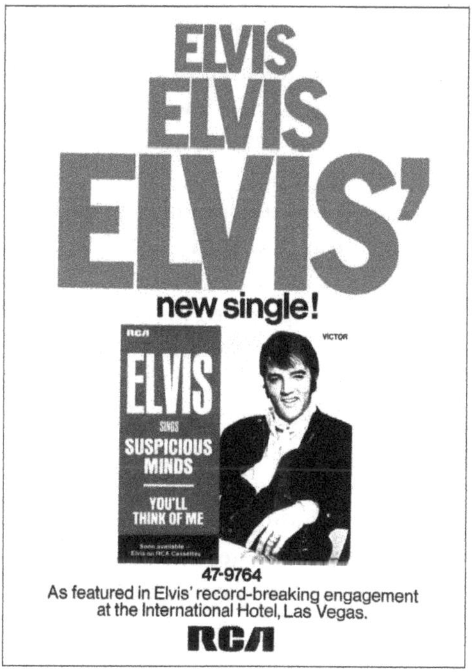

FIGURE 8.4 RCA ad in *Billboard* promoting "Suspicious Minds"

large part to its Vegas-inspired style, "Suspicious Minds" became Presley's first number-one hit in more than seven years.

For the critics, Vegas exemplified everything that was manufactured and phony, and no matter how much they may have enjoyed Presley's performance, they simply did not value the older, straitlaced audience that now seemed to constitute his fan base. Yet with a dedicated two-thousand-seat venue, the ability to host a four-week residency, and the bankroll to pay its star a hefty appearance fee, Las Vegas was the only logical place for Presley to stage his comeback. And in the end, the city once again revitalized Presley's career, first by giving him a platform to reach his fans, and then by helping "Suspicious Minds" become a national best seller.

The Later Vegas Residencies

Presley used the success of his first International appearances as a launching pad into a lucrative return to live performances, and from 1970 up to his untimely death in 1977, he split his time between his biannual Las Vegas residencies, short national tours, and recording new music. His stage show also continued to evolve throughout, as Presley leaned more heavily into a Vegas aesthetic, a move that further deepened the divide between the critics and his fans.

Starting in 1970, Presley began performing in the one-piece jumpsuits that have now come to symbolize his Vegas years (fig. 8.5). Echoing the advice that Liberace had given him back in 1956, these increasingly elaborate outfits became an integral part of Presley's stage show. According to Susan Doll, their "excess" and "extravagance" were a form of conspicuous consumption that conveyed Presley's status as a superstar.[36] This conspicuous consumption also clearly represented a class fantasy, both for the singer and for his audience. For Presley, such overt displays of wealth were the outward manifestations of his rags-to-riches life story, a success that his fans could then also vicariously celebrate. Musically, Presley also regularly updated his set lists to incorporate more songs that he actually enjoyed singing, which further de-emphasized his early material. Embracing the dramatic, grandiose musical style that had made "Suspicious Minds" a hit, Presley's renditions of songs such as "You've Lost That Lovin' Feelin'," "An American Trilogy," and "See See Rider" became the aural counterpart to his ostentatious costumes. Taken together, this new image and musical style expressed Presley's full embrace of Las Vegas show business.[37]

For his fans, Presley's Vegas performances continued to be a cause for celebration. However, as might be expected, most critics treated each of Presley's subsequent Vegas residencies as an intensifying disappointment.[38] The purest

FIGURE 8.5 Presley performing in a jumpsuit onstage at the International Hotel, 1970.

distillation of this sentiment comes from Mark Tan's review of a Presley performance from 1971:

> As performances go, Elvis Presley's . . . is sloppy, hurriedly rehearsed, mundanely lit, poorly amplified, occasionally monotonous, often silly, and haphazardly coordinated. Elvis looked drawn, tired, and noticeably heavier—weight-wise, not musically—than in his last Vegas appearance. He wasn't in his strongest voice, his costume of studded white slacks and vest with black satin high collar scarf was not his sexiest or most flattering. And do you know what? The packed to over-capacity audience—the first 2,000 of the usual 120,000 he'll draw for his month-long engagement—positively couldn't have cared less about any pros, cons, or comparisons. They absolutely loved, honored, and obeyed his every whim with screams, shrieks, whistles and dashes to the stage apron whenever Elvis decided to wander downstage to kiss, touch, or wipe his brow amidst the adoring throng.[39]

As with the reviews of Presley's first residency, Tan disparages the audience as a bunch of rubes too mystified to see that they have been duped. However, he adds a new piece of evidence: Presley's physical appearance. As would become commonplace in the seventies, Tan explicitly fat-shames Presley, pointing to the singer's weight gain as an outward indicator of his performative deficiencies. As Mark Duffett demonstrates, such critiques were inherently classist, as they implicitly connected Presley's lack of dieting to the low social status of his upbringing; for the critics, Duffett argues, Presley's "dogged determination to maintain a lack of culinary sophistication distinguished him as someone who gained the material wealth of a different class, but not its cultural trappings." By emphasizing his increasing weight, the press thus found yet another way to treat Presley as an irredeemable hillbilly. However, Presley's publicized indulgences in food can also be more charitably interpreted as part of the aforementioned conspicuous consumption that characterized his Vegas years. Like the lavish outfits he wore onstage, his weight in some ways actually epitomized his triumph over his low-class origins—he had gone from being someone who grew up on government food assistance to now being able to eat whatever he wanted. Duffett also points out that "if the journalists who wrote about Elvis's shows cared [about his weight], there was much less evidence that his audiences shared their views."[40] This can be proven by ticket sales alone: regardless of the critics' pronouncements, every single one of Presley's Vegas performances sold out—an estimated 636 shows in total.[41]

The platform that Vegas provided Presley fundamentally reinvigorated the final years of his career and cemented his status as one of America's most famous entertainers. It gave him the freedom to experiment with new musical and visual styles and the ability to reach hundreds of thousands of fans each year. Even if critics and historians continue to present this era of Presley's career as increasingly inauthentic, it is important to note that his fans simply did not experience it that way.

Conclusion

Rock historians have tended to view Presley's relationship with Las Vegas as an embarrassment. They'd prefer to remember Presley as a young, rebellious rock 'n' roller rather than the aging, jumpsuited figure that inspired countless Elvis impersonators. But those two images are not mutually exclusive. Although it may not easily fit prevailing narratives of rock authenticity, Las Vegas show business repeatedly played a crucial role in helping Presley remain culturally relevant—so much so that without Vegas, Presley might not remain a household name today.

Whether they recognize it or not, those that are uncomfortable with Presley's later Vegas years are simply parroting the same dismissals that were promoted by his contemporary critics. Yet, under the surface of this discourse has always resided an elitism and classism that is problematically disconnected from the opinions of Presley's fans. An accurate historical account of Presley's status as a cultural icon thus requires an approach that values the perspectives of his mass audience. For as with any popular artist, it was Presley's fans who were ultimately responsible for his continuing success.

Following the model that Presley established, multiple musicians have turned to Las Vegas to revitalize their careers, including everyone from Cher,

Céline Dion, Elton John, and Britney Spears, to Mötley Crüe, Def Leppard, and Aerosmith. Ultimately, perhaps this is the greatest legacy of Presley's later years: he established Las Vegas as a place where performers and their fans can come together in joyous, communal celebration—critics be damned.

Notes

1. Kays Gary, "Elvis Defends Low-Down Style," *Charlotte Observer*, June 27, 1956, 1B.

2. For more on Presley's "Southernness," see Susan Doll, *Understanding Elvis: Southern Roots vs. Star Image* (New York: Garland, 1998).

3. Peter Guralnick, *Last Train to Memphis: The Rise of Elvis Presley* (Boston: Little, Brown, 1994), 62–63.

4. With its roots in African American musical traditions, Presley's vocal style also fulfilled Philips's infamous dictate that "If I could find a white man who had the Negro sound and the Negro feel, I could make a billion dollars." For a thorough interrogation of this quote, see Gilbert B. Rodman, "A Hero to Most? Elvis, Myth, and the Politics of Race," *Cultural Studies* 8, no. 3 (1994): 457–83. For an analysis of Presley's relationship with the African American community and its subsequent interpretations, see Michael T. Bertrand, *Race, Rock, and Elvis* (Urbana: University of Illinois Press, 2005).

5. Describing Presley and "Heartbreak Hotel," a *Life* magazine article explained that "the 21-year-old hillbilly who howls, mumbles, coos and cries his way through [the recording] has overnight become the biggest singing attraction for teen-agers in the U.S." "A Howling Hillbilly Success: Young Elvis Presley's Complaint Becomes Nation's Top Pop Tune," *Life*, April 30, 1956, 64.

6. "The Top 100 [for survey week ending April 25]," *Billboard*, May 5, 1956, 40.

7. Bill Willard, "Elvis Is a Bore," *Las Vegas Sun*, April 28, 1956.

8. Richard Zoglin, *Elvis in Vegas: How the King Reinvented the Las Vegas Show* (New York: Simon & Schuster Paperbacks, 2019), 5.

9. This performance was commercially released in 1980 as part of the limited-edition retrospective box set Elvis Presley, *Elvis Aron Presley (1955–1980) 25th Anniversary* (RCA CPL8-3699, LP).

10. "Hillbilly on a Pedestal," *Newsweek*, May 14, 1956, 82.

11. Bob Johnson, "The Golden Boy Reaches for a Star While the Music Goes Round and Round," *Memphis Press-Scimitar*, May 4, 1956, 25.

12. Darden Asbury Pyron, *Liberace: An American Boy* (Chicago: University of Chicago Press, 2000), 264–65.

13. Zoglin, *Elvis in Vegas*, 50.

14. Quoted in Mike Weatherford, *Cult Vegas: The Weirdest! The Wildest! The Swingin'est Town on Earth!* (Las Vegas: Huntington Press, 2001), 120.

15. Guralnick, *Last Train to Memphis*, 273.

16. For further discussions of Presley's film career, see Mark Feeney, "Elvis Movies," *American Scholar* 70, no. 1 (2001): 53–60; Douglas Brode, *Elvis Cinema and Popular Culture* (Jefferson, NC: McFarland, 2006); David Baker, "Elvis Goes to Hollywood: Authenticity, Resistance, Commodification, and the Mainstream," in *Redefining*

Mainstream Popular Music, ed. Sarah Baker, Andy Bennett, and Jodie Taylor, 89–101 (New York: Routledge, 2013); and James L. Neibaur, *The Elvis Movies* (Lanham, MD: Rowman & Littlefield, 2014).

17. Baker argues that Lucky Jackson's loose relationship with work also inscribes the film with a distinct working-class Southernness. Baker, "Elvis Goes to Hollywood," 99.

18. "Big Rental Pictures of 1964," *Variety*, January 6, 1965, 39; "Feature Reviews: *Viva Las Vegas*," *Boxoffice*, May 25, 1964; "The Way-Out West," *Time*, May 29, 1964, 86; Howard Thompson, "Elvis Presley Teams with Ann-Margret," *New York Times*, May 21, 1964; "Film Reviews: *Viva Las Vegas*," *Variety*, May 20, 1964, 20.

19. Brode, *Elvis Cinema and Popular Culture*, 151.

20. Zoglin writes that "*Viva Las Vegas* has endured as the quintessential Las Vegas film" and "serves as a good travel brochure for Vegas in its classic era," but that it "has attained its iconic status mainly because of its title song." As he explains, "The bongo-driven beat, catchy melody, and Elvis's energetic vocal performance seemed to perfectly capture the fun-loving, high-flying spirit of Vegas in its golden age." Zoglin, *Elvis in Vegas*, 106.

21. "Big Rental Pictures of 1964." According to *Variety*, by the end of 1964, *A Hard Day's Night* had grossed only $4,473,000 domestically.

22. Zoglin, *Elvis in Vegas*, 169.

23. Ken Sharp, *Elvis: Vegas '69* (n.p.: Jetfighter, 2009), 55.

24. Peter Guralnick, *Careless Love: The Unmaking of Elvis Presley* (Boston: Little, Brown, 1999), 341–47.

25. For the fiftieth anniversary of Presley's first performances at the International Hotel, RCA released a box set containing recordings of eleven full shows, each of which has a nearly identical set list. See Elvis Presley, *Live 1969* (RCA Records, 2019, CD).

26. Quoted in Sharp, *Elvis: Vegas '69*, 91, 105.

27. Zoglin, *Elvis in Vegas*, 170. As part of his new contract with the International Hotel, Presley was also given "favored nations" status, meaning that if any other performer in Vegas was contracted at a higher rate, Presley's would be raised to match it. Guralnick, *Careless Love*, 354–55.

28. Presley, *Live 1969*.

29. Guralnick, *Careless Love*, 358.

30. Zoglin, *Elvis in Vegas*, 216.

31. "Return of the Big Beat," *Time*, August 15, 1969, 57; David Dalton, "Elvis," *Rolling Stone* February 21, 1970, 27.

32. The contradictions of rock authenticity are explored in Keir Keightley, "Reconsidering Rock," in *The Cambridge Companion to Pop and Rock*, ed. Simon Frith, Will Straw, and John Street, 109–42 (Cambridge: Cambridge University Press, 2001).

33. Richard Goldstein, "A White Boy with Black Hips," *New York Times*, August 10, 1969, D22.

34. Presley, *Live 1969*.

35. Ellen Willis, "Rock, Etc.," *New Yorker*, August 30, 1969, 78.

36. Doll, *Understanding Elvis*, 165, 174.

37. The evolution of Presley's musical and visual style are apparent in the multiple live audio and video recordings from this era, especially the documentary *Elvis Presley: That's the Way It Is* (1970), the concert film *Elvis on Tour* (1972), and the televised concert special *Elvis: Aloha from Hawaii* (1973).

38. This increasing dissatisfaction is perhaps best witnessed in Robert Hilburn's multiple reviews of Presley's performances for the *Los Angeles Times*. See, for instance, Robert Hilburn, "Fan to Fan: What's Happened to Elvis?" *Los Angeles Times*, February 6, 1972, Y44.

39. Mark Tan, "Uninspired Elvis Delights in Vegas," *Hollywood Reporter*, August 12, 1971, 3. Describing Presley's second 1973 Vegas residency, the *Hollywood Reporter* was even more demeaning, stating that "[Presley is] not just a little out of shape, not just a little chubbier than usual, the Living Legend is fat. . . . His voice, opening night, was thin, uncertain, and strained. His . . . personality . . . was lost in one of the most ill-prepared, unsteady, and most disappointing performances of his Las Vegas career." Guralnick contrasts this review with the audience's positive reaction to the very same performances: "Fan reports suggested that Elvis was 'much happier,' 'full of fun for the most part,' and seemed to be 'enjoying the shows much more.'" Both review and fan reports are quoted in Guralnick, *Careless Love*, 504.

40. Mark Duffett, "Elvis Presley and Susan Boyle: Bodies of Controversy," *Journal of Popular Music Studies* 23, no. 2 (2011): 173, 175.

41. John Katsilometes, "Was Number of Elvis's Consecutive Sold-Out Shows in Las Vegas 636 or 837?" *Las Vegas Sun*, April 26, 2015, https://lasvegassun.com/blogs/kats-report/2015/apr/26/was-number-elvis-consecutive-sold-out-shows-vegas-/.

9

Céline Dion's and Cher's Vegas Residencies

The Envoiced and Embodied Spectacle of Feminine Aging on the Vegas Stage

JESSICA A. HOLMES AND MICHAEL KINNEY

With musical careers spanning several decades, numerous Grammy Awards, accolades, and record-breaking achievements, pop divas Céline Dion and Cher have both maintained mass appeal in the face of a perpetually youthful pop music industry and the deeply misogynist logics of ageism. Crucially, Las Vegas has been key to their continued appeal, as the singers have held successive Vegas concert "residencies" during the latter half of their careers. With its roots in the mythology of the American West as a land of opportunity, Vegas has long served as a nostalgic space where headliners perform their greatest hits night after night in the manner of concert residencies for vacationers staying at one of the many luxury resort hotels that line the famous Strip. While formerly stigmatized as a place where "singers go to die," in recent years, Vegas has experienced a musical revitalization, due in no small part to Dion's pathbreaking influence, which has seen the concert residency reemerge as a glamorous and profitable opportunity for singers, young and old, to strengthen and capitalize on their iconic status.

In this chapter, we situate Céline Dion's and Cher's Vegas residencies as a type of embodied musical tourism that at once reifies and resists cultural attitudes toward the aging female voice and body, bridging work in pop music studies, age studies, disability studies, and voice studies in the process. In both cases, we explore the various onstage performance strategies and offstage conditioning these singers undertake to mitigate the oftentimes disabling physical demands of successive live shows to protect their voices and fortify their musical longevity. Lest the manufactured dimensions of their brands fool you, we ultimately celebrate their creative agency and professional autonomy as women entertainers and entrepreneurs who have leveraged their Vegas residencies to maintain their stronghold as cultural touchstones. In the process, they challenge straightforward ideas of aging as a process of decline and its uneven gendered logics, while foregrounding the creative multiplicities of what it means to grow older.

To be sure, while age studies scholars caution against equating aging with disability wholesale—particularly the mistaken idea that aging *is* a disability or that aging necessarily causes disability—the lived experiences of aging and disability intersect in significant ways.[1] Accordingly, age studies finds common ground with disability studies in its critique of bodily norms and biomedical pathologization through a sociocultural lens that challenges the customary Western neoliberalist construction of aging as an "immutable material" process of decline marked by discrete biological substrata corresponding to naturalized age-based categories.[2] To the extent that it is culturally marked, "aging," like disability, becomes part of one's identity only when social contexts fail to account for and accommodate it, hailing it into the present as a stigmatized spectacle.[3]

As Abigail Gardner explains, the centrality of spectacle in pop music combined with the "continuing nexus of youthfulness as/and desire" in the pop music industry are inherently gendered in ways that paradoxically render aging women performers—like Dion, Cher, and others—at once hypervisible and invisible through what Alexandra Apolloni notes is a process of "gradual sexual disqualification" that promptly begins in a woman's thirties.[4] Indeed, Tiffany Naiman argues that "the very acts and traits that qualify an artist to be a pop star (such as suggestive costume or performances and more generally making a spectacle of one's body) disrupt common ideas of appropriate behavior for middle-aged women."[5] Even as ageism is unevenly gendered and racialized in pop music, there is need to avoid generalizing, as these disparities do not always divide along expected male/female and black/white lines of power.[6]

Unequivocally, the cultural spectacle of the disabled body and the cultural spectacle of the aging body—and the resulting stigma associated with both—have been framed as predominantly *visual* phenomena in disability, aging, and popular music studies. Céline Dion's and Cher's Vegas residencies offer an opportunity to further ponder the sonic dimensions of the interlocking cultural spectacle of aging and disability as manifest in perceived vocal and bodily "decline" in their more recent performances in Vegas. Our chapter thus positions the singing *voice* as a locus in which naturalized markers of age, musical ability, and gender intersect, just as they do in the body—an acoustical site onto which fans project anxieties and fantasies about who these singers were, who they have become, and the culturally gendered spectacle of aging.

Ultimately, by attending to the evolution and reception of Céline Dion's and Cher's voices on the Vegas stage, we position Vegas as a liminal musical space where nostalgia, stardom, and camp overlap with and often belie the misogynist logics of ageism in the pop mainstream and the disabling capacities of the music industry. Calling forth from these Vegas stages is an insistence to continue, to be seen and heard with dignity and power in a music industry where aging women are too often subject to scrutiny, shame, stigma, and even ridicule. Building on the work of scholars like Nicole Naimon, George MacKay, and Laurie Stras, as well as Naiman and Ros Jennings, we position Cher and Dion as pioneers of an *empowered late feminine pop style* that originates in, is facilitated by, and is inextricably tied to Vegas as the "city of second chances." Rather than understand Vegas as a place where aging performers "go to die," or play at being "young" again, we hear Dion's and Cher's performances as resisting tropes of aging femininity and restructuring their aging as a process of possibility.

Feminine Age, Aging, and Ageism in Dion's Vegas Residencies

To date, five-time Grammy Award–winning French Canadian vocal juggernaut, queen of the blockbuster power ballad, and best-selling Canadian artist of all time Céline Dion has delivered two *multi*year concert residencies in Las Vegas, amounting to 1,141 shows performed over a sixteen-year period (2003–19). With a combined gross revenue of 681.31 million U.S. dollars with over 4.5 million tickets sold, her first residency, *A New Day . . .* (2003–7), and her second residency, *Celine* (2011–19), are "the highest grossing and best-selling Las Vegas residencies of all time," according to *Billboard*.[7] The record-breaking success of Dion's residencies is all the more extraordinary given the fact that historically, the Vegas concert residency had suffered from a notably ageist stigma, derided by the theater establishment for its low production value, conjuring "images of early-bird dinner specials, corny magicians and Cole Porter standards sung to happily clapping coach parties," in the words of critic Ben Beaumont-Thomas, or, as critic Martin Chilton explains, "a retirement home for musical careers, a place where a washed-up old crooner would go for a residency, forlornly singing medleys of their old hits night after night to a few hundred bored or drunk punters and tourists, resting between visits to the slot machine."[8]

Under the creative leadership of former Cirque du Soleil director Franco Dragone and the strategic oversight of Dion's husband and manager, impresario René Angélil, Dion's inaugural residency presented a ninety-minute show replete with flying acrobats, dancers, and dreamy stagecraft with Dion's powerhouse singing and emotionally emphatic stage presence front and center at the brand-new Colosseum Showroom at Caesars Palace, specially built to house *A New Day . . .*[9] Through centralizing and capitalizing on world-leading creative talent and state-of-the-art infrastructure, Dion and Angélil ultimately established the blueprint for what quickly became a "glamorous and lucrative rite of pop passage" for singers young and old, in the words of Beaumont-Thomas, significantly revitalizing the Vegas entertainment industry, while positioning Dion as "pilgrimage site," to borrow media studies scholar Erin Hurley's characterization.[10]

Dion's iconic status has only grown as she has grown older on the Vegas stage. Indeed, at the close of her second residency in 2019, the then fifty-one-year-old Dion was experiencing new popularity among millennial fans who were flocking to her Vegas shows as a "once-in-a-lifetime" "bucket-list item," having "latched onto" her as an "icon to 'stan,'" in the words of critic Katie Connor. Known among fans as the "Célinaissance," this resurgence in Dion's popularity centers on a *defiant* embrace of the very qualities Dion's detractors have long ridiculed as corny, bombastic, annoying, wholly contrived, and decidedly uncool: not least, her larger-than-life voice, her unabated appeals to emotion, and, increasingly, her unapologetic musical longevity in an unapologetically ageist industry, evident from Dion's own assertion: "I am a woman assuming her own destiny, full of energy and *in* love with life. . . . At 51, I have the sense that I am at my pinnacle!"[11]

Dion's Vegas residencies thus offer a fruitful opportunity to interrogate the long-standing centrality of ageism in the singer's image, fandom, and censure relative to debates over the politics of musical taste and gendered and classed consumption. Analyzing the reception of Dion's Vegas performances also provides insight into broader cultural expectations regarding so-called age-appropriate behavior among middle-aged white women, where questions of technological innovation, spectacle, and sexual autonomy are at stake in Dion's case. Finally, Dion's longevity as a performer on the Vegas stage reveals much about the function of vocal damage in musical perceptions of authenticity: among fans, evidence of vocal strain in her more recent Vegas performances further authenticates her vocal prowess, emotionality, and sense of feminine resilience, while her authority as a vocalist remains uncontested, even among her harshest critics.[12]

Age and ageism have been uniquely central to Dion's celebrity image since the very beginning of her career, from controversy over the twenty-six-year age gap between Dion and Angélil with critics framing Dion as the ingénue-protégé to Angélil's presumed Svengali, to moral panic in the late aughts over the pair's failed IVF attempts on account of Dion's "geriatric" reproductive age and Angélil's old age and precarious health, to more recent suggestions that Dion throw in the towel, following the repeated postponement of the start of her *third* Vegas residency due to chronic muscle spasms, and her more recent announcement that she had been diagnosed with "stiff-person syndrome," a rare neurological disorder.[13] Also relevant is the fact that fifty-eight-year-old French comedian Valérie Lemercier played Dion from age five onward in the unauthorized 2021 Dion biopic *Aline*, a seemingly absurdist strategy that made for an uncanny spectacle of the fraught politics of age in Dion's celebrity image.[14]

Crucially, ageism and sexism also figure prominently in Dion's legacy as the quintessential punching bag for cultural gatekeepers of musical taste in the late nineties and early aughts who bemoaned her ubiquity and bombast. Critic Cintra Wilson described Dion and the *Titanic* theme in violently ableist, misogynist, and infantilizing terms, remarking that the "morbidly shriveled and schoolmarmish Dion, despite her sexual handicap," "has totally capsized the vocal world" with a song that "distills the emotional torpor and the whining indignities of puberty and filters it through hundreds of thousands of dollars in production value into a kind of sap-like audio cologne, which, for reasons of stunted maturity, appeals to billions of adults as well as the emotionally hairless teen."[15] In his soaring manifesto on musical taste, critic Carl Wilson observed that Dion's predominantly middle-aged suburban woman fan base significantly contributed to the widespread perception of Dion's music as cheesy, admitting, "It's hard to imagine an audience that could confer less cool on a musician."[16] Hurley explains that Dion's self-identifying "haters" customarily describe being involuntarily subject to Dion's music and "(redundant) displays of emotion" through their mother, mother-in-law, or aunt and often in domestic spaces like "the family car or home."[17] The ageism in these examples works in both chronological directions then, whether through the infantilization of Dion fans of all ages as emotionally underdeveloped, or through a simultaneously generational, gendered, and class-bound disavowal of their musical tastes, where Dion's sentimentality is further denigrated through its ties to middle-aged suburban womanhood.

While perhaps young relative to the Vegas stereotype, at thirty-six, Dion was already "old" by pop standards when she embarked on her first residency in 2003, where the aforementioned ageist, gendered, and classist logics significantly colored early reception of *A New Day* . . . To be clear, Dion's authenticity has long been a point of contention between fans and critics: the same assimilated, Americanized sense of French Canadian alterity and rural, working-class roots that Dion's fans embrace as wholly *authentic* rings hollow among detractors, including those in Quebec who ridicule her music as *quétaine*, that is, garish, unfashionable, and unsophisticated. For Dion's harshest critics, her purported schmaltz and "*manufactured* authenticity" finds its ultimate expression in her Vegas residencies and the commercialism and hyperreal aesthetic of Vegas more generally, as Hurley explains.[18] Indeed, initial reception of *A New Day* . . . bemoaned the production's emphasis on visually extravagant set design and "over-the-top theatrics" at the expense of musical substance and "nuance." *Variety* critic Phil Gallo wrote: "The most egregious example comes during 'My Heart Will Go On,' in which the backdrop of a rotating moon with a meteor shower sits behind two parallel scrims of seating boxes at an opera house. It's just plain goofy."[19] Such critique is ultimately laden with gendered value judgments about the ostensible performativity and musical inferiority of the pop diva show relative to the idealization of masculine authenticity in the rock stadium show.[20] It also reinforces long-standing anxieties around technological mediation as an encroachment on musical authenticity, where it intersects with ageist, sexist stereotypes about acceptable levels of technological innovation on the part of middle-aged women musicians. Indeed, Gallo further remarked that whereas Dion's "bold" vocals "never waver," "the music, though, is another story. The amplified instruments sound *wholly unnatural* beyond the occasional flute or violin passage; the sound is clear, even the synthesized string sections, but they have no 'live' textures. It often sounds recorded."[21] Here the seeming technological subterfuge of the recorded instrumentals compromises on the musical integrity of Dion's seemingly unaltered live singing voice. This reception has only intensified as Dion has aged, evident in frequent derision of her audible use of digital vocal production techniques and foray into a hip-hop and dance-inflected sound as *cheesy* attempts to pander to youth culture in a way that is unbecoming for a woman of her age.[22] Indeed, as Naiman explains, "middle aged women are not expected to be aligned with trends in youth culture, or to be savvy in the use of innovative technologies."[23]

Where an aging woman pop artist's performance of sexuality is concerned, age studies scholars make clear that white womanhood is bound by a paradoxical set of expectations requiring that women resist and reverse the outward markers of aging in order to cultivate a youthful appearance, but crucially with modesty, propriety, and grace, that is, without sexualizing themselves. A woman musician's susceptibility to ageist critique on sexual grounds depends, in large part, on the politics of authenticity associated with a given genre and individual persona. For instance, Naiman explains that Madonna's detractors view her continued displays of female sexual prowess into her middle age as an utterly repugnant and "desperate attempt to maintain youthfulness" that mirrors long-standing denigration of her musical abilities.[24] By contrast, Gardner argues that Dolly Parton evades ageist critique by virtue of the authenticity associated with her country legacy, combined with her well-established performance of hypersexualized feminine bodily artifice through the logics of camp.[25]

Crucially, Dion fulfills cultural expectations regarding age-appropriate sexual behavior among middle-aged white women through a simultaneous camping up of her sexuality and performance of monogamous heteronormative love, sensibilities clearly on display in Vegas. By far the raciest number in *A New Day . . .*, "Seduces Me" has Dion seated in a black leather armchair with dozens of shirtless men writhing on the floor, crawling toward and encircling her. All the while, Dion remains poised and largely unperturbed, her gaze fixed on the audience as she longingly sings of the singular pleasures of her lover's embrace. While Dion is the centerpiece, her own expression of sexual desire is overshadowed and subsumed by the sensuous display of male homoerotic corporeal pleasure. Offstage, Dion is steadfast in her public declarations of love for the late Angélil and devotion to her three sons, cultivating the image of a chaste widow and dutiful matriarch who embodies the propriety, grace, and sexual modesty associated with respectable articulations of middle-aged white womanhood, while establishing continuity between her life onstage and offstage—with manager-husband Angélil serving as the natural link between the two spheres—in a way that endears her to her fans.

In Vegas, Dion's apparent devotion seemingly verges on self-sacrifice in ways that further solidifies her credibility among fans, where performing five consecutive nights a week for several months at a time over many years has often proved physically punishing for the singer. Dion began rehearsing for her second residency, *Celine*, three months after the birth of her twin boys following what she explains was a significant lapse in her vocal training during her pregnancy, where singing induced dangerous premature contractions.[26] During the start of the residency, Dion experienced rapid weight loss as a result of having to pump breast milk backstage. This grueling start ultimately resulted in chronic vocal cord strain and muscle spasms, leading Dion to cancel multiple legs of the residency at different points during its eight-year run. In 2012, one year into the residency, the singer's physician ordered that she take an eight-week vocal rest after discovering a "weakness in her right vocal cord."[27] In March 2018, at age fifty, Dion had to once again cancel several show dates in order to undergo "minimally invasive ear surgery," having been diagnosed with patulous eustachian tube, "which causes hearing irregularities, and makes it extremely difficult to sing."[28]

Interestingly, despite enduring elitist attacks on Dion's authenticity and the aesthetic of her music, critics have seldom questioned her vocal prowess, even following her ongoing vocal health–related setbacks, a cultural consensus that arguably hinges on knowledge that Dion came of age as a live performer and recording artist prior to the ubiquitous adoption of Auto-Tune as a pitch correction device.[29] Whereas Dion's live performances in the late '90s and early 2000s were characterized by a five-octave lyric soprano, a large open belt, bright sound, precisely executed modulations, seamless transitions between registers, and an ability to project over large instrumental forces, over the years she has developed a tendency to strain when belting, resulting in an audible vocal crack.[30] To be sure, changes in the vocal musculature associated with the physiological process of aging are further compounded by any ongoing wear and tear resulting from performing with the kind of intensity and regularity that Dion does, making it difficult to separate the envoiced markers of aging from those related to Dion's longevity as a professional singer. Among Dion's fans, such vocal *foibles*, for lack of a better term, by no means diminish her vocal prowess, but further authenticate her sentimentality and sense of feminine resilience in keeping with Laurie Stras's assertions that audible vocal damage often strengthens perception of a singer's authority, engendering a sense of reverence among fans, who may well interpret these vocal foibles as evidence of Dion's commitment to them.[31] We also want to make the case that a singer's *emotional* state can also compound any existing acoustical damage or age-related changes, further contributing to the perception of authenticity.

These dynamics were evident in reception of Dion's highly anticipated return to the Colosseum following Angélil's death in 2016, where she paid him tribute with a performance of Barbra Streisand's "One More Look at You," a performance in the markers of longevity and age further colored by her palpable grief: her pitchy, scratchy tone; breathlessness; and strained facial expressions made for an emotional performance that was met with a standing ovation, with critics later praising Dion for her "strength" and "courage," while fans on YouTube remarked, "Her voice had never sounded so weak . . . and yet it made it her most powerful performance ever," "Ms Dion is the definition of pure grace," "a *true* diva in every way."[32]

Dion's enduring vocal prowess and consistent appeals to emotion are central to her increasing popularity among self-identifying "empath" millennial fans, like critic Katie Underwood, who notes that Dion's "ability to exist in perpetual catharsis" and feminine resilience helped her through the COVID-19 pandemic.[33] In queer spaces, Dion's campy flamboyance—what Connor calls her "extra-ness"—serve as prime drag inspiration and meme fodder. On the popular Instagram account @drinksforgayz, she appears in empowering memes that highlight her tendency to emphatically gesticulate in live performances, whether by dramatically thrusting her arms skyward in synch with rhythmic punctuations, or through what Connor describes as her habit of "*shoulder pressing* key changes, and *lunging, backbending,* and *squatting* into crescendos."[34] Crucially, we interpret this queer camp appeal as a liberatory antidote to the punitive visual logics of ageism, one that allows Dion and her fans to embrace the ambiguity and incongruence of an aging female body, subverting the sexist, ageist, and ableist expectations of what is acceptable of women who are deemed "too old" (read: ungendered, asexual, undesirable, valueless).

To that end, Dion's Vegas residencies raise important questions about the politics of class*ed* consumption in pop, and how they shift as a performer ages alongside evolving generational temporalities and tastes. For many in Dion's original fan base, attending one of her residencies has significant cultural value akin to going to the opera, whether in terms of the unprecedented quality and scale of its production as a near-totalizing work of art, the transcendent power of Dion's voice, or the high price of admission. Dion's new fandom is defiantly unbounded by the former classed distinctions and the legacy of cultural elitism and sexism that plagued Dion's early reception, to the extent that she has been firmly ensconced in the pop canon as what producer Jamie Lambert recently described as "arguably the best vocal technician of all time" and what one fan termed "the quirky matron saint of pop."[35] Reflecting on this generational resurgence in Dion's popularity—that is, the Célinaissance—relative to his own former public disdain for Dion, music critic Carl Wilson aptly suggested that "the world 'has finally aged into [Céline].'"[36] Ultimately, Dion's unapologetic longevity as a woman performer amid a perpetually ageist industry is due not only to her fans' devotion, but also to the creative affordances of the residency model that she pioneered, one that has sustained her throughout the last two decades of her career.

"There's No Turning Back": Aging Cyborgs and the Creation of Future Being in Cher's "Believe"

If Dion reinvigorated the Vegas residency, then Cher capitalized on this format for extreme longevity. Cher's first Las Vegas residency, titled *Cher in Concert*, debuted in 1979 when she was thirty-three years old, though, this residency was also a concert tour associated with the album *Take Me Home*. Her second residency in 2008, simply called *Cher*, had two hundred performances with a $60 million contract at Caesars Palace. In 2017 Cher began a joint three-city residency based out of the Park MGM's Park Theatre at the age of seventy-one. While the first two residencies drew on her iconicity as pop music royalty to bring in audiences, the third, titled *Classic Cher*, frames her career in retrospective terms, centering her legendary status as one of pop's oldest divas. About the show's title, Cher told reporters prior to the February 2017 debut: "Oh, it's just some bullshit word. It's because I'm going to try and distill my career and let everybody remember and see who I was, what I did and try not to disappoint people."[37] On its surface, *Classic Cher* is representative of traditional Las Vegas shows that entice a generation who grew up with this music to travel to Vegas for "nostalgia: to help make them make it through the night, to cry a tear for the good times they've lost."[38] The performance of sentimentality is very much present in how Cher frames the show. She, for example, sings a duet using a mix of live and recorded vocals to perform "I've Got You Babe" with a black-and-white video of now-passed ex-husband and former performing partner, Sonny Bono. While *Classic Cher* promotes the promise of revealing something about the past in the present, bringing fans closer to some sort of truth about Cher, the fabrication of this story using a type of life narrative through song is possible, we argue, only in the context of the Las Vegas residency. This platform provides a space for self-(re)invention as well as the molding of a path toward longevity.

Despite Cher's pop icon status, reactions to *Classic Cher* were mixed. Many felt lucky to have the opportunity to see Cher live while she was still performing and considered her age an asset. YouTube commenters remark how her performance is exemplary of her image as a living legend. One comment suggests that the performance and Cher's vocal expertise are didactic, "showing the younger ones what's up!!!"[39] Others express amazed disbelief at Cher's age: "Omg I'm so impressed and proud at the same moment, it's like she don't have 71 years old, she's such a beautiful woman and a beautiful performer, it's a completely artist," commented one viewer on a YouTube video of a February 2017 show. Another fan wrote, "IT'S AMAZING THIS WOMAN IS 71 YEARS OLD. WOW!" Such comments also allude to a special "X factor" stating that "after so many years, she still has it!" confessing, "[I] saw her, she was amazing! definitely worth it." Others, however, were much more critical of Cher's performance and the show in general. A French viewer writes, "She doesn't move like she used to, the earlier energy has disappeared, and her costumes at 71 years old in 2017 are ridiculous. We are bored."[40] Others suggest that her musical and vocal abilities were declining with age: "love her," one fan wrote, "but she needs to work on her breathing. out of breath most of the time," while another reiterates that they were bored while disparaging Cher for supposedly lip synching, labeling the performance as not a "real authentic concert." Such reviews express the ageist idea that older performers are somehow deceiving fans by insisting that these performers remain virtually unchanged in their appearance or vocal/performance abilities.[41]

These comments, both positive and negative, turn to Cher's aging body and voice as suspect and tenuous sites of both success and failure, a dialectic that we argue is emblematic of a certain type of Las Vegas performance for aging female singers. Those who celebrate Cher's performance find her abilities amazing *despite* her aging, as if it is something that she has *overcome* to remain entertaining (not unlike the problematic logics of the "overcoming" narrative that disability studies scholars note haunts cultural portrayals of disability).[42] Those who disparage the performance lay blame on her age as a reason for their dissatisfaction. Both reactions are predicated on what one expects from the aging body in terms of vocal and performance ability; those who just want to see Cher in the flesh because of her iconic status before it is "too late" tend to hear her voice and age as the source of success, while those who expect an unchanged, unaged performance are disappointed by the aging body. Both modes of listening bring people to Vegas to confirm or contradict their expectations of the aging body and voice. In other words, Cher's Las Vegas residencies capitalize on the "mysteries of aging" and turn the process into an audiovisual spectacle of the body.

Uncertainty surrounding Cher as a performer is not new. Skepticism abounds her multiple reinventions, which has thrown into question her "realness" and "authenticity" as a pop performer. Her ability to adapt to the changing pop music landscapes of the twentieth and twenty-first centuries has at once garnered her the label of cultural panderer, but, as Mitchell Morris celebrates, her career malleability and "inauthentic" camp have become part of her diva allure.[43] One such reinvention we wish to pause over is her turn to electro-pop with her 1998 smash hit "Believe." The song's success was in part due to the new and overt use of Auto-Tune technology that, as Catherine Provenzano writes, "furnishes not just pitch correction, which normally goes unnoticed (and had already gone unnoticed in hundreds of pop songs since the tool's commercial release the previous year), but also a distinctive sonic effect the program creates when dialed away from 'natural'-sounding parameters toward an impossibly fast, pitch-jumping effect."[44] Auto-Tune was (and is) a tool of smoothing over vocal "defects," but also became a tool of aesthetic expression, what Provenzano calls "The Auto Tune Effect," or TATE.[45] And while Provenzano has masterfully explored the gender politics in the use of Auto-Tune as an artistic tool, we might also understand its use in Cher's "Believe" as constructing a technological future for the aging female voice and body in popular music.[46]

The technofantastic sound world of "Believe" was a departure from Cher's previous rock and light pop hits like "If I Could Turn Back Time," "The Shoop Shoop Song (It's in His Kiss)," and her cover of Marc Cohn's "Walking in Memphis" from the late 1980s and early 1990s. The now iconic Auto-Tuned vocals were heard first after a performance and recording hiatus due to Cher's chronic fatigue caused by the Epstein-Barr virus in the early 1990s.[47] Given this context, we might read the technology as a type of aid for performance. In this sense, Cher's use of Auto-Tune can be heard as an experiment of the voice where the reinvention of her voice-body shows audiences a way forward after her experience with disability as well as a way forward in pop music as an aging woman. Her swerve into dance pop was couched in the sentiment of reminiscence and nostalgia, with many noting how "Believe" brought us back to the disco dance-club feel of "Take Me Home" (1979). This incongruous mixing of then (disco-era dance-hall Cher) and now (electro-pop Cher) gave cause for critics to comment on Cher's age (she was fifty-two when "Believe" was released). Barry Walters for the *Village Voice* wrote about Cher's entrance into "hi-NRG Euro," stating that in this type of music "our beloved female vets can belt an old-school schmaltzcore codependency-for-days ballad and get away with it because the club-targeted bottom booms, the lushy aggressive arrangement soars, and *the instrumentation flaunts a computerized nowness* few studio hacks could achieve with conventional *sonic airbrushing*."[48] Thinking of Auto-Tune, TATE, and Cher's "nowness" in terms of "sonic airbrushing" raises questions about the technologics of aging and strategies that singers might undertake to achieve longevity in the misogynist and ageist logics of the pop music industry.

We see an important parallel that helps us think through Cher's continued use of voice-altering technology (and sound and visual technology more generally) in Vegas in the discourse and panic around Cher's use of cosmetic surgery as a strategy of visual aesthetic longevity in the public eye. As early as her thirties (ca. the mid-1980s), Cher has been made to field questions about her aging and the possibility of longevity in the American entertainment industry. In a 1984 interview for the British TV talk show *Wogan*, Cher was asked about the reason for seeking cosmetic surgery. Responding to a question about the unnaturalness of plastic surgery, she noted, "I think it's worse in America [than in the United Kingdom]. Women get older, and men get . . . dignified or character. But it's hard to be older in this business."[49] More than ten years later, she explained in an interview that critics and gossip that label her image as inauthentic and artificial are upsetting and, again, exemplify a beauty double standard for female celebrities. "[People say] the reason Cher looks good is because she's had everything snipped and tucked and whatever. And if I came on and I looked bad, everyone would say, 'Oh poor Cher, have you seen her?'"[50] Cher has, over the past forty years, been made to explain herself for the panic over plastic surgery. The body marked by plastic surgery, many have noted, only reveals a body with something shameful to hide.[51] Furthermore, cosmetic surgery was (and still is) often criticized for what it says about the construction of "natural" femininity of bodies, framing enhancement as a form of social subterfuge and distortion of self-worth.[52]

There has been no hiding the fact of Cher's age through plastic surgery since she has been open about her procedures and that they are the result of living in a world that values youth over age. Kathleen Woodward notes that, in age-related cosmetic surgery, the act of "masquerade" can be an ambivalent reaction to aging, both a "submission to dominant social codes and as resistance to them."[53] Thinking about cosmetic surgery as a corrective for aging, we are at once left with the reification of ageist tropes about the worthlessness of aging bodies, though, as Woodward asks, "What about [cosmetic surgery] at its best? Is there not something moralistically puritanical about this injunction against cosmetic surgery . . .? Why judge those who wish to alter their bodies and their body-images through surgery?"[54] On the one hand, aging should not be seen as a physical defect. But, on the other hand, what is one to do when one's livelihood and access to the stage are contingent on the power of youth in an ageist society? Who are we to dictate what aging looks like?

The fear of the modified body harks back to a general fear of the aided body. Technology becomes integral to keep the body alive, leading Don Idhe to argue, for example, that he would rather be a cyborg than dead.[55] Both voice and body manipulation, as we see it, help keep Cher's career alive. They conserve her financial livelihood while also making her desire to perform in an ageist industry possible. As a result, she maintains some cultural status in a society that could have easily forgotten her long ago. The cyborgian aesthetics of body modification and technological vocal manipulation perform what Woodward argues is a "postmodern body." And while it "remains in the register of reaction *against* the aging body,"[56] the technologic paired with Cher's awareness of pop music's ageist, ableist, and misogynist logics affords an agency to continue and to define her aging on her own terms.[57] Technologies of voice manipulation parallel the act of body modification that evokes a cyborgian aesthetic that characterizes Cher both in and of the musical moment of "Believe." The looming specter of Y2K and the panic over technological catastrophe made the aesthetics of "Believe" *au courante* for late-twentieth-century audiences. The new sonic space offered by the vocal manipulations of Auto-Tune ironically drew listeners of American pop into "Believe" despite the long-standing belief that pop music is all about vocal and performance authenticity. While, as Provenzano points out, Auto-Tune "threatens the labor value of the pop singing voice," Cher's use of this technology demonstrates the type of unequal gendered labor aging female pop vocalists often turn to in order to remain relevant.[58] By establishing a futuristic performance aesthetic that hears the Auto-Tuned voice and its artificiality as entirely plausible and appropriate within the domain of Cher's ever-shifting identity as a performer, the aging body and the voice are given a space to persist and not fade.

The Las Vegas show in the twenty-first century, through its emphasis on the use of costumes, stagecraft and design, acrobatic and athletic dancing, and incomparable technological forces that maximize acoustic and visual display becomes a playground for the performer to imagine and become their own version of their aging self. By way of example, we turn to more recent performances of "Believe" in Las Vegas that update Cher's cyborgian aesthetic, demonstrating in her performances of the song some twenty years later that Cher—the image, the celebrity, the icon of pop music—will age on her own terms. The song appears in her 2017 residency (and in most tours and residencies since the early 2000s) as an encore. This placement is significant, given the framing devices of Cher's recent performances as acts of remembrance and nostalgia. Placing the song outside of this frame, we are invited to hear Cher's technological voice as future oriented. The new musical setting also connotes a space of perpetual futurity: in the song's intro, Cher's voice is sampled and digitally manipulated, fractured, and unintelligible, though identifiable as Cher's, and accompanied by a generic rock-pop beat. The show design indexes a futuristic aesthetic: while the introduction plays out, dancers clad in white and glow-wear perform in a hip-hop style. A buildup leads to a break in the music as we hear Cher's vocals from "Believe" clearly sampled ("And maybe I'm too . . ."). Before the lyric can finish on the word *good*, the bass drops, giving way to a dubstep remix of "Believe" where Cher's vocals are heard singing the familiar refrains "so sad," and "takes time." Importantly, these are the lyric moments where, in the original "Believe," the Auto-Tune effect is first heard. In other words, this whole introduction, much like the introduction to the studio version of the song, is focused on the technologic and places Cher in the middle of it. It is playful, self-referential, and completely aware of its manipulated construction.

The continued use of the technologic in Cher's performance of "Believe" maintains the possibility of an everlasting future for the aging pop icon, giving her vocal presence a certain degree of indestructibility. While Cher could have easily "legitimized" her late-career dance pop hit through a musical style change that uses a slower tempo, acoustic instrumentation, and refocuses the lyrics in an attempt to index the modesty of a woman who knows how to "act her age," Vegas affords her the space to reject this age narrative.[59] And her continued performance in this space invites audiences to understand that she will keep going as long as she can, even if that means being aided by technological intervention in the form of vocal manipulations, cosmetic surgery, sets, staging, costumes, and more. Vegas, as an enabling force for both Dion and Cher's late careers, informs a special type of feminist approach to aging, voice, and performance that discards the concern with expected performances of authenticity and celebrates the idea that we are who we make ourselves to be. Vegas becomes a place in which the aging female pop singer can create a future in a world that routinely tells aging women there is none.

Conclusion

We wish to return to our opening assertion that Dion and Cher are the trailblazers of a late feminine pop style. Tiffany Naiman's definition of pop music's late style, one rooted in the experience of out-of-timeness associated with illness, aging, and death, relates to both Dion's and Cher's experiences and representations of aging in their Vegas residencies.[60] But unique to this space is their creative license to enact their own individual version of empowered feminine lateness in the pop music industry. Over the years, Dion has ultimately defied the stigma and ageist stereotypes historically associated with Vegas concert residencies of generations past, blazing a trail for her peers and successors, while using her residencies to further solidify her unique eminence among an elite class of twentieth- and twenty-first-century female vocal powerhouses. Likewise, Cher takes up the freedom created by Dion's reinvigoration of the Vegas scene and uses a network of technological resources, staging, sound engineering, backup dancers, and vocalists to create a sense of indestructibility and malleability that was already a part of her iconicity. In other words, these two performers created their own longevity in a misogynistic, ageist, and ableist industry where aging women are not meant to have longevity. In turn, Las Vegas emerges as a major player in their development of a uniquely feminine late pop style due to the city's embrace of theatricality (in Dion's case) and technology and artificiality (in Cher's case), and as a destination for the spectacle of the aging body. Vegas, then, as an entertainment capital of the United States, has an important role to play in the development of creating a more age-diverse pop music industry.

One way we see Vegas emerge as a location for age diversity is in how it engenders intergenerational community, or intergenerational "bonding en masse," to borrow Underwood's apt characterization. Dion's and Cher's shows bring in new generations of fans, upending the trope of the Vegas performer and audience being overly concerned about growing older, desperately clinging to a lost past. Younger fans are drawn to these divas' residencies precisely because of their theatricality, sentimentality, emotionality, and nostalgia, and because of a genuine desire to witness and celebrate a living musical legend together with her older, original fans who are themselves searching for ways to age creatively. In these ways, fans help redefine the Vegas residency as a space of musical longevity, creative vibrancy, and intergenerational musical legacy building. We understand this assembly as crucially important where Vegas provides freedom for redefining what it means to age, but also becomes a space where fans can speak across and challenge naturalized generational differences by coming together around a shared devotion to a female musical icon.[61]

Along those lines, we also want to note that Dion's and Cher's approaches to aging differ significantly from one another and show that there is as much diversity within generations of performers and audiences as there is between them. This shows that perhaps the most unifying element of late-feminine pop style, like Las Vegas itself, is its multiplicity—its platform of possibility. Each employs their iconicity in Vegas in a way that supports their own individual ideals of what it means to get older. While Cher resists normative understandings of aging by using technological aids in the form of cosmetic surgery and vocal technology to articulate a pop style that startles the (cultural) understandings of aging bodies, Dion turns to a performance of authenticity that showcases her quirkiness and effusiveness and a refusal to abide by traditional age narratives in pop. Ultimately, both reject the script of decline as a fundamental commonality in the late-feminine pop style, fashioning "lateness" as a site of entrepreneurial risk taking, feminine bodily autonomy, and creative empowerment.

Notes

1. See Christine Overall, "Old Age and Ageism, Impairment and Ableism: Exploring the Conceptual and Material Connections," *NWSA Journal* 18, no. 1 (2006): 127.

2. Aging, as Jane Gallop asserts, is neither fixed nor static, though, more than disability, aging typically unfolds as a constantly evolving process of becoming. She writes:

"Indeed I would say that aging is all about temporality, is literally the lived experience of temporality. To add aging to our analysis is not so much to add another identity group as to add temporality to our crip theory, to add temporality to our understandings of sexuality and the body." For this reason, Gallop draws on theories of queer temporality employed in crip theory of the early 2000s in productive dialogue to understand the intersections of aging, sexuality, and disability. See Jane Gallop, *Sexuality, Disability, and Aging: Queer Temporalities of the Phallus* (Durham, NC: Duke University Press, 2019), 9–10. See also Kathleen Woodward, "Aging," in *Keywords for Disability Studies*, ed. Rachel Adams, Benjamin Reiss, and David Serlin (New York: New York University Press, 2015), 33–34.

3. See Rosemarie Garland-Thomson, *Staring: How We Look* (New York: Oxford University Press, 2009); and Rosemarie Garland-Thomson, ed., *Freakery: The Cultural Spectacles of the Extraordinary Body* (New York: New York University Press, 1996).

4. Abigail Gardner, *Ageing and Contemporary Female Musicians* (New York: Routledge, 2019), 2; Alexandra Apolloni, "Authority, Ability, and the Aging Ingénue's Voice," in *Voicing Girlhood in Popular Music*, edited by Jacqueline Warwick and Allison Adrian (New York: Routledge, 2016), 147.

5. Tiffany Naiman, "Resisting the Politics of Aging: Madonna and the Value of Female Labor in Popular Music," in *Popular Music and the Politics of Hope: Queer and Feminist Interventions*, edited by Susan Fast and Craig Jennex (New York: Routledge, 2019), 267.

6. See Sweta Rajan-Rankin, "Race, Embodiment and Later Life: Re-animating Aging Bodies of Color," *Journal of Aging Studies* 45 (2018): 32–38.

7. Eric Frankenberg, "Las Vegas with Record-Breaking $681 Million in Ticket Sales," *Billboard Pro*, June 13, 2019, https://www.billboard.com/pro/celine-dion-wraps-historic-16-year-run-las-vegas-681-million/.

8. See Ben Beaumont-Thomas, "Security, Intimacy and Money: Why Adele Is Going to Las Vegas," *Guardian*, December 3, 2021, https://www.theguardian.com/music/2021/dec/03/security-intimacy-and-money-why-adele-is-going-to-las-vegas; and Martin Chilton, "Viva Las Vegas: A History of Sin City's Musical Residencies," udiscovermusic, May 15, 2021, https://www.udiscovermusic.com/in-depth-features/las-vegas-residencies-history/.

9. Phil Gallo, "Celine Dion: A New Day . . .," *Variety*, March 26, 2003, https://variety.com/2003/music/reviews/celine-dion-a-new-day-1200542553/; "Celine Dion Says Goodbye to Her Groundbreaking Las Vegas Residency at the Colosseum at Caesar's Palace," June 9, 2019, https://www.celinedion.com/news-en/celine-dion-says-goodbye-to-her-groundbreaking-las-vegas-residency-at-the-colosseum-at-caesars-palace/.

10. Erin Hurley, *National Performance: Representing Quebec from Expo 67 to Céline Dion* (Toronto: University of Toronto Press, 2011), 178. See also Luc Plamondon in Melena Ryzik, "Celine Dion, She Went On and On," *New York Times*, December 17, 2007, https://www.nytimes.com/2007/12/17/arts/music/17celi.html.

11. Dion in Katie Connor, "Celine Dion Is Living Her Best Life," *Elle*, May 1, 2019, https://www.elle.com/culture/celebrities/a27288491/celine-dion-elle-interview/.

12. For a discussion of sentimentality, see Emily Gale, "Sounding Sentimental: American Popular Song from Nineteenth-Century Ballads to 1970s Soft Rock" (PhD diss., University of Virginia, 2014), 16.

13. See Alice Kelly, "Céline Dion Movie 'Aline' Examines Her Relationship with René Angélil—and How They Met When She Was 12," *Your Tango*, June 4, 2021, https://www.yourtango.com/entertainment/celine-dion-rene-angelils-age-difference-examined-movie-aline; Hannah Hangrave, "What Is Wrong with Celine Dion? All We Know about the Singer's Recent Health Battle," *Hello! Canada*, February 28, 2022, https://www.hellomagazine.com/healthandbeauty/health-and-fitness/20220228134243/what-is-wrong-with-celine-dion-heartbreaking-health-update-revealed-tour-canceled-las-vegas/; Nici de Wet, "She Just Can't Go On—Celine Dion Pulls Out of Vegas Residency Due to Health Woes," *You/News24*, October 21, 2022, https://www.news24.com/you/celebs/international/she-just-cant-go-on-celine-dions-pulls-out-of-vegas-residency-due-to-health-woes-20211021; and Rachel Avery, "Celine Dion's Traumatic IVF Battle Detailed amid Shock Health Diagnosis," *Hello! Canada*, December 9, 2022, https://www.hellomagazine.com/healthandbeauty/mother-and-baby/20221209159185/celine-dion-ivf-battles-details/.

14. K. Austin Collins, "'Aline' Is a Biopic That's Not about Céline Dion, Nope, Not about Her at All," *Rolling Stone*, April 6, 2022, https://www.rollingstone.com/tv-movies/tv-movie-reviews/aline-review-1332488/.

15. Cintra Wilson, "Sickened by Celine Dion's Audio Cologne," *Connecticut Insider*, January 8, 1999, https://www.ctinsider.com/news/article/Sickened-by-Celine-Dion-s-audio-cologne-3309465.php.

16. Carl Wilson, *Celine Dion's Let's Talk about Love: A Journey to the End of Taste* (New York: Continuum, 2007), as quoted in Sam Anderson, "Taster's Choice," *New York Magazine*, December 13, 2007, https://nymag.com/arts/books/reviews/42082/.

17. Hurley, *National Performance*, 158–59.

18. Hurley, *National Performance*, 146.

19. Gallo, "Celine Dion: A New Day . . ."

20. For a discussion of the denigration of the pop diva show relative to the rock show, see Constantine Chatzipapatheodoridis, *The Music Diva Spectacle: Camp, Female Performers and Queer Audiences in the Arena Tour Show* (Chicago: Intellect Books, 2021).

21. Chatzipapatheodoridis, *Music Diva Spectacle*.

22. For instance, in a 2007 article in the *Guardian* decisively titled "Celine Dion Is Not Cool," critic Caroline Sullivan bemoaned hip-hop producer Timbaland's announcement that he would be producing Dion's next album: "Enough, already. Enough of this critical rehabilitation of singers that every sentient human being knows are unrehabbable. . . . Last week she [Dion] was the standard bearer for pop naffness—the only big name bellower that you could rely on to produce music that was unfailingly cheesy, bombastic and insincere. . . . And now she's cool. Is nothing sacred?" Note the implicit centrality of ageism in Sullivan's notion of "critical *rehabilitation*" and the youthfulness associated with notions of cool. See Caroline Sullivan, "Celine Dion Is Not Cool," *Guardian*, August 8, 2007, https://www.theguardian.com/music/musicblog/2007/aug/08/celinedionisnotcool.

23. Naiman, "Resisting the Politics of Aging," 267.

24. Naiman, "Resisting the Politics of Aging," 268.

25. Abigail Gardener, "Grit, Glitter and Glamour: Tracing Authenticity in the Aging Artifice of Dolly Parton," in *Aging Femininities: Troubling Representations*, edited by

Josephine Dolan and Estella Tincknell, 183–94 (Cambridge: Cambridge Scholars Press, 2012).

26. *Celine: 3 Boys and a New Show*, documentary film (Las Vegas: Productions J, 2011). For the full documentary see, Celine Dion Brasil, "Céline Dion—3 Boys and a New Show [LEGENDADO]," YouTube, September 8, 2016, https://www.youtube.com/watch?v=8q9NXzmin4U.

27. "Celine Dion Cancels Las Vegas Shows on Doctor's Orders," *BBC News*, March 1, 2012, https://www.bbc.com/news/entertainment-arts-17219599.

28. "Céline Dion, Set for 'Minimally Invasive' Ear Surgery, Cancels More Shows," *CBC News*, March 22, 2018, https://www.cbc.ca/news/entertainment/celine-cancels-ear-surgery-1.4587583.

29. This reveals as much about Dion's vocal prowess as it does the extent to which conceptions of vocal ability in pop are still rooted in a false idealization of a technologically unmediated voice. As Catherine Provenzano has exquisitely detailed, "tuning" arguably obscures and consequently marginalizes the labor of singing, resulting in its false equation with an underlying inability to sing and a lack of emotional sincerity on the part of women pop artists. See Catherine Provenzano, "Making Voices: The Gendering of Pitch Correction and the Auto-Tune Effect in Contemporary Pop Music," *Journal of Popular Music Studies* 31, no. 2 (2019): 63–84. See also the recent uproar among Dion fans over *Rolling Stone*'s omission of Dion from their recent "The 200 Greatest Singers of All Time" list. Griffin Jaeger, "Celine Dion Was Left Off Rolling Stone's Greatest Singers List and Fans Are Furious," *CBC News*, January 2, 2023, https://www.cbc.ca/news/entertainment/celine-dion-rolling-stone-snub-1.6701708.

30. Freya Casey—Master Your Voice, "Vocal Coach Reacts to Celine Dion—Her Voice Now and Then," YouTube, July 16, 2019, https://www.youtube.com/watch?v=8Vg4fpkOszU.

31. Laurie Stras, "The Voice as Organ of the Soul," in *Sounding Off: Theorizing Disability in Music*, edited by Joseph N. Straus and Neil Lerner (New York: Routledge, 2006), 175. William Cheng has elaborated on these gendered double standards in his analysis of the ridicule Britney Spears faced upon the viral leak of her ostensibly "un-Auto-Tuned" vocals for her track "Alien" (2013) as it connects with the reception of her body and psychological well-being. See William Cheng, "So You've Been Musically Shamed," *Journal of Popular Music Studies* 30, no. 3 (2018): 63–98.

32. John W., "Celine Dion Returns to Las Vegas after Death of Husband Rene," YouTube, February 24, 2016, https://www.youtube.com/watch?v=AsVFAe-dMFI.

33. Katie Underwood, "Coming Back to Us Now: Céline Dion Is the Emotional Defibrillator for This Exact Moment. And We've Never Needed Her More," *McLean's*, December 1, 2021, https://archive.macleans.ca/article/2021/12/01/coming-back-to-us-now. Among Dion's younger superfans is pop diva Ariana Grande, who is famous for her uncanny and loving imitations of Dion's voice and affect, whether on *The Late Night Show Starring Jimmy Fallon* (2015), *Carpool Karaoke with James Corden* (2018), or multiple episodes of *The Voice*.

34. Connor, "Celine Dion Is Living Her Best Life."

35. Jamie Collabro Tweet quoted in Johnny Oleksinksi, "Celine Dion Snubbed by Rolling Stone's Greatest Singers List—and Fans Are Outraged: 'A Crime against Humanity,'"

New York Post, January 3, 2023, https://nypost.com/2023/01/02/celine-dion-snubbed-by-rolling-stones-greatest-singers-list/; and *Célinaissance* (blog), accessed November 11, 2022, https://celinaissance.wordpress.com.

36. Carl Wilson in Connor, "Celine Dion Is Living Her Best Life."

37. "Cher Talks Donald Trump, Emojis, and 'American Horror Story,'" *Billboard*, October 20, 2016, https://www.billboard.com/music/pop/cher-donald-trump-emojis-american-horror-story-7549849/.

38. Larry Gragg, *Bright Light City: Las Vegas in Popular Culture* (Lawrence: University Press of Kansas, 2013), 136.

39. All comments this paragraph in Classic Cher France, "Classic Cher—Las Vegas, 2017 (Live Complet)," YouTube, 51:50, August 20, 2017, https://www.youtube.com/watch?v=9iX9W2y1c9Y&ab_channel=ClassicCherFrance.

40. The original French comment reads: "Elle ne bouge plus comme avant, l'énergie d'antan a disparu, et ces accoutrements à 71 ans en 2017 sont ridicules. On s'ennuie."

41. Full comment reads: "Just saw her last night in Vegas. Bored, lip sync, it was a Cher show starring in her own musical. Go see Diana ross or Rod Stewart if you want a real authentic concert. The crowd was dancing more to the disco music being played before the show. lol. Awful. The balcony seats were empty. Mind you this is a Friday night."

42. For a discussion about how the overcoming narrative operates in the context of sung live performances (in televised singing competitions), see William Cheng, "Staging Overcoming: Narratives of Disability and Meritocracy in Reality Singing Competitions," *Journal of the Society for American Music* 11, no. 2 (2017): 184–214.

43. Mitchell Morris, *The Persistence of Sentiment: Display and Feeling in Popular Music of the 1970s* (Berkeley: University of California Press, 2013), 168, 170–72.

44. Catherine Provenzano, "Auto-Tune, Labor, and the Pop-Music Voice," in *The Relentless Pursuit of Tone: Timbre in Popular Music*, ed. Robert Fink, Melinda Latour, and Zachary Wallmark (New York: Oxford University Press, 2018), 163.

45. What Provenzano calls "The Auto Tune Effect," or "TATE," might act as a sonic corollary to Vivian Sobchak's analysis of women's aging in monster films that seek to hide the special effects that turn the older woman into a younger woman. For Provenzano's discussion of TATE and its aesthetics, see Provenzano, "Making Voices." On the visual effects of cinematic depictions of aging women, see Vivian Sobchak, "Scary Women: Cinema, Surgery, and Special Effects," in *Figuring Age: Women, Bodies, Generations*, ed. Kathleen Woodward, 200–213 (Bloomington: Indiana University Press, 1999).

46. Provenzano, "Making Voices."

47. Mary Anne Cassata, *The Cher Scrapbook* (New York: Citadel Press, 2002), 77–78.

48. Barry Walter, "The Beat Goes On," *Village Voice*, February 2, 1999, 127 (emphasis added).

49. Cher News, "Cher Talks Plastic Surgery, Her Image & Aging (1984) ('Wogan')," YouTube, 4:49, June 7, 2018, https://www.youtube.com/watch?v=hlSW4oP21eo&ab_channel=CherNews.

50. CherFan91, "Cher 1995 Interview," YouTube, 5:14, August 23, 2019, https://www.youtube.com/watch?v=VVryFi33uqc&ab_channel=CherFan91.

51. For such critiques of cosmetic surgery among older people (especially women), see Kathleen Woodward, "Youthfulness as a Masquerade," *Discourse* 11, no. 1 (1989): 119–42; and Sobchak, "Scary Women."

52. For a reflection of feminist commentary on plastic surgery from the past thirty years, see Susan Bordo, "Twenty Years in the Twilight Zone," in *Cosmetic Surgery: A Feminist Primer*, ed. Cressida J. Heyes and Meredith Jones (New York: Routledge, 2009), 21.

53. Woodward, "Youthfulness as a Masquerade," 125–26. Woodward writes about defiance that "by destabilizing the image [of masculinity through drag (that is, the denial of womanliness in patriarchal visuality)], the masquerade confounds the masculine structure of the look. It effects a defamiliarization of female iconography."

54. Woodward, "Youthfulness as a Masquerade," 134.

55. For a phenomenological account of aging with technology, see Don Idhe, *Medical Technics* (Minneapolis: University of Minnesota Press, 2019), 34–39.

56. Woodward, "Youthfulness as a Masquerade," 136.

57. Naiman, "Resisting the Politics of Aging," 277. With respect to Madonna's aging, Naiman writes, "Madonna is not chasing the fountain of youth; rather, she is redefining what an aging woman in popular music can look, sound, and act like. . . . [Her] refusal to allow the western mentality of aging to unduly influence her behavior and identity is a type of rebellion; she is self-fashioning in a way that is resistant to the norms and narratives of aging."

58. Provenzano, "Auto-Tune, Labor, and the Pop-Music Voice," 161.

59. Adam Lambert in his 2018 Kennedy Center Honors tribute to Cher performs "Believe" as an acoustic ballad. It is an example of how Cher could "act her age" by giving legitimacy to a song that is seemingly at odds with what one expects from a pillar of American artistry. It is important to note that Cher has never tried to change "Believe" to adapt to her aging self, and rather rejects normative narratives of musical aging that foreground modesty through new arrangements that sound more "age appropriate."

60. Tiffany Naiman, "Singing at Death's Door: Late Style, Disability, and the Temporality of Illness in Popular Music" (PhD diss., University of California at Los Angeles, 2017).

61. Margaret Gullette, speaking on the "generation wars," notes that conflict between generations is a form of ageism. Where one generation seeks to blame another generation, we must always look to where the real oppressive power comes from. See Gullette, *Aged by Culture* (Chicago: University of Chicago Press, 2004).

PART IV

Virtuoso Fantastique

These, as the angler at the silent brook,
Or mountain-shepherd leaning on his crook,
Or gaping plowman, from the vale descries,
They stare, and view 'em with religious eyes,
And strait conclude 'em Gods; since none, but they,
Thro' their own azure skies cou'd find a way.

10

Viva Viagra

Vegas, Elvis, and a "Little Blue Pill"

JAMES DEAVILLE AND KIRSTIN BEWS

The bond between Elvis Presley and Las Vegas persists in the popular imaginary; for decades both city and celebrity cultivated the public image of a close relationship that was mutually advantageous to their intersecting mythologies. Enterprising entities have recognized the value of exploiting the Elvis-Vegas link, not least among them the pharmaceutical giant Pfizer, which invoked the myths surrounding the city and celebrity in its "Viva Viagra" promotional campaign of 2007–9.

This chapter positions one of Pfizer's "Viva Viagra" commercials within broader discourses of Presley's musical style and sexual persona, his relationship with Las Vegas, and direct-to-consumer (DTC) pharmaceutical marketing. The commercial in question parodies the song "Viva Las Vegas" from the eponymous 1964 movie. By situating the spot within the historical reality and prevailing myths of Elvis and Vegas, we consider how it draws on male fantasies of (hetero)sexual license and freedom and fosters nostalgia for bygone virility while accessing the culture of (over)medicating for age-related bodily dysfunction.

The Elvis Phenomenon

Elvis Presley had a particularly tantalizing stage presence that both infatuated his young audiences and threatened the traditional values and sexual mores of older generations.[1] For American youth who felt a stifling dissatisfaction with societal, cultural, and moral norms, and who yearned for more excitement,

Elvis served as an idol, not only for his sex appeal, but also for the destruction of reactionary "White American" society.[2]

In the late 1950s, American psychologist Martin Reiser wrote about the "Elvis Presley Phenomenon," hypothesizing that while the craze around Elvis may have appeared to be a "form of insanity," it was actually the result of puberty giving rise to a second phallic phase. For Freud, this phase brings about a conflict between the ego and the id, which creates a desire for gratification in the face of a fear of castration and defiance against anxiety, that is, an abnormal degree of "dependence on the cathected objects." Due to the teenager's incessant need for independence from parents, the old ego ideal must be externalized, and therefore replaced. Reiser concluded that Elvis became the externalized personification and fulfillment of these needs for a generation of youth, yet he sympathized with the "disapproving attitude of adults on the subject of Elvis Presley and 'Rock 'n' Roll.'"[3]

Though no longer current in discussions of the Elvis phenomenon, Reiser's work provides an important contribution to our understanding of the cultural context within which it unfolded. Noting the threat that Elvis posed to parental figures and prevailing mores, Reiser situated Elvis as a figure representing a crude transition from childhood to adulthood, one that demonstrated the "replacement" that solidified Elvis's image as a rock 'n' roll sex symbol.

Elvis produced a new kind of performance, one that quickly became the focus of a generalized anxiety among middle-aged Americans, that teenagers were becoming sexually obsessed with carnal pleasures and that rock 'n' roll exploited the power of libido through pulsating beats and erotic vocal lines. Reiser fed into this anxiety with his notion that Elvis's sultry voice was reminiscent of "a mother crooning to her baby to allay the separation anxiety before sleep," that is, that the music acquires a "soothing quality of the mother, essentially replacing her as a source of pleasure."[4] As historian Glenn Altschuler put it, with Elvis "the sexual genie was climbing out of the bottle, with the cork nowhere in sight."[5]

The genie flew to film. Elvis scored his acting debut in Robert Webb's *Love Me Tender* (1956), a film that was well received by critics, with the initial screenings providing a curious new hybrid of cinema and concert, as Elvis could not shake his identity as a serenading sex symbol. This would be the start of a secondary career, as he would star in twenty-eight more films, including the consequential *Viva Las Vegas* (1964).

Filmed in and around Las Vegas, *Viva Las Vegas* was hailed as Elvis's best on-screen work, due largely to the chemistry between race-car driver Lucky Jackson (played by Elvis) and swimming instructor Rusty Martin (played by Ann-Margret). The film's tagline cites the reputation of the city as America's mecca of pleasure and entertainment: "It's that go-go guy and that bye-bye gal in the fun capital of the world!" Moreover, as Brian Wright posits, "Vegas is presented . . . [as] a place of possibility and reinvention where anyone could be just one big win away from changing their lot in life."[6] In the song's lyrics, Vegas is further personified as the "ultimate woman," boasting flashing lights and encouraging gambling, intoxication, and sex. If audiences were expecting a gyrating Elvis, they may have been disappointed with Lucky. Still shot primarily above the waist, with no "uhhh-huhh-huhhh" and no shaking hips, Elvis sticks to his character; his on-screen performance as Lucky is more likely to bring a conga line to mind than a pelvis trip.[7]

While the film was a hot commodity, "a working-class fantasy" in the words of Wright, the *Viva Las Vegas* LP did not do as well, climbing only to a modest summit of number ninety-two on the 1964 *Billboard* charts (making it the lowest-charting release of Elvis's career to date).[8] Although Elvis never sang the track live, "Viva Las Vegas" eventually become one of his best-known and most recognizable songs, and it has heavily infiltrated popular culture in its various forms and renditions.[9] Its "coverability" can hardly be attributed to Elvis alone, for Las Vegas's cultural reputation (or stigma, depending on your perspective) is one of high-ball gambling, flashy entertainment, frivolous spending, reprobative nights out, and glamour, all captured by the popular mantra "what happens in Vegas, stays in Vegas." To use "Viva Las Vegas" in a twenty-first-century context is therefore not only to emulate Elvis, but to capitalize on the artist's own valorization as a cultural icon and sex symbol, while simultaneously pointing to the enduring notion of Las Vegas as a party town.[10]

With strong box-office numbers eclipsing his *Billboard* chart numbers, Elvis took a nine-year hiatus from live performance to appear solely on the movie screen. When he was approached about considering a Las Vegas residency, he saw this as an opportunity for a comeback. The Vegas residency allowed an aging Elvis to cement his legacy as a sex symbol through his iconic sound and rock 'n' roll music. The stage was set for the corporate appropriation of that sexuality, and in 2007 the pharmaceutical giant Pfizer sought to cash in.

Advertising Viagra

Media psychologists and marketing specialists have long argued for the effectiveness of music in audiovisual promotion, especially in enhancing product recall.[11] From its start in the late 1940s, American broadcast television has relied on music to support its advertising messages. At first the musical jingle carried over from radio—its short, catchy tune and memorable lyrics identified the product in an attempt to capture consumer attention. Television advertisers have also scored commercials with library tracks (typically instrumental), which are sold by music production companies according to the desired affect. A third use of music in promotion on the small screen has occurred through quotation and parody techniques that count on consumer recognition of preexisting music. Depending on the product and the audience, the source music could originate in either the classical or the popular realm, old or new, as long as it is readily identifiable by the target market. For example, film promotion via trailers has prominently deployed covers of current and past popular songs, as has the pharmaceutical industry in its direct-to-consumer television ads that have aired in recent decades.

In 1997 the Federal Drug Administration consolidated its standards for audiovisual DTC promotion to three guidelines: the spot must present a "fair balance" between effectiveness and risk, include a "major statement" of the most serious risks, and inform the public about the product's "indications" (that is, usefulness in treating a condition).[12] The FDA had periodically chastised Pfizer concerning Viagra advertising for failing to adhere to these guidelines. In response Pfizer ran a staid erectile-dysfunction (ED) awareness campaign from 2005 to 2007, and then ad agency McCann Erickson rolled out the firm's "Viva Viagra" commercial in 2007. Pfizer claims that a focus group rated the spot 40 percent higher than more reserved commercials: spokesperson Francisco Gebauer remarked, "It's extremely motivating," helping persuade men to "engage in dialogue with their physician."[13]

With Viagra revenues at $1.7 billion for 2007, Pfizer could afford to spend more than $100 million advertising its pharmaceutical solution to ED.[14] The sixty-second spot, "Roadhouse"—debuted during the *NBC Nightly News* on July 23, 2007—presents what looks like a live performance of "Viva Viagra" (a parody of the title song from *Viva Las Vegas*) by a group of middle-aged men (four white and two Black) singing and playing acoustic guitars, piano, stand-up bass, and drums.[15] Table 10.1 gives a breakdown of the commercial.

Pfizer aimed for the highest creative standard, signing experienced music-video director Bob Giraldi and hiring two groups of top musicians, one on the set and the other in the recording studio.[16] "Roadhouse" intentionally portrays these performers as ordinary men—like the target consumers—who happen to enjoy making music together. The site of this indoor performance is a country roadhouse, and the performers are casually dressed, as if jamming or rehearsing, yet the musicians on-screen and on the soundtrack are professionals from New York and Los Angeles. Their performance of the parody verses fills the spot's first twenty-five seconds, with two guitarists and the bass player taking turns singing the new text. After the chorus "Viva Viagra" at 0:22, the male voice-over provides the usual DTC advertising exhortation: "Talk to your doctor . . ." The recitation of dangers is primarily narrated during an overhead shot of the group, background riffing to the tune. The voice-over ends just before the extended climactic chorus, accompanied by footage of the musicians "bromantically" parting in their vehicles, presumably for their "honeys."

TABLE 10.1. "Viva Viagra"

Time	Element				
	Visual	Lyrics	Music	Voice-over	Graphic lettering
0:00	Roadhouse interior, medium close-up of guitarist/singer Man 1	[Line 1, Man 1]*	Verse A		
0:08	Medium close-up of guitarist/singer Man 2, intercut with pianist hands	[Line 2, Man 2]	Verse A		
0:16	Medium close-up of bassist/singer Man 3, intercut with medium shot at chorus	[Line 3, Man 3]	Verse B		
0:22	Medium shot of group, intercut with close-ups of pianist	[Chorus]	Chorus		
0:24	Close-ups of pianist, guitarist/ harmonica player, Man 1, Man 2		Background riffing	Talk to your doctor about Viagra, America's most prescribed treatment for Erectile Dysfunction. Learn more at Viagra.com.	[gray screen:] Viagra (sildenafil citrate). For men with Erectile Dysfunction (ED) by prescription only. [large, blue:] Viagra.com
0:30	Medium shots of group	[Chorus]	Chorus		[large, blue:] Viagra.com
0:32	Medium shots of pianist, harmonica player		Background riffing	Ask your doctor if your heart is healthy enough for sex.	
0:35	Extreme close-up of bass strings			Don't take Viagra if you take nitrates for chest pain as it may cause an unsafe drop in blood pressure.	[centered, bold:] Do not take Viagra if you take nitrates for chest pain as it may cause an unsafe drop in blood pressure.
0:41	Overhead shot of group			Side effects may include headache, flushing, upset stomach, and abnormal vision.	[gray screen:] Viagra does not protect against sexually transmitted diseases including HIV.

(*continued*)

TABLE 10.1 *(continued)*

Time	Visual	Lyrics	Music	Voice-over	Graphic lettering
	Element				
0:45				To avoid long term injuries stop taking Viagra and call your doctor right away if you experience a sudden decrease in vision or an erection lasting more than four hours.	
0:46					[gray screen:] See our ad in *Golf Magazine*.
0:51	Medium shot of Man 1, dog				
0:53	Medium shots of men with parting gestures, long shot of vehicles departing	[Extended chorus]	Chorus (extended)		
0:55					[large, blue] Viva
0:56					[large, blue:] Viva Viagra (sildenafil citrate) tablets

* See Table 10.2 for the lyrics.

Meika Loe's 2004 study of Pfizer's Viagra ads argues that they "reveal cultural investments in . . . whiteness."[17] Similarly, the ads emphasize what Botz-Bornstein classifies as the "Viagra body," which is "the normal, white, middle-class body."[18] The two Black musicians in the spot reflect Pfizer's exploitative desire to extend its target audience beyond the primarily white and middle-class men who would relate to Elvis and Vegas. Yet Botz-Bornstein neglects the most obvious identifying aspect of the Viagra man: age. As Joy Fuqua observes, "The commercial points to a utopian vision of the aging male maintaining sexual practices commonly associated with younger men."[19] In this context, the throwback to Elvis and Vegas purposefully recalls the youthful association between the singer and the Strip, while the commercial's restrained exuberance symbolizes the attempt to recapture that vitality within boundaries of respectability in aging.

The "Viva Viagra" lyrics are loosely based on the original song "Viva Las Vegas" (by Doc Pomus and Mort Shuman), and the music is an abridged version of Elvis's track.[20] (See table 10.2 for a comparison.)

The primary link back to Elvis/Vegas is the simple, recognizable chorus "Viva Viagra." Through musical skill and advertising savvy, the arranger replaces the verses' glorification of the Strip with middle-aged domestic bliss. Immediately following the opening line, both versions present the fervent wish "gonna set my soul, gonna set my soul on fire." This sets up divergent lyrical paths, one toward excitement over gambling and promiscuous sex, the other toward the expression of love for one partner. Such lyric divergences parallel an equally striking musical shift from early 1960s Vegas show culture, embodied in the original song, to Pfizer's concept of how middle-aged male sensibility sounds in the mid-2000s, as reflected in the advertisement's cover version.

Of the original "Viva Las Vegas," Elvis biographer Richard Zoglin observes, "The bongo-driven beat, catchy melody, and Elvis's energetic vocal performance seemed to perfectly capture the fun-loving, high-flying spirit of Vegas in its golden age," likening it to "a good travel brochure for Vegas in its classic era."[21] Cementing the bond between Elvis and Vegas, the song became the city's unofficial theme song.[22] But the ad also cost the city and song. The commercial exchanges the youthful rock 'n' roll world of Elvis in Vegas with a middle-aged, countrified mellowness; the almost frenetic drive of Presley's "live" performance is replaced by a moderately paced "Texas Roadhouse" style, combining blues, classic rock, and outlaw country.

TABLE 10.2 "Viva Viagra" lyrics

"Viva Las Vegas," First Verse/Chorus	"Roadhouse," Verse/Chorus
[Elvis:] Bright light city gonna set my soul,	[Man 1:] Got me a honey gonna set my soul,
Gonna set my soul on fire.	Gonna set my soul on fire.
Got a whole lot of money that's ready to burn,	[Man 2:] At the end of the day, I'm not a guy who'll stray.
So get those stakes up higher.	'Cuz she's my heart's desire.
There's a thousand pretty women waitin' out there,	[Man 3:] Now this lonesome toad is sick of the road,
And they're all livin' the devil may care,	I can't wait / [Chorus:] Can't wait /
And I'm just the devil with love to spare.	[Man 3:] I can't wait to go home.
[Elvis & Chorus:] Viva Las Vegas, Viva Las Vegas	[Chorus:] Viva Viagra / [Voice-over] /
	[Chorus:] Viva Viagra / [Voice-over] /
	[Chorus:] Viva, Viva Viagra

By engaging male consumer attention through a recognizable oldie, "Roadhouse" relies on the consumer's embodied experience of past sexual performance to make its pitch. The spot's reference to Elvis nostalgically captures what Fuqua calls the "Playboy moment, in which . . . sex was simply sex, without the need for sexuopharmaceutical intervention," carrying "connotations of sexual liberation and frivolity associated with the city."[23] At the same time, the commercial positions those prevailing mythologies as (paradoxically) embodying unacceptable excesses of sexual performance for the "Viagra man."[24] Pfizer had to find a balance between the promiscuity nostalgically associated with Elvis and Vegas and an enhanced monogamous heterosexual desire. The textual and musical reworking of "Viva Las Vegas" into the parody "Viva Viagra" provided the surreptitious mechanism to accomplish that goal.

Notes

We thank Professor James Wright (Carleton University) for his generous assistance in preparing this article.

1. Patsy G. Hammontree, "Audience Amplitude: The Cultural Phenomenon of Elvis Presley," *Southern Quarterly* 18, no. 1 (1979): 54; Benson P. Fraser and William J. Brown, "Media, Celebrities, and Social Influence: Identification with Elvis Presley," *Mass Communication and Society* 5, no. 2 (2002): 184.

2. Glen Jeansonne, David Luhrssen, and Dan Sokolovic, "Love Me Tender," in *Elvis Presley, Reluctant Rebel: His Life and Our Times*, ed. Glen Jeansonne, David Luhrssen, and Dan Sokolovic, 1–17 (Santa Barbara: ABC-CLIO, 2011).

3. Martin Reiser, "A Note on the Analysis of the 'Elvis Presley' Phenomenon," *American Imago* 15, no. 1 (1958): 97–100.

4. Reiser, "A Note on the Analysis of the 'Elvis Presley' Phenomenon," 99.

5. Glenn Altschuler, "Great Balls of Fire," in *All Shook Up: How Rock 'n' Roll Changed America*, ed. Glenn Altschuler, 67–99 (New York: Oxford University Press, 2004).

6. See Brian F. Wright's chapter in this volume for a discussion of the film's shooting locations in Vegas.

7. It was common throughout the 1950s and '60s for Elvis to be filmed only from the waist up to avoid offending older viewers.

8. Ernst Jorgensen, ed., *Elvis Presley: A Life in Music: The Complete Recording Sessions* (New York: St. Martin's Press, 1998), 146.

9. Including, of course, Pfizer's Viagra campaign.

10. Jac Tharpe, "Will the Real Elvis Presley . . . ?" *Southern Quarterly* 18, no. 1 (1979): 3.

11. Various chapters in *The Oxford Handbook of Music and Advertising* address the role of music and sound in audiovisual promotion. James Deaville, Siu-Lan Tan, and Ronald Rodman, eds., *The Oxford Handbook of Music and Advertising* (New York: Oxford University Press, 2021).

12. Kim Bartel Sheehan, *Controversies in Contemporary Advertising*, 2nd ed. (Thousand Oaks, CA: Sage, 2013).

13. Matthew Arnold, "Pfizer Seeks to Put Some Elvis into Viagra's Share of Voice," *Medical Marketing and Media* (*MM+M*) (July 24, 2007), https://www.mmm-online.com/welcome/8781/single/~home~channel~pfizer-seeks-to-put-some-elvis-into-viagras-share-of-voice/.

14. Matej Mikulic, "Worldwide Revenue of Pfizer's Viagra from 2003 to 2019," *Statista* (March 1, 2021), https://www.statista.com/statistics/264827/pfizers-worldwide-viagra-revenue-since-2003/. See also Keith Winstein and Suzanne Vranica, "Drug Firms' Spending on Consumer Ads Fell 8% in '08," *Wall Street Journal*, April 16, 2009.

15. A video of the commercial was posted on YouTube on April 19, 2009, by bass player Mark Shelton (marknation) at https://www.youtube.com/watch?v=NyMXahpRVV4.

16. Giraldi directed the video for Michael Jackson's "Beat It" (1983) and the film *Dinner Rush* (2000). According to Shelton and guitarist Mike Simpkins, the studio musicians first recorded the track and the onscreen group then finger- and lip-synched to the recording. See their comments to the YouTube video.

17. Meika Loe, *The Rise of Viagra* (New York: New York University Press, 2004), 56.

18. Thorsten Botz-Bornstein, "America and Viagra; or, How the White Negro Became a Little Whiter: Viagra as an Afro-Disiac," in *Philosophy of Viagra*, ed. Thorsten Botz-Bornstein (New York: Rodopi, 2011), 145.

19. Joy V. Fuqua, *Prescription TV: Therapeutic Discourse in the Hospital and at Home* (Durham, NC: Duke University Press, 2012), 136.

20. A film excerpt is available at https://www.youtube.com/watch?v=ui0EgRsFVN8.

21. Richard Zoglin, *Elvis in Vegas: How the King Reinvented the Las Vegas Show* (New York: Simon & Schuster, 2020), 106.

22. In 2002 Las Vegas unsuccessfully attempted to make "Viva Las Vegas" its official theme song. David McGrath Schwartz, "Our Song, Wronged: Look What Viagra's Done to Elvis' Vegas Anthem," *Las Vegas Sun*, April 3, 2008, https://lasvegassun.com/news/2008/apr/03/our-song-wronged/.

23. Fuqua, *Prescription TV*, 134–35.

24. Cecilia Åsberg and Ericka Johnson, "Viagra Selfhood: Pharmaceutical Advertising and the Visual Formation of Swedish Masculinity," *Health Care Analysis* 17 (2009): 144–57.

11

Shall We Go for It?

The Viral Hermeneutics of Céline Dion's Las Vegas Show

SAM MURRAY

In 2003 Céline Dion was invited to perform a residency in the Colosseum at the infamous Caesars Palace Hotel. The Vegas residency has become somewhat synonymous with grandeur and high production value as much as it has with being the affirmation of an artist's status as a heritage act. As *Rolling Stone Australia* journalist Tyler Jenke once remarked: "Heritage acts are those artists who have always been there, have long been considered as iconic, have managed to outlive most of their contemporaries."[1] Not only do such acts outlive contemporaries, but in many cases they outsell them and continue to garner large record sales, mostly through virtue of their status as opposed to solely being about the music.

Glancing past the musical value of Dion's Vegas residency, this chapter thus examines the dialogues and interactions she has with her audience. Such interactions take on new meanings when placed in contexts outside of the moment of the show and exist in new spaces beyond the Colosseum at Caesars Palace. In fact, while audiences may respond to such interactions as positive life-affirming experiences, such interactions have also led to Dion becoming the subject of parody. Céline Dion's Las Vegas residency has become more culturally significant, helping to amplify Dion's persona as a cultural figure beyond her music and, by extension, the Vegas residency as a porous, unbounded phenomenon. In developing Erving Goffman's theories of audience-performer interaction, this chapter thus seeks to push forward these hermeneutic approaches to audience-performer interactions to look beyond the immediate and into the meanings taken on postevent. The result is an image of how Vegas spills beyond itself and carries its mystique and mythical values further into the everyday world.

Céline Dion's Las Vegas residency fully embraces the fantastic nature of its surroundings, drawing on the expectations of creating something so remarkable that disbelief is suspended and the unreal becomes the real. Although the show is performed night after night with the same script, audiences embrace the fantasy of their experience. In his book *Zeropolis*, Bruce Bégout remarks that Las Vegas's "pseudo-edifices of fantasy contain the formula for our lives to come," a space that allows one to live an idealized existence and experience the extraordinary. Vegas is an unbounded fantastical space in which the impossible seems possible, so when Céline Dion interacts with an audience it becomes a meaningful, sincere conversation and a personal connection they arguably couldn't get at any of her other shows. Dion also embraces the possibilities of Las Vegas existing beyond its geographical borders, as Bégout suggests: "We are all inhabitants of Las Vegas, however far away we are from southern Nevada. Its name is no longer a fantasy. It lives in our heads, is expressed in our ordinary gestures."[2] If the experience, the gesture, the mind-set of Las Vegas can exist outside of the city boundaries, then it is reasonable to believe audience-performer interactions can as well. These interactions can tell the story of Dion's Las Vegas residency, and in particular tell us how she has existed within that space and who she has become as a result of engaging the fantastical. Such interactions, it could be suggested, may even carry more weight in defining Dion as performer than her songs do.

Examining audience-performer interactions can be a crucial way to find out more about the personality of an artist and the meaning and intent of their performances. It can also set boundaries to where performances begin and end. Ethnomusicologist John Bealle, through his study of audience-performer interaction in bluegrass performances, utilizes the work of Erving Goffman in his analysis of what he terms "stage talk," drawing on Goffman's concept of "keyings" to explain what he describes as "specific spoken images that are to be associated with the performance," suggesting that the concept is as much about register as voicings.[3] He also further engages Goffman in observing that "we might also consider that by using stage talk to circumscribe the boundaries of performance, speaker/performers also maintain a space within which the conventions of musical performance do not reach," alluding to the process of text brackets marking out the spaces of performance, but perhaps going further to suggest that it also can elicit particular crowd responses.[4] Such boundaries can also create a sense of authority for the performer who had control of the direction of a performance. If a performer introduces a song, they can prescribe it with a particular meaning and indeed ask an audience to remain within the confines of such a meaning. It is naturally difficult to measure if such a request is successful, but if not wholly adopted the placing of a meaning on a song will at least be acknowledged by an audience, if not wholly received. Many of these techniques are clearly witnessed in Dion's interaction, as this chapter will further discuss.

Goffman's notions of audience interaction are conceptually based in a present experience and seek to give the control of the flow of meaning into the authoritarian hands of the performer who can rely on conventions and stock phrases. But this is merely one part of the equation. There needs to be a notional sense of not only reception of audience-performer interaction but indeed dialogue, exploring how the audience can construct meaning in response to such conventions. It is this focus on audience reception that is crucial in bringing live performances beyond the confines of the space in which they exist and lead them to a fantastical space of infinite reproduction, as Dion's interactions demonstrate.

To analyze the audience-performer interaction involved in Céline Dion's Las Vegas residency show *A New Day . . .*, I will consider not only the live performance but also the existing postevent through recordings, retelling, and parody. I analyze key interactions for their viral quality and how such interactions are journeyed out of context and given new meanings through impersonation and parody in Kathy Griffin's comedy routine about the *A New Day . . .* residency, as well as Ariana Grande's impression of Dion on late-night U.S. television. This will draw on the work of Goffman, Bealle, and Barbara Bradby, all of whom have analyzed audience-performer interactions as a conversation in the moment of performance and consider how such interactions are replicated and retold for a variety of audiences beyond Las Vegas.[5]

In her controversially titled comedy stand-up special *Strong Black Woman* performed at the Orpheum Theatre in Los Angeles, California, on May 9, 2006, comedian Kathy Griffin included a segment about Dion's *A New Day . . .* residency that told the story of meeting Dion at a performance in 2005. During this segment, Griffin satirizes and jokes about the meaning of various segments of *A New Day . . .* She begins by commenting on the show's combination of Cirque du Soleil–style performance art, branding the performance "Cirque de Céline" and exclaiming that "it makes no sense, like she'll be standing there singing 'Titanic,' right, and it's beautiful and wonderful, and for no reason a giant Styrofoam piano floats by over her head with a French Canadian clown playing it on a harness."[6] The floating-piano scene is incorrectly ascribed to a performance of the song "My Heart Will Go On" from *Titanic*, but it is in fact taking place during a performance of "If I Could." This misremembering adds humor, as wider audiences will be more familiar with the *Titanic* theme due to its mainstream success. There is also no discernible reason for a clown to float across a stage with a piano during a song used in a tragic film.

Griffin then turns her attention to two particular audience-performer interactions during which she mimics Céline Dion with a fake French Canadian accent. The first is about Dion's entrance: "I've seen the show several times. Every single time she walks out at the beginning of the show . . . every night, every time she walks out, she acts like she shocked anyone showed up . . . as if every single day at about three o'clock she's like, you know, René, maybe tonight is the night they do not come."

Again, this is a slight misremembering of the *A New Day* . . . residency, as this point does not come until the first medley of songs is performed and Dion has had a costume change, but indeed she does look shocked and surprised when the crowd cheers and gives her an ovation. Griffin's misremembering again adds humor by creating the impression that Dion worries about her audience numbers despite being a highly successful artist, and this in some way humanizes Dion through such a joke.

The final joke about audience-performer interaction in the show focuses on the aforementioned interaction in which Dion dedicates the song "If I Could" to the parents and children of the world. This particular interaction seems to highly amuse Griffin, who retells this interaction as follows: "So, Céline says this one thing . . . she comes out and she goes like this: 'Is it okay if I come and sit with you for a moment?' and everybody goes ape [beep] . . . she goes and she sits down to the front of the stage and she goes like this: 'This next song is for all the parents in the audience and also the children.' That's just everybody, right?!"

There is only a slight misremembering of the words, but this retelling is more accurate than the others, although she leaves off a specific dedication made to her son René-Charles Angélil that would have effectively made Griffin's punch line pointless. Griffin takes what is an emotive touching moment of interaction and mercilessly mocks it, intimating that such interactions are prescripted and disingenuous while also suggesting she herself fell for it when she was part of the audience. Griffin also distorts the contextual meaning this utterance is meant to give. To someone who has yet to see the show, such satirical retellings could warp the meanings Dion had intended in these interactions and encourage a cynical approach to them.

The satirical reading of such interactions not only recontextualizes performer-audience interactions for the purpose of parody and humor, but can also involve restructuring and retelling in a way that is not quoting such interactions verbatim. These retellings are subject to either intentional or unintentional misremembering to allow the structure of a joke to be formed. The satirical adds a humorous and critical meaning to such interactions and could be perceived as inviting cynicism about how genuine such interactions actually are.

While the satirical can recontextualize interactions outside of the space they inhabit, it also considers the context and environment in which they happen, which are crucial to such retellings. Thus, the retelling of the *A New Day* . . .

residency is a retelling and resituating of Las Vegas itself. The already parodic existence of Las Vegas is something Bégout considers when he remarks that "Las Vegas makes fun of everything. It makes every reality an object of mockery. Without any concern for history, it pulps all human event into an electrochemical swill of parody which leaves absolutely nothing in one piece."[7] It is no surprise that Las Vegas residencies are no exception to this rule and are subject to the mockery that Dion has received for her performance. It is almost as if the boundaries pushed by a performance that combines big hit songs with large-scale production and modern circus performance cannot be computed by the various audiences who receive this. Outside of Vegas, the *A New Day . . .* residency appears absurd. Audiences in Las Vegas, already surrounded by multitudes of absurd and fantastical experiences, may not necessarily mock Dion's residency, as they are already immersed in expecting the unexpected. Umberto Eco explained such a phenomenon, suggesting that "the consumer finds himself participating in the fantasy because of his own authenticity as a consumer."[8] Therefore, a concertgoer to the *A New Day . . .* residency will believe in the authenticity and sincerity of audience-performer interactions that come from Dion, even if such interactions are scripted and repeated. It is only when such interactions are removed from the Vegas environment that interactions are critiqued and their sincerity questioned and mocked. Griffin throughout her stand-up section about Céline Dion even positions herself as a willing audience member, seemingly gullible to the audience-performer interactions as special unique moments in a special Vegas environment. It is only through critical reflection (and distance) that Griffin can mock such interactions, resituating *A New Day . . .* outside of Las Vegas.

While the satirical resituates and retells audience-performer interactions, parodies take such interactions and replicate them at speed through direct imitations. It is such repetition of Dion's audience-performer interactions that have given a new meaning and life to the *A New Day . . .* residency. Sangeet Kumar, in his examination of viral political parody videos and memes in India, argues, "The text's parodic content deploys the power of repetition with difference to implode an argument or social practice from within." By altering a text and repeating it, such an altered meaning can gain traction and success and have a meaning that could displace that of the original, taking away any notion of the artist's control over how meaning is interpreted in such interactions. Thus, the audience-performer interaction happening within a moment for specific reason is given different and new interpretations. Kumar also asserts, "This critical power is then amplified by its ability to replicate infinitely, as easily as with a single click, through a diffused network of creators and participants."[9] This points to a quality of replication, between a variety of digital channels on the Internet—meaning that if it is taken down in one place, it may resurrect in another. It may also suggest critique that is inherent in parodying being a motivation for such replication. There is a sense of meanings surrounding a text becoming infinite through constant replication and recontextualizing by the individual user when they may share content in a public way, such as sharing or posting a video/meme with added context. The audience-performer interaction within the *A New Day*... residency has indeed been subject to such viral parody and as a result replicates new meanings to new consumers of such interactions on the internet.

One such progenitor of parody is Ariana Grande, whose impression of Dion has gained infinite replication as viral parody shared through video streaming channels. Grande's impression of Dion first came to light during her appearance in 2015 on *The Tonight Show Starring Jimmy Fallon* during a segment called "Wheel of Musical Impressions," where Grande battles Jimmy Fallon by doing impromptu impersonations of artists singing songs they are not known for.[10] Alongside a version of "Mary Had a Little Lamb" in the style of Britney Spears and "The Wheels on the Bus" as if it were done by Christina Aguilera, Grande is asked to perform a version of the Weeknd's "I Can't Feel My Face" in the style of Céline Dion. In this impression, as with Dion's performance of "I'm Alive" in her Vegas show, Grande interrupts her singing by speaking the phrase "SO much" to emphasize the song lyrics, then says "So much" exactly the way Dion does during "I'm Alive" before using the phrase "Shall we go for it?" as a way to signal Jimmy Fallon to join in with his Sting impression. It is through these small audience-performer phrases that the illusion of Dion is constructed to inject her personality into the impression and to help differentiate her voice form the other diva impressions that Grande attempts. By doing this, Grande takes the phrase "Shall we go for it?" out of the conventional introduction to a song and into viral parody by taking a phrase intended to seek permission from a live audience to go on with the show and turning it into a quirky phrase that can immediately mark an impression of Céline Dion far outside the space and place where it originally held meaning.

Grande's impression was resurrected for a skit during her appearance as the host and musical guest of *Saturday Night Live* in March 2016.[11] In the skit, Grande plays Chloe, an intern working at Tidal, who is asked to cover songs for different artists whose streams go down due to a technical fault. This in reality is a vehicle for Grande to give impressions of divas. When it is declared that they have lost Céline Dion, Grande's character stands in to perform "It's All Coming Back to Me Now" with remarkable accuracy. During this brief skit, Grande mimics Dion's common audience-performer interactions by parroting in a mock French Canadian accent her famous introduction line "Shall we go for it?" while doing a chest bump, another symbol synonymous with Dion's performance, as seen in her *A New Day*... residency. In these two short moments, Ariana Grande used

Dion's *A New Day* . . . residency audience-performer interactions to create clear signifiers that her impressions were of Dion. Both of these clips went viral.[12]

Grande's parodies have resulted in a new caricature of Céline Dion based on retellings of Dion's audience-performer interactions, introducing a new generation to the personality behind the music. Grande's impression has been so successful that Dion herself has responded in an appearance on *The Tonight Show Starring Jimmy Fallon* in July 2016.[13] When asked about the impression, she not only parrots it back but says of Grande, "She's so good, I love her," before agreeing to participate herself in "The Wheel of Musical Impressions" segment, bringing the impression full circle.[14] The only trick missed is that Dion is not invited to parody Ariana Grande in return.

These impressions mirror Las Vegas, which in itself replicates and impersonates culture in a variety of ways. Within Las Vegas, many have found careers in impersonation, keeping Vegas legends like Elvis and Sinatra alive. If viral parody is focused, as Kumar suggests, on the constant replication of ideas, then Las Vegas is a consistent proponent of replication. In her book *Multivocality: Singing on the Borders of Identity*, Katherine Meizel recalls an encounter of seeing a Tina Turner impersonator, noting, "Tina Turner hadn't sung in Las Vegas for years. But in October of 2013 I heard her voice there—issuing from a petite blonde French-Canadian woman . . . for an ephemeral moment."[15] For a moment in time, a star performer is channeled and paid tribute for an audience who cannot see the real thing. This fits well with the architecture of Vegas in which simulations of the wonders of the world, from the pyramids of Giza to the Venice Grand Canal, are situated all in one place and made available to all. Audiences suspend disbelief to access these landmarks, even if they are not the real thing. This culture of simulation and impersonation can often be projected outward, and it is somewhat fitting that the *A New Day* . . . residency has been useful in crafting an impersonation of Céline Dion.

The impact of the viral parody has been to create a new personal connection for audiences with Céline Dion. Any previous preconceived notions of how Dion reacts and responds to her audience have become defined by parody and homage to the point where Dion has leaned into the impression and has almost allowed the parody to replace original reality by now providing audiences with the now expected turns of phrase popularized by Grande.

Ariana Grande's impressions, though parodies, are clearly a homage, and by doing so she is exposing her own personal fan base to Céline Dion's personality, encouraging fans to connect with Dion's work, all through a reconstruction of the audience-performer interactions captured within the *A New Day* . . . residency. As Meizel explains, "Whilst an impersonator may rely on oculo-centric techniques to match the body language or superficial physical features of a chosen artist, they must also depend upon the imagination of another's interior space, the assumption of its familiarity and the perception of minute variance."[16]

Ariana Grande performs, in the given instances, without oculo-centric signifiers of impersonating Céline Dion, and so relies on the minute detail of audience-performer interactions.

Through the satirical and the viral parody hermeneutic categories, Céline Dion's *A New Day* . . . residency has found new meaning beyond the walls of the Colosseum at the Caesars Palace Hotel, helping further cement Dion's iconic status as a French Canadian megastar. The viral parody in particular has allowed broader and wider consumption of Dion's artistry and personality as captured in her audience-performer interactions. Dion's Las Vegas residency is set to live on in years to come as the many interpretations of her original Vegas residency also go through a digital mitosis through YouTube and streaming platforms.

What this chapter reveals is how viral parodies allow Vegas performers to spill out of the confines of Las Vegas itself, making clear a broader ecosystem of fantasy and possibility in the world. This emanates from the inherent values of replication, recontextualization, and simulation that create the hyperreality that is Las Vegas. Audiences suspend disbelief when present in the city and become wrapped up in the performances they experience around them. It is not until the city boundaries are left that we see the unlimited replication of meaning that can occur. New meanings are constructed out of retelling (replication), recontextualization of performances, and interactions and simulations of performers themselves. Kathy Griffin and Ariana Grande are only the tip of an iceberg of meaning that has already begun to redefine Céline Dion as a personality. Dion is not likely to be the last artist subjected to such viral replications, and with new residencies being announced year on year, the very idea of the residency will soon come to be seen as a moment that redefines an artist. The mythologies of Las Vegas will only continue to be exploited and subjected to viral replications, and as technology grows and develops, the possibilities seem endless.

Notes

1. Tyler Jenke, "The Nostalgia Cash Cow: Are Heritage Acts Funding the Musical Economy?" *Rolling Stone Australia*, February 13, 2020, https://au.rollingstone.com/music/music-features/nostalgia-cash-cow-heritage-acts-funding-musical-economy-6075/.

2. Bruce Bégout, *Zeropolis: The Experience of Las Vegas* (London: Reaktion Books, 2003), 12.

3. See Erving Goffman, *Forms of Talk* (Oxford: Oxford University Press, 1981); and John Bealle, "Self-Involvement in Musical Performance: Stage Talk and Interpretive Control at a Bluegrass Festival," *Ethnomusicology* 37, no. 1 (1993): 71.

4. Bealle, "Self-Involvement in Musical Performance," 82.

5. Barbara Bradby, "Performer-Audience Interaction in Live Concerts: Ritual of Conversation?" in *Musicians and Their Audiences: Performance, Speech and Mediation*, ed. Ioannis Tsioulakis and Elina Hytonens-Ng (London: Routledge, 217), 89.

6. Kathy Griffin, "Céline Dion Vegas Kathy Griffin Parody (with Céline Clips)," *YouTube*, 2015, https://www.youtube.com/watch?v=uGqVPT-BFUg.

7. Bégout, *Zeropolis*, 13.

8. Umberto Eco, *Travels in Hyper Reality* (Orlando: Harcourt Bruce Jovanovich, 1986), 41.

9. Sangeet Kumar, "Contagious Memes, Viral Videos and Subversive Parody: The Grammar of Contention on the Indian Web," *International Communication Gazette* 77, no. 3 (2015): 243.

10. *Saturday Night Live*, "Ariana Grande Saturday Night Live [Legendado]," YouTube, 2016, https://www.youtube.com/watch?v=K0OIoUF4wjE; *The Tonight Show Starring Jimmy Fallon*, "Wheel of Musical Impressions with Ariana Grande," YouTube, 2015, https://www.youtube.com/watch?app=desktop&v=ss9ygQqqL2Q.

11. *Saturday Night Live*, "Ariana Grande."

12. *The Tonight Show Starring Jimmy Fallon*, "Wheel of Musical Impressions with Ariana Grande"; *Saturday Night Live*, "Ariana Grande."

13. *The Tonight Show Starring Jimmy Fallon*, "Céline Dion Never Wanted to Record 'My Heart Will Go On,'" YouTube, 2016, https://www.youtube.com/watch?v=sJLaaqUgzvM.

14. *The Tonight Show Starring Jimmy Fallon*, "Wheel of Musical Impressions with Céline Dion," YouTube, 2016, https://www.youtube.com/watch?v=hFDHryC6Vwg.

15. Katherine Meizel, *Multivocality: Singing on the Borders of Identity* (New York: Oxford University Press, 2020), 74.

16. Meizel, *Multivocality*, 74.

12

Liberace's Surfaces

Democratic Virtuosity, American Fantasies, and Vegas Pianism

PHEAROSS GRAHAM

Aptly, the piano metaphorizes Las Vegas. Like the carte blanche city—a "zeropolis"—the instrument lends itself to unrestrained fantasy powered by its own nuclear cores ushering fundamental blankness, bestowed character by superimposed, often fleeting imagination.[1] Stretches of the Mojave Desert bear unending sameness, much like Vegas's practically identical hotel rooms and casinos, differentiated by surfaces of flashing lights, elaborate facades, and outlandish themes. The piano's tonal landscape prevails of uniformity; in its upkeep, skilled technicians voice each key to sound the same, iron out registral differences, and tune with standardized, equal temperament. Vegas allures of the American Dream of riches and material pleasures, in harmony with the piano's beckoning of bourgeois distinction.

Postwar years saw pianos gracing American living rooms alongside television sets, flashing glimpses of haute, often ascendant culture. From this context, Władziu Valentino Liberace lent himself to public fantasies of an upwardly mobile-minded listening public, which led to his act ultimately exploding in Las Vegas, America's city of illusion. Liberace hailed from West Allis, Wisconsin, and understood his proletariat audience well. The community that shaped him consisted of working-class, conservative capitalists who appreciated but did not necessarily like classical music, preferring instead social outings to relish regional favorites: deep-fried cheese curds, kielbasa, and Pabst Blue Ribbon. Not to pass over audiences otherwise dismissed by "serious" artists, Liberace fashioned a democratic pianistic strategy that foregrounded surfaces to engage and include listeners otherwise deterred by formal, straitlaced concert halls, and perhaps hard-to-follow repertory.[2]

At its core, Liberace's publicly oriented piano style remained consistent throughout his career, notwithstanding his ever-changing theatrics and extra-musical elements.[3] On account of his prominence, his pianism often presupposes comparisons with "the greats"—Rubenstein, Horowitz, and Hofmann. Yet his performance parameters were not equivalent. Unlike them, Liberace dismissed the work concept and cult of the composer.[4] Early on, he freed himself from the bonds of the titles of "concert pianist" and "artist," preferring instead "entertainer."[5] Contrary to the "great pianists," Liberace, the "evangelist of kitsch," reached the greatest number of listeners possible through inclusive virtuosity.[6] In doing so, he often scrubbed away the structuralism, architectural development, fine-graded nuances, counterpoint, and inner complexities of his classical repertoire, in his own words, to skip the "spiritual struggle," giving audiences what he believed they wanted—directness, lack of suggestion, and instant gratification. This chapter connects aspects of Liberace's pianism and musicianship with fantasies of Vegas itself, examined through a representative medley performed for *The Tonight Show Starring Johnny Carson* in 1984.[7]

As the world's chief fantasy hub, Las Vegas attracts flocks of tourists for its juxtapositions of heterogeneous cultural simulacra. In one day going down the Strip, tourists might journey to Paris, Venice, Egypt, ancient Rome, and King Arthur's court, concluding with an excursion to the circus, a burlesque show, or tropical shark reef. Instant, splendid gratification distinguishes Vegas as a variety-show city. Liberace's musical acts, especially those featuring medleys, anticipated and set a precedent for much of Vegas's metropolitan tendencies. There is something for everybody as Liberace binds together excerpts from extremely famous piano compositions in four minutes, catering to fleeting attention spans. In recognizing or resonating with at least one excerpt, emblematic listeners may feel personally accomplished rather than uncultured or baffled, as they might in formal concert halls. Like a tourist awash in Vegas's cosmopolitan architecture, Liberace tours Vienna (likelier Lake Lucerne?), Málaga (possibly Havana?), Moscow, and Hollywood's Warsaw in his medley—a musical Vegas-style buffet united simply by the steam table key of C-sharp minor.

Liberace begins his medley with the opening movement of Beethoven's "Moonlight" Sonata, reduced to a mere forty-eight seconds, compared to a typical six minutes. He retains only the most characteristic portions, cutting from measures (mm.) 1–4 to a lightly embellished mm. 60–63, and finishing with mm. 66–68 (example 12.1). In effect, Liberace turns this into an appetizer before the main entrée, presenting a nineteenth-century preluding exercise readying himself and the audience for the rest of the performance. Preluding as a practice began to fade by the earlier twentieth century as stable textual paradigms boosted the composer's primacy over the performer.[8] Liberace held to the erstwhile practice, opening paths to freer imagination and almost improvisatory

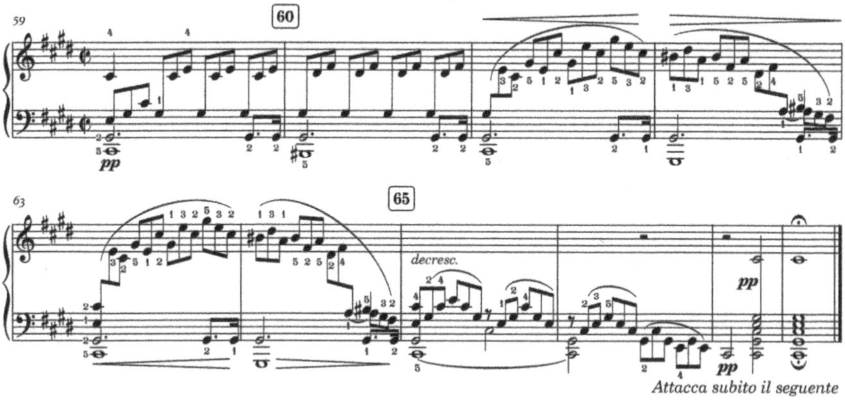

EXAMPLE 12.1 Beethoven: conclusion of "Moonlight" Sonata, opening movement.

fantasy. He gives only the surface of Beethoven in extreme terseness, eliminating development and presenting a Vegas frontage to reel listeners into his personality's orbit.

Liberace's decision to feature the "Moonlight" Sonata was on account of popularity; most anyone who has ever attempted the piano would have tried their hands at the piece, given its relative straightforwardness marked by repetitive figurations and nonawkward, close-position triads. A generous work, it offers immediacy in accessing Romantic pathos.[9] Liberace's use does not take the listener through a journey but signals to, as a quick topos, "cultured" listeners apparently in the know of recognizing a veritable masterpiece.

Giving only a few bites to allow for a greater overall indulgence of his musical smorgasbord, Liberace elides the downbeat of m. 68 into the second full bar of Rachmaninoff's famous Prelude in C-sharp Minor, a work the composer grew to loathe, as audiences incessantly demanded it as an encore (example 12.2). Liberace's approach excises the soft, "boring bits" (as he called them) that might lose audience members not yet phasing into attention. Rachmaninoff distinctively marks the prelude pianississimo (*ppp*), yet throughout Liberace's performance, he primarily resides within a mezzo forte to forte range, consistent with his avoidance of compositional development that highlights architecture. A primary attribute of Rachmaninoff's prelude is sonic transformation; with the return, Rachmaninoff aggrandizes the initially inward motif to fortississimo (*fff*), writes *pesante*, and expands to four full staves from the usual two to accommodate more densely written music (example 12.3). Liberace bypasses Rachmaninoff's unfolding.

Las Vegas is littered with an abundance of gentlemen's clubs and, perhaps, overzealous models handing out dirty advertisement cards. Liberace's strategy

EXAMPLE 12.2 Rachmaninoff: Prelude in C-sharp Minor, opening.

EXAMPLE 12.3 Rachmaninoff: Prelude in C-sharp Minor, opening theme aggrandized to four staves.

may resonate with the city's libidinal obsession, manifesting with his aesthetic of directness. In his youth, he performed at raunchy stag parties with nude women; he also provided piano accompaniment for pornographic films and live strippers dancing with "weird gyrations."[10] Thus, Liberace would select only the most titillating high points of musical works, skipping the "spiritual struggle" and tapping into a lucrative entertainment aesthetic many other pianists dismissed as kitsch and cheap theatrics. Liberace removes the work's unique architecture, as with the other excerpts, and renders it like one of many identical hotel rooms behind a grand facade. The graphical abstraction is based on the dynamic and textural parameters set in Rachmaninoff's score (fig. 12.1). In the performance waveform from 00:48–02:16, Liberace's performance resembles a solid block, especially as seen in the context of his other musical selections (fig.

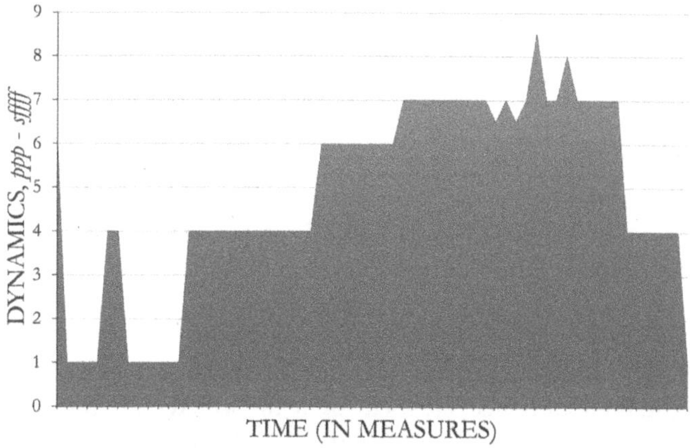

FIGURE 12.1 Structure of Rachmaninoff's (original) prelude as plotted by dynamics.

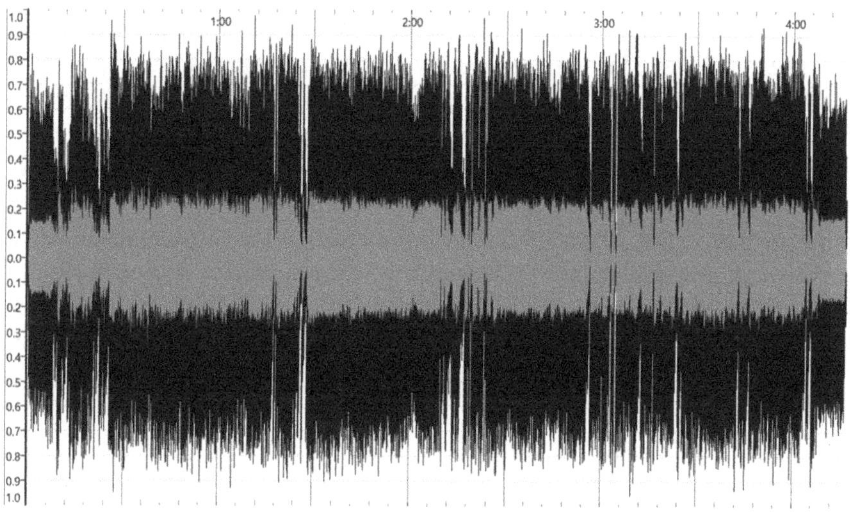

FIGURE 12.2 Waveform: Liberace's medley (applause immediately before and after).

12.2). Shapewise, this excerpt, like the others that follow and the one preceding, has an element of sameness, distinguished chiefly by the quick zest of a surface flavor. Larger emerging shapes are not characteristic here, hence the general lack of peaks and valleys, making the waveform unremarkable.

Liberace keeps intact the agitato middle section, as the brisk tempo would impress a listening audience more readily. A socialite not sequestering himself to isolated practice booths to excise all technical difficulties, he alters some of the riskier left-hand jumps of the interval of a quick fourteenth, marked in the score with brackets. Liberace sits on the lower C-sharp octave for approximately two beats rather than moving his hand instantly to play the upper B (example 12.4). In avoiding difficulties that might involve "antisocial" complexities, he

EXAMPLE 12.4 Rachmaninoff: Prelude in C-sharp Minor, left hand fourteenth.

morphs some of the otherwise interlocking chords into duplets from the original triplets, performing with a democratic but not transcendental virtuosity that might put off or frighten an audience. (Just consider the nineteenth-century super-virtuoso violinist Niccolò Paganini, whom the church anathematized for his diabolical, superhuman virtuosity.)

Liberace then transitions from m. 45 (example 12.5) of the prelude to the downbeat of Ernesto Lecuona's massively popular "Malagueña" (example 12.6). Well known in its many pop love-song instantiations, this piece had been one of Liberace's go-to staples throughout his career and may have opened doors to high-yield, sparkling pianism that would wow an audience. "Malagueña" presents an accessible, democratic bravura with its relatively straightforward yet impressive arpeggios that ripple up the keyboard, besides its fast, repeated figuration of quintuplets fitting comfortably under the hand's five fingers (example 12.7).

As with Rachmaninoff's prelude, Liberace avoids low points, texturally and dynamically speaking. He leaves out the "boring," contemplative *cante jondo*

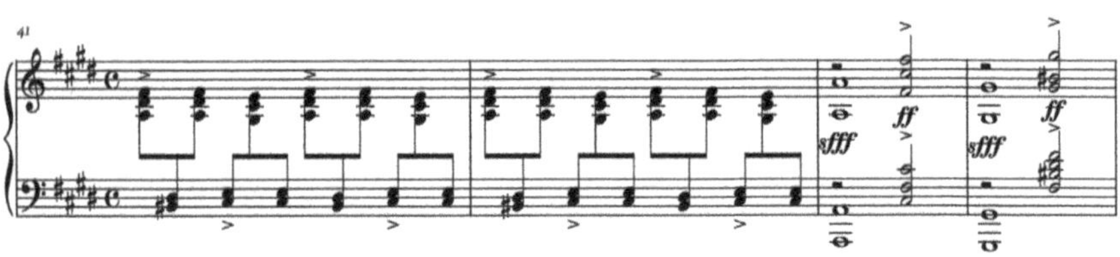

EXAMPLE 12.5 Rachmaninoff: Prelude in C-sharp Minor, retransition to A', where Liberace segues.

EXAMPLE 12.6 Lecuona: "Malagueña," opening.

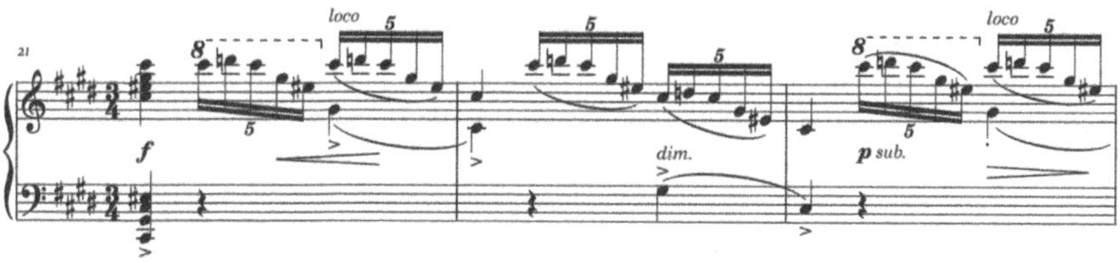

EXAMPLE 12.7 Lecuona: "Malagueña," quintuplets.

section near the center of the piece, distinguished by a monodic *recitativo* accompanied by upward flourishes that recall a guitar. In general, Liberace abstains from playing single-note melodic lines, which might not register with listeners as virtuosic or impressive. Instead, he jumps to the melody's filled-out reappearance at m. 111, the high point of the piece, yielding instant gratification (example 12.8).

With its exotic harmonies and tone moves, "Malagueña" may sound authentically Spanish, despite its being a simulation written through Lecuona's Cuban gaze. Lecuona's source material is not necessarily Spanish. He borrowed from

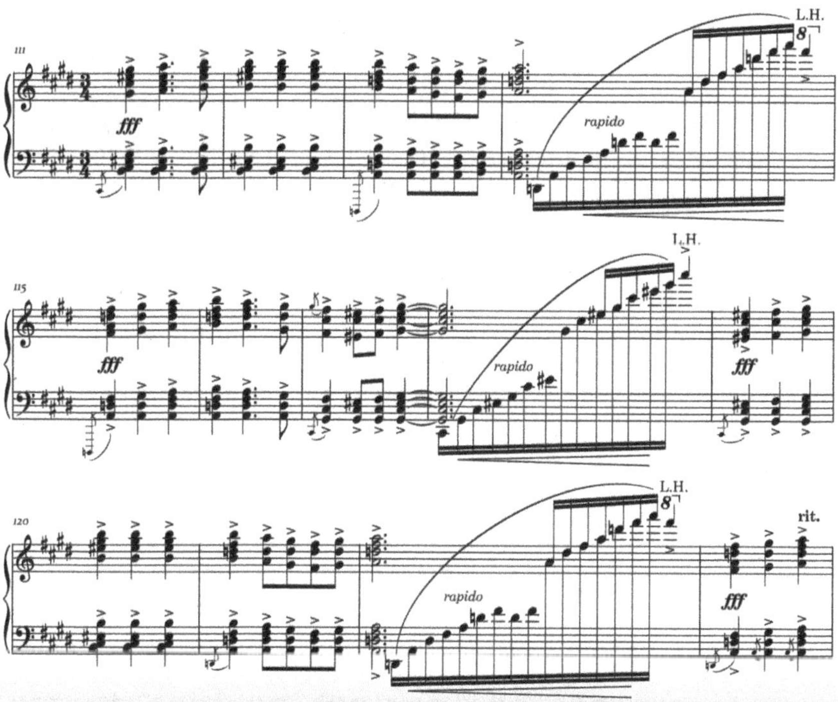

EXAMPLE 12.8 Lecuona: "Malagueña," filled-out recitativo.

the Louisianan Creole pianist-composer Louis Moreau Gottschalk, specifically the theme from his "Souvenirs d'Andalousie" (example 12.9), a work among his others that reminisced on his tours to lands afar. Given Liberace's Vegas penchant for surface simulations, he harks to Gottschalk's creation through Lecuona. Rather than conclude the Andalusian-esque piece as written—only seventeen bars remain—Liberace reshapes what was supposed to be the resolution at m. 125 (vivace) to the opening of the English composer Richard Addinsell's *Warsaw Concerto*, another cultural simulation written for the Hollywood screen as a stylistic imitation of Rachmaninoff, who refused to compose for the associated film, *Dangerous Moonlight* (1941). Addinsell's emulation takes only the most topical of gestures, avoiding inner complexities and long-term structural unfolding, given its utilitarian aim for the film's immediacy. The most characteristic gestures of a surging melody against lush strings, dramatic blocked chords, a large registral compass, and its minor key translate as the principal elements that Addinsell and his orchestrator, Roy Douglas, adopted. Micro-level hard-to-hear details, like subtle counterpoint and intense, inner chromatics found in Rachmaninoff, are not present; only aspects of the most zoomed-out perspective of stylistic features remain in the *Warsaw Concerto*. Much of this approach aligns squarely with Liberace's stylistic tendencies. For a viewing audience needing to grasp an overall affect quickly, the music serves its purpose, like a building's facade. With Liberace's interpolation of Lecuona and Addinsell's music, a pianistic "Vegas" cultural simulation prevails in a stitched-together souvenir that appeals to various interests, with brevity and immediacy being of the essence.

Contrary to his preceding excerpts, Liberace's conclusion is comparatively more challenging for the listener to pin down. It shares qualities with the ending of a classical Hollywood film score flavored by improvisatory, Lisztian harmonic shifts. Its fleeting nature renders it a musical chameleon pliable to fantastical projection. Liberace extensively employs a device that might be termed the "Liberace arpeggio," heard almost ubiquitously in his performances when a distinct melody appears. Within his well-oiled performance practice, the longer the melodic note value, the more likely Liberace inserts an arpeggiated chord. He doubles melodic pitches and fills in the resulting right-hand octaves with related chord members. As time permits, he extends the arpeggios as far up the keyboard as he can, possibly moving two or three octaves higher. More often

EXAMPLE 12.9 Gottschalk, "Souvenirs de Andalousie" (NB: left-hand theme).

on Vegas stages as he performs with this approach, the sequins on his costumes sparkle, as do his ring-covered fingers rippling up the keyboard. He sounds like what he looks like; each key's glittery ping accompanies light refracted from the crystals of his costumes. The "Liberace arpeggio" also recalls Vegas's twinkling lights from the tiny bulbs of the city's signage.[11]

While employing this device, Liberace eliminates inner complexity, including hidden contrapuntal lines the typical listener may not hear, as in the previous excerpt. Liberace likely recognizes that a greater shading, imposing "dull" softness, will not register for most listeners accustomed to amplified popular music, which tends to have fewer dynamic levels. In eliminating the obligation to hold contrapuntal voices down physically with the piano's keys, he liberates his hands to enhance the visual impact of his fingers unrestrictedly glistening across the keyboard, which is vital to those watching at a distance in a Vegas performance venue or watching on a low-resolution television set, as viewers would have seen him on *The Tonight Show*. With his hands whizzing up and down, his performance looks and sounds more complicated than it is, foregrounding make-believe and fancy.

Democratic virtuosity emerges as a chief factor behind the medley, which in many ways traces to nineteenth-century Romantic pianism, however ostentatiously transformed, even relative to "Lisztomania." In his essence, Liberace was a nineteenth-century pianist.[12] His free, surface-level appropriation of themes recall older pastiche "souvenirs," as did aspects of preluding, theatricality, and exaggeration to make immediate impressions on listeners. Nineteenth-century ephemerality often entailed only once-in-a-lifetime listening opportunities; Romantic pianists often augmented surfaces to translate effects for greater immediacy. Even the classicist Brahms advocated for exaggeration to teach unfamiliar audiences.[13] Hyperbolic parameters were sonic and theatrical, as were those of Liszt, who stockpiled multiple pianos on stage for performative backups in the wake of his awe-inspiring, instrument-wrecking paths of destruction. If he was not snapping strings through his *tutta forza con stepito* passages, he would nearly dance during orchestral tuttis of concerti as his jewelry clanged rhythmically, like other pianists of the era.[14] Divergently, Liberace surpassed Romantic excess; Mae West's "too much of a good thing is wonderful" became his creed.

In his modern adaption of the aristocratic salon, Liberace narrowed the audience-performer divide, encouraging greater back-and-forth exchange. Liberace's medley for *The Tonight Show* smoothly lent itself to a subsequent conversation and public orientation. More widely, Liberace's democratic virtuosity and exaltation of surfaces exerted an inescapable pull over other superstars, encouraging greater self-determination and liberated fantasy. The likes of Elvis Presley, Little Richard, David Bowie, Barbra Streisand, Elton John, and others, either directly or indirectly, were under his thrall. As seen in an iconic photograph taken in 1956 at the Riviera Hotel, for instance, Liberace and Elvis adopt veneers of each other's persona. Notably, Elvis dons Liberace's signature sparkling coat and takes his advice to add more "glitz," a move that helped catapult him into stardom.[15]

Liberace also influenced classical organists, who pushed against the sober, ecclesiastic connotations of their instrument, including the "Liberace of the organ loft," Virgil Fox, known for his "heavy organ" Bach performances with light shows, and more recently, the rhinestone-studded Cameron Carpenter, who would eventually perform Chopin's "Revolutionary" piano étude with his feet on the organ's pedal board. Superstar concert pianist Lang Lang channels Liberace, freely contorting his face as he gazes toward the heavens onstage. In sacred spaces, pianist-evangelist Dino Kartsonakis continues to reach a sector of Liberace's audience today as his near clone in Branson, Missouri—a sanitized hologram of Las Vegas—as he brings Jesus to bedazzled audiences hypnotized by his burnished arpeggios and digital bling.

Liberace wrought his performance tactics when contemplating his boyhood idol, the nineteenth- and twentieth-century-straddling superstar concert pianist Ignacy Jan Paderewski, who actively aspired to reach a broad listening public. (Consider his pioneering outreach through the film *Moonlight Sonata* [1937].) The enamored Polish public so awesomely venerated Paderewski that they inaugurated him prime minister. Liberace aspired to his condition, emulating his publicly minded bravura and tending to overt American fantasies, drawing awe through his astonishingly large fortune amassed as the world's highest-paid performer. Through the same artery, nineteenth-century pianism's pull worked its way via Liberace to another Vegas magnate drawn to surface dreaming: Donald Trump. Attracted to Liberace's larger-than-life charisma and prosperity, Trump came to adopt aspects of his predecessor's trademark qualities—not only a love of pink marble and gold leaf, but also his democratic traits and "calculated outrage," which he distinctly modulated to populism in shaping his political performances.

Liberace preinterpreted works that might not reach an audience disposed to find entry points, masticating for them the music and contracting multivalence. Perhaps, Liberace's approach might invite comparisons to universal design, a concept championing accessibility for the greatest number of individuals.[16] Trump would endeavor to reach many, but not necessarily as many as possible, contrasting to Liberace's "something for everybody" paradigm. Paralleling Liberace's musical medleys of musical fragments, Trump selects the most provocative of surfaces of others in his speeches, less concerned with veracity or consistency than generating visceral responses, often at the expense of the marginalized, however. While Liberace invited more open fantasizing on narrowed surfaces of truth, Trump moves further toward personal abstraction, imposing his own fantasies as reality and further reducing his audience's range of more individual, democratic propensity to dream. Both Liberace and Trump have appealed to the same audience, yet the former invited them to play along, while the latter played them.

Singing praises to Western culture in a speech in Warsaw, Trump proclaimed, "We write symphonies. We pursue innovation. We celebrate our ancient heroes, embrace our timeless traditions and customs, and always seek to explore and discover brand-new frontiers. We reward brilliance. We strive for excellence, and cherish inspiring works of art that honor God."[17] Yet foregrounding surfaces of surfaces, Trump proposed eliminating funding for the National Endowment for the Arts to make America rich again.[18] Trumping aesthetic experiences, the politician's idea of classical music extolled power.[19]

Liberace's musical surfaces translated to aspects of his accessible public persona. He seldom disclosed the intimate details of his personal life, suing for libel and defamation those suggesting fundamental unavailability to women. Out in plain view, though, Liberace's leanings were "as democratically invisible as the emperor's new clothes," Dave Hickey writes.[20] Liberace imaginatively directed public interpretation of his outward surfaces as wholesomely epicene, catering to the idealized, amorous fantasies of his conservative, middle-aged female audience disillusioned by their boorish, farting-in-the-bed husbands.[21] Analogously, a litigiously oriented Trump would pivot his illusions to pronounce sterling, upstanding Christian virtuousness. Illuminating commonalities and departures, a photograph by David McGough taken in 1984 shows Trump and Liberace standing together in the lobby of a boutique in Trump Tower. Liberace dons a genuine fur coat, charmed by the surface hide, not the whole, living animal, as he paralleled with his performances of skinned musical works. Trump, however, stands closer to a giant stuffed animal with a *faux*-taxidermized surface, suggesting further favor of artifice.

Liberace's wide-reaching musical inclusivity lent itself to populist transformation under the hands of Trump, shifting narratives as a Vegas-turned-world performer selectively satisfying the masses chasing their American Dreams. Liberace's democratic Vegas pianism, archetypally labeled unworthy of conversation within serious spheres, unexpectedly shaped much of the cultural and political landscape of the twentieth and twenty-first centuries. How his legacy will continue to morph and reach into the future can, perhaps, only be left to active fantasy.

Notes

1. Bégout introduces the term *zeropolis* for Las Vegas in Bruce Bégout, *Zeropolis: The Experience of Las Vegas* (London: Reaktion Books, 2003).

2. On a metaphorical basis, this chapter works with the "surface-depth" model prevalent in music analysis. For an ontological evaluation of the idea, see Robert Fink, "Going

Flat: Post-Hierarchical Music Theory and the Musical Surface," in *Rethinking Music*, ed. Nicholas Cook and Mark Everist (New York: Oxford University Press, 1999).

3. See Darden Asbury Pyron, *Liberace: An American Boy* (Chicago: University of Chicago Press, 2000), 270–71.

4. See Lydia Goehr, *The Imaginary Museum of Musical Works: An Essay in the Philosophy of Music* (Oxford: Clarendon Press, 1994).

5. Pyron, *Liberace: An American Boy*, 179.

6. Richard Corliss, "Liberace: The Evangelist of Kitsch," *Time*, November 3, 1986.

7. Liberace Girl, "Liberace Plays the Moonlight Sonata at the Johnny Carson Show (1984)," 2019, https://www.youtube.com/watch?v=A02JIliHgGk.

8. Kenneth Hamilton, "A Suitable Prelude," in *After the Golden Age: Romantic Pianism and Modern Performance* (New York: Oxford University Press, 2008).

9. Cf. Mitchell Morris, *The Persistence of Sentiment: Display and Feeling in Popular Music of the 1970s* (Berkeley: University of California Press, 2013), 99.

10. Pyron, *Liberace: An American Boy*, 54.

11. See Ivan Raykoff, *Liberace's Musical/Material Appeal*, vol. 1 (New York: Oxford University Press, 2018).

12. Nicholas Mathew, "Gould and Liberace; or, The Fate of Nineteenth-Century Performance Culture," *Journal of Musicological Research* 39, nos. 2–3 (2020): 231–45.

13. Brahms (in 1886), *Johannes Brahms im Briefwechsel mit Joseph Joachim*, ed. Andreas Moser (Berlin, 1912), 220.

14. Cf. Busoni's recollection of pianist Friedheim performing in Edward Dent, *Ferruccio Busoni, a Biography* (London: Eulenburg, 1974), 47.

15. For more on Liberace's influence on Elvis, see Richard Zoglin, *Elvis in Vegas: How the King Reinvented the Las Vegas Show* (New York: Simon & Schuster, 2019).

16. Corliss, "Liberace." See also Aimi Hamraie, *Building Access: Universal Design and the Politics of Disability* (Minneapolis: University of Minnesota Press, 2017).

17. Ryan Teague Beckwith, "Read Trump's Remarks on 'Defending Civilization' in Poland," *Time*, July 6, 2017, https://time.com/4846924/read-president-trumps-remarks-on-defending-civilization-in-poland/.

18. Eileen Kinsella, "President Trump Is Trying to Eliminate the National Endowment for the Arts—Again—in His Just-Released 2021 Budget Proposal," Artnet News, February 10, 2020, https://news.artnet.com/art-world/trump-proposes-eliminating-nea-and-neh-again-1774236.

19. Alex Ross, "Toscanini, Trump, and Classical Music as a Symbol of Power," *New Yorker*, July 12, 2017, https://www.newyorker.com/culture/cultural-comment/toscanini-trump-and-classical-music-as-a-symbol-of-power.

20. Dave Hickey, *Air Guitar: Essays on Art & Democracy* (Los Angeles: Art Issues Press, 1997), 55.

21. Cf. Morris, *Persistence of Sentiment*, 95–108.

PART V

Making Book

When now the boy, whose childish thoughts aspire
To loftier aims, and make him ramble high'r,
Grown wild, and wanton, more embolden'd flies
Far from his guide, and soars among the skies.
The soft'ning wax, that felt a nearer sun,
Dissolv'd apace, and soon began to run.
The youth in vain his melting pinions shakes,
His feathers gone, no longer air he takes:
Oh! Father, father, as he strove to cry,
Down to the sea he tumbled from on high,
And found his Fate; yet still subsists by fame,
Among those waters that retain his name.

13

Comedy Tonight

Broadway Musicals on the Las Vegas Strip

ARREANNA ROSTOSKY

In their 1955 book, *Playtown, U.S.A.*, journalists Katharine Best and Katharine Hillyer recall a flight into Las Vegas: "In the early morning hours, when Broadway is dim to airplanes above . . . little Las Vegas presents such a pulsing dazzle of incandescence that the most sophisticated air traveler is apt to cry out in childlike wonder. 'Like an embezzler's dream, these diamonds in the desert,' one poetic passenger murmured upon seeing the show for the first time. Another, less poetic, simply bawled, 'There she is! There's Vegas!'"[1] Less than fifteen years after the first major casino opened in the area, Las Vegas was established as a sparkling, glittering man-made mecca in the middle of the harsh southwestern desert, a place where tourists sought to lose themselves in the surreal swirl of lights, entertainment, and excess the gleaming city had to offer. And this city, drawing in visitors from all over, managed, according to Best and Hillyer, to outshine the other major cultural mecca of the United States: Broadway.

What feeds into the magnetic aura of Las Vegas? An obvious answer is that a portion of the city's allure stems from its long history of being *the* American town where living on the edge is the norm. Lucius Beebe describes it as "the national dream of something for nothing, [finding] quintessential expression in dice, roulettes, and decks of painted cards."[2] Another answer comes in the form of the incredibly dynamic culture that grew up around the city to protect and supplement its image as the place where morals are ignored, drinks cannot be drunk fast enough, and money cannot be bet quick enough. In the midst of this whirlwind of cultural development, an entertainment industry also grew up around Las Vegas. Naturally, various entertainers and impresarios wanted a piece of the disreputable pie the Strip had to offer, resulting in an influx of acts, which included cut-down versions of Broadway musicals. But why, of all available options, were *musicals* chosen? Vegas's moniker of "Sin City" more readily conjures images of smoky jazz bars and burlesque acts than a sprightly dance number like "The Cowman and the Farmer Should Be Friends" from *Oklahoma!* (1943). Yet the resonance between Vegas and Broadway is undeniable. They are very much kindred spirits, cities that hum with the perpetual promise of escape and fantasy. They offer the chance to witness the impossible.

Despite their relatively early entry onto the Las Vegas entertainment scene, however, Broadway shows have failed to establish strong roots along the Strip; the relationship began somewhat tentatively and remains fragile, with transferred shows generally failing to match the success of their New York counterparts. Most of these productions were not just shipped in from Broadway unchanged, however: the score and book were typically cut down to run ninety minutes without an intermission, almost half the length of a typical two-act show. The practice of creating shortened "tab shows" took off around the turn of the twentieth century in vaudeville circuits and became the dominant method for adapting Broadway musicals for Vegas casinos. The table below offers a catalog of the musicals that have played on the Strip in tab form.[3]

TABLE 13.1 Musicals that have played on the Las Vegas Strip

Year	Show Title	Casino
1953	*Annie Get Your Gun*	Flamingo
1953	*Panama Hattie*	Frontier
1955	*Guys and Dolls*	Royal Nevada
1956	*Pajama Game*	Riviera; later transferred to the Dunes
1957	*Damn Yankees*	Riviera
1958	*Li'l Abner*	Riviera
1960	*Destry Rides Again*	Riviera
1960	*La Plume de Ma Tante*	Riviera
1960	*The World of Suzy Wong*	Riviera
1961	*Flower Drum Song*	Thunderbird
1961	*Gypsy*	Riviera
1961	*Irma La Douce*	Riviera
1961	*Tenderloin*	The Dunes
1962	*Bye Bye Birdie*	Riviera
1962	*Guys and Dolls*	The Dunes
1962	*South Pacific*	Thunderbird
1963	*Anything Goes/High Button (double bill)*	Thunderbird
1963	*Flower Drum Song*	Thunderbird

Year	Show Title	Casino
1964	*A Funny Thing Happened on the Way to the Forum*	Riviera
1965	*Hello, Dolly!*	Riviera
1967	*Fiddler on the Roof*	Caesars Palace
1967	*Funny Girl*	Riviera
1967	*Hello, Dolly!*	Riviera
1967	*Sweet Charity*	Caesars Palace
1967	*That Certain Girl*	Thunderbird
1968	*Mame*	Caesars Palace
1969	*Flower Drum Song*	Thunderbird
1969	*Many Happy Returns*	Desert Inn
1971	*Fiddler on the Roof*	Union Plaza
1972	*Cabaret*	Union Plaza
1973	*Funny Girl*	Union Plaza
1973	*Oklahoma!*	Union Plaza
1973	*Promises, Promises*	Union Plaza
1973	*The Sound of Music*	Union Plaza
1973	*South Pacific*	Union Plaza
1974	*Hello, Dolly!*	Union Plaza
1974	*The Music Man*	Union Plaza
1974	*Oklahoma!*	Union Plaza
1974	*The Unsinkable Molly Brown*	Union Plaza
1977	*Grease*	Aladdin
1978	*Can-Can*	Union Plaza
1979	*Anything Goes*	Union Plaza
1980	*George M!*	Union Plaza
1980	*Top Banana*	Union Plaza
1982	*42nd Street*	Caesars Palace
1982	*I Love My Wife*	Union Plaza
1983	*Chicago*	Union Plaza
1984	*The Best Little Whorehouse in Texas*	Union Plaza
1985	*A Chorus Line*	Sahara Las Vegas
1985	*Fiddler on the Roof*	Union Plaza
1986	*A Funny Thing Happened on the Way to the Forum*	Union Plaza
1986	*Gypsy*	Union Plaza
1987	*Ain't Misbehavin'*	Sahara Las Vegas
1987	*Never Too Late*	Union Plaza
1988	*42nd Street*	Sahara Las Vegas
1993	*Starlight Express*	Las Vegas Hilton
1995	*Guys and Dolls*	Desert Inn
1999	*Chicago**	Mandalay Bay
1999	*Rent**	Las Vegas Hilton
2000	*Footloose*	Rio
2000	*Smokey Joe's Cafe*	Caesars Palace

(*continued*)

TABLE 13.1 *(continued)*

Year	Show Title	Casino
2003	*Mamma Mia!**	Mandalay Bay
2004	*Saturday Night Fever*	Sahara Las Vegas
2004	*We Will Rock You!*	Paris Las Vegas
2005	*Avenue Q*	Wynn Las Vegas
2006	*Hairspray*	Luxor
2006	*Phantom—The Las Vegas Spectacular*	Venetian
2007	*The Producers*	Paris Las Vegas
2007	*Spamalot*	Wynn Las Vegas
2008	*Jersey Boys**	The Palazzo
2009	*The Lion King*	Mandalay Bay
2011	*Jersey Boys**	Paris Las Vegas
2012	*The Best Little Whorehouse in Texas*	The Plaza (formerly the Union Plaza)
2012	*Rock of Ages*	The Venetian; later transferred to the Rio
2013	*Million Dollar Quartet*	Harrah's Las Vegas
2014	*Mamma Mia!**	Tropicana

*Musicals that ran as a standard two-act show as the sit-down (permanent) production in a casino.

The phenomenon of the Broadway-Vegas transfer is something that remains relatively unconsidered in musical theater scholarship, a situation that is due in part to the lack of significant documentation of these shows. Yet some primary source material for these productions does exist, in the form of edited scripts and business letters; an analysis of this material sheds some light on the decision-making process for bringing Broadway productions to Las Vegas and on how the casinos benefited from producing such entertainment for their guests. Using these materials and others, this chapter explores the emergence and evolution of Broadway shows in Las Vegas and considers how "success" for these shows has been redefined over the years.

The Ascent of Sin City

Historically, Las Vegas served as a place where travelers took a brief respite from the harsh environment of the desert, but the region really found its stride as a tourist destination by the early 1940s following decades of infrastructure expansion in the Southwest.[4] After Thomas Hull opened El Rancho Vegas just off Highway 91 in 1941, a flurry of other casino and resort openings in the following years established Las Vegas's famous Strip. In addition to the Flamingo, opened in 1946 by the ill-fated mobster Benjamin "Bugsy" Siegel, the next decade saw the opening of nineteen other casinos, including the Thunderbird, the Desert

Inn (with an eighteen-hole golf course), the Sahara (housing a "full Broadway musical-comedy size" stage),[5] the Royal Nevada, the Riviera, the Moulin Rouge (the only interracial resort on the Strip), and the Dunes (boasting an ice-skating rink).

With the influx of new casinos, each establishment sought to draw tourists through *their* doors, spending money and building special facilities to house celebrity acts. The earliest of these included Jimmy Durante, who played the unfortunate opening of the Flamingo.[6] Abbott and Costello (also at the Flamingo), Eartha Kitt and Liberace (El Rancho Vegas), Betty Hutton and Patti Page (the Desert Inn), Rosemary Clooney (the Thunderbird), Zsa Zsa Gabor and Elvis (both at the New Frontier), Red Skelton and the Andrews Sisters (the Sahara), and Frank Sinatra (at the Sands) were just a few of the numerous performers to set foot on a casino stage. Many of the artists who spent any significant amount of time in Las Vegas, Liberace in particular, headlined at various casinos throughout their career.

Entertainers in Las Vegas were often the premiere performers in the country and were paid premiere prices accordingly. Liberace was the first performer to be paid $50,000 per week for his services at the Riviera (up from $6,500 per week at El Rancho just a few years earlier).[7] Other performers were often paid upwards of $20,000. And these shows were kept on a tight schedule—mostly for the benefit of the casinos, who wanted the audience back gambling at the slots and tables.[8] Such steep performance fees were not sustainable for most casinos long-term, and the lack of headline entertainment plaguing entertainment establishments across the country by the early 1950s compounded the issue. In response, nightclub owners toyed with the idea of bringing in tab shows to supplement their performance roster early on and to help make up for lost revenue.[9] Although by this time tab shows had faded in popularity alongside the decline of vaudeville, the genre would become a powerful tool for Vegas producers looking for an economical entertainment option that could also fit within the desired runtime constraints set by casinos.

The Pre-Vegas History of Tab Shows

The tabloid show (or tab show, as they were soon called) arose as a new development in theater entertainment earlier in the century. H. A. Peterman, in a 1917 article for *Billboard*, provides a basic understanding of how the genre developed and offers information about the business of tab shows.[10] According to Peterman's account, and those of other theater journalists, it is evident that the tab show did not have an auspicious beginning.

The tab show was developed as a new and less expensive alternative to vaudeville shows—a stepsibling of what Peterman terms "vest pocket editions" of stage productions.[11] In the earliest days, managers provided cheap costumes made of cheesecloth for their, at best, modestly talented cast, who in turn performed traditional vaudeville-esque bit parts, typically involving popular blackface routines. Peterman notes that at this time some managers were beginning to adapt farce comedies, with moderate success, by cutting them down to a shorter duration while retaining the crucial plot material; this truncated format would eventually become a standard tactic for translating major theater productions to the tab-show stage.[12]

At the time he was writing, Peterman estimated that there were at least two hundred tab-show companies touring the United States, with cast and crew sizes of between ten and twenty-five people. The average weekly salary paid to these companies hovered just under $300 for a company of about ten people. He also noted that larger tab companies of eighteen to twenty people were growing in popularity and in financial success, which he took as a sign that tab shows were gaining significant traction as a legitimate form of entertainment.[13]

Peterman and other journalists writing between 1910 and the mid-1920s communicate a sense of urgency to prove the cultural worth of the tab genre. As Peterman writes, the tab show was firmly rooted in the vaudeville tradition, bringing with it several associations with cheaper, less artful entertainment. Part of what marred the genre's reception early on was the practice by many tab companies of pirating material; managers would often produce shows without paying royalties, most specifically when the tab shows were shortened versions of popular stage productions, such as musicals and plays. This practice, however, was in the process of being rectified by the mid-1920s, which Al Bridge poetically acknowledges in a 1926 article: "The black stigma of piracy that has clung like an evil odor to tabloid for so long is gradually beginning to blow away."[14]

By the mid-1920s, several articles in *Billboard*, which by then had a dedicated tabloid department, addressed the tab show's improving status in the entertainment world.[15] In addition to tab producers being forced to pay royalties on borrowed material, the overall quality of the productions seemed to be improving to observers, which was reflected in the substantial increase in the weekly salaries offered to tab companies (up to $1,000–$2,000 per week for the best companies).[16] Producers, managers, and performers were beginning to take pride in what they were offering to the theatergoing public, whereas audiences were seeking more elaborate (or at least more substantive) productions. Perhaps Bridge states it best: "[The tabloid] is—or should be—the best seller, reduced to bargain rates, without diminishing their original luster."[17] This conscious move to demand a certain level of excellence translated into a call for quality control for productions as well as a call for a professional organization for tab-show developers.[18]

While it is unclear whether a professional organization was developed specifically for tab-show producers, there was a sudden move to legitimize the genre and its business model. In 1927 a new professional association affiliated with the National Amusement Association, the Southeastern Manager's Association, was established to assist in booking tab shows.[19] The Actors' Equity Association made a ruling as to the maximum running time of tab shows (seventy minutes were allowed; shows exceeding this duration would be contracted under a stock contract, which allowed a maximum of ten shows per week).[20] Each of these moves toward regulating tab-show companies and their productions speaks to the popularity of the genre by the close of the 1920s.

Tab Shows in Las Vegas

Around mid-1952, casino owners in Las Vegas produced tab versions of musical comedies starring legit stage stars, hoping the combination of light entertainment and known stage personalities would bring in audiences while costing the casino much less than hosting a single headliner. The gamble was a success for Hal Braudis at the Thunderbird Casino and Hotel. His concoction required an in-house cast and set, only changing out the main star as needed, unlike package shows booked by fellow impresario Frank Sennes (at the Desert Inn), which required high transportation costs for the whole production and cast.[21]

Less than a year later, in early 1953, other casinos were developing alternative forms of entertainment to fill the void left by a limited supply of headline performers; an article in *Variety* noted that "there aren't enough names to go around, and since the needs of this gaming centre [*sic*] are so great, new entertainment formats must be developed." Water shows and ice shows were developed or at least considered by a few casinos. Beyond these more unusual solutions, casino impresarios primarily considered "cafe units" (referring to tab or package shows) to be drawn from legit stage material.[22] Tab versions of the Broadway shows *Panama Hattie* and *Annie Get Your Gun* were under development concurrently in 1953, with *Hattie* set to open March 23 at the Frontier Hotel and *Annie* on March 19 at the Flamingo.

The Flamingo's production of *Annie Get Your Gun* met with moderate success. In the media, the show was depicted as a litmus test for the practicality of producing tab versions of legit musicals in Las Vegas: "First of a series of tabshows [*sic*] from w.k. [well known] musicals, [*Annie*] will be a good test booking for this nitery [*sic*] mecca on the prowl for something different. Without top names in lead roles, management is also taking a close gander to find out whether pop musicomedies [*sic*] can offset dwindling supply of headliners." The review, by Bill Willard, is favorable overall, noting the quality of the performers and the production. He adds that the "choice of *Annie* to begin the series [of tab shows at the Flamingo] was wise. Filled with fave tunes, many of which have become standards, the production has sparkle in its 80-minute running time."[23]

Although the show appeared poised for success, by the end of 1953 it was clear that the Las Vegas tab-show experiment was over. An article in *Billboard* announced the closure of the most recent tab show, a version of *The Student Prince* (1924), after only a week of performances at the Sands, concluding that the closure "emphasized the inability of musical comedy packages to make it in this town." Other planned tab shows, including one derived from *Follow the Girls* (1944), were either canceled or, in the case of *Girls*, restructured into a more conventional vaudeville structure. The *Billboard* article suggests that the same type of package shows produced by Sennes at the Desert Inn were more likely to be successful than the ill-fated tab shows, "either because there's no book to clutter up an hour show, or the book is given only a token nod, plus the fact that the pattern is girls and more girls, then flash and some obvious comedy. . . . It doesn't run more than an hour and it puts dining room occupants in a good enough frame of mind so they stop off in the casino [to] gamble. And that, after all, is the reason for the show."[24]

It was not until 1955 that Vegas saw another tab version of a Broadway hit. Producer Sid Kuller, for the Royal Nevada Casino, brought the recent hit *Guys and Dolls* (1953) straight from Broadway, complete with most of the show's original leads intact. Boasting a cast with Vivian Blaine, Robert Alda, Sam Levene, Stubby Kaye, and B. S. Pully, *Guys and Dolls* was still a wager. In Willard's review of the show, he remarked on the risk involved in mounting such a production: "There have been other tab shows (with moderate reception accorded) along the Strip, but with the mounting frenzy for almost any form of entertainment and most spots battling for name talent, this venture was bound to make either bums or heroes out of producers Kuller and [director Manny] Frank."[25]

The risk was not merely for Kuller's and Frank's reputations; it was a financial risk, too. Earlier tab productions ran at a fairly high cost, upwards of roughly $20,000 per week. This new production of *Guys and Dolls* was revealed to cost more than $47,000 per week for the casino, with costs going down if the show were to play for its full twelve-week booking. Lucky for the Royal Nevada and Kuller, their attempt to bring musical tab shows to Vegas was remarkably successful, with its three-month run extended to five months.[26]

After the success of *Guys and Dolls*, Broadway tab shows joined the standard Las Vegas entertainment lineup, with a handful of productions mounted roughly every year following 1955. The Riviera emerged as the first major casino to regularly produce tab musicals, championed by general manager Ben Goffstein and entertainment director Sammy Lewis. After the success of *Pajama Game* (Riviera, 1956), *Damn Yankees* (Riviera, 1957), and *Li'l Abner* (Riviera, 1958), Goffstein and Lewis entered a contract with Broadway producer David Merrick in 1960 to transfer any Merrick-produced musicals to the Riviera.[27] On paper the arrangement was perfect: it provided Merrick with a production (and revenue) pipeline for his shows at the conclusion of their Broadway runs, and it provided a steady stream of proven box-office hits to bring in patrons for the Riviera. In practice, the results were anything but, and the deal came to an abrupt end in early 1962, with only two of the eight shows produced under the agreement turning a profit.[28] Undeterred, the casino continued to mount tab productions through the 1960s, including *A Funny Thing Happened on the Way to the Forum* (Riviera, 1964) and multiple runs of *Hello, Dolly!* (Riviera, 1965, 1967). Other casinos attempted to match the Riviera's Broadway lineup with productions such as *Flower Drum Song* (Thunderbird; 1963, 1969) and *Fiddler on the Roof* (Caesars Palace, 1967), among others, but none would approach the prolific output of producer Maynard Sloate and the Union Plaza starting in the 1970s.

Before being crowned "the king of the tabs," Sloate got his start in Vegas as a top jazz talent booker and later produced such shows as *Les Folies Bergere* at the Tropicana. It was when he moved to the Union Plaza in 1972 that he gained renown for his successful run of tab shows, mercilessly cutting the works of Richard Rodgers and Oscar Hammerstein II, among others, to fit the ninety-minute requirement of the casino stage.[29] Unlike other productions where the show's creators often made the necessary edits, Sloate primarily made the revisions solo. The underlying principle for him was, "We want to keep [the audience] laughing for 90 minutes and send them to the crap tables happy," so he typically adapted material that was more upbeat. The more dancing it had, the better. But, ultimately, no matter the show's subject matter, tab shows were always a loss leader necessary to getting people in the door. Per Sloate, "We realize we're going to take a loss on a musical. A musical costs three times as much. We don't do three times the business. We do one musical per year to give integrity."[30] His tab shows were a dominant force on the Strip and continued to be produced at the Union Plaza and later the Sahara through the 1980s.

Looking to the state of Vegas tab shows of the 1990s and 2000s, Broadway transplants in Vegas saw a new period of reinvention with the rebranding of Vegas as a family-friendly destination. Whereas the Sloate-era productions involved musicals that were typically a few years removed from their Broadway debut (translation: lower licensing costs), casino owners and entertainment directors returned their gaze to staging musicals that were fresh from Broadway, or even still running there. Choosing to bring brand-new productions to Las Vegas was a very pointed attempt to legitimize casinos as entertainment centers, where they now boasted custom-built theaters for shows.[31] As then president and chief operator office of the Luxor, Felix Rappaport, remarked in 2005, "We're no longer in the casino or hospitality or tourism business. Entertainment is our business." Excitement over the future of Broadway in Las Vegas in the new millennium was palpable in various press outlets, including Jesse Green's assertion,

"If it isn't already, Las Vegas will soon be the second city of Broadway, home to more New York musicals than any market outside Manhattan."[32]

After the flurry of Broadway arrivals in the mid-2000s (including *Mamma Mia!* [2003], *Avenue Q* [2005], *Phantom—The Las Vegas Spectacular* [2006], and *Spamalot* [2007], among others), demand for Broadway shows as headline casino entertainment abated. In recent years, *Jersey Boys* (2008, 2011) and *Rock of Ages* (2012) managed to run through 2017 and 2018, respectively, though no new long-term Broadway transplants have opened since.[33]

Defining Show Business "Success" on the Strip

Live shows in Vegas were always designed to attract gambling clientele, but there exists a tension about how a show's "success" on the Strip is measured. Looking at the Riviera's production agreement with Merrick, success was measured as much by a show's box-office figures as the crowds flowing to the casino floor. Conversely, for Sloate and the Union Plaza, tab shows were a means to an end, a customer recruitment tool where box-office success was secondary. Although not diametrically opposed, the Riviera's and the Union Plaza's different models point to the difficulty in defining what a Broadway musical's "success" is in the casino environment. After all, musicals have been a steady presence on the Strip since 1953, yet myriad media articles over the decades have claimed that Broadway's Vegas reign was now truly imminent.[34]

In the new millennium, profit and run length have reemerged as the key metrics of a show's success in Vegas. Unlike the early days where Broadway tab-show runs were scheduled by weeks instead of years, now many shows are scheduled to fulfill a contracted run of several years. Being unable to meet that obligation due to poor ticket sales creates a very public "failure" of the show, even if it did enjoy a comfortably long run of a few years (a feat that is not easy to achieve on Broadway!).[35] This shift in how Broadway shows are positioned in Las Vegas—from customer acquisition to profit generation—lies at the crux of the uneasy existence musicals have had on the Strip. Gambling may be risky, but as Rappaport points out, "Broadway, which arguably has the greatest concentration of live entertainment in the country, also has a failure rate of 90 percent. . . . Face it, the financial model here is much better."[36] Although he may have been right that Broadway sees more misses than hits, his comment speaks to what might be the fatal flaw for musicals in Las Vegas: a hit in show business is never guaranteed, and the house *does not* always win, even if that house is in Vegas.

In viewing Broadway musicals as a guaranteed crowd-pleaser, many casino impresarios have ignored the clear fact that, historically, long runs for Broadway shows in Vegas are rare. The Broadway tab show instead found greatest success as an ever-renewing oasis of new productions, which in many ways aligns perfectly with the constant motion and reinvention of the Strip. Ultimately, though, memory is short, and the allure of defying the odds is integral to the way of life in Vegas; we can be sure that casinos will continue to take a gamble on Broadway.

Notes

1. Katharine Best and Katharine Hillyer, *Las Vegas, Playtown U.S.A.* (New York: David McKay, 1955), 4.

2. Lucius Beebe, foreword to *Las Vegas, Playtown U.S.A.*, xi.

3. Although the listing is thought to be as complete as possible, the research process is not infallible and the potential of having missed a production, particularly if it was short-lived, is possible. All shows listed were tab productions except those that are asterisked, which indicates musicals that ran as a standard two-act show as the sit-down (permanent) production in a casino. National tours that played in casino theaters such as the tour series held at the Desert Inn and the Aladdin in the 1980s and 1990s, respectively, were omitted from the list, as those were neither tab productions nor intended to be permanent installments at the given casino.

4. For a brief video documentary on the history of Las Vegas, see the *Las Vegas Sun*'s eleven-part documentary series titled "Boomtown: The Story behind Sin City," http://www.lasvegassun.com/history/video/.

5. Best and Hillyer, *Las Vegas, Playtown U.S.A.*, 67.

6. Poor weather and timing made the opening of the Flamingo a complete disaster, a disaster from which Bugsy would never recover (he was murdered not too long after for his failure).

7. Best and Hillyer, *Las Vegas, Playtown U.S.A.*, 98.

8. Another amusing tale from Best and Hillyer: "Among other things, . . . dinner shows are timed to a tight hour and fifteen minutes so that patrons can't stay away from those lonely old crap tables too long. It is not beyond imagination that a Judy Garland would be bagged by the stage manager should she respond too often to encores, or at least be carried bodily offstage. If it hadn't been Grand Opening night for the Riviera one memorable evening . . ., it surely would have happened to Liberace, who so enraptured himself and audience with his appearances . . . that he joyously overstayed his time by an hour. Reliable sources report that even the cash registers broke out in a cold sweat." Best and Hillyer, *Las Vegas, Playtown U.S.A.*, 10–11.

9. See "Shortage of Headliners May Cue Tab Productions," *Variety*, January 31, 1952, 45; and "Cafe Packages Pay Off Again," *Billboard*, May 10, 1952, 15.

10. According to a later byline, Peterman at some point served as a manager, producer, and performer for tab shows. See H. A. Peterman, "The Tabloid Show," *Billboard*, January 10, 1920, 9.

11. A 1915 *Billboard* article about the growing popularity of tab shows in the South notes: "Vaudeville is too costly for the small-town manager. Ergo, the tab. show." Julian T. Baber, "Tab. Craze in the South," *Billboard*, December 18, 1915, 115.

12. H. A. Peterman, "The 'Tab' Show," *Billboard*, December 22, 1917, 21.

13. Peterman, "The 'Tab' Show," 160. The rest of Peterman's article contains practical advice and observations about how tab shows have been managed historically, detailing corrupt managerial tactics to extract money from towns and aspiring performers, and solutions for avoiding such problems should the reader go into tab show business.

14. Al Bridge, "'Tabs' on Eve of Recognition," *Billboard*, August 14, 1926, 55.

15. See "'Pay or Play' Contracts for Tab. Musical Shows," *Billboard*, August 30, 1924, 6; Ray Adair, "Vital Facts about Tab Show Business," *Billboard*, October 2, 1926, 31; and Al Bridge, "'Tabs' on Eve of Recognition," *Billboard*, August 14, 1926, 55, 129.

16. Peterman, "The Tabloid Show," 9.

17. Bridge, "'Tabs' on Eve of Recognition," 129.

18. A Tab Artist, "The Forum: Organizing the 'Tab.' Field," *Billboard*, April 24, 1926, 49.

19. "Newly Organized Association to Give Tab. Shows More Work," *Billboard*, June 25, 1927, 30.

20. "Actors' Equity Association: Tab. Show Limit 70 Minutes," *Billboard*, October 15, 1927, 38.

21. Bill Smith, "Stage Stars Give Clubs Big Results," *Billboard*, October 25, 1952, 1, 17.

22. "Booking of Ted Mack Amateur Hour Shows Las Vegas in Foraging Mood," *Variety*, February 18, 1953, 51. The article notes, "Las Vegas is the top purchaser of cafe units. The show current in the Latin Quarter, NY, is expected to be packaged for Las Vegas."

23. Bill Willard, "Unit Review—'Annie Get Your Gun' (Flamingo, Las Vegas)," *Variety*, March 25, 1953, 69. Willard mentions that the Flamingo, in anticipation of *Annie*'s success, ordered several other tab versions of legit shows, including *Girl Crazy* (1930), *Where's Charley?* (1952), *Gentlemen Prefer Blondes* (1949), and *On Your Toes* (1936). None of these would reach fruition.

24. "Tab Shows Fail to Make Vegas Grade," *Billboard*, December 19, 1953, 18.

25. Bill Willard, "Royal Nevada—'Guys and Dolls,'" *Variety*, August 17, 1955, 59.

26. The show's success was owed in part to its successful (and long) Broadway run as well as upcoming movie version, which meant that it had a significant amount of positive buzz surrounding its opening in Vegas. These points are noted in Willard's review.

27. "Broadway Musical Shows New Vegas Riviera Policy," *Hollywood Reporter*, February 4, 1960, 1.

28. Herb Stein, "January 12, 1962 (Page 11 of 36)," *Philadelphia Inquirer Public Ledger*, January 12, 1962.

29. William B. Collins, "He's the Show-Stripper at the Casinos," *Philadelphia Inquirer*, July 4, 1984.

30. Laura Deni, "Broadway in Las Vegas," *Billboard*, January 29, 1983, B39.

31. Custom-designed theaters during this period include a $42 million venue for *Phantom—The Las Vegas Spectacular* at the Venetian (1,815 seats) and a $40 million venue for *Avenue Q* (1,200 seats, expanded to 1,500 for *Spamalot*). Brock Radke, "Encore Theater's Headliners Expand Wynn's Entertainment Dynasty," *Las Vegas Weekly*, December 6, 2017.

32. Jesse Green, "Live on the Strip: Broadway's Second City," *New York Times*, October 2, 2005.

33. The 2012 opening of the Smith Center, Las Vegas's current hub for Broadway tours, may have satiated locals' appetites for musical theater and potentially reduced some demand for Broadway tab shows on the Strip. However, given the differences in dramatic structure (two acts versus ninety minutes) and audiences (locals versus casino-goers/tourists), the Smith Center's touring slate is likely not cannibalizing the market for Broadway tab productions. Additionally, one can likely expect more tab shows to be announced in the coming years as the effects of the COVID-19 pandemic lessen on the entertainment industry.

34. Examples include Vernon Scott, "All Good Productions Go to Desert Heaven," *Washington Post Times-Herald*, June 18, 1961. Diane Haithman writes, "The city reinvents itself again, gambling that Broadway-style shows and stage stars will lure new visitors," in "Vegas Ups the Ante," *Los Angeles Times*, July 18, 1999. See also Robert Hofler, "Road Report: Las Vegas: Sin City Gives Broadway Another Roll," *Variety*, September 9–15, 2002, A4; and Jeff Lunden, "Broadway's Latest Frontier: Las Vegas," *Morning Edition*, September 28, 2005, https://www.npr.org/transcripts/4857945.

35. On the issue of runs cut short by poor sales, Michael Paskevich remarks, "A shortened but well-staged version of Andrew Lloyd Webber's flimsy *Starlight Express* was derailed in 1997 at the Las Vegas Hilton some two years ahead of schedule. Just not enough tickets sold." Paskevich, "Hopes Placed on 'Chicago' to Keep Broadway in Town," *Las Vegas Review-Journal*, February 21, 1999.

36. Green, "Live on the Strip."

14

"Trouble Is, We Don't Make the Rules"

The Las Vegas Years of Jazz and Classical Violinist Ginger Smock

LAURA RISK

"Guess, I've *given up* being a contender in the jazz field. It's rough and I got tired of so many 'doors' being closed in my face, so now, I'm making myself content to be an orchestral musician," wrote violinist Ginger Smock to Canadian jazz violin collector John Reeves in May 1974 (fig. 14.1).[1] This letter, penned backstage between shows at the Flamingo Hotel in Las Vegas, marks the early months of a correspondence that was to last for more than two decades. Smock's discouraged tone belies the rich musical life that she led before becoming an orchestra musician in Las Vegas showrooms, however. Smock was a popular stage, radio, and television performer in Los Angeles from the 1940s through the 1960s. She toured nationally in the mid-1950s. She was the first African American woman to record hot-jazz improvisations on the violin and one of the first African American women bandleaders on television.

After moving to Las Vegas in 1971, Smock stepped out of the spotlight. Playing in the orchestra for Sammy Davis Jr., Frank Sinatra, Diana Ross, and many others, Smock helped turn the wheels of fantasy but rarely felt the heat of those lights herself. Instead, she dreamed of an alternate future, one that would put her back on the jazz stages where she felt she belonged. In this chapter, I map Smock's career in Las Vegas from the 1950s until the Musicians' Union strike of 1989 and document her struggles—made more challenging by gender, race, and age—for increased recognition. My sources include two formerly private collections recently deposited at the Smithsonian National Museum of African American History and Culture (NMAAHC). In 2013 I connected with Lydia Bennett, a member of Smock's extended family, and Dean Reeves, the son of

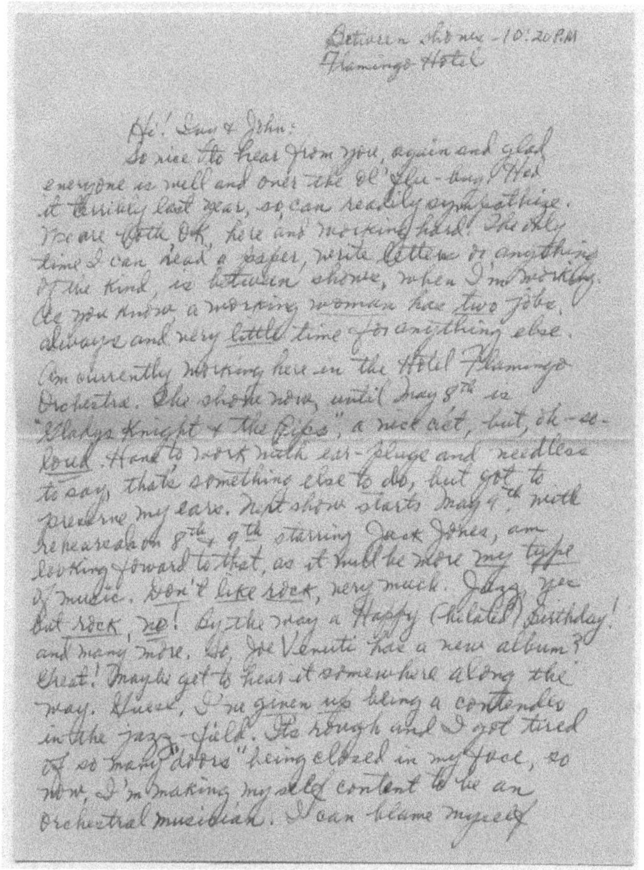

Between shows – 10:20 P.M.
Flamingo Hotel

Hi! Ivy & John:
So nice to hear from you, again and glad everyone is well and over the ol' flu-bug! Had it terribly last year, so, can readily sympathize. We are both OK, here and working hard! The only time I can read a paper, write letters or anything of the kind, is between shows, when I'm working. As you know, a working woman has two jobs, always and very little time for anything else. Am currently working here in the Hotel Flamingo Orchestra. The show now, until May 8th is "Gladys Knight & the Pips", a nice act, but, oh-so-loud. Have to work with ear-plugs and needless to say, that's something else to do, but got to preserve my ears. Next show starts May 9th with rehearsals on 8th & 9th starring Jack Jones, am looking forward to that, as it will be more my type of music. Don't like rock, very much. Jazz, yes but rock, no! By the way a Happy (belated) Birthday! and many more. So, Joe Venuti has a new album? Great! Maybe get to hear it somewhere along the way. Guess, I've given up being a contender in the jazz-field. It's rough and I got tired of so many "doors" being closed in my face, so now, I'm making myself content to be an orchestral musician. I can blame myself

FIGURE 14.1 Ginger Smock to Ivy and John Reeves, undated letter (postmarked May 3, 1974). Ginger Smock Archives, Collection of the Smithsonian National Museum of African American History and Culture, Gift of Ivy G. and Dean Tatam Reeves in memory of John Reeves. Digital copy reprinted with permission from the personal collection of Ivy G. and Dean Tatam Reeves.

John Reeves. I worked with them to digitize their family collections of Smock-related materials and, at their request, coordinate the transfer of these materials to the NMAAHC. The Bennett collection contains handwritten manuscripts and printed compositions, several studio and live recordings, and various personal and professional effects, including Smock's violin. The Reeves collection contains Smock's correspondence with John Reeves from 1973 to 1994, press clippings, photos, and a number of homemade recordings. Together, these collections now make up the Ginger Smock Archives at the NMAAHC.

The story of Smock's Las Vegas years exemplifies the importance of proactively building out the content of public archives to include underrepresented voices, or what I term proactive public archiving.[2] As Joan M. Schwartz and Terry Cook have noted, records and archives are "dynamic technologies of rule which actually *create* the histories and social realities they ostensibly only *describe*."[3] Ginger Smock is absent from jazz violin histories in part because of her lack of recordings—and this lack resulted, in part, from the "social realities" of her working life, notably her restricted opportunities as a racialized woman violinist. The materials in the Bennett and Reeves collections tell Smock's story in her own words. Proactive public archiving in a case such as this means first adding Smock's voice to the archive—for instance, to the NMAAHC archives—and then using the archive to amplify her voice in the public sphere. This chapter uses Smock's correspondence with John Reeves and additional archival sources to recount the complex lived experience of one Las Vegas violinist in the 1970s and '80s, and trace the story of an African American woman who successfully navigated a multifaceted musical career across five decades and broke ground for a new generation of performers.

Remembering in Vegas

Ginger Smock grew up in Los Angeles in the close-knit African American community—delimited by race-restrictive housing covenants—centered around Central Avenue.[4] She studied classical violin privately and was drum majorette in her high school band, all the while improvising to jazz violin records "for fun" at home.[5] On the avenue, she attended big-band performances by Duke Ellington, Count Basie, Benny Goodman, and others.[6] As an adolescent, she played with several youth orchestras, including the All-City Orchestra and the Junior Philharmonic under conductor Otto Klemperer, and later attended the Zoellner Conservatory of Music. After graduating, she led a forty-eight-member ensemble, Symphonetta, which performed "light concert music."[7] As she would later tell *DownBeat*, her goal was the classical "concert stage," presumably either as a soloist or as an orchestral musician.[8] In the early 1940s, when Smock graduated from conservatory, however, professional orchestras in the United States did not hire African American musicians, and she turned in other musical directions.[9]

From the early 1940s, Smock performed with bands such as the Sepia Tones and Ginger and Her Magic Notes, playing repertoire that ranged from hot jazz to novelty to light classical. She was bandleader with the short-lived CBS production *The Chicks and the Fiddle* in 1951 and a favorite on the local variety show *Dixie Showboat* from 1951 to 1953. She performed up and down the West Coast with the Jackson Brothers Orchestra in 1953 and from 1953 to 1955 toured nationally with Steve Gibson and his Red Caps, including a run at El Rancho in Las Vegas in 1954. By all accounts, Smock was a stunning performer: she had a "gingervating" stage presence, and her solos combined a hard-driving rhythmic sensibility with impeccable classical technique and a blues-based improvisational language punctuated by special effects, including left-hand pizzicato, trills, and glissandi.[10]

Smock's career underscores the close connections between musicians in Los Angeles and Las Vegas in the midcentury. She first performed in Las Vegas in late 1951 with the J. C. Heard Trio at the Jungle Club.[11] In 1955 she and pianist Charlie Pryme, a frequent LA collaborator, played both the Sands and the newly opened Moulin Rouge, Las Vegas's first integrated casino.[12] In 1958 she was again in Las Vegas, this time with saxophonist Jack McVea's band at Town Tavern, the only Black-owned and -operated club in the city at the time. Advertisements in the *Los Angeles Tribune* for the Town Tavern's "New Year's Party" point to an easy back-and-forth between Los Angeles and Las Vegas for both musicians and audience members: "Start the New Year off with a *Bang*!" reads one ad, promising, "Everything . . . Everybody will be there!" For the occasion, a forty-seat airplane had been chartered to fly from Los Angeles to Las Vegas and return a scant nineteen hours later.[13] The African American readership of the *Tribune* were encouraged to begin their "New Year's Eve 'partying' in Los Angeles," board the plane at midnight, join "all of the stars 'on the Strip'" for a full day of revelry at Town Tavern, and return to Los Angeles in time for dinner.[14] Events like this suggest a robust interstate gigging circuit for freelance musicians, and their audiences, that rendered the miles of mountains and desert between the two cities seemingly inconsequential.

In January 1960, Smock launched a new band, the Aristocats, with a gig at the Flamingo Hotel in Las Vegas.[15] By March talent scouts were "raving" about Smock and band, according to *Jet*, which described her jazz violin as "the hottest since Stuff Smith."[16] Two months later, the Aristocats were contracted as the house band on the SS *Catalina*, a daytime cruise ship between San Pedro (Los Angeles) and Catalina Island.[17] They renamed themselves "the Shipmates and Ginger" and for several years in the early 1960s spent their summers on the ship and their winters in Las Vegas playing venues such as the Flamingo, the Frontier, and El Cortez. The band recorded one LP, *On the S.S.* Catalina *with the Shipmates and Ginger*, of what Smock called "original island music."[18] While she took pride in this recording, her correspondence with John Reeves indicates that, musically, it was not the album she wished to "leave for posterity."[19]

After three decades as a jazz player, Smock returned to orchestral work part-time in 1970. Invited to join the George Rhodes Orchestra at the Now Grove in Los Angeles, she accompanied Sammy Davis Jr., Johnny Mathis (Smock was a featured performer), and Connie Stevens in quick succession.[20] During a preshow dance set for Dionne Warwick in February 1971, Rhodes signaled to Smock to "go up front to the mike and 'blow'" on "Bye-Bye Blackbird," and she played a "splendid ad lib violin solo."[21] Smock moved to Las Vegas later in 1971 to pursue this line of work full-time and was a successful showroom orchestra musician for more than a decade. Still, she saw this career shift as a step down and linked it to the many opportunities that she felt had been denied her. As she wrote to Reeves in the letter cited above, she had encountered too many "closed . . . doors" as a jazz player and so had decided to "content" herself with orchestral work.[22]

John Reeves was originally from England and a plumber, pipe fitter, and tile setter by trade. His interest in the jazz violin had begun in the 1930s courtesy of French radio broadcasts of Stéphane Grappelli and Django Reinhardt, and he became an avid collector. Reeves immigrated to Winnipeg, Manitoba, in 1956 with his wife, Ivy, and son, Dean, and by the early 1960s was an occasional guest on the vintage jazz shows of CBC host Gren Marsh. Later in the decade, Reeves and his family moved to Edmonton, where he was a frequent guest on local station CKUA.[23] Among the items now deposited at the NMAAHC is a tape of Reeves's first phone call to Smock, in 1973. In their conversation, Smock repeatedly associates her move into orchestral work with a lack of recording opportunities:

> JR: I read something in *Jazz Journal*. . . . [The author] said that if you'd ever heard Stuff Smith play violin, there is someone whose name is Ginger Smock who is a Stuff Smith all over again. And in his opinion, you were better than Stuff Smith. . . . This made me wonder if you had recorded or if, as a collector, I could get a tape or something.
>
> GS: . . . [I] never did have anything out that was really worthwhile because I never got a chance to. I never had anyone to record me, in other words. And I just don't happen to have anything that's even a tape that's decent. I've been doing orchestral work here now for quite a while. . . .
>
> [My demos] were little homemade things to take around trying to think that some recording company would have just listened to the fiddle and would have given me a decent session. But I didn't have that luck. So I gave up trying. And I guess I shouldn't've, but I did. I got discouraged and I went on into orchestral work.[24]

When Smock speaks of her "little homemade" recordings, she is likely referring to the ten-plus demo sides that she recorded between 1946 and 1954, as documented by jazz violin historian Anthony Barnett; many of these may be heard on the posthumous release *Strange Blues*.[25] Although Smock doesn't mention gender- or race-based discrimination outright in the above phone conversation, her description of her demos as "little homemade things" and her desire for a "decent session" suggest that she did not have the financial backing to make recordings to a high production standard, while her statement that record companies never "just listened to the fiddle" implies that they never read her as "just" a jazz violinist—presumably gendered as male—but always as a racialized woman. A 1974 letter to Reeves gives credence to this reading:

> Several years ago, when I was touring . . . many, many people asked for records then. An executive of RCA-Victor came to San Francisco, liked my playing

> so well, he rented a studio, made the tape, took it back to Hollywood to RCA. He played it for the rest of the execs there, they listened, said it was superb . . . and asked him who was the artist. He said it was a girl from L.A. and they told him I had *no-name* and they could get Joe Venuti instead. Needless to say, that "took the wind out of my sails" in more ways than one.[26]

Striking in this anecdote is the shift in the executives' tone when they discover the gender identity of the artist to whom they are listening. Whereas the performance initially strikes them as "superb," they lose interest when told that they are listening to a "girl from L.A." Presumably Smock sounded like a man to their ears, and we can imagine their discomfort at discovering that they have misgendered the soloist. Yet the story is still more complex: when Smock recounted this experience to historian Sherrie Tucker two decades later, she located the executives' rejection of her demo at the intersection of gender and race:

> In San Francisco . . . I was appearing at a place called Say When. . . . And this tall gentleman walks in and gave us his card. He was from RCA Victor. He was so impressed. He said, "Hey, Saturday I want to record you kids. I want to take it back to let the big wigs at Victor hear this." So he did. . . . He told the executives, "Sit down, I want you to hear something." So when he finished playing the two numbers, these guys were so impressed, they said, "Who on earth is playing the violin? We've never heard anything like this." And he says, "A colored girl up there in San Francisco." They said, "Aw, forget it. We've got Joe Venuti."[27]

Both anecdotes leave numerous questions unanswered. How did Smock learn about the backroom conversations of RCA Victor executives? Why did she mention race to Sherrie Tucker and not to John Reeves? What exactly does Smock mean when she writes that this rejection "took the wind out of my sails," and should we associate that with the fact that she stopped making demos around 1954? Beyond these details, however, is the fact that Smock told this story on at least two occasions, at twenty years' distance, to support her claim that there were "just too many closed doors. A lot of talent went down the drain."[28] Living and working in Las Vegas, Smock remembered her Los Angeles years not only through her many achievements but also by the opportunities denied to her.

Working in Vegas

Smock stepped easily into full-time gigging in Las Vegas after her move. Her early letters to John Reeves are often on hotel postcards, and she casually boasts of her successes, as on a Tropicana postcard that reads, "This is Hotel where I am currently working. I am concert-mistress of the Geo. Rhodes Orch. in the new Super Star Theater—working 6 nites per wk. 2 shows nitely" (fig. 14.2).[29] She also occasionally shared her opinions on the many celebrities that she worked

FIGURE 14.2 Ginger Smock to Ivy, John, Dean, and David Reeves, undated (likely December 1973). Ginger Smock Archives, Collection of the Smithsonian National Museum of African American History and Culture, Gift of Ivy G. and Dean Tatam Reeves in memory of John Reeves. Digital copy reprinted with permission from the personal collection of Ivy G. and Dean Tatam Reeves.

alongside. Playing for Gladys Knight and the Pips in 1974, she described them as "a nice act, but, oh-so-*loud*."[30] In 1976 she accompanied Julie Andrews, who was "terrific! . . . What an artist!"[31] Smock's favorite performer by far, however, was Sammy Davis Jr., whom she would later describe as "the most fantastic and the most fabulous person on stage today."[32]

As an African American woman, Smock faced a particular set of challenges in Las Vegas. Janis McKay notes that there were few women musicians in showroom orchestras before the 1970s and that even after desegregation, the "old ways [of racial and gender discrimination] died hard."[33] In fact, the archive suggests that Smock may have had a hand in integrating showroom orchestras: a passing notice in the *Los Angeles Sentinel* reads, "DON'T know when we have heard such great news as learning that violinist Ginger Smock is now a full member of the Antonio Morrelli Orchestra at the Las Vegas Sands. . . . Of course, this is a first."[34] What exactly that "first" was, however, is unknown. Still, her early successes in Vegas are attested to by a 1980 notice in the Los Angeles musicians' union newsletter: "*Ginger* has enjoyed tremendous success during her 9 years in Las Vegas, where she is playing all of the major hotel show-rooms and has been at Caesar's Palace with the Al Ramsay Orchestra for almost 5 years."[35]

Although Smock rarely described the day-to-day of her working life to John Reeves, her letters provide enough detail to roughly map her Las Vegas orchestral career from 1973 until 1989. Table 14.1 points to the diversity of her work in the 1970s followed by the ever-leaner years of the 1980s, when her gigs shrank to the single star of Sammy Davis Jr.

TABLE 14.1 Ginger Smock orchestral work, 1974–1989, as documented in her letters to John Reeves (NMAAHC-Reeves).

Date	Location	Featured Performers
November 2–22, 1973	Tropicana, Super Star Theater	Jack Benny, Pearl Bailey Show, with Louie Bellson
Closing May 8, 1974	The Flamingo	Gladys Knight and the Pips
Opening May 9, 1974	The Flamingo	Jack Jones
Closing June 5, 1974	The Flamingo	unknown
Closing July 9, 1974	The Flamingo	unknown
Opening July 11, 1974 (rehearsals on July 10)	The Flamingo	Tony Bennett
Including September 19, 1974	The Flamingo	unknown
Before April 28, 1977	Caesars Palace	Diana Ross[1]
Including August 9, 1975 (two-week run)	Las Vegas Hilton	unknown
Including October 18, 1975 (possible three-week run)	Flamingo	unknown
ca. December 30, 1975	Caesars Palace	unknown
Opening February 26, 1976 (two-week run)	Caesars Palace	Frank Sinatra
ca. March 11, 1976	Caesars Palace	Sammy Davis Jr.
Including May 30, 1976	Caesars Palace	Tom Jones
Including June 11, 1976	Caesars Palace	Sammy Davis Jr.
Including June 24, 1976	unknown, possibly Caesars Palace	Paul Anka
Including August 18, 1976 (one-week run)	Caesars Palace	Julie Andrews
Opening August 21, 1976 (one-week run)	Caesars Palace	Steve & Eydie
ca. October 18, 1976	Caesars Palace	unknown

(*continued*)

TABLE 14.1 *(continued)*

Date	Location	Featured Performers
Opening November 18, 1976	unknown, possibly Caesars Palace	Tom Jones
Including February 12, 1977	Caesars Palace	unknown
Including February 28, 1977	Caesars Palace	Andy Williams and the Pointer Sisters
Late May 1977	unknown, possibly Caesars Palace	Tom Jones
Including June 7, 1977	unknown	Lena Horne and Vic Damone
From August 26, 1977	Caesars Palace	unknown; at Caesars Palace through end of year
Including March 7, 1978	Caesars Palace	unknown
Including June 29, 1978 (one-week run)	unknown, possibly Caesars Palace	Linda Carter, TV's Wonder Woman
ca. July 6, 1978 (two-week run)	unknown, possibly Caesars Palace	Andy Williams
Including July 12, 1978	Caesars Palace	unknown
Including September 14, 1978	Caesars Palace	Sammy Davis Jr.
Opening January 25, 1979	Caesars Palace	Sammy Davis Jr.
Including October 11, 1979	unknown, possibly Caesars Palace	Tom Jones
Including June 30, 1980	Caesars Palace	unknown
Closing October 8, 1980	Caesars Palace	Frank Sinatra
Opening October 23, 1980 (two-week run)	Caesars Palace	Sammy Davis Jr.
Including April 26, 1981, show closes April 29	unknown, possibly Caesars Palace	Sammy Davis Jr. with Rip Taylor
Opening June 4, 1981	unknown, possibly Caesars Palace	Sammy Davis Jr.
September 3–9, 1981	unknown, possibly Caesars Palace	Paul Anka
September 17–23, 1981	unknown, possibly Caesars Palace	Paul Anka
May 6–19, 1981	Caesars Palace	Sammy Davis Jr. with Count Basie's Orchestra
July 23–August 5, 1982	Harrah's, Lake Tahoe, CA	Sammy Davis Jr
October 31–November 20, 1982	Harrah's, Lake Tahoe	Sammy Davis Jr. and Count Basie
January 28–February 3, 1983	Harrah's, Lake Tahoe	Sammy Davis Jr. and Count Basie
March 1983	Lake Tahoe	Sammy Davis Jr.[2]
June 24–July 7, 1983	Lake Tahoe	unknown, likely Sammy Davis Jr.

Date	Location	Featured Performers
Opening around September 10, 1984 (4 nights only)	Caesars Palace	Sammy Davis Jr. and Bill Cosby
March 5–31, 1985	Desert Inn Hotel	Sammy Davis Jr.
Opening May 8, 1985 (for two or three weeks)	Caesars Palace	Sammy Davis Jr.
Opening May 22, 1986	The Desert	Sammy Davis Jr.
November 20–26, 1986	The Desert	Sammy Davis Jr.
Closing January 29, 1987	Caesars Palace	Sammy Davis Jr. and Bill Cosby
Opening March 19 (two-week run)	Bally's Grand	Sammy Davis Jr. and Jerry Lewis
October 26–28, 1987	unknown	Sammy Davis Jr. and Jerry Lewis
November 5–11, 1987	unknown	unknown
June 2–15, 1988	unknown	Sammy Davis Jr. and Jerry Lewis
August 18–31, 1988	Bally's Grand	Sammy Davis Jr. and Jerry Lewis
February 17–19, 1989	Riverside Resort Hotel & Casino, Laughlin, NV	Eddy Arnold Show; Smock hired to contract seven string players (five violins, one viola, one cello)
Two weeks in 1989	unknown	Sammy Davis Jr. and Jerry Lewis

[1] Bill Lane, "people—places—'n' situwayshuns," *Los Angeles Sentinel*, April 28, 1977. Sources for all other items in this table are correspondence between Smock and Reeves except as noted.

[2] Peggy Gilbert, "Tuning in on Femme Musicians," *Overture*, March 1983, NMAAHC-Reeves.

By the late 1970s, Smock's work situation was precarious. When Reeves suggested a possible jazz gig in Edmonton, she expressed interest but wrote that she "[couldn't] afford to offend in any way that will 'blow my gig.' . . . The jobs are funny here and they will replace you *permanently* and *quickly*."[36] Several months later, she expressed concern that she might be "out" in the "political" Vegas milieu after missing work due to health issues.[37] This letter is remarkable for her detailed description of day-to-day life as an orchestra musician in Vegas:

> I'm trying to "hang-on," but each year becomes *harder* and *harder*. . . . I get very *little* sleep. As an example—will get home from work and try to rush to bed by *3:30 AM*, set alarm for *9:30 AM* make beds, make breakfast, clean up, dress and be back onstage at *11:45 AM*. . . . Then rehearse probably till 6:00 PM, rush home take care of Duke [their dog] and home chores . . . in concert *8:00 PM* and onstage at *7:45 PM*. . . . Just praying I can have the strength to *last*.[38]

Smock moved to Las Vegas at a transitional moment for the city. Although work was still good, the 1970s were the beginning of the "downslide of Las Vegas entertainment," a shift that McKay attributes to multiple factors: a "gradual exodus" of the Mob bosses who had run the hotel-casinos and their replacement by "corporate [owners]," an industry turn toward rock 'n' roll and away from big bands and crooners, the growing social importance of television, the disappearance of late-night lounges, and the city's unprecedented growth.[39] As the decade progressed, Smock increasingly worried what her next gig would be and, eventually, if she would have one at all. In August 1977, she wrote to Reeves that she was booked through the end of the year at Caesars Palace but hoping that nothing "*unforeseen*" would happen: "Trouble is, we don't make the rules, we just have to abide by them. Old thing called—*survival*. Right?" She and her husband briefly took on work managing apartments because, as she wrote, "Got to learn something besides the so-called show-biz routine. It's getting to be something else!"[40]

Smock found that her aging body was also a liability. In 1978 she and her husband pooled their finances, including vacation savings, to pay for a face-lift because, as she wrote, "everything nowdays [*sic*], especially in my business is geared to the *young*. They've been laying off the older and older-looking ones like 'mad' here. So, pain and all, I don't have much choice."[41] Even so, her orchestral work continued to diminish. Two years later, in February 1980, she wrote that the orchestra contractor at Caesars Palace had hired "all (mostly) very young fiddlers" and put Smock "out to pasture" with "a bunch of very unnecessary *lies*. . . . Everything has become so political here, it's *who* you know, not *what* or how *well* you can perform."[42]

Las Vegas performance styles were changing too, as documented in her letters from the early 1980s. "Not too much work for strings lately," she wrote in April 1981. "Lots of acts are cutting us out and bringing in their own musicians."[43] By February of the following year, there was "[not] a job in *sight*. First time in the 10 yrs. I've been here that there's *nothing*. Geez! They've about cut out *all* the strings in the shows."[44] In December 1982, Smock sent Reeves a newspaper article about the decline in orchestral work and added a handwritten note: "It's rough for string players, here, especially."[45] For most of the 1980s, Smock's one steady gig was with Sammy Davis Jr., who seems to have requested her for his orchestra when he played Las Vegas or nearby Lake Tahoe (fig. 14.3). When, in 1986, Sammy Davis Jr. opened in Las Vegas without Smock in the orchestra, it was "the *first* time in 16 yrs.," she wrote—and only because she had been in the hospital for surgery. She was back onstage in time to play the third and final week of the run.[46]

The late 1980s was a time of loss for Smock personally as well as for the industry in which she worked. George Rhodes—"the *best* friend I ever had in the business"—died unexpectedly in December 1985.[47] After the passing of Sammy Davis Jr. in May 1990, she shared her grief with Reeves: "He was not only the greatest and *most* talented star but a loving (to *everyone*) and caring

FIGURE 14.3 Ginger Smock and Sammy Davis Jr. backstage at Caesars Palace, November 5, 1980. Ginger Smock Archives, Collection of the Smithsonian National Museum of African American History and Culture, Gift of Ivy G. and Dean Tatam Reeves in memory of John Reeves. Digital copy reprinted with permission from the personal collection of Ivy G. and Dean Tatam Reeves.

human being. Yes, *I* miss him—always."[48] Meanwhile, the Musicians' Union strike of 1989–90 was taking its toll. Although Smock was by then semiretired, she followed the strike closely. "The hotels are trying to use all-tapes for the shows instead of live orchestras and the 'fight' is on," she wrote to Reeves. "Only thing,—the hotels are still operating and the musicians are *not*. . . . Most of the [musicians] are suffering and I feel badly for them."[49] A letter from February 1990 reads: "Well, if you haven't heard the *hotels*, here, have *destroyed* the Musicians Union. We (the union) *lost* the strike of 8 months with most of the hotel orchestras being dissolved and replaced with *taped* and synthesizers for music."[50] With Sammy Davis Jr. gone and the city's orchestras disbanded, Smock's orchestral career in Las Vegas showrooms came to an end.

Dreaming in Vegas

Throughout Smock's years in Las Vegas orchestras, she lived a double life: on the one hand, playing showrooms nightly, and on the other, imagining herself a jazz violinist again, performing and recording at the highest levels. These dreams were stoked by Reeves, who set out to relaunch her jazz career. His enthusiasm rekindled her hope that "maybe someday, somewhere, it will happen."[51] For more than a decade, in letter after letter, he reported on his attempts to secure her a recording contract and a spot at a major jazz festival, and Smock responded with cautious optimism. Yet in the end, in the words of his son, Dean, it was "a breakthrough that never was to be."[52]

Reeves first reached out to Joachim Berendt with MPS Records in Germany. Berendt was, it seems, "thrilled to bits" with Smock's playing and sent Reeves a tentative yes. "I think I've hit pay dirt," Reeves wrote to Smock in December 1975, and added a note for her husband: "So Bob—my little gal with the fiddle!—! I think she's on the brink!"[53] Smock wrote back between shows at Caesars Palace, with enthusiasm: "It's thrilling to know that people are mentioning my name in Europe . . . Who knows? Maybe it'll happen sooner than we think. In answer to Mr. Berendt, if things are right and time, ect. [*sic*] right, will be more than happy to perform in his dear country. Would absolutely *love it*!"[54] The following March, however, Berendt wrote to Reeves that MPS Records had "decided not to do it. . . . [T]hey told me: We anyway have the great violinists on MPS, even when we do not have Ginger. I'm sorry about that. I would have loved to do this record."[55] This vision of jazz violinists as interchangeable reads as an unlikely excuse from MPS given that their recent LP *Violin-Summit*, which Berendt produced, showcased the individual styles of four jazz violinists.[56] It may be that MPS, and perhaps Berendt, heard Smock's playing as derivative and therefore not deserving of a solo recording. In her December 1975 letter to Reeves, Smock opposes an implied statement, presumably by Berendt, that her playing emulates that of Stuff Smith: "Yes, at times I may sound a bit like Stuff, *but* to *me* I sound only like *Smock* . . . and *that's* the impression I hope to leave in this ole' world, before retiring to the *greatest* orchestra of all—*heaven's*."[57]

Reeves continued his efforts. He contacted Claude Nobs at the Montreux Jazz Festival, who expressed interest but did not hire Smock because she lacked a record deal.[58] He tried Norman Granz at Pablo Records, who had helped restart Stuff Smith's career in the late 1950s, but received no response.[59] He wrote to Rounder Records, Stash Records, Chiaroscuro Records, and Music Minus One, and he penned a press release–style document headed "Ginger Smock, Legendary Female Jazz Violinist, This Fairy Tale is True! It Concerns a Real 'Cinderella' of Jazz."[60] Smock, hopeful, returned to the recording studio and, in May 1980, cut a seven-song demo in Los Angeles. "Sure wish that I could get an *album* from this," she wrote to Reeves. "I'm kind of excited wish the record companies would feel the same. Only want to leave at least *one* album before it's too late and it's getting later and later."[61] But by 1982, when Reeves's efforts had still not yielded results, Smock asked him to stop trying, writing that "I'm doing *all* that I want to now. I don't want any Jazz gigs. . . . After all, they're interested in '*names*,' I can understand that and I've come to the conclusion, that everyone who has a talent, was not meant to be a *Star*."[62] Even so, she recorded one more demo in 1985, this time with a pianist—"couldn't afford anything [more]"—and asked Reeves to send a copy "overseas." "Try to envision 3 or 4 swinging guys behind me," she wrote, "also some snazzy-duds (*clothes*) ect. [*sic*], and I think we could do it. . . . Let's say a *prayer* that someone, somewhere on this globe will 'dig-it!'"[63] Reeves send the tape to Erhard Kayser in Germany the following month but seems to have received no reply.[64]

Smock's letters to Reeves suggest that, while much of her time in Las Vegas was consumed by the everyday practicalities of making a living, the city was also a site of personal fantasy and mythmaking. She wrote many letters just before going onstage or between shows, and it may be that her conversations with Reeves about record deals and European tours were spaces for her to dream into existence a continued creative life in spite of an increasingly challenging work environment.

Conclusion

Reading Smock's letters during the ten-year span in which Reeves tried to restart her jazz career, one senses a race against time. Even as he sought gigs and recording contracts for her, and as she continued recording demos, her hands were stiffening with arthritis and her eyesight deteriorating. Yet her letters also document her determination to continue playing violin for as long as she could. As her orchestral work diminished and Reeves's efforts failed to bear fruit, Smock refocused her musical energies on service work, performing at nursing homes and at church, where she was concertmaster for Christmas cantatas, played piano, sang and led the congregation in song, and played violin solos to prerecorded accompaniment on cassette tape.[65] She also received a degree of late-career recognition in her hometown of Los Angeles via Bette Yarborough Cox's BEEM Foundation and performed and spoke for that organization on several occasions.[66] Smock expressed deep gratitude for these opportunities but still dreamed of a solo album and a spot at a high-profile jazz festival.

Listening to Smock's voice through the archive, we hear aspects of her musical life that would have remained hidden otherwise, including the day-to-day grind of orchestral musicians in Las Vegas in the 1970s and the ways in which the many "closed doors" that she encountered tainted her remembering and telling of her five decades as a gigging musician. We also hear her hopes for the same late-in-life successes bestowed on her male jazz violin peers, such as Stuff Smith, Joe Venuti, and Johnny Creach, all of whom accessed a new level of stardom in their later years. Yet her letters leave much unsaid, including, for the most part, her experiences as a racialized woman in the industry. Like all archives, the Ginger Smock Archives at the NMAAHC are silent on many counts. Bringing Smock back into the public archive works to counter the narratives of invisibility that followed her across her career but is only a first step toward a full, rich reading of the complexity of her lived experience.

Notes

1. Ginger Smock to Ivy and John Reeves, undated (postmarked May 3, 1974), Ginger Smock Archives, Collection of the Smithsonian National Museum of African American History and Culture, Gift of Ivy G. and Dean Tatam Reeves in memory of John Reeves (all correspondence to/from John Reeves cited hereafter is from the Ginger Smock Archives at the NMAAHC; additional items from these archives cited as NMAAHC-Reeves) (emphasis in the original).

2. "Proactive public archiving" extends the concept of "proactive archiving" proposed by Carolyn Landau and Janet Topp Fargion in "We're All Archivists Now: Towards a More Equitable Ethnomusicology," *Ethnomusicology Forum* 21, no. 2 (2012): 126. See also Ray Edmondson, *Audiovisual Archiving: Philosophy and Principles; Commemorating the 25th Anniversary of the UNESCO Recommendation for the Safeguarding and Preservation of Moving Images* (Paris: United Nations Educational, Scientific, and Cultural Organization, 2004), 20.

3. Joan M. Schwartz and Terry Cook, "Archives, Records, and Power: The Making of Modern Memory," *Archival Science* 2, nos. 1–2 (2002): 7 (emphasis in the original).

4. See Clora Bryant et al., eds., *Central Avenue Sounds: Jazz in Los Angeles* (Berkeley: University of California Press, 1998); and Bette Yarbrough Cox, *Central Avenue—Its Rise and Fall, 1890–c. 1955: Including the Musical Renaissance of Black Los Angeles* (Los Angeles: BEEM, 1996).

5. Hal Holly [Charles Emge], "Addition to 'Girls in Jazz' Found on Coast by Holly," *DownBeat*, June 15, 1951, 8.

6. Ginger Smock, unpublished interview by Sherrie Tucker, October 28, 1993, Las Vegas (hereafter cited as Tucker interview).

7. "Bright Future Predicted for Ginger Smock," *Pittsburgh Courier*, September 20, 1947; "Fiddlin' Around," *Tele-Views* (March 1953): 36, NMAAHC-Reeves; "Aristocats Claim a Century of Musical Know-How," *Los Angeles Sentinel*, January 14, 1960.

8. Holly, "Addition to 'Girls in Jazz.'"

9. "About Us | Southeast-Symphony," Southeast Symphony, accessed August 11, 2021, https://www.southeastsymphony.com/aboutus.

10. "'Hot' Violinist Is TV Hit in Los Angeles," *Jet*, April 24, 1952, 63. For more on Smock's early career, see liner notes to Ginger Smock, *Strange Blues: Ginger Smock, the Lovely Lady with the Violin, Los Angeles Studio & Demo Recordings, 1946–1958*, compact disc (AB Fable, ABCD1-010, 2005); Anthony Barnett, "Ginger Smock: Issued and Unissued Sessions on Disc and Tape," *Fable Bulletin Violin Improvisation Studies*, no. 3 (1994): 1–12; and Laura Risk, "Ginger Smock: Narratives of Perpetual Discovery, Jazz Historiography, and the 'Swinging Lady of the Violin,'" *Journal of the Society for American Music* 17, no. 2.

11. Barnett, "Ginger Smock, 4.

12. Florence Cadrez, "Mostly 'bout Musicians" (column), *Los Angeles Sentinel*, June 30 and July 7, 1955. See also Kevin Cook, "The Vegas Hotspot That Broke All the Rules," *Smithsonian Magazine*, January 2013, https://www.smithsonianmag.com/history/the-vegas-hotspot-that-broke-all-the-rules-165807434/.

13. Display ad, *Los Angeles Tribune*, December 19 and 26, 1958 (emphasis in the original).

14. "'Way Out' New Year's in Vegas Offered," *Los Angeles Tribune*, December 26, 1958.

15. "Aristocats Claim a Century"; "Theat: People and Places," *California Eagle*, January 28, 1960.

16. Major Robinson, "New York Beat," *Jet*, March 31, 1960, 64.

17. "Aristocats, Ginger Smock on 'Catalina,'" *Los Angeles Sentinel*, May 12, 1960; untitled photo captioned "Change of Professional Name," *Los Angeles Sentinel*, September 8, 1960.

18. Cox, *Central Avenue*, 310–12.

19. Smock to Reeves, undated (postmarked May 3, 1974).

20. Gertrude Gipson, "Candid Comments from G. G.," *Los Angeles Sentinel*, April 23, 1970; "Johnny Mathis in Starry Opener at the NOW Grove," *Los Angeles Sentinel*, August 27, 1970; Bill Lane, "Fred MacMurray Denies Rental Bias; Connie Stevens Clicks; Carmen McRae Opens," *Los Angeles Sentinel*, January 7, 1971.

21. Barnett, "Ginger Smock," 7; Leonard Feather, "Dionne Warwick at Grove," *Los Angeles Times*, March 2, 1971, NMAAHC-Reeves.

22. Smock to Reeves, undated (postmarked May 3, 1974).

23. John Henry Tatum Reeves, obituary, *Globe and Mail*, September 1, 2011, https://www.legacy.com/obituaries/theglobeandmail/obituary.aspx?n=john-henry-tatam-reeves&pid=189949406; John Reeves to Ginger Smock, October 20, 1973; Dean Reeves, personal communication, January 27, 2016.

24. "Ginger's Phone Call #1," cassette tape, NMAAHC-Reeves.

25. Barnett, "Ginger Smock," 2–4; Smock, *Strange Blues*.

26. Smock to Reeves, undated (postmarked May 3, 1974) (emphasis in the original).

27. Tucker interview.

28. Tucker interview.

29. Ginger Smock to Ivy, John, Dean, and David Reeves, undated (likely December 1973).

30. Smock to Reeves, undated (postmarked May 3, 1974) (emphasis in the original).

31. Ginger Smock to Ivy and John Reeves, August 18, 1976.

32. Bette Yarbrough Cox, "Ginger Smock Interviewed by Bette Yarbrough Cox," filmed February 24, 1983, University of California, Los Angeles, Ethnomusicology Archive video, posted September 23, 2015, https://archive.org/details/calauem_000206. A letter from Ginger Smock to Ivy and John Reeves dated November 1, 1983, places this interview on November 7, 1983, rather than in February.

33. Janis L. McKay, *Played Out on the Strip: The Rise and Fall of Las Vegas Casino Bands* (Reno: University of Nevada Press, 2016), 116–17.

34. "Gertrude Gipson's Candid Comments," *Los Angeles Sentinel*, May 18, 1972.

35. Peggy Gilbert, "Tuning in on Femme Musicians," *Overture*, November 1980, NMAAHC-Reeves (emphasis in the original).

36. Ginger Smock to Ivy and John Reeves, April 1, 1977 (emphasis in the original).

37. Ginger Smock to Ivy and John Reeves, June 7, 1977.

38. Smock to Reeves, June 7, 1977 (emphasis in the original)

39. McKay, *Played Out on the Strip*, 79, 85–90.

40. Ginger Smock to Ivy and John Reeves, August 26, 1977 (emphasis in the original).

41. Ginger Smock to Ivy and John Reeves, July 23, 1978 (emphasis in the original).

42. Ginger Smock to Ivy and John Reeves, February 11, 1980 (emphasis in the original).

43. Ginger Smock to Ivy and John Reeves, April 26, 1981.

44. Ginger Smock to Ivy and John Reeves, February 17, 1982.

45. Handwritten note on newspaper clipping headlined "LV Is No Longer 'Pot at the End of the Rainbow' for Musicians," *Nevadan*, December 12, 1982, NMAAHC-Reeves.

46. Ginger Smock to Ivy and John Reeves, November 16, 1986 (emphasis in the original).

47. Ginger Smock to Ivy and John Reeves, February 9, 1986 (emphasis in the original).

48. Ginger Smock to Ivy and John Reeves, June 24, 1990 (emphasis in the original).

49. Ginger Smock to Ivy and John Reeves, September 6, 1989 (emphasis in the original).

50. Ginger Smock to Ivy and John Reeves, February 8, 1990 (emphasis in the original).

51. Smock to Reeves, undated (postmarked May 3, 1974).

52. Dean Reeves, email to the author, September 2, 2020.

53. John Reeves to Ginger Smock and Bob Shipp, December 11, 1975.

54. Ginger Smock to Ivy and John Reeves, December 30, 1975.

55. Joachim E. Berendt to John Reeves, March 29, 1976.

56. Stuff Smith et al., *Violin-Summit* (SABA Records, SB 15 099 ST, 1967).

57. Smock to Reeves, December 30, 1975.

58. Johnny Simmen to John Reeves, August 1, 1978; John Reeves to Claude Nobs, October 3, 1978 (draft), and October 4, 1978 ("2nd copy"); Claude Nobs to John Reeves, letters dated November 1, 1978, and May 29, 1979; John Reeves to Harold Jackson, June 4, 1980.

59. John Reeves to Norman Granz, November 16, 1976; John Reeves to Harold Jackson, June 4, 1980.

60. John Reeves to the Rounder Collective, April 17, 1976 (draft); Bernard Brightman (Stash Records) to John Reeves, July 10, 1978; John Reeves to Hank O'Neal (Chiaroscuro Records), November 20, 1978 (draft); John Reeves to Irv Kratka (Music Minus One), June 30, 1981 (draft); John Reeves, "Ginger Smock, Legendary Female Jazz Violinist," typewritten document, June 1980, NMAAHC-Reeves.

61. Ginger Smock to Ivy and John Reeves, May 28, 1980 (emphasis in the original).

62. Ginger Smock to Ivy and John Reeves, November 1, 1982.

63. Ginger Smock to Ivy and John Reeves, January 24 and February 1, 1985.

64. Ginger Smock to Ivy and John Reeves, July 8, 1985; Anthony Barnett, personal communication, August 25, 2021.

65. Ginger Smock to Ivy and John Reeves, May 23, 1990, February 16, 1991, February 15, 1992, and July 26, 1993.

66. The BEEM Foundation (the Black Experience as Expressed through Music) documented and celebrated the history of African American musical life in Los Angeles in Central Avenue's heyday. Cox, "Ginger Smock Interviewed."

15

"For Adult Audiences Only"

A History of LGBTQ Performers on the Las Vegas Stage

LOUIS NIEBUR

Throughout its relatively brief history, Las Vegas has featured entertainers who have taken advantage of its "wide-open" reputation to perform unconventional sexualities and gender representations onstage. When Hot Chocolate (the alter ego of drag performer Larry Edwards) was awarded the key to the city by Mayor Carolyn Goodman in 2000 for service to the tourism industry, she was only the latest in a long line of artists to unlock gender in ways that were new to many visitors to the city. While the more raucous, risqué gay performers of the 1950s and 1960s such as T. C. Jones, Ty Bennett, and Lynne Carter moved between the bar scenes of Los Angeles, New York, and San Francisco, performing for mostly queer audiences, in Las Vegas "female impersonator" shows tended to focus on glamour and illusion for largely straight crowds. At the same time, queer singers on the cabaret and supper-club circuit of the 1950s, 1960s, and 1970s were frequently and surprisingly open about issues of sexuality, using comedy and artistry to contain any potential controversy. Queer entertainers in Las Vegas have never been a universal bloc with essentialized queerness embodied in their performances. And Las Vegas has never been a queer destination on the level of Fire Island, San Francisco, or Provincetown. But some queer performances have embraced aspects of the kind of freedom Vegas did encourage while negotiating the unique challenges of that city's otherwise conservative show world.

In this chapter, I will survey a collection of LGBTQ artists in Las Vegas in the postwar years who challenged traditional notions of gender and sexuality onstage to varying degrees as an integral part of their act. From the largest stages of the Strip to the smaller-scale environment of the Las Vegas supper-club circuit, these performances serve as examples of a kind of visual and sonic spectacle that presented alternative sexualities through same-gendered song dedications, costuming, and modes of performance that contradicted their assumed gender presentation. These challenges to audiences included Jim Bailey's impersonations of female gay icons at the Flamingo, including Barbra Streisand, Carol Channing, and Judy Garland, which mesmerized audiences with their verisimilitude and beauty. Rusty Warren, though publicly closeted, presented a stage show that built on her reputation as the party-record queen, allowing otherwise conservative heterosexual couples a chance to sample a freer life through her "Knockers Up!" persona. Frances Faye at the Thunderbird Casino, in both the "masculine" strength of her vocal style and her regular dedications to her longtime partner, Teri Shepherd, scandalized and enthralled audiences in equal measure. Finally, Johnnie Ray, the "King of Wails," offered listeners at the Desert Inn a feminized, irrational mode that nevertheless drew out tears of sympathy alongside him. These performers capitalized on Las Vegas's reputation for adult spectacle to offer straitlaced audiences a chance to experience, however vicariously, different kinds of gender and sexuality.

A Double Life

Las Vegas, despite its infamy as "Sin City," is, in comparison to some other metropolitan areas, notoriously conservative toward its LGBTQ populations. By the early 1980s, by which time most other states had eliminated antisodomy laws, Nevada still had some of the harshest on the books.[1] In fact, in the wake of the Stonewall uprising in 1969 in New York City, Nevada "refined the state's sodomy law making it applicable only to gay people and increasing penalties."[2] Three separate laws were still used against queer people well into the 1970s, which included vague descriptions of misdemeanor "gross lewdness" in addition to more specific felonies of "crimes against nature": "anal intercourse, cunnilingus, or fellatio between consenting adults of the same sex."[3]

Las Vegas earned its reputation among more "enlightened" gay activists as a place to be avoided, as this tourist acknowledged in 1971: "They told me Las Vegas would turn any Gay Insider to a Sad Outsider. Just no gay life to speak of there at all. And this from gay friends in the show biz who'd worked the Babylon of the Great American Desert. In all my years in the profession, I had avoided Las Vegas as a gourmet might eschew candied ants." One gay resident of the city reminded this visitor, "There's still a life penalty for sodomy in Nevada. They're working to legalize prostitution in this county as they have in Carson City and elsewhere, and that will probably happen, but homosexuality is not about to enjoy open indulgence any time soon." Ultimately, they found a vibrant gay scene in the local bars, mostly "conducted in the closet, with marriage being the rule. Couples who are stashing away the bread as waiters or dealers have to present a super-straight image on duty and in their home neighborhoods," and that "there are no Gay Lib groups, nor a very keen awareness that there is oppression of gays on all sides."[4]

By the early 1960s, there were eleven casinos on the Strip (Tropicana, Flamingo, Sands, Desert Inn, Riviera, Thunderbird, Sahara, Stardust, New Frontier, Dunes, and Hacienda), each with their own stage shows. The entertainment, like the city, had a reputation for slightly seedy, risqué acts designed to titillate between bouts of gambling. As the famous "exposé" of Vegas *The Green Felt Jungle* revealed with hyperbole typical of the time:

> At night, except for a brief (from an hour to an hour and a quarter) floor show, there is no place to go but the casino. . . . There are the lounge shows adjoining the casino in every hotel, but they are noisy and crude, and the drinks are watery and the cocktail waitresses keep them coming (at standard prices). . . . Unless you are addicted to gambling, drinking, or fornication, the Las Vegas action soon becomes a bore, and most sensible guests find themselves getting restless after two or three days and are ready to call it quits and go home.[5]

Las Vegas had, then, a double life, one in which a licentious reputation existed side-by-side against a reactionary state government and conservative visitors in town for a good time. Acts that played against conventional norms were to be expected, as long as they didn't push *too* far, and homosexuality was that step too far. Likewise, despite an active but relatively small local gay entertainment scene, which included provincial drag shows and nightclub acts, very little overlap existed between them and the casino's main stages. Consequently, those queer artists living in the mainstream had to be quite careful about their public personae. Some, like Rusty Warren, lived deeply in the closet, but nevertheless pursued a controversial "sex positive" agenda in her stage act for "Mr. and Mrs. America." Similarly, Johnnie Ray and Liberace, while not openly gay, performed visibly antimasculine characters onstage, Ray weeping and carrying on as the "Cry Guy" and Liberace campily referencing his mother throughout his shows. Others who seemed to be challenging gender norms more directly, such as drag performers Jim Bailey and the androgynous Frances Faye, walked a more delicate line in their acts. As each of these performers navigated a careful line of gender expression in their acts, also on the line was Las Vegas's unspoken promise of endless possibility and an American mythos of acceptance.

Female Impersonators as "Illusionists"

Female impersonation acts had had a surprisingly difficult time in Las Vegas until the success of Kenny Kerr's drag spectacular "This Is Boy-Lesque" at the

Silver Slipper in 1977 and Jim Bailey's subsequent long run at the Flamingo Hotel. As queer Las Vegas historian Dennis McBride has observed, "Female impersonation has always lurked at the edge of Las Vegas entertainment culture."[6] While all the big names in drag had appeared there since at least the 1950s—T. C. Jones, Lynne Carter, Craig Russell—they were never invited to stay more than a few weeks. Jim Bailey, in his first attempt to conquer the city, probably came the closest, when he was named "Most Promising Male Newcomer" in the *Fabulous Las Vegas Magazine* critic's poll in 1971, but even his brilliant act survived only a few months at the Flamingo Hotel.[7]

Of course, drag was a vibrant part of Las Vegas's local gay scene, where, like in all cities, even amateur performances helped create a feeling of community. But both Bailey and Kerr ultimately achieved success with mainstream Vegas audiences where others had failed by marketing themselves as "illusionists" rather than drag artists through their impressions of familiar famous women. They avoided the issue of homosexuality by presenting themselves as a kind of magician, similar perhaps to the popular but harmless David Copperfield, and by filling their shows with a professionalism and glamour audiences had come to expect from Las Vegas. All this deflected attention away from the subversive gender play at work through the dazzling artistry of dancers, lighting, costuming, and impressive musicianship. They actively denied their homosexuality in the press in the 1970s, since, as McBride has reminded, casinos were not allowed to hire anyone with a criminal record, nor could they cater to criminals: "Nevada's sodomy law was enforced so that Kerr, and all other gay entertainers and gaming personnel in Las Vegas were de facto criminals."[8]

There was always, however, a frisson of danger and the freak show about their acts, which doubtlessly added to the allure. For example, Bailey played a version of himself, "Jeremy Welles, World's Greatest Illusionist," when he guest starred in an episode of the crime procedural *Vega$* in 1980.[9] Bailey's character was understood as a brilliant artist able to channel the spirit of gay icons Judy Garland and Barbra Streisand, but, perhaps inevitably, also a psychotic "split personality," a divided soul who attempts murder in their confused mental state. As we will see, little had changed since Johnnie Ray was accused of a similar "war of the sexes" raging within his body twenty years earlier.

Bailey's musicianship (he was a conservatory-trained singer) and uncanny ability to mimic the stars he performed endeared him to audiences, and his "wounded" freak persona disarmed those who would have condemned these shows, since on some level they confirmed the mainstream belief that homosexuals were mentally ill, but of a danger to no one but themselves. By the later part of the 1980s, however, as laws changed, and attitudes began to change, both Kerr and Bailey were able to be open about their sexuality. In particular, Kerr brought the local gay community of Las Vegas and the tourist industry together through his work with AIDS charities.

A Very Particular Kind of "Risqué"

Comic vocalist Rusty Warren also understood that most of her audience were made up of "traditional" American couples, often newlyweds, in Las Vegas to experience a bit of risqué humor. She had become famous as a singer of best-selling "party records," the most notorious of which were her albums from the end of the 1950s and early 1960s, including *Songs for Sinners* and *Knocker's Up!* as well as *Sinsational* and featuring songs like "Bounce Your Boobies" and "Knockers Up!" Her *Knockers Up!* album was the eighteenth best selling of all records sold in 1961. She had honed her brand of observational humor throughout the 1950s, where, initially as a pianist, she found that her banter with the audience was the most satisfying and successful part of the show. Gradually, she moved out from behind the piano and began relating to the women in her audience, most of whom were there with husbands or boyfriends. The slightly off-color nature of the comedy developed into more ribald humor, and by 1960 she had become a nightclub draw, touring all over the country, finally making her Las Vegas debut in the Persian Room at the Dunes in 1963. The *Las Vegas Review* introduced Warren to the city, noting, "She talks about s-e-x and the anatomy. She holds a mirror up to life and exhorts her cohorts to 'laugh at yourselves.' This is not double entendre, or sotto voce. It is one-dimensional. Every adult understands it."[10]

Despite her inability to be open about her own lesbian identity at the time, Warren placed herself in the tradition of Jewish vaudeville women like Sophie Tucker who with their brash and unapologetic manner were able to express themselves onstage in a way that would have been impossible in real life. "I didn't 'intend' to, but my audience was 'Mr and Mrs America' and it was to them that I spoke: suburbanites, married couples, newlyweds," Warren explains. "That meant that I only talked about 'the husband' and 'the wife.' I didn't talk about gay people or use gay humor in my act. I didn't talk about race. . . . I just talked about a universally sensitive subject in an honest and humorous way that was also topical, creative and inclusive. I was accepted by 'Mr and Mrs America' in a way that [fellow party-record artists] Belle [Barth] and Pearl Williams . . . were not."[11]

While avoiding the issue of homosexuality in her act, she nevertheless challenged midcentury audiences and their provincial notions of sexuality, prompting them to think, if only while in Vegas, that alternatives, particularly for women, existed. At the end of each show, the women would get up and form a conga line to her famous anthem, "Knockers Up," dancing around the theater, and know for a few minutes what female solidarity felt like, what "being a rebel" felt like. "So when the women came by the busloads to see my show in the 1960s and 1970s," Warren recalls, "they dragged their husbands along and everybody had a good time."[12] This had the effect of reinforcing Las Vegas's reputation as a place with loose morals, but one where such transgressions were contained within the city's limits. Once back home in their more straitlaced communities, both women and their husbands knew Vegas was the exception that proved the rule of law.

As careful as she was, like all queer public figures in the 1950s and 1960s, Warren was susceptible to the damaging influence of gossip magazines, which during those years became less coded in their language about closeted performers and more aggressive in outing them. In the early 1960s, a blackmailer threatened to sell some photos to the most notorious of gossip rags, *Confidential*. In some of the photos, Warren was acting as master of ceremonies for a gay wedding, dressed in a tuxedo, and in others from the same event, she was walking down the aisle with another woman in male drag. Warren understood that these photos could effectively end her career: "'Rusty Warren' was supposed to be the after dinner darling of 'Mr and Mrs America' but she was absolutely not supposed to be queer—which I absolutely am. . . . It was the wrong timing for 'Mr and Mrs America' to find out that 'Rusty Warren' was a lesbian in real life. . . . After I hung up the phone with Stan [Warren's manager], I cried myself sick," she acknowledged many years later.[13] While the blackmailer never followed through with their threat, the incident shows that even in the seemingly wide-open town of Las Vegas, queer performers were never safe and had to keep hidden their sexuality if they wanted to stay employed.

Thriving in the Margins

Another artist who pushed those boundaries to the limit (and occasionally past them) was Frances Faye. Like Rusty Warren, Faye started in small-time nightclubs in cities across the United States before becoming a Vegas regular in the early 1960s. During Prohibition, she had been a favorite entertainer in Mob-owned speakeasies and became comfortable around gangsters. She recalled, "The gangsters were great guys. Men like Legs Diamond. Names so big in the underworld that I still don't even like to talk about them. But they loved me and that was wonderful for any teenage girl's morale. I'd sing and dance for them and they'd come and see me as my fans."[14] Also like Warren, Faye never tried to be the ingenue, and in fact presented herself in a shockingly androgynous manner for the time. With buzz cut, pants, and button-down top, Faye was constantly the subject of reporters who consistently referred to her looks as an analog to her "strange" ability to draw an audience. One journalist noted, "The woman at the table next to mine said she looked like a butch teapot." Another reporter described how "her hair is cropped so short she must comb it with a toothbrush. A slash of fire-engine red for a mouth, two enormous black olives for eyes . . . her looks are so startling that you almost forget how talented and musically creative she is."[15]

Throughout the 1950s and 1960s, Faye appeared in a number of prominent venues around the city, including the Gay Nineties Bar at the New Frontier Hotel, Nero's Nook at Caesars Palace, and the Bagdad Theatre in the Aladdin Hotel, with *Nudes on Ice*. But she was most at home at the Thunderbird, where she frequently performed three shows a night. She recorded a live album there in 1962, *Caught in the Act, Vol. 2*, a follow-up to her first live album recorded three years earlier at Los Angeles's Crescendo club. But her reputation as a performer who challenged audience's sensibilities had been established long before, and she remained what one reporter called "right in the vanguard of the new hipsters. Miss Faye expresses the new and growing revolutionary spirit abroad in the land, reshaping attitudes."[16] Her Vegas shows legendarily attracted both celebrities and a heavily queer tourist audience. One woman recalled that for lesbians like her, "*Caught in the Act* was a very popular album among us. It was a big deal that she was so blatant, so publicly open. We had so little. This was so precious."[17] Stevie Philips, Judy Garland's personal assistant, remembers that in the early 1960s,

> By three in the morning . . . we typically found ourselves, yet again, watching Frances Faye do her lounge act at the Thunderbird. Judy . . . was going strong and growing stronger pill by pill. I'm embarrassed to report that our third time there I fell asleep at the little cocktail table directly in front of the tiny stage where Miss Faye performed. Judy attempted to prod me awake; that is to say she gave me a well-deserved shove and in so doing pushed me onto the dance floor. I lay there, spread eagle in my customary fashion, apparently looking like I needed help from everyone present. And they all jumped in. I was carried into Miss Faye's dressing room, where a group of women with a strong sexual preference for one another started pawing at me—in my interest, of course—which woke me up fast![18]

It's easy to understand her appeal to LGBTQ audiences in the midcentury. Cloaked in the performance language of the lounge act, her show encourages a polyvalent reading. Faye's interpretations of jazz standards cry out for a queer subtext. For example, one notable constant in a Faye performance is a glint of irony, a sheen of guarded impersonality in the characters she performs. But in "(All of a Sudden) My Heart Sings," from *I'm Wild Again* (1955), she allows for a moment of honest vulnerability as she recalls "the secret way you press my hand to let me know you understand," and it's hard to imagine that the song is directed to anyone but a woman. She continues with the feminized imagery of "your little laugh and half surprise" and "the way your hair won't stay in place." Often she was less guarded in her lyrics than upfront about her emotions. In "Love Is Just around the Corner," from *Relaxin' with Frances Faye* (1957), she blatantly refuses to change the genders in the lyrics as she growls in a deep tenor, "strictly between us, you're cuter than Venus." Most famously, in her tune "Frances and Her Friends," which formed a central part of her nightclub act, the singer recites a chain of polyamorous relationships that would impress anyone today: "I know a girl named Shirley. Shirley goes with Helen. And Helen goes with Janie. And Janie goes with Mamie. And Mamie goes with Angelo. And Angelo goes with Robin. And Robin goes with Jamie. And Jamie goes with Seymour. And Seymour goes with Georgie. And Georgie goes with Orgy . . . [and so on]." She had included this song in her act at least as early as a live recording made in 1956 for a *DownBeat* radio broadcast, a time when a conviction for homosexuality could easily have resulted in prison time. One woman recalls, "When we were a rowdy bunch of young lesbians, we went up to Vegas to hang with some friends and see some shows and we accomplished what we set out to do. . . . We went to Caesars Palace, she [Faye] was performing in the lounge. . . . Two drink minimum and we saw her play the keys, fine jazz, plenty of eye contact."[19] A performance like this would always have also included her version of Cole Porter's "Night and Day," with her proudly interjecting her own lyrics, "gay gay gay, is there another way?" to loud cheering from the audience night after night.

A Language of Vulnerability

The stage had been set for many of Las Vegas's queer performers by Johnnie Ray, who had one of the city's longest careers, starting with the rise of the Strip casinos in the early 1950s and continuing until the late 1980s. Having suffered severe hearing loss either genetically caused or from a childhood accident and made worse by ear surgery in adulthood, he wore a prominent hearing aid in one or both ears throughout his performing career. Born in rural Oregon, he spent his early professional life playing nightclubs across the United States before landing his first recording contract with OKeh Records in 1951, one of the only white artists to do so with a repertoire of R&B songs. His first hit, "Whisky and Gin" (1951), was a success in both white and Black markets across the United States and was followed that same year by his one-two punch of "Cry" and "The Little Cloud That Cried," establishing his reputation as a balladeer, with drawn-out, emphatic vocals his trademark, often reducing himself to tears in his own performances. His bisexuality was frequently alluded to in scandal sheets throughout his career, as one aspect of a remarkable "difference" that marked him as unusual and unpredictable, desirable and dangerous.

Ray had been scheduled to open the Copa Room at the Sands Hotel in Las Vegas in 1952, but with delay after delay that honor ultimately fell to Frank Sinatra, with the cancellation of Sinatra's contract at the Flamingo after its owner's murder in 1953. Ray's debut ended up at the Desert Inn that year, earning a record breaking $15,000 a week. This was the start of a long-standing relationship with that casino. He then followed Sinatra, Dean Martin and Jerry Lewis, and Sammy Davis Jr. at the Sands three months after his Desert Inn debut.

His immediate appeal for Vegas audiences can be understood as an extension of his larger worldwide popularity among women, who heard in Ray that rarest of 1950s masculine traits: vulnerability. Ray had written "The Little Cloud That Cried" before he was famous, and that song, like "Cry," drew from the performer a kind of effusive outpouring of emotion that encouraged empathy and longing from his audience. "I just show people the emotion they're afraid to show," Ray explained to the press after the massive success of "Cry." "People are too crowded inside themselves these days. They're afraid to show any love. And boy, what is the primary existence for existing? It's beauty and love."[20] Ray explained his need to perform as originating in an isolated childhood: "I was a mighty sad and lonely boy who needed something to keep me going, to make me feel adjusted to the narrow little world into which I had been shoved."[21]

As this quote alludes, it wasn't simple emotion that people responded to; there was, to 1950s eyes and ears, something "different" about Ray. A white singer performing Black music, with a visible marker of his deafness in the bulky hearing aid, Ray represented a new kind of man in the 1950s, what biographer Jonny Whiteside described as "America's first culture-shocking misfit, the earliest nationally recognized prototype model for those the press tagged, as de-mystifyingly and unemphatically as possible, 'anti-hero.'"[22] His deafness was fascinating to audiences and press alike, from his first mention in the trade press, where it had marked him as "odd."[23] Reviewers struggled to understand his overtly emotive performance style, but noted his ability to draw his audiences into his emotional world: "While cry-boy delivers his lachrymose songs, the on-lookers stamp and clap, weep and groan, and by the time Mr Ray completes his whining, stammering performance an indescribably hypnotic spell seems to have been cast over the entire audience."[24]

Perhaps the easiest way to understand how Ray negotiated his many modes of difference is through Robert McRuer's "crip theory," which posits the 1950s and 1960s as a period where both "heterosexuality and able-bodiedness were wedded but invisible (and in need of embodied, visible, pathologized, and policed homosexuality and disabilities)." In this context, discussion by critics frequently understand his unusual mode of performance by substituting a discussion of his suspect sexuality with observations about his disability. Concerning a government scandal of 1953, McRuer notes that the press conflated homosexuality and disability, but conveniently substituted one for the other, since "the spectacle of sexual, bodily, or mental difference was preferable to that of a visibly threatened masculinity or heterosexuality requiring deviance to define and sustain itself."[25] Vincent Lamar Stephens relates this back to Ray's reviewers who "chiefly described Ray's extroverted performing style by surveying how his body and its movement signify emotiveness and vulnerability. Ray's voice, gestures and audience were an index of what appears unusual or queer to male observers many of whom found him disturbing."[26] And, as Cheryl Herr has observed, this unique style was often directly connected to his disability, as a way of understanding both his mode of performance and his reasons for performing such material in the first place.[27] Ray himself understood his appeal as related to his difference, noting at the time, "They come out to see what the freak is like. . . . They want to know what this cat has got. I know what it is. I make them feel, I reach in and grab one of their controlled emotions, the deeply buried stuff, and yank it to the surface."[28]

Ray set the stage for other Las Vegas artists who challenged traditional gender roles. Throughout his career, Liberace performed at the Riviera, the Sahara, Caesars Palace, and MGM Grand, where his brand of middlebrow music appealed to a similar demographic as Ray. Liberace's image as an eternal mama's boy "reveled in a type of 'soft' emotional delicacy and stylistic 'excess' counter to the era's emphasis on masculine hardness,"[29] but without Ray's air of desperation and frisson of racial transgression.

In 1956 Elvis Presley, in residence at the New Frontier, would frequently watch Ray's Desert Inn act across the street and picked up his habit of gesticulating and kissing the girls and women in the front row, particularly during Ray's performance of "Walkin' My Baby Back Home."[30] But where Ray's performance was perceived as chaste and nonthreatening, Presley's sexualized gestures embodied a new kind of virile masculinity. And as rock 'n' roll conquered the charts, Ray found his style of crooning labeled old-fashioned. Rather than move in the new, sexualized direction, however, he began to rein in his performances with new, slower, and thicker arrangements, focusing on his nightclub act. In 1957 he recorded a live album at the Desert Inn with his new, more understated material. But if anything, his refined style appears *more* emotionally engaged, an introverted expression of heartbreak and loneliness he is barely able to contain. In his rendition of "Don't Worry 'bout Me," he opens confidently, but quickly descends, through dramatic downward-sliding melismas, and gasping breathlessness, to his trademark tears on the words "Why should we cling to some silly thing that used to be?" His struggle to contain his emotions bursts out in the final part of the song as he shouts the last chorus to wild applause. From here he introduces a medley of his two biggest hits, "The Little Cloud That Cried" and "Cry," by way of a modest apology: "If we may, hoping we haven't worn out the welcome mat. This is once more for your approval, these tunes . . ."

Reviews of the new show and album praised his new understated approach, while pointedly making a subtle dig at his sexuality, as when this critic observed: "Wisely, he's dropped the femme kissing routine because last time many husbands and boyfriends took a dim view of the demonstration, especially when he left some of his make-up on faces and furs."[31] This kind of insinuation had dogged Ray his whole career. A 1953 "tell-all" in *Confidential* magazine had attempted to out the singer, erroneously reporting that he had performed as a drag artist in Detroit before he became famous, and featured an interview with "eminent psychiatrist" Dr. Louis Berg, who reported that in Ray, "we have a case of a personality in which the 'war of the sexes' is waged within a single body."[32] Ray had been arrested in 1951 for "accosting and soliciting" in a men's room; while this initial article didn't mention that arrest, subsequent articles in rags like *Uncensored*, *Anything Goes*, and *On the QT* (which featured an article titled "Why Johnny [*sic*] Ray Likes to Go in Drag") were less timid. After Liberace successfully sued *Confidential* in 1957 and the *London Daily Mirror* in 1959, gossip magazines were less blatant in their accusations, but by then, for Ray, the damage had been done. After another arrest in 1959 in which he was entrapped by an undercover police officer, Ray's career suffered, and he never again achieved mainstream success in the United States outside of his Las Vegas, Reno, and South Lake Tahoe touring nightclub act. He continued to perform in Las Vegas, at the Golden Nugget and the Desert Inn, until 1987.

• • •

The three decades after the Second World War were profoundly difficult for LGBTQ people, and queer performers faced especially difficult and seemingly intractable problems, particularly as regards the expression of their identity through their art. But Las Vegas presented unique opportunities for some of these artists to express a kind of openness, where a certain licentiousness was expected. Despite constantly pushing against the boundaries of acceptable behavior, for the most part, queer performers in the hothouse of Las Vegas were allowed to present alternative modes of expression and gave audiences permission, if only for the duration of their time in Sin City, to imagine what such identities might be like.

Notes

1. Thomas B. Stoddard et al., *The Rights of Gay People* (Toronto: Bantam Books, 1983), 151.
2. Dennis McBride, *Out of the Neon Closet: Queer Community in the Silver State* (North Charleston, SC: CreateSpace, 2016), vii.
3. Stoddard, *Rights of Gay People*, 151.
4. John Francis Hunter, "A Vagabond in Vegas," *Gay*, May 10, 1971, 9.
5. Ed Reid and Ovid Demaris, *The Green Felt Jungle* (New York: Pocket Books, 1963), 3.
6. Dennis McBride, "Las Vegas and Female Impersonation," Gay History in Nevada and Las Vegas, updated 2009, https://outhistory.org/exhibits/show/las-vegas/articles/boylesque.
7. Ad, *Fabulous Las Vegas Magazine*, October 30, 1971, 4.

8. McBride, "Las Vegas and Female Impersonation."

9. "The Man Who Was Twice," *Vega$*, directed by Alf Kjellin, written by Michael Mann and Judy Burns, March 12, 1980, ABC.

10. "Dunes Hotel," *Las Vegas Review*, December 4, 1963, quoted in Elizabeth Rizzo Dubois, *Rusty Warren: The "Knockers Up" Gal* (self-published, 2018), 60.

11. Dubois, *Rusty Warren*, 181, reprinted from *Daeida* 413 (June 2008).

12. Dubois, *Rusty Warren*, 182.

13. Dubois, *Rusty Warren*, 186.

14. Tyler Alpern and Rex Strother, "Frances Faye: No Regrets," liner notes to *No Regrets* (Jasmine Records, 2006).

15. Rex Reed, *Daily News*, October, 17, 1975.

16. Tyler Alpern, "Fabulous Frances Faye Archive," last modified 2020, http://www.tyleralpern.com/francesfaye.html.

17. Alpern, "Fabulous Frances Faye Archive."

18. Stevie Phillips, *Judy and Liza and Robert and Freddie and David and Sue and Me . . .* (New York: St. Martin's Press, 2015), 71–72.

19. "Nearly Normalized: Ramblings of the Slightly Askewed," updated February 13, 2011, https://nearlynormalized.wordpress.com/2011/02/13/frances-faye-she-showed-me-her-tracks/.

20. Jonny Whiteside, *Cry: The Johnnie Ray Story* (New York: Barricade Books, 1994), 25; Johnnie Ray, "Negroes Taught Me to Sing: Famous Cry Crooner Tells What Blues Taught Him," *Ebony*, March 1953.

21. Whiteside, *Cry*, 84.

22. Whiteside, *Cry*, 83.

23. "The Ray Story: $90 to $1,750," *Billboard*, October 6, 1951, 1, 45.

24. Cheryl Herr, "Roll-over-Beethoven: Johnnie Ray in Context," *Popular Music* 28, no. 3 (2009): 326.

25. Robert McRuer, *Crip Theory: Cultural Signs of Queerness and Disability* (New York: New York University Press, 2006), 2, 11.

26. Vincent Lamar Stephens, "Queering the Textures of Rock and Roll History" (PhD diss., University of Maryland, 2005), 295.

27. Herr, "Roll-over-Beethoven," 327.

28. Whiteside, *Cry*, 133.

29. Stephens, "Queering the Textures," 245.

30. Whiteside, *Cry*, 206–7.

31. Whiteside, *Cry*, 234.

32. Jay Williams, "Johnnie Ray: Is It True?" *Confidential*, April 1953, 37.

PART VI

Leaving Vegas

The father, now no more a father, cries,
Ho Icarus! where are you? as he flies;
Where shall I seek my boy? he cries again,
And saw his feathers scatter'd on the main.
Then curs'd his art; and fun'ral rites confer'd,
Naming the country from the youth interr'd.

A partridge, from a neighb'ring stump, beheld
The sire his monumental marble build;
Who, with peculiar call, and flutt'ring wing,
Chirpt joyful, and malicious seem'd to sing:
The only bird of all its kind, and late
Transform'd in pity to a feather'd state:
From whence, O Daedalus, thy guilt we date.

16

The Real Deal

Impersonation and the American Dream in Branson and Vegas

JOANNA DEE DAS AND MADDIE HOUSE-TUCK

Imagine driving along a Strip with neon signs encouraging you to enter palaces of delight. You pass by a glowing Ferris wheel and a replica of New York's Empire State Building. You are one of millions visiting what many have called the "most American" of U.S. cities. This city has also been called tacky, cheesy, and the "elephant's graveyard of entertainment," but the individuals and corporations who built it gambled correctly that many people would embrace the vision of America performed on its stages. The question is: Are you in Las Vegas or Branson, Missouri?

This question may come as a surprise, given that not many people would speak of the two cities in the same breath. Vegas has become a global brand, one of the most visited cities on the planet with forty-two million annual guests in 2019. Branson, despite its respectable nine million that same year (more than the Eiffel Tower), lacks name recognition beyond the midwestern and southern United States. Vegas has historically claimed the nickname "Sin City" with an emphasis on gambling, drinking, drugs, prostitution, and seminude burlesque shows. Branson emphasizes patriotism, Christianity, prohibitions against gambling, and "clean" shows: no profanity or bare bosoms in sight. Vegas boasts of drawing a racially diverse and international crowd (though 77 percent of visitors in 2019 were white and 86 percent from the United States, revealing a disjuncture between branding and reality). Branson's tourists are demographically more than 95 percent white and mostly from within a six-hundred-mile radius.[1]

Despite such differences, the fact that these two cities share a claim to quintessential Americanness via an economy dependent on live performance warrants a comparison. Since 2004 an average of 78 percent of Branson's annual visitors see at least one performance, the most common tourist activity. In Las Vegas, shopping is the number-one draw, but entertainment surpassed gambling for second place in the early 2000s.[2] More specifically than the broad category of live entertainment, Vegas and Branson have come to rely on the same models of performance that aesthetes have historically derided: the spectacular, where spectacle is the end goal rather than the means to an end; the variety show, featuring thematically disparate short acts by jugglers, magicians, singers, instrumentalists, dancers, and comedians; and the tribute show, featuring celebrity impersonations.

This chapter charts the intertwined history of the Vegas and Branson entertainment industries from the mid-twentieth century to the present, focusing on one tribute show that runs year-round in both places: *Legends in Concert*. While scholars of theater and performance have tended to dismiss Vegas and to overlook Branson entirely, we place the two cities in conversation vis-à-vis *Legends* to uncover their shared investment in the surreality of contemporary political and cultural life. Impersonation, or the act of pretend, emerges not only as the bedrock of *Legends*' ethos and allure, but also as a useful frame for encountering Vegas and Branson together. The two cities' entertainment economies impersonate each other (it seems that what happens in Vegas never actually stays in Vegas after all), recurrently echoing each other's histories, methods, and even slogans to reach the top of the entertainment ladder. Concurrently, *Legends* persists in both cities to defend an Americanism reliant on pretend, on franchise facsimile and gossamer visions of "truth." This chapter investigates impersonation and how the *Legends* show constructs a particular vision of America as a place of self-made individuals whose success relies on their ability to sell a multilayered performance of inauthenticity. Tribute shows, and *Legends* in particular, stage fantasies of communion with celebrity; these fantasies, while technically a ploy with pretend, achieve the feeling of encountering what audience members call "the real deal."[3] Accordingly, *Legends* provides insight into the "post-truth" phenomenon that has roots in the poststructuralist, postmodern turn of the 1970s but has captivated American media attention since the election of Donald Trump to the presidency in 2016.

This chapter thus emphasizes the inseparable relationship between performance aesthetics and questions of political economy. In the 1970s and 1980s, as the rest of the United States scrambled from the fallout of deindustrialization and global outsourcing, Vegas and Branson experienced explosive growth, primed by decades of honing entertainment as a tourist commodity. Their growth coincided with the turn from the industrial to the service economy in the late twentieth century; by some metrics, tourism is still the largest segment of the service economy in the 2020s.[4] Ironically, tourism's anchoring in local experience, what makes it an industry not easily outsourced like manufacturing or technology, contrasts with late capitalism's insistence on labor flexibility. In the 1960s, Las Vegas and Branson had divergent artistic labor pools—Frank Sinatra versus local Ozark musicians. By the 1990s, these pools had merged, with performers at all tiers—from headliners such as Tony Orlando to *Legends* impersonators to backup dancers/singers—shuttling back and forth between the two cities.[5]

Despite performers' flexibility according to capitalist labor standards, they paradoxically remain core to audience investment in tourist entertainment as a localized, "real" experience. Scholar Jane Desmond has compellingly argued that embodied experience is, indeed, at the very heart of tourism. She claims that tourists view bodies in performance as sites of the "real" and thus that "physical foundationalism is with us now as much as it was a century ago . . . [despite] our own anti-essentialist postmodernist artistic and scholarly interventions."[6] For Desmond, the political implications here involve the extension of colonialist frames of thinking about power in the United States. For us, they involve a particular staging of America that emphasizes intimacy with imitation and impersonation. Vegas and Branson capitalize on a vanishing horizon between the authentic and its facsimile, primed by an economy that no longer manufactures durable goods, but rather repackaged ephemera like financial services and touristic experiences. *Legends in Concert* emphasizes a contemporary landscape wherein authentic celebrity matters less than the feeling produced by its impersonation and approximation; in both cities, the tribute show remains eager to sell facsimile, and the facsimile of that facsimile, as the only "real" and a constituent component of the American way.

Origins

Both Vegas's and Branson's live entertainment industries began similarly: with a dam. In 1930 the federal government began construction on the Hoover Dam near Las Vegas. Tourists flocked to see this marvel of modern engineering but stayed for the gambling (legalized in 1931), the air-conditioning (provided by the dam and not available in many other places in the United States), the liberal divorce laws, and, finally, the live performances. In 1947 Bugsy Siegel built the Flamingo, which precipitated a wave of new themed resort-casinos that mixed "leisure and fantasy."[7] While gambling lay at the heart of these businesses, live performance was a mandatory component of every new hotel that opened on the Strip and often made the difference between its success or failure. By the 1960s, "the bounty of top entertainers who could be found on the Las Vegas

Strip on almost any given week" was incomparable, and Vegas started to call itself the Entertainment Capital of the World.[8] In 1969 Elvis Presley began his legendary five-year run of sold-out performances at the International (later Hilton) Hotel; his garish costumes and unabashed sentimentality solidified Vegas's reputation as a city for "middlebrow bad taste." As Vegas's star rose for middle-class, predominantly white American tourists, its cachet with the emerging counterculture fell precipitously.[9]

Echoing Vegas, Branson's live performance industry blossomed after the construction of a federally funded dam. The White River area of the Ozarks had long been a local tourist attraction for its outdoor recreation opportunities—hunting, fishing, and boating—but the dam, completed by the Army Corps of Engineers in 1958, made entertainment possible by providing electricity and controlling flooding, even as it forced numerous small farmers off their land. The dam destroyed rural life and jump-started tourism based on an impersonation of that way of life. Thousands traveled by car to see variety shows featuring country music, gospel, and comedic "hillbilly" characters that harked back to rural social gatherings displaced by modern infrastructure.[10]

Despite the emphasis on humble roots, the first families to produce live variety shows in Branson got their start on radio, belying the image of isolated, antimodern hill folk. Nearby Springfield, Missouri, known as the "Queen City of the Ozarks," was nationally recognized for mediated dissemination of country music in the 1940s and 1950s, including the 1954–58 television show *Ozark Jubilee* starring Red Foley. Members of the Presley and Mabe families enjoyed successful runs on Springfield radio stations before opening their own shows in Branson in the 1960s, buoyed by national interest in "the folk" and television shows like *The Beverly Hillbillies*, *The Andy Griffith Show*, *Green Acres*, and *Hee Haw*. Conservative white Americans saw in rural southern culture a counter to the counterculture; left-leaning white Americans saw in it an authenticity they felt was lacking in consumption-driven, conformist suburbia. In 1960 one hundred thousand tourists visited Branson annually. By the end of the decade, that number had increased tenfold to over one million a year.[11] In both their radio and their live shows, the Mabe and Presley families drew upon a nationally recognized repertoire of country music hits, gospel tunes, and other popular songs, overlaid with an emphasis on Ozarkian humor and a nostalgic ethos that claimed that Americans were more patriotic, God fearing, and family oriented in the Good Old Days.

While Branson's geographic placement evokes a rural sentimentality emulated in its performance oeuvre, the city's placement of entertainment events within theater spaces impersonates Vegas's tourist ethos. Theater scholar Jessica Howard links Branson to the "ethnographic village" model of tourism given that the simulacra of rural Ozarkian life happens in the same geographic location as the purported original, unlike Vegas's themed resorts.[12] Nonetheless, Branson carves out a layer of remove from the so-called authentic, placing most of its performances in theaters that physically and figuratively distinguish themselves from the natural landscape.[13] This move differentiates Branson from ethnographic villages such as Colonial Williamsburg, which attempt to re-create architectural and environmental surround, and aligns it with Vegas, catering toward cultivating a certain structure of feeling rather than ethnographic display.

The Convergence: *Legends* Unites Vegas and Branson

Elvis tribute artist Jonathon Von Brana walks onstage in a white jumpsuit emblazoned with a sparkly bald eagle on its back. He grins knowingly and begins in a deep baritone: "Oh See/See See Rider." He grinds his hips as sweat runs rivulets down his shaved chest, soaking into a silk scarf that he eventually wraps around the neck of a thrilled elderly audience member.[14] By the time this segment was filmed in the late 1980s, Von Brana had repeated this performance hundreds of times—twelve nights a week, most weeks of the year, since *Legends in Concert* opened in 1983 at the Imperial Palace Hotel & Casino in Las Vegas. *Legends* was the brainchild of John Stuart, a successful insurance salesman who grew up in Southern California with dreams of becoming a famous singer. The tribute show initially featured impersonations of five entertainers who had all died young: Bobby Darin, Buddy Holly, Janis Joplin, Marilyn Monroe, and, of course, Elvis. While celebrity impersonators had long existed, especially of Elvis, the assemblage of five acts in one show, along with a live band, backup dancers and singers, state-of-the-art lighting, special effects, performers who actually sang rather than lip-synched, and Stuart's rebranding of impersonators as "tribute artists," was novel.[15]

It was also a gamble in a gambling town at a nadir. The glory days of the Rat Pack and Elvis had ended, while the corporate boom inaugurated by Steve Wynn's Mirage Resort was still several years away. Journalists at the time mocked impersonation shows, with one asserting that Vegas entertainment in the 1980s was leading Nevada to becoming "the Rodney Dangerfield of states" (that is, a disrespected laughingstock). Even scholars who champion Las Vegas consider the decade a period of decline, with shows becoming "cheaper, sleazier, and cheesier."[16] But Stuart defied such critics. *Legends*' initial six-week run turned into thirty-seven years and counting; as of 2023, it is the longest-running show in Las Vegas.

While nostalgia explained *Legends*' initial appeal, it fails to fully account for its endurance. Within a year, the show evolved to include celebrities who did not die young, and by the end of the 1980s, to include celebrities who were still alive. *Legends*' shape-shifting investment in celebrity reflects a deep understanding of the value placed on celebrity as itself a facsimile of American life. Karen Sternheimer tracks the importance of American celebrity as a tool in meaning making: "Celebrity stories can help us make sense of our identities—not simply by telling us how we should look, feel, think, or act, but through a social process of negotiation." Sternheimer continues connecting celebrity's role in identity crafting to the continuance of the "American Dream," arguing that the "myth of mobility makes Americans feel good about ourselves," and that celebrity stories (especially those that chart a "rise" from the bottom to the top) allow for vicarious enjoyment of this quintessential trope of Americanness.[17]

For *Legends*, the idea of celebrity seems just as important as particular individuals themselves. The show is willing to evolve, including whatever acts will presumably appeal to the public at any moment in time.[18] What reigns supreme then is an insistence on proximity to celebrity as that which makes audiences *feel* good, through both its role in social identity construction (after all, we are in a theater) and its staging of an encounter with America vis-à-vis the American Dream. These encounters keep celebrities frozen in time (performers can switch or alternate as needed to emulate the "original" in their prime), producing an experience that is simultaneously flexible and can be consumed over and over again. Obviously, though, these are not "real" celebrities. *Legends* offered a model that knowingly relies on facsimile, on a self-aware and multilayered performance of the inauthentic that still satiates audience desires for celebrity and, hidden within, Americanness.

Stuart made savvy choices to give audiences a feeling of being proximate to celebrity. To begin, historically inaccurate technology creates the sensation that one is sharing the atmosphere of a given celebrity. To gain the sensory aspect of *being there* or *being elsewhere*, audiences must connect to their contemporary moment, rather than feel simply plunked into an alien historical time line. Dressing the images in a way that comports to the "now" reflects a commingling of the past and the present that induces the desired effect. Then, of course, the performer must look and sound like the original. Costuming, hair, general body shape, and vocal intonations must create a plausible sense that the audiences are seeing a version of the celebrity. In his discussion of hyperreality and the bio-musical, Ben MacPherson outlines the significance of vocal performance in producing nostalgic affects (similar to those *Legends* desires): "The affective agency of meaning resides in a space between the 'original' voice as embodied by the 'copy,' and the 'copy' which, in a limited way, offers a simulation of the (hyperreal) 'original.'"[19] Performers must evoke this in-between space to produce a temporal simultaneity required for *Legends*' affective success: they must impersonate in the present the sound and image of a celebrity from the past, a celebrity already rooted in the construction of "celebrity" itself.

Stuart also understood that *Legends* would have to manufacture *complete* atmospheres to make audiences feel connected to celebrity. He set a new precedent by insisting on live singing and an onstage band. This live aspect was seemingly key; numerous studies have shown that live music creates more intense physiological responses than recorded music does, and live singing carries the potential for creating the original/copy blur that produces "affective agency" à la MacPherson.[20] Stuart was also relentless in publicizing about liveness; how it was featured in press releases and critics' reviews created the perception that it made for superior entertainment. Ultimately, Stuart's creation convinced many, with one journalist stating that the show "recreate[s] the total aura of the stars, the stage presence and charisma. And those qualities are startlingly real."[21]

Legends also used exaggeration as, paradoxically, a tool to underscore the original. Stuart claimed that the show had to go "beyond" the talents of the originals, since "the entertainment level is higher today [1988] than in the 40s or 50s. Today you're competing with Michael Jackson or Mick Jagger, so we exaggerate the original."[22] For example, Von Brana in the 1980s exaggerates Elvis's 1973 performance in Hawaii. The YouTube clip from Hawaii shows Elvis with a lugubrious physicality, slightly pulsing his chest and closing his eyes to five cymbal crashes in the brief instrumental break of "See See Rider." In contrast, during the same instrumental break, Von Brana vigorously circles his arm, thrusts his pelvis, and whips his hair according to eighteen accelerating cymbal crashes, following it all up with twelve full-bodied orgasmic shakes.[23] Strategies like Von Brana's comment on the ways in which celebrity is visually and gesturally manufactured, while emphasizing spectator pleasure as more important than the "fact" of celebrity itself. Marketed as "tribute" rather than "imitation," Stuart emphasized re-creating the positive emotions and connections that audience members felt with the celebrities, harking back to Sternheimer's claims about vicarious enjoyment and feeling good. Charles Supin of the *Las Vegas Review-Journal* noted that the "enthusiastic" response of the crowd, only six weeks into the production's run, "surely takes away any of your possible fears about carbons and imitations, because, while it is this, it is very much more. . . . [T]his is . . . full of life and vigor."[24]

This show, full of life, was also fully clothed. Long marketed as Sin City, Vegas in the early 1980s had not yet capitalized on the nation's largest tourist market: families. Stuart, a devout Mormon with five children, exploited this new market, which also meant advertising the show as budget friendly.[25] Stuart billed *Legends* in its first year as "The Million Dollar Show for only $9.95."[26] Of the twenty-five shows in the *Las Vegas Review-Journal* Show Guide for the summer of 1988, fourteen were more expensive, one at the exact same price, and nine less expensive; *Legends* was squarely in the middle lane.[27] After the first few years, advertisements started to include that children twelve and under were half price and stated that the ticket price included tax and tip—"no surprises" when the bill came.[28]

The other secret to Stuart's success was homing in on the American tradition of interchangeable parts.[29] In order to satiate audience desires for proximity to whatever celebrity was hot at the moment, specific legends could indeed disappear when they no longer fitted the zeitgeist. Stuart changed the lineup every three months to keep it fresh and ensure repeat customers. This model relies on labor flexibility. Performers in the *Legends* "stable," as many called it (notably comparing performers to horses),[30] were seen as interchangeable, an irony for a show that epitomizes celebrity influence (though potentially placing in stark relief the creation of celebrity itself). Helmed by this interchangeable labor model and grounded by its reputation for wholesome entertainment at middle-range ticket prices, *Legends* set itself up as easily replicable in other tourist destinations. In 1987 it opened in Atlantic City and began a national tour; in 1989 it became the first Vegas show to appear on Broadway; in 1991 it toured to Russia; in 1995 it established residence in Myrtle Beach, South Carolina; and in 1998 it went to Branson.[31]

Branson's opening of *Legends* came at a transformative time in the city's entertainment economy. The same year that *Legends* opened in Vegas (1983), Jim Thomas, local entrepreneur, took a chance on expanding beyond local Ozark entertainers to bring country music star and *Hee Haw* host Roy Clark to his theater. The venture's success attracted other aging country music stars like Boxcar Willie, Mel Tillis, Mickey Gilley, Glen Campbell, and Conway Twitty.[32] Within a few years, Branson boasted of rivaling Nashville as a center for country music.[33] Branson's transition to national prominence prompted a change in its marketing. Known as Ozark Mountain Country in the 1960s and 1970s, in the 1980s boosters rebranded Branson as "America's Hometown" or the "Live Music Show Capital of the World."[34]

The CBS television show *60 Minutes* ushered in a phase of even greater national recognition. On December 8, 1991, and May 24, 1992, national audiences watched an eleven-minute segment on Branson called "$ound of Music." Host Morley Safer emphasized the economic aspects of the American Dream that were possible in Branson: a get-rich-quick, be-your-own-boss individualist capitalist ethos. Safer also attempted to explain why this out-of-the-way place had become an entertainment mecca. This attempt is in some ways ironic, given that Branson's geographic placement is not much more isolated than Las Vegas; furthermore, in both locations, making something from seemingly nothing (a branding that ignores histories of displacement and the genocide of Indigenous communities) feeds into the fantasy that one can achieve the American Dream anywhere. Featuring shots of largely white audiences cackling at corny jokes, praying at lunch tables, and booking hotel rooms, the segment paints Branson's white middle- and working-class audiences as "the American audience." This way of life is decidedly "family friendly" and seeks to be the place where audiences could be comforted by the familiar at cheap entertainment rates. According to *60 Minutes*, if you really cared about "true" American entertainment at a discounted price, you were on your way to Branson.

After the *60 Minutes* segment, Branson's name recognition and popularity exploded. A building frenzy ensued in the 1990s, with the number of theaters, hotel rooms, restaurants, and amenities more than doubling over the next few years. Now explicitly impersonating Vegas, Branson rebranded itself as the "Live Entertainment Capital of the World," a near-replica of Las Vegas's moniker, "Entertainment Capital of the World."[35] Branson's ethos fitted the *Legends* brand perfectly. In addition to the show's emphasis on "family-friendly" entertainment and discounted prices, *Legends* slotted easily into Branson's care for "second chances": the "glory days" of the past-their-prime stars that helmed Branson's success could be frozen in time, maintained via their impersonation. Overall, Branson's social, economic, and aesthetic orientations made it a prime market for the expansion of Stuart's brand.

Despite this boom, Branson could not keep up with Vegas's emerging corporate economy. By the 1990s in Vegas, smaller hotels and casinos were being overtaken by grander money-making machines (such as the newly instantiated Luxor, Excalibur, and the Bellagio), many of which catered to the city's reputation as a place of extreme excess, novel experience, and adult-level fun. The cash flow gave rise to aesthetic dominance. Ada Louise Huxtable's 1997 article "Living with the Fake, and Liking It" addresses an evolution in cultural attitudes wherein "surrogate experience" and "synthetic settings" became the preferred way to access the American Dream. Las Vegas, according to Huxtable, reflects the apogee of the "real fake": "A singular confluence of desire, flash and the big sell has created its character and destiny. Built to be exactly what it is, this is the real, real fake at the highest, loudest, and most authentically inauthentic level of illusion and invention."[36] By the dawn of the new millennium, Vegas's fake real had conquered American culture. Critics who had once called it the "elephant's graveyard of entertainment" now worried that the Strip would eclipse Broadway to become the nation's premiere location for live performance.[37]

Las Vegas, once known as the place where has-been stars kept their fading careers alive, now sent its own has-beens, squeezed out by the corporate turn, to Branson. In the 1990s, singers Tony Orlando and Wayne Newton, comedian Yakov Smirnoff, magician Kirby VanBurch, and other "former regulars on the [Vegas] Strip" decamped for the Branson Strip. "For several Las Vegas headliners," one journalist mused in 1996, Branson was "a rebirth."[38] Yet Branson's cultural cachet could not keep up, and performers knew it. Longtime Vegas entertainer Bob Anderson decamped for Branson in 2003, "discouraged by the lack of opportunities for his classy style of entertainment" by the new "mega-resorts" opened by Steve Wynn and his ilk. In Branson Anderson opened his own 250-seat venue at the Lodge of the Ozarks and found a groove playing five nights a week. Nonetheless, he repeatedly returned to Vegas to perform gigs and attempt to secure a lengthier contract, ultimately leaving Branson for good after eleven years. In 2022 Anderson's website makes no mention of his time in Branson, instead focusing on his Vegas performance history and his plans for a Sinatra tribute show.[39] He seemingly deemed the city embarrassing enough to ghost from his biography, even though its tourist industry had supported his career for more than a decade. Like carbon copies that blur with each iteration, the facsimile of facsimile cities had less luster.

Anderson's publicity decisions reflect a savviness about changing tides in cultural preoccupations around Vegas and Branson beginning at the turn of the twenty-first century. While both cities' straightforward insistence on pleasure makes them easy targets for continuing ridicule, the "Vegas-bashing" of the 1980s has steadily declined. Branson-bashing has remained a popular journalistic sport. Branson's down-home earnestness fails to fit the bill for cultural attitudes that prioritize poststructuralist investments in irony. A widely circulated social media meme from 2020 expresses Branson's low-rung status. A "letter" from (Democratic) Blue States to (Republican) Red States announces secession, with Blue States divvying up America's assets and Red States gratuitously coming up short. In one of its comparisons, the letter states, "We get the Statue of Liberty. You get Branson, Missouri."[40] Nonetheless, *Legends* persists by harnessing claims to the real fake wherever it goes. While Branson's emphasis on humble beginnings may contrast with Vegas's orgy of money and global cosmopolitanism, audiences in both places can still reap a dose of facsimile inside the air-conditioned space of the theater. And of course, this illusion marks the preferred American package: one where the real and the fake fail to test as separate entities, and instead become one in the same.

TripAdvisor reviews of *Legends* confirm this conflation. The phrase "the real deal" appears as a popular mention within the Branson reviews, taking up about six TripAdvisor pages. Its first mention is from 2011: "latrippers" titles their review "Must See—REAL DEAL," writing, "The performers did about three songs each and talked for a bit to the audience. It felt like you were with the real deal." In 2016 "Michelle S" wrote, "Escape to a world where you can find the likes of Kenny Chesney, MJ, and Elvis all on the same stage. Unheard of, right? Not at The Legends; some of the performers are so talented you almost forget they are not 'the real deal.'" While these reviews point to the deployment of the "real deal" as a way to describe how performers accurately enflesh the celebrities they emulate, they also evoke *Legends* as an entire experience that cultivates this atmosphere (in Michelle S's words, where you can "escape to a world"). *Legends* continues to place audiences in close contact with "real deal" celebrities, a contact far greater defined by the affective tenors of impersonation than whether the "actual" celebrity was there. *Legends* sells an experience of entanglement with celebrity, where authenticity pales in comparison to nostalgia and American craving.[41]

This vision of the American way is racialized. *Legends*' audiences are overwhelmingly white, at least in Branson and in Las Vegas.[42] Black scholars and artists have long criticized one of the most enduring traditions of the fake real in American performance—minstrelsy—and its afterlives in the continued practices of impersonation and appropriation of Black cultural practices by white entertainers. The most beloved figure in the celebrity impersonation world, Elvis, is a major lightning rod for critique of cultural theft. While most scholars of Black culture acknowledge the limitations of representation as a mode of politics, calls for racial authenticity in performance have increased dramatically since the rise of social media and the groundswell of the Black Lives Matter movement in the 2010s. In contrast, *Legends* and its audiences find the question of authenticity irrelevant, even as they desire to see physical likeness in their impersonators. The desire for accuracy stems from different impulses: *Legends* audiences want it to better engage in the fantasy of intimacy with celebrity, whereas artist-activists demand it for a political project of decentering whiteness. *Legends* props up impersonation and its affective resonances as a vehicle for transmitting an American project, while other calls for racial authenticity are geared toward dismantling this version of the American project altogether.

In the 2020s, Branson and Vegas still see tribute shows dotting their Strips. The real fake has become a driving force in American entertainment across the country. Bruce Bégout's words resonate: "We are all inhabitants of Las Vegas, however far away we are from southern Nevada. Its name is no longer a fantasy. It lives in our heads, is expressed in our ordinary gestures."[43] Driven by a craving for the inauthentic, encapsulated in the figure of the impersonated celebrity in *Legends*' case, audiences seek to find, experience, and express the Vegas fantasy of unreality whether they are in the city proper or not. To sell to this craving is to replicate Vegas as an idea, an idea that sells a vision of America where facsimile reigns supreme and corroborates with a post-truth moment in which the "real" and "fake" are blurred, intertwined, and indiscernible. The tourist experience metabolizes a vision of America that prioritizes the inauthentic as, ironically, the only form of authenticity at all. *Legends*' persistence encourages a view of entertainment as a vehicle for transmission of a gossamer American Dream, one that comments on its status as a mythology while encouraging its proliferation.

Notes

1. GLS Research, "Las Vegas Visitor Profile Study," prepared for Las Vegas Convention and Visitors Authority, 2019, 54; Branson Convention & Visitors Bureau 2019 Branson Visitor Profile and DMA.

2. Branson Convention and Visitors Bureau, "2019 Year End Marketing Report," March 10, 2020, 16; William A. Douglass and Paulina Raento, "The Tradition of Invention:

Conceiving Las Vegas," *Annals of Tourism Research* 31, no. 1 (2004): 17; Adam Nagourney, "Headliners and Headdresses Return to Las Vegas. Will Tourists Follow?" *New York Times*, June 10, 2021, https://www.nytimes.com/2021/06/10/theater/las-vegas-shows-reopening.html.

3. TripAdvisor reviews in Branson starting in 2011.

4. In 2019 travelers spent $1.1 trillion in the United States, which supported 9 million jobs directly and 6.8 million indirectly. The onset of the COVID-19 pandemic in 2020 obviously tested that growth, uprooting tourism's localized stability. See U.S. Travel Association, "U.S. Travel and Tourism Overview (2019)," March 2020, https://www.ustravel.org/system/files/media_root/document/Research_Fact-Sheet_US-Travel-and-Tourism-Overview.pdf.

5. For an overview of this phenomenon, see Mike Weatherford, "Postcards from Branson, MO," *Las Vegas Review-Journal*, December 1, 1996. For more on the labor flexibility of performers, see Anusha Kedhar, *Flexible Bodies: British South Asian Dancers in an Age of Neoliberalism* (New York: Oxford University Press, 2020).

6. Jane Desmond, *Staging Tourism: Bodies on Display from Waikiki to Sea World* (Chicago: University of Chicago Press, 1999), xxv.

7. Eugene P. Moehring, *Resort City in the Sunbelt: Las Vegas, 1930–2000*, 2nd ed. (Reno: University of Nevada Press, 2000), 13–49; Richard Zoglin, *Elvis in Vegas: How the King Reinvented the Las Vegas Show* (New York: Simon & Schuster, 2019), 25.

8. Moehring, *Resort City in the Sunbelt*, 76–77; Zoglin, *Elvis in Vegas*, 10, 12.

9. Zoglin, *Elvis in Vegas*, 16, 18, 174, 238.

10. For more on this early history, see Bob McGill, *Branson's Entertainment Pioneers: A Success Story for Our Times* (Reed Spring, MO: White Oak, 2011).

11. There are several sources that tell the origin stories of the Mabe and Presley families. See Arline Chandler, *The Heart of Branson: The Entertaining Families of America's Live Music Show Capital* (Charleston, SC: History Press, 2010); James D. Lancaster Jr., *Branson: The Music Show Capital of the World* (Branson, MO: James D. Lancaster, 1986); and McGill, *Branson's Entertainment Pioneers*. For more on the revived interest in southern folk in the 1960s, see Zachary J. Lechner, *The South of the Mind: American Imaginings of White Southernness, 1960–1980* (Athens: University of Georgia Press, 2018), 40. Tourism numbers from Jessica Howard, "America's Hometown: Performance and Entertainment in Branson, Missouri" (PhD diss, New York University, 1997), 46.

12. Howard, "America's Hometown," 20.

13. The most obvious exception to this remove is Silver Dollar City, a theme park that integrates a re-creation of an 1880s village with roller coasters.

14. *Legends*, documentary directed by Ilana Giannini, filmed ca. 1987, YouTube, posted October 24, 2015, https://www.youtube.com/watch?v=0XQzDrtl9Ms. On Elvis's vocal range, see Henry Pleasants, "Elvis Presley," in *Popular Music: Critical Concepts in Media and Cultural Studies*, ed. Simon Frith (New York: Routledge, 2004).

15. It is unclear if Stuart was the first person to rebrand impersonation shows as tribute shows, but from our research the language of "tribute" started appearing in newspapers only after *Legends in Concert*.

16. Quoted in Robert Reinhold, "*Las Vegas Journal*: Nevada Draws the Line: No Hitler in the Casinos," *New York Times*, April 3, 1989. See Janis McKay, "It Was Better When the Mob Ran the Town," chap. 3 in this volume.

17. Karen Sternheimer, *Celebrity Culture and the American Dream: Stardom and Social Mobility* (Oxfordshire: Routledge, 2015), 5, 9.

18. Some celebrities continue to possess cultural capital that outlasts celebrity interchangeability. For example, *Legends* almost always includes Elvis in its lineup. For more on the large market for Elvis impersonators (and Stuart's hand in creating this market!), see Leslie Rubinkowski, *Impersonating Elvis* (London: Faber & Faber, 1997).

19. Ben MacPherson, "Baudrillard on Broadway: Bio-musicals, the Hyperreal, and the Cultural Politics of Simuloquism," *Journal of Interdisciplinary Voice Studies* 5, no. 1 (2020), 9.

20. Töres Theorell and Eva Bojner Horwitz, "Emotional Effects of Live and Recorded Music in Various Audiences and Listening Situations," *Medicines (Basel)* 6, no. 1 (2019): 16.

21. Dan Collett, "Legends Never Die," *What's On in Las Vegas,* September 1983, 16.

22. Bill Moody, "The Fall and Rise of Stuart," *Las Vegas Review-Journal*, December 4, 1988.

23. Elvis Presley, "See See Rider," Aloha from Hawaii, Live in Honolulu, 1973, YouTube, uploaded March 15, 2019, https://www.youtube.com/watch?v=Jzc0MhZXXzg.

24. Charles Supin, "Legends in Concert' Is Tribute to 5 Stars," *Las Vegas Review-Journal*, June 17, 1983.

25. Bill Moody, "The Fall and Rise of Stuart."

26. Collett, "Legends Never Die."

27. "Show Guide," *Las Vegas Review-Journal*, July 20, 1988. A twenty-sixth show, *Men of Paradise* at Vegas World, had no price listed.

28. *Legends in Concert* advertisements, *Today in Las Vegas*, 1994, *Tour Guide* magazine, 1995, UNLV Archives. Documentary filmmaker Ilana Giannini observes that *Legends*' audiences in the 1980s seemed to be predominantly working-class Americans. Ilana Giannini, telephone interview by Joanna Dee Das, June 9, 2021.

29. We thank Raymond Knapp for bringing this relationship to our attention.

30. Merry Lynn Starling, "Musical Legends Live on in Stage Show," *Las Vegas Review-Journal*, April 13, 1984.

31. As of 2022, *Legends* is not only still in residence in Atlantic City, Myrtle Beach, and Branson, but also has year-round venues in Alabama, Hawaii, and on the Norwegian Pearl cruise ship. It also has seasonal productions in Wisconsin, Connecticut, Long Island, Australia, and Niagara Falls, as well as international and national tours.

32. Joy Thomas, telephone interview by Joanna Dee Das, February 13, 2020.

33. Quoted on *60 Minutes*, https://www.youtube.com/watch?v=x7uUQhloVwc.

34. Howard, "America's Hometown," 88.

35. It is unclear exactly when Branson adopted this new moniker. See Connie Farrow, "Showtown, U.S.A.: Branson Isn't Lawrence Welk Anymore. Variety Attracts Visitors of All Ages," *Press of Atlantic City*, August 1, 2004; and Hal Rothman, *Devil's Bargains:*

Tourism in the Twentieth-Century American West (Lawrence: University Press of Kansas, 1998), 333.

36. Ada Louise Huxtable, "Living with the Fake, and Liking It," *New York Times*, March 30, 1997. Huxtable's emphasis on the "real fake" echoes the claims of French philosopher Jean Baudrillard, whose now oft-cited 1994 work *Simulacra and Simulation* argues that media and the postmodern turn brought the increased erosion of the boundary between "originals" and "copies." See Jean Baudrillard, *Simulacra and Simulation* (Ann Arbor: University of Michigan Press, 1994).

37. Les Spindle, "Give Our Regards to Vegas? Theatre in the Gambling Capital Elicits Controversy," *Back Stage*, December 17, 2004, 26, 45, 51.

38. Weatherford, "Postcards from Branson, MO."

39. "Bob Anderson Biography," Bobanderson.com/bio, accessed May 20, 2021.

40. "Dear Red States; We're Leaving," attributed to John Vodonick, on *Medium*, September 21, 2020, https://suehirsch.medium.com/dear-red-states-were-leaving-by-john-vodonick-33895bb6ffb4. An earlier version of this letter was published on October 26, 2012, in the *Roanoke Times*, with "OpryLand" instead of "Branson." https://roanoke.com/news/local/an-open-letter-to-the-red-states/article_7d8b97a1–0c05–59a9–820b-1b3c79ca4081.html.

41. "Legends in Concert (Branson)," TripAdvisor, accessed March 3, 2021, https://www.tripadvisor.com/Attraction_Review-g44160-d1116560-Reviews-Legends_In_Concert-Branson_Missouri.html; and "Legends in Concert (Las Vegas)," accessed March 3, 2021, https://www.tripadvisor.com/Attraction_Review-g45963-d257192-Reviews-Legends_in_Concert-Las_Vegas_Nevada.html.

42. While relying on the visual is a fraught way to determine another person's racial identity, it can serve as a useful proxy in absence of or as supplement to demographic data. From Joanna's observations at the live performances of *Legends* in 2021, more than 90 percent of the audiences in both Branson and Las Vegas visually appeared as white or white passing. This estimation is corroborated by Branson visitor demographics overall (95 percent white from 2017 onward). In Las Vegas, Ilana Giannini, director of the *Legends* documentary who attended several shows and interviewed audience members, characterized the *Legends* audience of the late 1980s as almost exclusively white and lower middle to working class, a characterization that matches the visuals of crowd shots in the documentary.

43. Bruce Bégout, *Zeropolis: The Experience of Las Vegas* (London: Reaktion Books, 2004), 12.

17

Salaciously Family Friendly

The Unlikely Porousness of Sin City and the American Boob Tube

KELLY KESSLER

The year 1957 may have seen Dick Clark's Philadelphia-based clean teen popular music and dance sensation *American Bandstand* become a national televised phenomenon and *I Love Lucy* toast its final season, but during that same year, Harold Minsky of the Burlesque Minskys launched the Desert City's first topless review and branded a new hot desert style of entertainment. Minsky's bare-breasted showgirls would have sent Congress, the Federal Communications Commission (FCC), and the National Association of Broadcasters (NAB) into rabid cases of the vapors. Despite the two stages' sharply deviating sensibilities, Vegas and television found and embraced common ground. Nevada's "Sin City" welcomed family-friendly TV icons like Danny Thomas (*Make Room for Daddy*), Tennessee Ernie Ford (*Tennessee Ernie Ford Show*), Milton Berle (*Texaco Star Theatre*), and Ed Sullivan (*Toast of the Town*); and Vegas regulars like Steve Lawrence and Eydie Gormé, Mitzi Gaynor, and the Rat Pack brought Vegas-esque variety into American living rooms via the small screen, even when sexy had its televisual limits. Stars slid from the glitzy edge of Vegas to the glow of the small screen, but they kept it clean for the kiddies; meanwhile, television stars brought a marketable cachet to the Strip, one increasingly desirable to Vegas promoters looking to sell the next big act. It was as if Vegas and television had a magical ability to negotiate a swirl of incongruities, transmogrify performers, and breathe cross-platform appeal into apparent ideological contradictions.

This chapter explores how performers moved into and out of established—and at times evolving—television genres and how changes within the television industry opened up spaces welcoming to these at times racy performers from the desert. Television allowed Vegas to become displaced from its actual geographical space and the erotics of the Nevada desert and transform into a valued ethos of energy, sparkle, and sex-lite, just right for a developing television industry and a shifting American culture. This give-and-take of television's cultural ubiquity and Vegas flesh and flash created an unexpected sense of symbiosis between the entertainment meccas. Television lineups and regulation, variety-show guest stars, TV-Vegas casino-club pairings, and Desert City entertainment reviews help to shed light on this unexpected marriage of conservatism and salacious excess that brought a whole new meaning to the term *boob tube.*

Context Is Everything: No Boobs on the Boob Tube

The Vegas Strip and U.S. television gained steam at the same time on different sides of the country. As mobsters brought a late 1940s influx of cash to Vegas, Hollywood stars made their way to the desert. Mark Gottdiner, Claudia Collins, and David Dickens's *Las Vegas: The Social Production of an All-American City* suggests that "by attracting movie star glamor to the desert, [Bugsy] Siegel merged earlier Las Vegas venture visions with those of Hollywood fantasies."[1] By 1953 it was estimated that Strip hotels were paying out $6 million a year in entertainment.[2] The year 1947, when Siegel opened the Fabulous Flamingo, also marked the debuts of iconic New York–based television series such as Berle's *Texaco Star Theatre*, *Toast of the Town* (more commonly known as *The Ed Sullivan Show*), and the lauded anthology drama series *Studio One*, as well as a slow rise in television penetration. By 1950 TV reached only 9 percent of homes, but by 1955—as Hollywood exploded into Vegas—that number would skyrocket to 64.5 percent.[3]

Although the two industries may have found their footing at similar times, they immediately took different paths. With Minsky bringing bare breasts to the Sands in 1957, other casinos were hot to follow. The Stardust premiered Donn Arden's iconic *Lido de Paris* in 1958, the Tropicana introduced its *Folies Bergere* and the El Rancho added *Nouvelle Eve* in 1959, and the Dunes launched *Casino de Paris* in 1963. Partial nudity, sequins, and feathers came to define the culture of Vegas entertainment as television dug its heels into a kinder and gentler milieu. Per the FCC, TV and radio license holders were "trustees" of the airwaves and "guests" in American homes, and they were expected to behave accordingly. The NAB took further steps to ensure proper decorum, developing and adopting their own puritanical "Code of Practices for Television Broadcasters" in 1951. Among a long list of cardinal sins of the tube, it shunned "profanity, obscenity, smut, and vulgarity" as well as "attacks on religion," and demanded "respect for the sanctity of marriage." As if casting direct side-eye toward Vegas, it strongly encouraged de-emphasizing the consumption of liquor and "the use of gambling devices" in any manner that could "excite interest in, or foster, betting." The

NAB proclaimed that "costuming of all performers shall be within the bounds of propriety and shall avoid such exposure or such emphasis on anatomical detail as would embarrass or offend home viewers" and that movements of dancers should "be kept within the bounds of decency."[4] Any direct exchange from Mr. Minsky or on-location telecast from many of the Strip's clubs would have caused an uproar.

Despite these apparent existential contradictions, TV and Vegas maintained a close bond, with TV stars and Vegas stalwarts flowing back and forth from stage to small screen. Comedian Danny Thomas, perhaps known best for his decade-long stint on *Make Room for Daddy* (alternately titled *The Danny Thomas Show* [1953–64]), made his Vegas debut at the Flamingo in 1948, headlined the Sands' grand opening in 1952, and appeared at that casino's anniversary show every year for the next twenty-two, performing alongside Vegas royalty like Sammy Davis Jr., Joey Bishop, and Frank Sinatra, even garnering top billing in a lineup with Sinatra and Jerry Lewis.[5] *Holiday in Vegas*, airing on NBC in November 1957, marked one of the first, if not *the* first, network TV special coming to living rooms direct from Sin City. Framing the city as the "entertainment capital of the world" and (devilishly) sponsored by the Exquisite Bra Company, the show featured the likes of crooner Vic Damone, the Will Mastin Trio (starring Davis Jr.), Tony Randall, and Hollywood bombshell Jayne Mansfield. Trendex reports showed *Holiday in Vegas* running away with the evening's ratings, with the second half of the show reeling in 53.3 percent of the total television audience, more than new episodes of ABC's *Sugarfoot* and CBS's *Dick and the Dutchess*.[6] Again and again, TV audiences proved their allegiance to or at least curiosity for desert excitement.

Vegas didn't just come to TV; TV came to the Desert City. Fifties shows like *The Lucy-Desi Comedy Hour* and *The Ed Sullivan Show* took turns shooting on location and showcasing Vegas casinos to capitalize on the town's allure. The 1958 hour-long special "Lucy Hunts Uranium" was shot partially on location at the Sands, the locale for Ricky's band's fictional gig. In 1958 and 1959, Sullivan brought his show to the Desert Inn, featuring a hot combo of standards, new talent, and Vegas acts. Guests included The Kirby Stone Four, "Professor Backwards," The Morlidors, Della Reese, Helene and Howard, Pinky and Perky, and Carol Burnett—not yet a standout solo performer on TV or the Vegas stage.[7] Sullivan packaged his 1958 shows into two broadcasts, one combining stage acts with a filmette jointly arranged by the impresario, the hotel's publicity director, and the Las Vegas News Bureau, and including among other attractions aerial shots of the Strip and Hoover Dam and footage of Fremont Street and local "dude ranching." In 1959 Sullivan upped the ante on Vegas iconicity, integrating Donn Arden's iconic designs into the show—while still maintaining decorum for broadcast.[8]

By the mid- to late 1960s, television was tiptoeing toward edgier content. Although still in the throes of the NAB Code, sexual innuendo and biting political commentary were pushing at the boundaries. By this point, Davis Jr., Sinatra, Martin, and Bishop had become Vegas institutions, performing as solo headliners and as the Rat Pack. By the late sixties, Davis Jr. had landed a string of one-off television specials and a short-lived television series, Martin was hosting *The Dean Martin Show* (1965–74), Sinatra was a decade removed from his two self-titled variety series (1950–52, 1957–59) and more than a quarter way into his nearly two dozen television specials, and Bishop had hopped off of his long-running situation comedy for a two-year stint as the nighttime host of *The Joey Bishop Show*, a variety talk show providing a small-screen welcome mat for Vegas music and comedy acts like Don Rickles, Rodney Dangerfield, Davis Jr., Charo, Louis Prima, Rich Little, Wayne Newton, and Sonny & Cher. Despite wall-to-wall contradictions, the Strip became a television outpost and vice versa.

I Used to Be a Club Act: But I Don't Play One On TV

Although the fifties, sixties, and seventies lacked the infinitely permeable boundaries enjoyed by twenty-first-century stars, television shows were filled with performers who had honed their crafts in radio, film, vaudeville, burlesque, and Broadway. Acts like Burns and Allen jumped from vaudeville and nightclubs to television with their fourth wall–busting situation comedy. Before helming television hits such as *The Admiral Broadway Revue* and *Your Show of Shows*, Max Liebman produced, directed, and wrote Broadway revues, including *The Straw Hat Revue*, *Crazy with the Heat*, and *Alive and Kicking*. Crooners like Sinatra and Bing Crosby slid from big screen and vinyl to the radio and small screen with ease. The stardom such performers found being piped into America's living rooms then translated into solid Vegas clout, as promoters, newspapers, and entertainment rags marketed them via their TV roles, running photos of their TV alter egos to draw on the cachet of prime-time celebrity.

Irene Ryan, known to viewers as Granny in *The Beverly Hillbillies* (CBS, 1962–71), provides an ideal example of these kinds of stage veterans who were sold to Vegas audiences via their television personae. Ryan had performed professionally for decades prior to playing the Ozarkian matriarch: headlining at the Palace with her husband, Tim, as part of the comedy duo "Tim and Irene"; starring in a string of comedic short films; and appearing as summer replacement hosts on the radio for Jack Benny. Although comedy had been her bread and butter, she sang as well, performing comedic songs on Benny's 1936 summer replacement series, *The Jell-O Summer Show*, and singing "The Happiest Girl in Town" in Hollywood's *Hot Rhythm* of 1944. But when she premiered as the country-fried grandmother in Paul Henning's ratings-smashing, fish-out-of-water situation comedy, everything changed. The show catapulted Ryan to a new level of fame and earned the actress two Emmy nominations.

During the summer hiatus following the show's third season, Ryan headed to a four-week stint in the Sahara's famed Congo Room, marking her first Vegas nightclub appearance. She knew who audiences were there to see, taking the stage with a show blending the Ozarkian wit of Granny, the glamour of Vegas, and a hint of geriatric sex appeal. With the help of veteran comedy writer and lyricist Sid Kuller (Broadway's *Meet the People* and *Ziegfeld Follies of 1943*, Hope and Crosby's *Road to Singapore*, TV's *The Colgate Comedy Hour*, and others), Ryan blended talents she had been cultivating since her girlhood and the character who had captivated American television audiences. According to *Fabulous Las Vegas* magazine, fans loved her "from the moment she [came] on stage as the adorable little lady," claiming she immediately had them "wrapped right around her darning needle."[9] Taking the stage in Granny's shapeless prairie-flavored wardrobe, wire-framed glasses, work boots, and tight bun, and using her hillbilly accent, she performed a down-home parody of Jerry Lieber and Mike Stoller's "I'm a Woman," integrating lyrics like:

> Now I can rub and scrub Jethro's boots until they're shinin' like a dime,
> Shuck the peas, shoo the fleas, and clean the outhouse at the same time,
> Get all dressed up, go out and dance 'til four a.m. and then,
> Lay down at five, jump up at six, and start all over again,
> 'Cause I'm a woman, W-O-M-A-N, I'll say it again.[10]

Partway through the act, Ryan's Granny performed a "side-splitting spoof of a striptease" to reveal herself, Irene, "chic in a chiffon and lace short evening dress."[11] Outside of her embodiment of Granny, the sixty-three-year-old veteran relied largely on nostalgia with musical parody; impressions of vaudevillians like Eddie Cantor, Fannie Brice, and Al Jolson; and what the *Las Vegas Sun* described as a "medley of tunes from the Roaring Twenties" and a "rain" soft-shoe medley.[12]

Despite the act's midway transition from Granny to Irene, Ryan and the audience knew who the real headliner was. Garnering top billing over Andy Russell in the show's *Fabulous Las Vegas* advertisement, Ryan could not escape her TV alter ego, with her name followed by "Granny of *The Beverly Hillbillies*."[13] The *Las Vegas Review-Journal* ran a similarly slanted spot, using a headshot of Ryan styled in full Granny garb.[14] Even the actress's thank-you to the Vegas audience came from her TV character, with *Fabulous Las Vegas* running a page-length spot with dual pictures: Granny in her traditional garb positioned atop a smartly coiffed Ryan in a chic knee-length dress of pleated chiffon and lace. The copy read, "To Stan Irwin—Thank ya, Stanley! Bein' here agin [*sic*] has pleasured me quite considerable! 'Granny.'" "Irene Ryan," in all capital letters, was emblazoned across the bottom of the page, but Granny remained the star (fig. 17.1).[15] Ryan may have brought decades of experience to the Congo Room, but three seasons on CBS sold the show.

Although Ryan may be one of the more extreme cases of seasoned stage veterans being sold through their television alter egos, she was by no means alone. *Chico and the Man*'s Jack Albertson and *Barney Miller*'s Hal Linden followed similar paths to the seventies Strip. Although their acts were less reliant on "Barney" and "the Man" than Ryan's was on "Granny," small-screen notoriety, more than their lengthier stage careers, put butts in seats. Albertson had played vaudeville, burlesque, and Broadway and was sitting pretty, just a Grammy shy of the elusive EGOT (Emmy, Grammy, Oscar, Tony). He was nonetheless saddled with sharing top billing with his television character, Ed Brown. Articles frequently ran pictures of *Chico and the Man*'s unkempt Brown, rather than the tuxedoed Albertson who took the Vegas stage, and repeatedly compared Albertson to the curmudgeonly television character. Linden experienced a similar transition to Vegas clubs. Before landing the title role of the ABC cop comedy *Barney Miller*, Linden had toured with Bobby Sherwood's and Sammy Kaye's dance bands, served as one of Broadway's "forever understudies," and eventually won the Tony for initiating the role of Mayer in Jerry Bock, Sheldon Harnick, and Sherman Yellen's musical *The Rothschilds.* Despite this, reviews of his club act consistently obscured his musical past. Barney was always at the fore. The *Van Nuys Valley News* joked that Linden's singing and dancing were "unbecoming

FIGURE 17.1 In one of the entertainment rag's frequent "thank-you" spots from exiting celebrities, *Fabulous Las Vegas Magazine* shows everyone just who filled the house for the Irene Ryan show at the Sahara. *The Beverly Hillbillies*' Granny Clampett takes the literal top spot over Ryan and her decades of show-business clout. (*Fabulous Las Vegas*, May 15, 1965)

his 'Barney Miller' character," noting it was always "surprising to hear Hal sing," before going on to highlight his quite established musical career.[16] No matter how much musical background some actors had, television remained their hook. A rapt television audience of millions easily trumped dues paid on the stage.

Did You Know I Have a TV Show: Come See It

Unlike Ryan, who used Granny as a kind of bait and switch to introduce audiences to veteran performer "Irene," stars who lacked significant experience within cabaret seemed to see their television alter egos as their main selling point for the club circuit. Lorne Greene, who played the Cartwright patriarch on the hit television Western *Bonanza*, was tapped to open the Strip's Western-flavored Bonanza Hotel. Despite the star's lack of cabaret acumen, hotel publicists took out a full-page ad in *Fabulous Las Vegas* hawking "the Star of *Bonanza* in An Evening with Lorne Greene," just below an illustration of Greene wearing Cartwright's iconic white cowboy hat atop a sheriff's badge.[17] Alongside the TV icon stood a scantily clad Vegas beauty brandishing a six-shooter and decked out in a black cowboy hat, skintight black pants, cowboy boots, a black brassiere with a drooping shoulder, and a Western-detailed holster (fig. 17.2). The NAB would

FIGURE 17.2 The Hotel Bonanza may have been new, but *Bonanza* the television series had been riding high in the Nielsen ratings, sitting in the number-one spot for three consecutive seasons. Lorne Greene may not have had cabaret chops to lean on, but the TV Western's patriarch Ben Cartwright and a sexy Vegas dame were just the ticket for the new Western-themed Vegas hotel's grand opening. (*Fabulous Las Vegas*, July 1, 1967)

have been none too pleased if such a starlet had moseyed onto the set of the prime-time Western, but at the Bonanza Hotel prime-time fame and Vegas flesh coexisted peacefully. In a similar fashion, Barbara Eden landed a Vegas gig after three years of playing the magical Jeannie on NBC's 1965–70 *I Dream of Jeannie*. Like Ryan's Granny, Eden's Jeannie took over her stage show. Entertainment reporter John "Mr. Las Vegas" Cronan begged Eden to abandon the Jeannie facade, noting the prominence of a "large oriental bottle" onstage, one similar to the one in which her TV alter ego resided. He pleaded, "Barbara, please get rid of the bottle."[18] By her 1969 bill, Eden had done just that, ditching the television gimmicks and selling what the *Las Vegas Review-Journal*'s Forest Duke called a "solid standup songalong" featuring a solid lineup of "freshies," including Jimmy Webb's "Didn't We"; Blood, Sweat, and Tears' "Spinning Wheel"; and "Good Morning Star Shine" and "Aquarius" from the counterculture musical *Hair*.[19]

Carroll O'Connor, who starred as the "lovable bigot" Archie Bunker in Norman Lear's 1970s smash hit *All in the Family*, perhaps best embodies the power of television's cachet for cabaret virgins in Vegas. O'Connor had come to TV from a theater background, so he was no stranger to live audiences. *All in the Family* was even videotaped in front of a live studio audience. But cabaret was something else. In the gear-up to his Vegas debut at the Riviera in June 1972, O'Connor told both a Friar's Club Roast audience and the *Nevada State Journal* that his act would largely be "myself, talking as myself, and talking to the audience."[20] By all accounts, however, the "myself" who took the stage was Archie Bunker. Following the actor's pre-Vegas Reno debut in April 1972, the *Oakland Tribune*'s Robert Taylor ruminated about the act's strange amalgamation of O'Connor and Bunker.

> Was it Carroll O'Connor with a cigar and a New York accent? Or Archie Bunker in a tuxedo and patent leather pumps? He was both and he was neither, more a left-wing than a right-wing Archie of *All in the Family* and not completely the "real" Carroll O'Connor, at least not for long. . . . If he felt he had to, O'Connor proved he could get by for an hour without his television cast and crew, without his arm chair and his slow burns, without Jean Stapleton. But as far as establishing his own identity . . ."[21]

Whether O'Connor wanted to believe he was the one appearing beneath a thin sheen of his racist, sexist alter ego or whether he just played the Reno odds and gave the audience what they wanted, Bunker was the draw and the actor ultimately seemed to know that.

When the act opened in Vegas, it maintained its Bunker bias, with O'Connor slipping into the shadows. The actor had developed the act in tandem with TV comedy-writer Pat McCormick, who had been making the rounds of television variety, with credits including *The Jimmy Dean Show*, *The Danny Kaye Show*, and *Kraft Music Hall.* No stranger to Vegas performers, he had written Kraft's 1967 "Mitzi Gaynor Christmas Show" and seventeen episodes of *The Don Rickles Show*, including those featuring Vegas performers like Thomas, Jim Nabors, Bishop, and Burnett. Although Vegas embodied everything O'Connor's puritanical Nixon-loving Archie abhorred—formal wear, public nudity, flagrant sexual innuendo, and everything that threatened the bedrock of his existence—the O'Connor/McCormick routine deftly blended Archie with the more liberal mores of the actor himself and Sin City. Taking the stage wearing a tuxedo, but donning Bunker's trademark tattered fedora and chewing his iconic cigar, Carroll/Archie proclaimed in his best Bunker Queens accent: "Dey said I had to wear dis here suit. Da only guys who wears dis in my neighborhood are German waiters and morticians."[22] The forty-five-minute act comprised *All in the Family* malapropisms, but flavored with left-leaning political commentary and sexual innuendo antithetical to Archie. Carroll/Archie joked about the 1971 Mike Nichols sex comedy/drama *Carnal Knowledge*, or "Cardinal Knowledge," and quipped that "If anything happens to Kissinger, Nixon becomes president."[23] Bunker would have never criticized Nixon, so O'Connor must have been there as well.

When the actor briefly stepped out of his sitcom guise, he sang Vernon Duke and Yip Harburg's 1936 *Ziegfeld Follies* tune "What Is There to Say" and Hogie Carmichael's 1939 "I Get Along without You Very Well," a number already covered by Vegas stalwarts Sinatra and Davis Jr. He rounded out his act by dragging the crowd back to TV, singing his original lyrics to *All in the Family*'s familiar closing piano number, "Remembering You." Notably, he had performed the same number for television audiences just months earlier in tux and bow tie on the hit *Sonny and Cher Comedy Hour.* Vegas crowds and reviewers gushed, dubbing O'Connor and his act "unusually strong," "the Strip's newest 'overnight sensation,'" and "every bit as popular in the mammoth Versailles Theatre" as on CBS.[24] The *Las Vegas Review-Journal* evoked Archie's frequent show-based insult and declared, "Okay, meatheads, get in line," and five days later proclaimed, "Not since Engelbert Humperdinck and Liza Minnelli literally came from out of nowhere (as café entertainers) [had] the Riviera come up with a 'discovery' like O'Connor."[25] The television transfer made a splash in both Vegas and the rest of the country, with O'Connor's Riviera opening covered by CBS network news and O'Connor reportedly turning down $50,000 in post-Vegas summer bookings.[26] He instead headed back to California to prepare for *All in the Family*'s third season, one that would become the second of five consecutive top-rated seasons and the lead-in to the CBS Saturday-night powerhouse 1972–73 liberal-leaning, increasingly Vegas-tinged lineup of *All in the Family, Bridget Loves Bernie, The Mary Tyler Moore Show, The Bob Newhart Show*, and *The Carol Burnett Show.*

The TV-to-Vegas crossovers went on and on, highlighting the salability of television personalities, even when they ran counter to the class and sass of Vegas. Andy Griffith and Don Knotts headlined with Jerry Van Dyke at Caesars, capitalizing on their down-home *Andy Griffith Show* fame. Soon after the CBS country music variety series *Hee Haw* launched, cast members flooded Vegas, with Buck Owens headlining the Western-tinged Frontier and Bonanza and cohost Roy Clark being deemed "much more than a hee haw" by *Panorama* magazine.[27] And then came television stars/comedians like Demond Wilson (*Sanford and Son*), McLean Stevenson (*M*A*S*H*), and Freddie Prinze (*Chico and the Man*) staging Vegas debuts alongside big-name musical acts, with Wilson and Stevenson performing on separate bills with Vegas superstar Glen Campbell at the Las Vegas Hilton and Prinze providing "spicy stuff not intended for the kiddies" alongside Paul Anka at Caesars. Prinze—Chico to Albertson's "the Man"—notably used this 1975 Vegas stint as an opportunity to perform bits on television censorship for NAB conventioneers. Apparently, Vegas was even an escape from television's conservatism for those *penning* the medium's puritanical code.[28] Ironically, Prinze's performance occurred within weeks of the NAB adding a statute to their code setting aside 7:00 to 9:00 p.m. as a "family hour," one free from "entertainment programs inappropriate for viewing by general family audiences."[29] In one stroke, TV-Vegas hybrids could provide the kind of national, mainstream notoriety tied to the "family" broadcast medium, just the thing promoters yearned for to draw a wide cabaret audience. As an added bonus, these same stars were often more than ready to push against the restraints of the medium that had made them famous.

Don't Bring Your Boobs to the Tube, but Come on Over

The television-to-Vegas route was no one-way street. Despite more restrictive NAB regulations, ABC's, CBS's, and NBC's 1970s push for individualized brands made the medium rife for toned-down transfers from the Strip. Before the "family hour" amendment of 1975, the networks had begun dipping their toes into a slightly more salacious pool of content. The sexual revolution and political dissent hit the airwaves in ways undreamed-of just a decade earlier. As the networks rolled into the seventies, battles for audiences, advertisers, and discernible and distinctive marketing identities helped lead a new sexiness into the living room. Elana Levine, television historian and author of *Wallowing in Sex: The New Sexual Culture of 1970s Television*, argues, "The shift in influence from the traditional arbiters of sexuality [such as the legal system and the church] to the market place may be the legacy of the sexual revolution most indebted to television."[30] Sex sold. CBS was targeting younger and more liberal audiences with a string of what American sociologist Todd Gitlin has referred to as "relevance" programming, including *All in the Family*, *Maude*, *The Jeffersons*, *Good Times*, and *M*A*S*H*.[31] Abandoning the "least objectionable programming" strategies linked to shows like *The Beverly Hillbillies*, the network embraced overt and implied discussions of abortion, premarital sex, homosexuality, divorce, menopause, birth control, and so on. By mid-decade, CBS's main competitor, ABC, was pushing CBS shows out of the top spots and riding high on an alternative split-focus style of branding, one balancing family programming (*Happy Days*, *Laverne & Shirley*) and what NBC executive Paul Klein disparagingly termed "jiggle TV" (*Charlie's Angels*, *Love Boat*, *Fantasy Island*) or sexy babes cavorting in less than effective foundation garments. The doors were wide open for Vegas.

Although a relatively neutered Liberace had helmed *The Liberace Show* from 1953 to 1959, Rat Packers had dotted the small screen for years, and Mitzi Gaynor had already helmed three NBC specials—the *Kraft Music Hall* Christmas special in 1967, *Mitzi* in 1968, and *Mitzi's Second Special* in 1969—the seventies opened the televisual floodgates for a bit of Vegas sex. Between 1970 and 1980, at least a dozen specials aired directly from the Strip, with *Petula*, *Steve & Eydie: On Stage*, *Cinderella at the Palace*, and *Sinatra: The First 40 Years* coming straight from Caesars; *Ann-Margret: When You're Smiling*, *Leapin' Lizards It's Liberace*, and *Liberace: A Valentine Special* all filmed at the Las Vegas Hilton; and specials like *Opening Night: USA* and *Happy Birthday Las Vegas* featuring the city and its performers writ large. By 1969, Vegas fixture and Welsh panty magnet Tom Jones had even landed his own network series, starring in ABC's *This Is Tom Jones*—chock-full of guest stars and tight pants.

Televised shades of the Strip brought various degrees of sex appeal, skin, and sexual innuendo to the small screen. Crossover celebrities like Gaynor, Sonny & Cher, and Ann-Margret perhaps best exemplify the unique interplay of Vegas sexuality and television's limitations. Both Sonny & Cher and Gaynor had used Vegas to rejuvenate their careers. After starring in 20th Century–Fox's *South Pacific*, Gaynor's movie career had stalled out, and despite *Billboard* hits like "I Got You Babe" (number one) and "The Beat Goes On" (number six), Sonny & Cher had found themselves afloat in a burgeoning counterculture scene fueled by drugs and psychedelic rock. Both turned to Vegas and parlayed that into crossover multiplatform success: one via variety series (*The Sonny and Cher Comedy Hour*) and the other a string of successful sparkling television specials. Although perhaps not suffering the lows of Sonny, Cher, and Gaynor, Ann-Margret too turned a lull in her career into decades of sold-out Vegas crowds and a string of Vegas-esque TV specials, all complementing her Academy Award–nominated sexcapades in *Carnal Knowledge* and The Who's *Tommy*.

When Gaynor's movie career stalled after *South Pacific*, she took the advice of Flamingo investor Morris Lansburgh and turned mainstream name recognition into a smash Vegas act.[32] In response to her 1961 Vegas debut, *Life* magazine proclaimed: "Mitzi Fractures Las Vegas!"[33] No longer a sinking Hollywood starlet, she became a Vegas institution, combining inextinguishable energy, show tunes, a Vegas-lite striptease, impersonations, and a lot of sparkle, leading *Fabulous Las Vegas* to dub her "Miss Sparkle Plenty."[34] She may have been underappreciated by Hollywood, but between Vegas and television, Gaynor *was* the seventies. A mainstay on the Strip, she followed 1973's televised *Mitzi . . . The First Time* with *Mitzi . . . A Tribute to the American Housewife* (1974), *Mitzi & 100 Guys* (1975), *Mitzi . . . Roarin' in the 20s* (1976), *Mitzi . . . Zings into Spring* (1977), and *Mitzi . . . What's Hot, What's Not* (1978). A combination of Vegas shtick and the pizzazz of legendary costume designer Bob Mackie marked her specials. As I argue in *Broadway in the Box: Television's Lasting Love Affair with the Musical*, "From beginning to end, Mackie's designs helped project the singer/dancer/actress as a comfortable synthesis of the girl next door, sex-kitten, and over-the-top showgirl."[35] He dressed her in spangles (or strips of fabric that danced along with her), jumpsuits, evening gowns, florals, and everything in between. In *Mitzi . . . What's Hot, What's Not,* Mackie's pharaoh-inspired spangle dress struck anxious CBS censors as perhaps *too* Vegas, leaving nothing to the imagination, and it resulted in a portion of Gaynor's dance number being broadcast from the waist up only, Elvis-on-*Sullivan* style.

Gaynor's specials not only featured Miss Sparkle Plenty in her full glory of frenetic head shaking, high kicking, and costume changing, but also helped hawk CBS with guest appearances by network stars such as Ted Knight, Ed Asner, and Gavin McLeod of *The Mary Tyler Moore Show* and Suzanne Pleshette of *The Bob Newhart Show*, as well as stars from other networks, Broadway, and Vegas or Vegas crossovers (Jim Nabors, Rich Little, Roy Clark) (fig. 17.3). Although distanced from the clubs and casinos, Vegas was never too far in the rearview mirror. In *Mitzi & 100 Guys*, Gaynor features Vegas import and *Chico and the Man* star Albertson singing a bizarre rendition of Barry Manilow's "Mandy," and *Mitzi: Zings into Spring* employs the assistance of the U.S. Olympic Men's Gymnastics team to bring a bit of Vegas flesh and muscle—in the guise of patriotic athleticism—to the screen. Her need to exhibit a bit more visual (or sexual) restraint for prime-time audiences perhaps explains why Gaynor's specials rely more fully on her inextinguishable energy, guest stars, and what the *Los Angeles Times* called "some of that TV technical wizardry,"[36] the kind not as likely on a Vegas stage: superimpositions, lens flares, dancing with multiple projections of herself, and an electronic performance paired with the Los Angeles Coliseum jumbo scoreboard. Her specials dotted the decade with Vegas skin, energy, and flash . . . but not too much.

Much like Gaynor, sex kitten Ann-Margret brought Vegas oomph into America's living rooms. She opened at the Riviera in 1967, immediately prompting the

FIGURE 17.3 This magazine ad for Mitzi Gaynor's third CBS special, *Mitzi and 100 Guys* (1975), exemplifies the televised synthesis of Vegas and the small screen: call-out to the sponsor Kraft, scads of television guest stars, crossover Vegas celebrities, a title chock-full of sexual innuendo, and a bejeweled "Miss Sparkle Plenty," displaying her signature smile and providing glimpses of four different Bob Mackie gowns.

fire department to respond in a panic when the performer had twelve real motorcycles revving on the Riv's stage.[37] She would come to be one of the top-selling acts of sixties and seventies Vegas and flood the television airwaves with sexy Vegas-esque variety, starring in seven specials between 1968 and 1980.[38] Mike Weatherford's *Cult Vegas* says the sultry singer/dancer/actress/motorcyclist's act "grew out of TV variety-show production numbers, not to mention the diva theatricality of Garland and Dietrich."[39] By the mid-seventies, Ann-Margret was Vegas box-office gold, earning the titles of "best show featuring a lady marquee headliner to ever play Las Vegas" and "Female Entertainer of the Year."[40] When she stepped outside of Sin City, she was equally in demand, performing "25 minutes of Las Vegas" at a 1976 White House state dinner with President Gerald Ford, Secretary of State Henry Kissinger, the shah of Iran, and Empress Farah, and slinking her "variety-show stylings" into America's living rooms in varying states of evening, period, and down-home dress.[41] Transferring her wildly successful act into something amenable to prime time, she sang and danced to everything from "Thank God I'm a Country Girl" with straw hat-wearing mimes (*Ann-Margret Smith*) and a frenetic "Nutbush City Limits" with Tina Turner (*Ann-Margret Olsson*) to *Sweet Charity*'s "Better than This" on a gigantic game board (*Ann-Margret: From Hollywood with Love*) and a sultry version of the 1928 standard "When You're Smiling" (*Ann-Margret: When You're Smiling*) to Swedish folk songs like "Violets for Mother" (*The Ann-Margret Show*). From mimes to motorcycles to a mod aesthetic, she took the energy and flair of her Vegas spectaculars and converted them into something (relatively) appropriate for television's family audiences.

But televised Vegas wasn't all the sex appeal of Gaynor and Ann-Margret. Sanitized acts like The Osmonds, Burnett, and Steve and Eydie provided the glitz and glamour of Vegas without the salaciousness. Mackie showered Burnett in sequins and feathers, and Vegas stalwarts Steve and Eydie brought a Vegas cachet to a string of largely Tin Pan Alley–inspired 1970s TV specials: *Steve and Eydie: On Stage* (1973), *Steve and Eydie: Our Love Is Here to Stay* (1975) celebrating the Gershwins, *Steve and Eydie: From This Moment On . . . Cole Porter* (1977), and *Steve and Eydie Celebrate Irving Berlin* (1978). Along with middle-aged veterans like Burnett, Gormé, and Lawrence, groups like The Osmonds and Tony Orlando and Dawn brought a more youthful angle to this kinder, gentler side of televised Vegas. Such acts could be television gold in a "family hour" slot. The *Donny & Marie* variety show would even go on to outlast the policy that welcomed the sanitized duo into prime time, airing until 1979. Despite the NAB and Mr. Minsky's best efforts, TV was Vegas and Vegas was TV.

And It Continued: Now Who's Family Friendly and Who's Salacious?

With shifts in Vegas and television, the dynamic between the two outlets has certainly evolved. The decline of variety shows and specials in the late seventies and early eighties made the back-and-forth flow of entertainers a bit more challenging. Gaynor's final special aired in 1978 and Ann-Margret's in 1980. Cher brought a number of specials direct from Vegas to broadcast and cable in the eighties and nineties, bringing her Vegas residency to Showtime with *Cher: A Celebration at Caesars* in 1983, *Cher: Extravaganza—Live at the Mirage* to CBS in 1992, and *Cher: Live in Concert* direct to Showtime from the MGM Grand in 1999, among others. The rise of cable television in the eighties and specifically the increased penetration of premium or pay channels like HBO and Showtime opened up new ways for Vegas veterans like Cher and comedian George Carlin to push the boundaries of televisual decorum without the watchful eye of the FCC and NAB.

The nineties brought an identity crisis to Sin City. New Strip hotels momentarily shelved the sex and attempted to target families and expand their customer base with kid-friendly gimmicks like Treasure Island's daily pirate battle, "Battle for Buccaneer Bay," and the Excalibur Hotel targeting families with its King Arthur theme and seventy-one-foot animatronic dragon fighting Merlin in the castle's moat. In the 2000s, Vegas returned to its roots, embracing a new "What Happens in Vegas, Stays in Vegas" motto and abandoning many of its family-friendly ventures for a return to more adult entertainment. Vegas residencies returned, and pop stars found new kinds of televisual homes in a post-variety-show era. Marginalizing the display of their talents but still capitalizing on their overall celebrity, the same big names that landed Vegas residencies found side hustles as judges on a spate of TV competition shows, with Katy Perry, Luke Bryan, Jennifer Lopez, Mariah Carey, and Steven Tyler all landing Vegas residencies, as well as taking turns judging *American Idol*. Christina Aguilera, Usher, and Gwen Stefani made similar moves, enjoying Vegas residencies and judging amateurs on NBC ratings winner *The Voice*.

But the sixties and seventies were something unique, with entertainers blowing in and out of Vegas and landing spots on a TV schedule dotted with variety series and specials. The television industry was muddling through the family hour and still clinging to the last vestiges of the NAB Code. In those moments, it was like Vegas and television had a magical relationship. Like Snoop Dogg and Martha Stewart's unlikely—but seemingly legit—friendship, the two performance meccas embraced their contradictory images and cultivated celebrity, sex, and a soothing sense of "just enough" conservatism to titillate but not overstimulate the viewing masses.

Notes

Thank you to DePaul University for awarding me the University Research Council grant that funded my on-site research for this project and Su Kim Chung and the rest of the University of Las Vegas Special Collections and Archives staff for all of their help and assistance.

1. Mark Gottdiener, Caludia C. Collins, and David R. Dickens, *Las Vegas: The Social Production of an All-American City* (Malden, MA: Blackwell, 1999), 13.

2. Richard English, "The Million Dollar Talent War," *Saturday Evening Post*, October 24, 1953, 68.

3. "TV Basics Online: A Report on the Growth and Scope of Television," Television Bureau of Advertising, 2012.

4. "Code of Practices for Television Broadcasters" National Association of Television and Radio Broadcasters, 1951.

5. "Record of Runs—Celebrities," Steno Book, David Fluke Papers on Las Vegas Entertainers, Special Collections, University Libraries, University of Nevada, Las Vegas (hereafter cited as Special Collections, UNLV).

6. Jack Entratter, *Holiday in Vegas* Memo, Sands Collection, box 49, Special Collections, UNLV.

7. "Sullivan Star of Great D.I. Show," *Las Vegas Review-Journal*, July 11, 1958; "Ed Sullivan Vegas TV Show Sunday," *Las Vegas Review-Journal*, July 20, 1958.

8. "Ed Sullivan" Program, UNLV University Libraries Collection on Las Vegas, Nevada, Show Programs, 1950–2012, MS-00333, Special Collections, UNLV.

9. "Sahara," *Fabulous Las Vegas*, May 15, 1965, 16.

10. Lyrics taken from a similar performance on ABC's *The Hollywood Palace*, January 18, 1969.

11. "Sahara," *Fabulous Las Vegas*, May 15, 1965, 26.

12. Ralph Pearl, "Vegas Days and Nites," *Las Vegas Sun*, April 20, 1965.

13. Irene Ryan advertisement, *Fabulous Las Vegas*, May 8, 1965.

14. Sahara advertisement, *Las Vegas Review-Journal*, May 8, 1965.

15. "Sahara," *Fabulous Las Vegas*, May 15, 1965, 14.

16. Vic Field, "Las Vegas Ventures," *Van Nuys Valley News and Green Sheet*, April 7, 1977.

17. Hotel Bonanza advertisement, *Fabulous Las Vegas*, July 1, 1967, 6.

18. John Cronan, "Mr. Las Vegas Says," *Van Nuys Valley News*, August 13, 1968.

19. Forest Duke, "Barbara Eden Joins 'Sugar Throat' Burns," *Las Vegas Review-Journal*, August 26, 1969.

20. "O'Connor Club Debut," *Nevada State Journal*, March 31, 1972.

21. Robert Taylor, "Stage and Screen," *Oakland Tribune*, April 4, 1972.

22. "Riviera 'Discovery' Carroll O'Connor in Las Vegas Debut," *Las Vegas Review-Journal*, June 29, 1972.

23. Forest Duke, "Riv's Rare Treat: Carroll O'Connor," *Las Vegas Review-Journal*, June 23, 1972.

24. "Archie in Debut as Riviera's Star," *Las Vegas Review-Journal*, June 24, 1972; "Riviera 'Discovery' Carroll O'Connor in Las Vegas Debut," *Las Vegas Review-Journal*, June 29, 1972; Duke, "Riv's Rare Treat: Carroll O'Connor."

25. "Archie in Debut as Riviera's Star"; Duke, "Riviera's 'Discovery.'"

26. Forest Duke, "The Duke of Las Vegas," *Las Vegas Review-Journal*, June 15, 1972; Forest Duke, "The Duke of Las Vegas," *Las Vegas Review-Journal*, June 28, 1972.

27. Joan Guertin, "Roy Clark Show Dazzles Frontier Hotel Audiences," *Las Vegas Panorama*, January 9, 1976, 10.

28. Forest Duke, "The Duke of Las Vegas," *Las Vegas Review-Journal*, April 18, 1975.

29. Les Brown, "TV Designates 7–9 P.M. as 'Family Time,'" *New York Times*, April 10, 1975, 1.

30. Elana Levine, *Wallowing in Sex: The New Sexual Culture of 1970s Television* (Dunham, NC: Duke University Press, 2007), 10.

31. Todd Gitlin, *Inside Prime Time* (Berkeley: University of California Press, 2000), 205–9.

32. *Mitzi Gaynor: Razzle Dazzle! The Special Years*, directed by David Stern (City Lights Pictures, 2008).

33. "Mitzi Fractures Las Vegas," *Life*, August 4, 1961, 48–49.

34. "Riviera," *Fabulous Las Vegas*, May 9, 1970, 22.

35. Kelly Kessler, *Broadway in the Box: Television's Lasting Love Affair with the Musical* (New York: Oxford University Press, 2020), 109.

36. Aleene MacMinn, "'The First Time' Is the Third Special for Mitzi Gaynor," *Los Angeles Times*, March 25, 1973.

37. Mike Weatherford, *Cult Vegas: The Weirdest! The Wildest! The Swingin'est Town on Earth* (Las Vegas: Huntington Press), 241.

38. Ralph Pearl, "Vegas Daze and Nights," *Las Vegas Sun*, December 9, 1969.

39. Weatherford, *Cult Vegas*, 238.

40. "Ann-Margret's Colorful Production at Hilton," *Las Vegas Sun*, July 25, 1975; Mary Anderson, "Newton Named' Top Entertainer," *Las Vegas Panorama*, December 19, 1975.

41. "Notes on People," *New York Times*, May 14, 1975.

18

Representation and Value in Michael Daugherty's Las Vegas Works

LAURA DALLMAN

The bassoonist threads his way through the audience, receiving warm applause as he approaches the stage. Laughter arises, becoming even more prevalent once the applause ends. The bassoonist prepares to play, the sequins on his white jumpsuit catching the light, and swaggers a bit to enhance the mood. The bassist in the ensemble strikes the first notes, slapping his strings with a drumstick. Soon the bassoonist begins, playing long tones that reach into the depths of his instrument's register.

We are witnessing the beginning of Michael Daugherty's *Dead Elvis* (1993), one of two works by Daugherty that evoke Elvis and one of eight that center on Las Vegas.[1] Yet in these eight works, listed in table 18.1, it is hard not to hear Daugherty. A composer who has experienced success in nearly every classical genre, Daugherty is a champion of Americana. Many of his compositions highlight iconic American figures and places, and his musical style in these compositions is distinctive. Short and repetitive phrases, additive layering of musical ideas, and frequent melodic quotation characterize his music, acting like aural landmarks. Once one can recognize Daugherty's style, it becomes as distinguishable as the fountains at the Bellagio.

But Las Vegas is undoubtedly in this music. In these eight works, Daugherty's approach to timbre evokes the flood of visual stimuli in the city. Performance indications of a visual nature also help create a populist flavor, suggesting the atmosphere of a place that thrives not only on commercial tourism, but on excess and theatricality. Most convincing, though, is Daugherty's inclusion of musical

TABLE 18.1 Daugherty's Las Vegas Works

Title	Year	Ensemble type
Firecracker	1991	Solo oboe and chamber ensemble
Dead Elvis	1993	Solo bassoon and chamber ensemble
Elvis Everywhere	1993	String quartet and prerecorded sound
Lounge Lizards	1994	Two pianos, two percussion
Le Tombeau de Liberace	1996	Piano and orchestra (concerto)
Route 66	1998	Orchestra
Sinatra Shag	1998	Solo violin and chamber ensemble
Lost Vegas	2011	Orchestra or symphonic band

Note: These ensemble designations are provided by Daugherty on his personal website. See https://michaeldaugherty.net.

quotations, which produce aural echoes of well-known performers associated with Las Vegas lounges and casinos.

Together, these characteristics produce clear vestiges of Las Vegas for listeners, though not without some provocation. Classical music is often associated with good taste and high art, which are not immediate descriptors typically afforded to Las Vegas or its performers. Daugherty brings the deliciously gaudy culture of Las Vegas to the traditionally refined performance hall, and in doing so forces listeners to consider that Las Vegas, a city known for overwhelming and sometimes tacky spectacle, has a place on the concert stage. I suggest that by putting Las Vegas on display in a "classical" setting, Daugherty entangles the essence of Las Vegas with the implied values of the concert hall, thus forcing listeners to reconsider values associated with classical music performance.

Evoking Las Vegas: Sonic Abundance and Visual Spectacle

In his Las Vegas–inspired works, Daugherty mimics the visual abundance of the city with timbral diversity. He also provides opportunities for musicians to engage in visual display; several indications in his Las Vegas scores produce striking gestures of showmanship, and two works traditionally include performers dressed like specific Las Vegas icons. Altogether, these characteristics evoke optical ostentatiousness, and perhaps even sensory overload, that seems inescapable in Las Vegas, but unexpected in the concert hall.

Regarding timbre, Daugherty uses a wide array of instrumental techniques. The variation of instrumental sounds echoes the various architectural styles, signs, and lights of Las Vegas that often change in quick succession. When standing at the famous Bellagio fountain, for example, and looking across the Strip, one can turn to the right and see the modernist Cosmopolitan. One can look straight ahead and see the Disneyesque Eiffel Tower replica. Then one can turn left and see the postmodernist Caesars Palace. During night hours, vibrant lighting also draws the eye, creating, along with the architecture, a sense of visual excess.

Sonically, Daugherty's listeners are treated to an auditory feast, and the impressive buffet of offerings is made abundantly clear with a quick inventory of techniques. With strings, Daugherty uses pizzicato, secco, *sul ponticello*, *sul tasto*, and *col legno*. He calls for slapped strings, slapped fingerboards, scratched bridges, and ricochets, and he also employs a range of vibrato styles. In *Elvis Everywhere*, for example, he indicates an "Elvis vibrato," which requires at least a cursory understanding of Elvis's recordings in order to mimic the vocal style. A "Las Vegas vib[rato]" in the second movement of *Le Tombeau de Liberace*, henceforth identified as *Tombeau*, suggests a schmaltzy style of playing, but, without further notes or instructions, leaves the interpretation up to either the string instrumentalists or the conductor. Similarly, a "mariachi vibrato" for trumpet in the final movement of *Tombeau* omits playing directions, giving interpretive license to the performers.

Percussion sections include a broad list of instruments. In *Tombeau* percussionists use splash, sizzle, and ride cymbals. *Firecracker* requires various mallet and percussive finger techniques, while *Lounge Lizards* requires maracas to be "swirled." *Route 66* calls specifically for wooden dowel rods to be used on cymbals and bongos. Regarding wind instruments, Daugherty often calls for brass to use straight metal mutes, Harmon mutes, or plungers. *Tombeau* and *Firecracker* include flutter-tonguing for woodwinds. Glissandi appear not only in every work of Daugherty's Las Vegas series, but in nearly every instrumental family.

One particularly intriguing timbral choice regards *Elvis Everywhere*. This work, written in 1993, is the only work in the Las Vegas series that includes prerecorded material. Written for string quartet and prerecorded tape, the tape, which is actually a CD, includes vocalizations by three Elvis impersonators and a baritone saxophone. This use of recorded material is especially significant because, as Janis L. McKay describes in her book *Played Out on the Strip*, the Las Vegas Musicians' Union held a strike from June 1989 into January 1990, protesting the replacement of musicians with taped material.[2] By August 1989, the strike had garnered attention across the United States. As the *Chicago Tribune* reported: "The dispute began in May, when the musicians union sat down to renegotiate its contract with the Big Five hotels: Bally's, Caesars Palace, the Flamingo Hilton, the Las Vegas Hilton and the Tropicana. The hotels announced that they wanted the right to unlimited use of tapes and synthesizers in their production rooms, where large revues are staged. Live music would continue in the rooms where celebrities perform, but the hotels would no longer guarantee work for local musicians."[3]

Initially, several star headliners, including Wayne Newton and Frank Sinatra, supported the union musicians, refusing to perform with recorded tapes. Yet as the strike continued for months without resolution, headliners increasingly crossed the picket line.[4] Although *Elvis Everywhere* does not come on the direct heels of the union strike, Daugherty wrote the work less than three years later, and it is possible that negative feelings regarding the strike still remained. As such, the work directly embodies Elvis, but could indirectly embody concerns of Las Vegas musicians: the voices representing Elvis, a headliner, are prerecorded, while the accompanying musicians, who would be comparable to union musicians, turn the tables and perform live.

A cultural turning of tables is also common in Daugherty's Las Vegas works. More specifically, classical patrons and musicians are trained not to call attention to themselves. Patrons engage in respectful concert etiquette. Musicians follow strict dress codes to make the ensemble look cohesive. String sections bow uniformly, generating a unified visual presentation. Audiences have been primed to hear, see, and even participate in certain codes of decorum in the concert hall, codes that the musicians in Daugherty's Las Vegas pieces frequently break. For example, at several points during "Fever" in *Lost Vegas*, Daugherty indicates for performers to stand or raise their bells in the air. He indicates raised bells, too, in the fourth movement of *Tombeau* and *Dead Elvis*, the latter of which also instructs the bassoon soloist to "get down on one knee" in the final measures. In "Ramada Inn" from *Lounge Lizards*, Daugherty concludes the movement with the instruction, "upon hearing rimshot leap off of piano bench in a startled fashion."[5]

Instrumentalists in a traditional symphony or chamber ensemble do not typically leap off the bench, take a knee, stand to play, or raise their bells. Such directives draw the eye, and the actions of leaping or kneeling, in particular, may draw differing audience, and even performer, reactions.[6] Some may find the actions humorous, perhaps recalling the antics of another Las Vegas showman, pianist Victor Borge. Others may find the actions kitschy or garish, viewing the directives as a form of pandering to the audience. One thing is certain, though: Daugherty's visually oriented instructions in his scores are optically arresting.

Some of Daugherty's visual spectacle, however, derives from more traditional means. For instance, *Lounge Lizards* and *Tombeau* include several gestures for the pianist that are meant to dazzle viewers, but these gestures derive from idiomatic writing for the piano. In *Lounge Lizards*, which is perhaps more subdued, Daugherty varies techniques throughout its four movements, including passages of rapid repeated notes, fast figuration, upward arpeggios, and both parallel and interlocking octaves. *Tombeau*, on the other hand, is a technical tour de force that includes sparkling arpeggiations, flashy arm crossings, cascading glissandi, and shimmering trills. In the finale, "Candelabra Rhumba," a variety of octave techniques—interlocking, broken, and contrary octaves—often occurs in quick succession and within a fast tempo. On the whole, the various piano techniques in *Tombeau* require the pianist to be all over the keyboard, emulating Liberace's glitzy, audience-pleasing style and clearly alluding to the spectacle of his Las Vegas performances.

To make the performance even more visually dramatic, performers of *Tombeau* also have the option of performing in costume. Although it is not required, enough performers have donned costumes or used props that such visual additions have become ingrained in the performance culture.[7] One of the most readily accessible performances was posted in a series of YouTube videos in October 2012 by pianist Kylan deGhetaldi. To begin his performance, deGhetaldi makes a grand entrance in a fur coat, which is removed by two stagehands.[8] Underneath the coat, he wears a costume reminiscent of Liberace's wardrobe: his pink suit features lacy ruffled sleeves, and his jacket sparkles with sequins and embroidery on the lapels, sleeves, and chest. The piano also displays Liberace's trademark candelabra.

In *Tombeau* both sight and sound become critical. Hearing *and* seeing become paramount as Las Vegas is evoked sonically and bodily. A similar situation happens with our opening vignette. In *Dead Elvis*, the bassoonist traditionally dresses as Elvis for the performance. Although in an interview with Martin Perlich, Daugherty affirms that the bassoonist is "an Elvis impersonator," and not Elvis himself, there is no indication in Daugherty's score or program notes that the bassoonist must dress like Elvis.[9] Yet impersonating Elvis seems like half the fun, as figure 18.1 shows, and one can find several examples of performers on YouTube that have donned a jumpsuit and coiffed a pompadour.

Dead Elvis, however, goes one step further than *Tombeau*. In *Dead Elvis*, Daugherty incorporates a clear quotation from Elvis's famous song "It's Now or Never," an anglicization of the Italian "O sole mio."[10] This straightforward musical reference all but reincarnates Elvis on the stage as he "sings" through the bassoon, upping the ante if the performer is costumed as an Elvis impersonator.

FIGURE 18.1 Dr. Shannon Lowe as Elvis (*Dead Elvis*), University of Florida, December 2018. Photograph by Peter Geldrich.

Daugherty is providing an undeniable representation of Elvis, but in doing so, he is also taking a gamble on how classically minded audiences may respond.

Beyond Impersonation: Including Musical Quotation

As with *Dead Elvis*, Daugherty's *Sinatra Shag* and *Elvis Everywhere* also utilize melodies sung by well-known Las Vegas performers. In these two works, snippets of popular songs not only generate an aural echo of music associated with Las Vegas acts, but also lend an air of authenticity to Daugherty's works. Yet while one might argue that these quotations provide legitimacy by sonically rendering a given entertainer, another may argue that Daugherty's use of popular styles thwarts convention by being too lowbrow for classical music, thus cheapening the works' artistic worth.

With *Sinatra Shag*, Daugherty begins thwarting expectations with his title. For most people, "Sinatra Shag" will likely bring Frank Sinatra to mind, but the work actually draws upon a popular song sung by Sinatra's daughter Nancy. Although Daugherty does not cite the quotation in his program notes, he does refer to both Frank and Nancy Sinatra: "The composition evokes the Las Vegas

EXAMPLE 18.1A Daugherty, *Sinatra Shag*, cello, mm. 6–7.

EXAMPLE 18.1B Author's transcription, Nancy Sinatra, "These Boots Are Made for Walkin'," Groove.

era when leading American popular music entertainers of the 1960s such as Frank Sinatra, and his daughter Nancy, performed at the Sands Hotel."[11]

To be more specific, in m. 6 of *Sinatra Shag*, Daugherty provides a "bass" line for the cello that sets up a catchy groove. This groove, provided in example 18.1a, is a paraphrase of the instrumental outro of Nancy Sinatra's "These Boots Are Made for Walkin'" (1966), with minimal changes to the original material. Daugherty writes for cello, as opposed to bass and trumpets, and omits an octave displacement of the second note; otherwise, the melodic and rhythmic patterns of Sinatra's material, transcribed in example 18.1b, are unchanged.

Additionally, Daugherty later writes a descending chromatic line in the violin that is reminiscent of the instrumental intro and interludes between verses of "These Boots." In Sinatra's song, the bass descends chromatically for the first sixteen beats, with each noted played and repeated over a downward span of a perfect fifth. Daugherty uses double-stops, keeping the tonic note of F sounding consistently under the descending line, but the gesture is clearly similar. He then repeats his idea several times. A comparison of the gestures is shown in examples 18.2a and 18.2b.

EXAMPLE 18.2A Daugherty, *Sinatra Shag*, violin, mm. 40–43.

EXAMPLE 18.2B Author's transcription, Nancy Sinatra, "These Boots Are Made for Walkin'," intro/interlude.

Although Daugherty does not use the groove (example 18.1b) constantly, he uses it often, providing a foundation for other instrumental material. At times the groove is enhanced by doubling in other instruments, including the flute and piano. Other times, the groove is layered or alternated with a host of other techniques, particularly in the violin. For example, functioning much like a soloist, or perhaps even a headliner, the violinist begins the entire work playing alone. Dissonant minor ninths shift to a melody near the top of the violin's range, followed by a seven-measure solo segment that includes ricochet, pizzicato, *col legno*, a glissando, double-stops, and triple-stops.

As *Sinatra Shag* continues, other instruments play dissonant intervals, including sevenths and tritones, and Daugherty layers musical motives using an additive texture. Such passages generate a subtler link to Las Vegas lounges, which were places where musicians could experiment with difficult or new music. In some cases, the playing level was higher in lounges than it was in the main showrooms, and lounges were frequently spaces where new artists or acts were allowed to try their material.[12] Ultimately, though, the alternation of dissonant, virtuosic, and layered musical materials with paraphrases of "These Boots" situates two performing traditions of Las Vegas side by side. Daugherty's compositional techniques imply innovative lounge acts, while "These Boots" recalls popular Las Vegas headliners and, by extension, their glamorous shows. Additionally, the phrases from "These Boots" provide audience members an aural anchor for *Sinatra Shag*. The presence of popular music does not devalue or mar the work; rather, it clarifies the work.

The same holds true for *Elvis Everywhere*. Here, Daugherty incorporates melodies and lyrics from Elvis's songs as well as words and phrases associated with both his legendary career and his death. Sonically, three Elvis impersonators enhance Daugherty's melodic and textual borrowings, immediately recalling the vocal sound of the performer. Yet, ironically, because the vocal parts are prerecorded, Elvis is not physically present onstage. One cannot escape his sound, but neither can one see him. Elvis is, in fact, now everywhere.

It is fairly easy to hear quotations of Elvis's songs in *Elvis Everywhere*, but the score makes the musical borrowings absolutely transparent. For example, in m. 77 Daugherty indicates "Hound Dog" above the staff, and the Elvis impersonators sing "I ain't nothing but a . . ."[13] Although the tempo is about half the speed of Elvis's original tempo, textual and melodic borrowing make the quotation clear. Over pickup notes into m. 91, Daugherty indicates "Dixie." This minstrel song, attributed to Daniel Emmett, appeared in a medley that Elvis incorporated into his act in early 1972.[14] The impersonators pass the melodic phrases of the song among themselves, then join together to conclude the song's melody. Later, in m. 165, Daugherty writes an instrumental quotation, indicating both "O sole mio" and "It's Now or Never" above the first violin's part. He uses only the first half of the song's famous chorus, however, trading melodic phrases between the violins.[15]

But Daugherty's use of quotation is only one noteworthy aspect of *Elvis Everywhere*. If one considers the complete instrumentation—strings, voice, and baritone saxophone—and compares it with Daugherty's other Elvis-inspired works, timbral connections emerge. In *Dead Elvis*, Elvis is impersonated specifically by the bassoonist. Although the bassoon is obviously not synonymous with the baritone saxophone, it has a similar range and reedy timbre. In "Viva," the opening movement to *Lost Vegas*, Daugherty opens with a groove in the baritone saxophone, which is quickly joined by the contrabassoon.[16] In "Fever," the last movement of *Lost Vegas*, the opening melody features solo bassoons. Daugherty does not indicate direct musical quotations of Elvis in either of these movements, but timbral similarities with *Elvis Everywhere* and *Dead Elvis* suggest that Elvis might be embedded in *Lost Vegas*.

This possibility is strengthened in two additional ways. In m. 65 of "Viva," bongos become prominent, making a timbral allusion to Elvis's song "Viva Las Vegas." In fact, in the film *Viva Las Vegas*, viewers see and hear five bongo players before Elvis begins to sing the title song. Thus, bongos could sonically stand in for Elvis. Additionally, Daugherty's program notes clearly refer to Elvis: *Lost Vegas* is "a swinging tribute to an earlier epoch, when legendary entertainers such as Elvis . . . performed in intimate and swanky showrooms" of Las Vegas.[17] Elvis is there, even though we do not see him.

This network of connections, and evident inclination toward representations of Elvis, suggests that Daugherty is creating his own compendium of Elvis lore. But Daugherty actually creates this lore by utilizing the compositional practice of musical borrowing, which is commonly found in "highbrow" music. Composers trained in Western practices have recycled and reworked music of various styles, including popular styles, for centuries. Additionally, Daugherty's network of connections is best heard through attentive listening. It is almost as if he is hiding sonic Easter eggs, which one can recognize only through purposeful aural engagement. If one casts aside Daugherty's music as cheap or lowbrow, these rich relationships could be easily overlooked.

The Value of Las Vegas

Undoubtedly, Daugherty prepares us to hear and see Las Vegas in his series of eight works. In this series, he constructs sonic suggestions of the city's visual excess with his clever use of timbral variety. Musical quotations produce aural resonances of famous performers. Physical cues in the scores generate a visual kind of showmanship common to Las Vegas, and costuming helps bring larger-than-life personas back to the stage. Flashy showmanship, fantastic personae, and popular styles of music, which are common in Vegas showrooms, then intersect with the more subdued decorum and class associated with today's concert halls.

The broader issue with Daugherty's series, though, regards value. Las Vegas captivates audiences with its colorful lights and entertainment, inviting people into a pulsing and vibrant world. But how real is Las Vegas? In truth, much of it is imagined and fabricated. Likewise, concert music traditions and attitudes in America are highly constructed. Classical musicians are trained not to call attention to themselves in the way they dress and perform, unless they are soloists. Ensembles must present as unified. Patrons are also expected to follow a code of polite social decorum. In classical spaces, values of surface and depth, accessibility and enigma, and the humorous and the sublime have come to seem antithetical. Whatever is imagined or understood as Las Vegas is not something that fits easily into what is imagined or understood in classical settings.

Yet Daugherty pushes against established classical behaviors, perceptions, and expectations with his representations of Las Vegas, a place where rules fly out the window in favor of entertainment and pleasure. We can smile at the accessible, surface layer of borrowed phrases in these glitzy, glamorous Las Vegas works while recognizing that Daugherty incorporates techniques of classical composition. He is not forsaking tradition; he is reminding us that it is conceivable to go to a concert simply to be amused, not edified. He encourages us to delight in and even laugh at a musical gag. He assures us it is possible to loosen decorum in the performance hall without burning it to the ground. What happens in Vegas, Daugherty shows, does not have to stay in Vegas.

Notes

1. "Dead Elvis Live at Change Music Festival 2016 with Fredrik Ekdahl," Change Music Festival, August 9, 2016, YouTube, https://www.youtube.com/watch?v=2yz0GATxSC8.

2. See Janis L. McKay, "The Strike of 1989," in *Played Out on the Strip: The Rise and Fall of Las Vegas Casino Bands* (Reno: University of Nevada Press, 2016), 161–91.

3. Mary T. Schmich, "Taped Tunes Put Musicians on Picket Lines in Vegas," *Chicago Tribune*, August 26, 1989, https://www.chicagotribune.com/news/ct-xpm-1989-08-21-8901060351-story.html.

4. McKay, *Played Out on the Strip*, 180–84.

5. "Ramada Inn," *Lounge Lizards*, m. 86.

6. Janet K. Halfyard has discussed similar issues regarding audience preconceptions of instrumental performance gestures in "Provoking Acts: The Theatre of Berio's *Sequenzas*," in *Berio's Sequenzas: Essays on Performance, Composition, and Analysis* (London: Ashgate, 2007), 110–11.

7. Some references to performers in costume come from Daugherty himself. See Frank Oteri, "NewMusicBox Icon Artist Interview," December 11, 2006, https://www

.youtube.com/watch?v=EaJNeqKO0-4; Jenny Raymond, Yale Oral History of American Music, "Interview I (Side C)," July 31, 1999, https://michaeldaugherty.net/interviews/yale-oral-history-of-american-music-interview-i-side-c-d/; and John Fleming, "Pop Goes the Composer," *St. Petersburg (FL) Times*, February 4, 2000, https://www.tampabay.com/archive/2000/02/04/pop-goes-the-composer/.

8. "Le Tombeau de Liberace (Michael Daugherty)—I. Rhinestone Kickstep," YouTube, October 29, 2012, https://www.youtube.com/watch?v=QJWPTux8CwM.

9. "Martin Perlich Interviews Michael Daugherty on Dead Elvis," December 11, 2004, https://michaeldaugherty.net/interviews/martin-perlich-interviews-michael-daugherty-on-dead-elvis/.

10. *Dead Elvis*, mm. 82–92. The song is unlabeled in the score, but the bassoon soloist is instructed to play with an "Elvis *vibrato*" and "*espr. â la Las Vegas*," tying the clear quotation to Elvis's Las Vegas shows. Elvis recorded "It's Now or Never," an adaptation of the Neapolitan song "O sole mio," in April 1960 after returning from his military tour in Germany. Freddy Bienstock, a music publisher's representative, commissioned the adaptation. See Peter Guralnick, *Careless Love: The Unmaking of Elvis Presley* (Boston: Little, Brown, 1999), 65.

11. *Sinatra Shag*, program note (New York: Boosey & Hawkes, 1998).

12. McKay, *Played Out on the Strip*, 63, 88.

13. Daugherty changes the pronoun from "you" to "I."

14. Guralnick, *Careless Love*, 455. The medley was crafted by Mickey Newberry.

15. This quotation occurs in a section Daugherty labels "Black Belt." Beginning with pickups into m. 154, the impersonators articulate "karate sounds," thus juxtaposing one of Elvis's most recognizable melodies with his interest in karate. Ultimately, he even incorporated karate demonstrations in his shows. Guralnick discusses Elvis and karate in several chapters of *Careless Love*.

16. Like *Sinatra Shag*, the groove sounds often, but is not consistent.

17. *Lost Vegas*, program (composer's) note.

19

Specters of Mine

Musicological Research in the Desert of the Opera

CARLO LANFOSSI

On November 25, 2014, I was driving through Ash Meadows Road in the state of California, the fastest way from the biggest town near the Death Valley desert, Pahrump, Nevada, to the place where I was supposed to meet with some of the ghosts I had been hunting for some time. I was headed in the direction of Death Valley Junction (current population, four). There—I was told by friends and colleagues—I would find a theater in the middle of the desert, the Amargosa Opera House and Hotel, run by an almost mythological figure who, back in the 1960s, decided to quit her career as a ballerina in New York to establish her art in the middle of nowhere in Death Valley. As soon as I arrived at Death Valley Junction, and as if on cue, the rented car I was driving got a flat tire.

In the spring of 1967, a forty-three-year-old ballerina from New York, Marta Becket, and her husband, Tom Williams, were driving through Death Valley as part of a performance tour. They were headed in the direction of Death Valley Junction. There—as told by the park ranger—they would find the only garage who could fix their car's sudden flat tire. While the car was being repaired, Marta found what looked like an abandoned building. As she walked down a colonnade, she noticed a mysterious back door and peered through a tiny hole in it, revealing what looked like an abandoned theater. She immediately felt as if she was "looking at the other half of [her] life."[1]

Like many writers, journalists, and graduate students before me—and as an Italian scholar living on the East Coast—I left the Las Vegas Strip and drove through the desert to leave behind the fantasies of a life modeled around academia and meet with the fantasy of another life, an Other life of musicological research where fieldwork and history, present and past, me and non-me would somehow be entangled. Marta left the Los Angeles highways to meet the fantasy of a real life in the desert and the Desert of the Real, where her performances would entangle with haunted histories and otherworldly spaces.

In the end, almost fifty years later, she met me.

• • •

My obsession for the quirky story of a ballerina and her theater in the middle of the desert stems from my interest in and understanding of opera as a genre inherently "haunted by instances of recurrence that had little to do with linear influences and more with issues of memory, replacement, and repression."[2] Moreover, opera houses are frequently imagined as haunted buildings, "powerful repositories of cultural memory" whose allure for audiences is built on the phantasmagoric quality of the experience of attending the reenactment of an ancient tradition.[3] This peculiar hauntological framework is thus inherently bound to overflow into the realm of the very subjects and objects of my "historical fieldwork," as ghosts seem to inhabit pretty much every theatrical space and time I have been researching—from the Orphic birth of opera to Lacanian insights on opera historiography, from the ghosting of previous music in Handel's pasticci to the Benjaminian *flâneries* of nineteenth-century Milan's galleries. I did not choose to stay among specters: we both failed to leave.

The Amargosa Opera House and Hotel lies at the intersection of State Routes 190 and 127, close to the border of California and Nevada, far enough from Vegas's loathing allure and near enough to live in fear of the ghost stories surrounding the valley's casinos and roadhouses. No wonder the place is called

FIGURE 19.1 The Amargosa Opera House and Hotel. Death Valley Junction, CA.

Death Valley Junction: much like the cathedral in the desert it conveniently hosts, the village is pure threshold; it is the place where you can only go left or right, as U-turning brings you back to the Other threshold—that is, the desert. In 1967 Marta Becket did what Orpheus could not: she chose not to turn back. She decided to stay.

Over the first few minutes of *Amargosa* (2000), an Academy Award finalist documentary dedicated to the story of Marta's theater in the desert, the voice of Mary McDonnell narrates the magical site as a "state of mind," a "deserted crossroad in the badlands of an uncertain future," reachable only "amongst the rubble of another time."[4] Of all the possible uncertain futures, Marta chose the most solitary one: entirely by herself, she renovated the lone Death Valley Junction building (once known as Corkhill Hall) and transformed it into a theater where she could perform her ballets and plays (also written by herself) for an audience yet to appear. And spectators did make an appearance: between 1967 and 1974, they (im)materialized as shadowy thirds over the walls of the opera house, thanks to the relentless work of this New York ballerina (by now in her fifties) who painted her own imagined community of simulacra. The uncanny interiors now display an array of present and past visitors, from Spanish rulers to local pets, with the aim of filling the empty theater with the ghosts of the valley's colonial histories and genealogies.

Back then, the few Mormon families living in the area showed little interest in Marta's plays and asked only for ballet classes for the kids. The crowdy murals were thus conceived not only to fill the void of an empty space, but also as a sort of artistic oddity to quench the thirst for those 1970s desert travelers seeking curiosities and out-of-body experiences. Rumors about this bizarre performance site in the middle of the desert began spreading, and in 1970 both *National Geographic* and *Life* had articles and photographs about Amargosa.[5] The myth had started.

By projecting a fictional collection of characters taken from the stories she used to dance to (kings and queens, ambassadors, nuns, and so on), Marta was gazed upon at first by only a multiplicity of her own selves but then eventually was observed by national discourse and wandering customers. This conflation of different times became one of the topics of conversation when I finally had the chance to speak with her during my stay at the Amargosa Opera House and Hotel in November 2014.

• • •

It was Thanksgiving week: roads were empty, and Las Vegas was cheap—one of the main reasons a graduate student like me could afford such remote and elaborate fieldwork. I decided to stay at the hotel connected to the opera house, hoping to speak to as many people as I could about the place and its owner. I did

FIGURE 19.2
The interior of the Amargosa Opera House.

not really know what I was trying to achieve, other than collecting voices and acting like a more informed visitor than I actually was. On Thanksgiving Day, the telephone rang as I was reading in the lobby. It was Marta (recently turned ninety), asking if she could have lunch with the women who were running the business. Suddenly, the atmosphere inside the hotel had turned from timeless stasis to frenzied action.

I was the only guest invited—mostly because I was the only one available. Marta Becket arrived in a wheelchair accompanied by a woman in her forties; she was dragging the "cart," thus leaving Marta facing toward the back, in the opposite direction of the opera house. The ballerina was a pale skin-and-bone reflection of the dancer she used to be. She barely talked. But when she did, her low voice seemed to come out of another dimension. "Life is a disappointment" was one of her refrains during the two hours we spent together. As I was listening to her voice during our conversation, I could hear her own younger voice juxtaposed by the speakers of the television that was showing nonstop the documentary *Amargosa*. It was as if an audible past kept breaking into our present. The effect was spooky, to say the least. "I like being alone," she said, to which one of the workers added, "But you always have all the crowd around you when you're performing, so you're still around a lot of people." "Yes, but they're too tame . . . in an invisible world . . ." were Marta's closing remarks.

During the Thanksgiving lunch I was seated with three women other than Marta. They volunteer to run the hotel and promote the business around the place (the gift shop, tours of the opera house, and so forth). Together they create

FIGURE 19.3 Marta Becket, November 2014.

a community that worships Marta and her art, as I can tell by the tears they still shed every time they glimpse a dramatic scene from the documentary screening in the hall. Over the years, they have promoted online campaigns and fundraisers to keep the business running, as Marta quit performing in 2011 and the place can rely only on the income from hotel revenues and tax-free donations. During our conversations, I could tell that, even though I stated from the very beginning the reason I was there, the attention I received hinged upon a silent request of economic support on my behalf. Soon, I realized that this sort of women-run "gift economy" permeated more than the walls of the hotel and opera house.

The economy of the valley was at the center of every conversation I had during my three days there. I was sent to the nearest town, twenty miles south of Death Valley Junction, called Shoshone Village (population, thirty-one) which still hosts a post office, a working gas station, a saloon, and the Shoshone Museum. As I entered the museum, I was greeted by Ethel, the local guide, who tells me everything she knows about Marta and points me in the direction of an entire wall devoted to the "Death Valley Women," which includes explorers, teachers, composers, and of course Marta Becket. Among the memorabilia, a playbill of one of the first events at the Amargosa Opera House: Marta was apparently dancing over nineteenth-century European classical music. The museum overflows with historical newspapers and articles that testify to the extent and relevance played by women's spheres and communal economy in Death Valley since the end of the nineteenth century. A few of them are dedicated to three of the major economic activities of the valley at the time: brothel management, mining companies, and stock markets.[6] Marta's family participated in such a narrative not only because she managed to run an art business almost by herself, but also because her mother "was addicted to the stock market," as she told everyone at the Thanksgiving lunch.

In the discourses surrounding women's cultural sphere in the valley, men are constantly described with a condescending tone. During our lunch, I am briefly joined by two men who I understand are regular handymen and also their partners: anytime they would take the floor, the women looked away with embarrassed faces. The stories of their male companions all follow this narrative of acquiescence and failure. Men are nullified to the point of being rendered as ghosts: across and aside from the "Women of Death Valley" wall at the Shoshone Museum, the gift-shop shelves have on display a few biographies and essays explicitly emphasizing the spectral quality of male discourses. Among them, I was able to spot titles such as *Ghost Riders in the Sky* and *These Canyons Are Full of Ghosts*.[7] The most recurring stories dealing with the ghosts of Death Valley center on the mining industry and the hard life conditions in which workers had to live. One of these is directly related to the Amargosa Opera House and Hotel. As indicated by the plaque still hanging outside, the theater "was originally built by the Pacific Coast Borax Company in 1924 . . . and was the social center for Death Valley Junction between 1924 to 1948." The sign was placed in 1988 by the fraternal organization "E Clampus Vitus," a "historical drinking society" whose "obsession" with plaquing is part of a larger mission to mark sites at the intersection of reality and absurdity, in line with the brotherhood's motto *Credo Quia Absurdum*, generally understood as "I believe because it is absurd."[8] It is certainly telling that a men-only organization was the one responsible for labeling one of the most special buildings in Death Valley as a liminal place, where even ghosts have to deal with sublimation through artistic means.

Back at my lunch at the hotel, Marta kept repeating how her husband was a complete disappointment (their troubled relationship had in fact ended in 1983). The person who replaced him as both stage assistant and lover was Tom Willett (amicably referred to as "Wilget"), a local character who started performing with Marta by playing the piano, then by entertaining the audience with all sorts of jokes, and finally by being Marta's dancing partner, almost always cross-dressed. In her autobiography, she recalls how Wilget "created a music machine. A sort of mechanized pipe organ that played several instruments at his commands. Wilget would put on a little show of his own. He loved the attention and people loved him. He didn't steal the show, I gave it to him."[9] In such emasculating narratives, even their musical instruments and music are soulless, mechanic, haunted. It is Marta who grants agency to men. In the desert, it is the female gaze that defines men.

One of the items that struck my curiosity at the Shoshone Museum was the vocal score for "An Ode to Death Valley." Song and lyrics were composed by Pauline Frederick, a woman who ran the Death Valley View Hotel and later our Amargosa Hotel, long before Marta did.[10] The piece starts with an eerie prelude consisting of sixteen arpeggios of dominant and diminished seventh chords and unfolds in *durchkomponiert* (or through-composed) style.

> You are a land of mystery
> Far, far away from the sea
> Grim mountains meet grey desert sand,
> Oh haunting, fascinating land
> Where sand dunes play
> And soft breezes stray,
> Oh land of mystery;
> Many have perished [*long pause*]
> While fanned by your breath,
> And thus you are called the Valley of Death!

FIGURE 19.4 Pauline Frederick, "An Ode to Death Valley" (1928), cover. Shoshone Museum, Shoshone, CA.

The song is mentioned as "inspired by scenes such as the one reproduced on the cover," a black-and-white shot "looking West from Zabriskie Point," without any trace of human activity.[11] Even though the Mojave Desert is certainly not home to the deadliest place on the planet, death here nevertheless informs every corner and discourse. For the women of the valley, coping with the trauma of living in such a hostile environment meant collectively disembodying men and producing art. A handwritten dedication on the front page of Pauline Frederick's score at the museum affectionately mentions one "Miss Cromwall, hoping that you have learned to love Death Valley as I do." The official printed dedication is instead to Christian Brevoort Zabriskie, vice president of Pacific Coast Borax Company and thus the boss of Harry P. Gower, Pauline's husband. His name still resonates in the valley at Zabriskie Point, named after him as representative of a haunted mining company. It is also still home to some of the best-known out-of-body experiences, from the protagonists of Michelangelo Antonioni's 1970 movie, *Zabriskie Point*, who "have no resonance as human beings,"[12] to Michel Foucault's famous 1975 acid trip listening to Richard Strauss's *Four Last Songs*, a trip mythologized as a turning point in his reflections on being and sexuality. "Is this perhaps death?"[13]

• • •

I left Death Valley Junction with much less self-transforming thoughts and with certainly less historically burdened music than Richard Strauss and local odes to the valley. The drive back to Las Vegas occurred almost entirely in complete darkness. "There's no such thing as a bad coincidence," I must have told myself as I stubbornly tried to weave together my flat tire with Marta's, operatic ghosts with the desert, even David Lynch's 1997 film, *Lost Highway*, as not only did I know his nonlinear movie had been filmed at the Amargosa Opera House and Hotel, but also because I knew its most iconic scene was literally unfolding in front of me.

FIGURE 19.5 Ash Meadows Road, Inyo County, CA.

I got to my Las Vegas hotel in need of a drink. I sat at the bar, when suddenly a rather spectral Britney Spears entered on a small stage and started singing "Oops! I Did It Again" in the company of a few male dancers. She was lip-synching throughout the song, while young adults in the audience were throwing money at her. As I recovered from the confusion of such a coincidence—not being sure where I was or if I had just entered one of David Lynch's "Club Silencio"—the bartender kept repeating to me, "You're very lucky!" The effect was uncanny: Spears's lively voice from the past adhered perfectly to the deathly context I had just left. It appeared to constitute a recurring event, one that happened every week, as Britney Spears was temporarily in residence in Vegas. Ghosts, after all, rely on repetition to exist—they always did it again. The time of young Britney Spears and our decaying present as well as the deathly presence of Marta Becket and her younger voice on TV at the same time collided and matched, in and out of joint.

Fast-forward to 2022. During a class on American Music, I show the brief clip of Britney Spears in Las Vegas that I took with my phone back in 2014. The video is blurry, but you can clearly distinguish who is onstage. A student comes up and lets me know that the artist they are watching onscreen is not really Britney Spears, but rather Derrick Barry, a Spears impersonator who at that time was opening for Lady Gaga in Vegas and making his way as a reality television personality after having participated in the third season of *America's Got Talent*.[14] As the student tells me that they recognized his characteristic wig, I realize not only that I have been the subject of a bartender's prank, but that such a revelation could not have been more appropriate, acting as a sort of double *après-coup* to make sense of both Britney's role in this story and my own ghosting. The epiphany I had as a young, naive graduate student would have made Foucault (and present-day students) laugh: fieldwork is the revealing of one single possible time-world in an infinite possible sets of times-worlds, while ghosts are the disembodied proof of separate times and spaces disclosing at once, the traces left by historiographical discourses. "Music is our theology," said Foucault in the desert listening to the voice of Elisabeth Schwarzkopf. "There's no such thing as a bad coincidence," added a detective at the end of *Lost Highway*, echoed by a Las Vegas bartender in 2014. The musicologist, for once, got lost in this game and at a drastic loss of words. Singing. Flat. Ghostlike.

Notes

1. Most of the background on Marta Becket's life comes from her autobiography, *To Dance on Sands: The Life and Art of Death Valley's Marta Becket* (Las Vegas: Stephens Press, 2007), esp. the section "Act Four: My Ship Comes in—in the Desert," 282–328.

2. Carlo Lanfossi, "Ghosting Agrippina: Genealogies of Performance in Italian Baroque Opera," *Journal of Musicology* 36, no. 1 (2019): 7.

3. Marvin Carlson, *The Haunted Stage: The Theatre as Memory Machine* (Ann Arbor: University of Michigan Press, 2003), 144.

4. *Amargosa*, documentary written and directed by Todd Robinson (Triple Play, 2000), transcript of 2:14–2:35.

5. Rowe Findley, "Death Valley, the Land and the Legend," *National Geographic*, January 1970, 69–103; "Ballet in Death Valley," *Life*, April 17, 1970, 42–43.

6. See Sally Zanjani, *A Mine of Her Own: Women Prospectors in the American West, 1850–1950* (Lincoln: University of Nebraska Press, 1997); and Robin Flinchum, *Red Light Women of Death Valley* (Charleston, SC: History Press, 2015).

7. Michael K. Ward, *Ghost Riders in the Sky: The Life of Stan Jones, the Singing Ranger* (Tucson: Rio Nuevo, 2014); Emmett Carl Harder, *These Canyons Are Full of Ghosts: The Last of the Death Valley Prospectors* (San Bernardino: Real Adventure, 2001).

8. Jesse McKinley, "Promoting Offbeat History between the Drinks," *New York Times*, October 14, 2008, https://www.nytimes.com/2008/10/14/us/14california.html. See also Lois Rather, *Men Will Be Boys: The Story of E Clampus Vitus* (Oakland: Rather Press, 1980).

9. Becket, *To Dance on Sands*, 325.

10. Richard E. Lingenfelter, *Death Valley & the Amargosa: A Land of Illusion* (Berkeley: University of California Press, 1986), 456.

11. Pauline Frederick Gower, *An Ode to Death Valley* (Ryan, CA: self-published, 1928), 6.

12. Roger Ebert, review of *Zabriskie Point*, directed by Michelangelo Antonioni, *Chicago-Sun Times*, January 1, 1970, www.rogerebert.com/reviews/zabriskie-point-1970.

13. The reference is to the last line of Richard Strauss's *Im Abendrot* as mentioned in the trip's memoir by Simeon Wade, *Foucault in California* (Berkeley: Heyday, 2019), 69. The actual relevance of the Death Valley trip within Foucault's philosophy has been recently critiqued and questioned by Kurt Borg, "Foucault on Drugs: The Personal, the Ethical and the Political in *Foucault in California*," *Foucault Studies* 28 (2020): 142–64.

14. See "Bio," Derrick Barry personal website, accessed October 5, 2022, http://derrickbarry.com/bio.html. I would like to thank Wilson Miller for their identification of the Spears impersonator.

Contributors

CELINE AYALA is a PhD candidate in the Department of Sociology and Criminology at the University of New Mexico. Her previous work focused on the Las Vegas Streetcar Scene as an alternative form of community. Celine currently examines Afrolatinx experiences framed within Black and Afrolatin feminist theories.

KIRSTIN BEWS holds a Master of Arts degree in comparative literature and art from Brock University, and she is currently in her second year of music and culture at Carleton University. Kirstin researches gender and sexuality in music, including the intertextual relationship between sound and image.

LAURA DALLMAN is currently an associate instructional professor at the University of Florida. Her research addresses issues of reception and accessibility, particularly regarding orchestral music and performance in the twentieth and twenty-first centuries. She has published book chapters on selected works by Michael Daugherty and Jennifer Higdon and presented her research at conferences in the United States, Ireland, England, and Wales.

JAMES DEAVILLE, professor of music at Carleton University, has published in the *Journal of the American Musicological Society*, *Journal of the Society for American Music*, *American Music*, *Journal of Musicological Research*, and *Music and Politics*, and has contributed to books published by Oxford, Cambridge, and Routledge, among others. He recently coedited the *Oxford Handbook of Music and Advertising* (2021) and is working on a monograph about music in cinematic trailers.

JOANNA DEE DAS is an assistant professor of dance at Washington University in St. Louis. Her research interests include dance in the African diaspora, musical theater dance, and the politics of performance in the twentieth and twenty-first centuries. She is the author of the award-winning *Katherine Dunham: Dance and the African Diaspora* (2017) and is currently working on a history of the entertainment industry in Branson, Missouri.

ROBERT FINK is a past chair of the UCLA Musicology Department and current chair of UCLA's interdepartmental degree program in Music Industry. His research focus is on music and culture after 1950, with special interests in the history and analysis of African American popular music, EDM, and the cultural politics of contemporary art music. His co-edited volume *The Relentless Pursuit of Tone: Timbre in Popular Music* was awarded the American Musicological Society's Ruth A. Solie Prize for best collection of essays in 2019.

PHEAROSS GRAHAM is a Mellon Postdoctoral Fellow in the Humanities and Lecturer in Music at Stanford University. As a musicologist and concert pianist, Dr. Graham explores the fault lines between theory and performance, focusing on pianism since the Romantic era, musicians' lived experiences, middlebrow and racial politics, and performance analysis. Currently, his musicological projects foreground Sergei Rachmaninoff and Donald Shirley.

JESSICA A. HOLMES is an assistant professor of musicology at the University of Copenhagen. Her research examines the representation of disability in contemporary musical practice, with attention to questions of embodiment, vocality, and identity formation. Her first book project, *Music at the Margins of Sense*, forthcoming from the University of Michigan Press, explores the relationship between music and deafness. Her peer-reviewed articles appear in the *Journal of American Musicological Society*, *Journal of the Society for American Music*, *Journal of Popular Music Studies*, and *Journal of Interdisciplinary Voice Studies*.

MADDIE HOUSE-TUCK has her MA in theater and performance studies from Washington University in St. Louis and is getting her PhD in American studies at George Washington University. Her research intersects studies of policing and performance, surveying forms of spectacle that proliferate images and ideas about police power.

JAKE JOHNSON is an assistant professor of musicology at the University of Oklahoma. A consummate musician, Jake brings his expertise as collaborative pianist, conductor, and musical director to his investigations of the lived experience of music-making in America. Much of this work centers belief and gathering. He is the author of *Mormons, Musical Theater, and Belonging in America* (2019) and *Lying in the Middle: Musical Theater and Belief at the Heart of America* (2021).

KELLY KESSLER is a professor of media and cinema studies at DePaul University and author of *Broadway in the Box: Television's Lasting Love Affair with the Musical* (2020) and *Destabilizing the Hollywood Musical: Music, Masculinity, and Mayhem* (2010). She is also the editor of *Gender, Sex, and Sexuality in Musical Theatre:*

He/She/They Could Have Danced All Night (2023), and her work can also be found in such diverse publications as *Wired*, the *Advocate*, and *Television and New Media*.

MICHAEL KINNEY is a PhD candidate in musicology at Stanford University. He is interested in music of the nineteenth, twentieth, and twenty-first centuries; aging; vocality; performance studies; and the medical humanities. His dissertation, supported by the Alvin H. Johnson AMS 50 Fellowship from the American Musicological Society, centers aging opera singers as culturally significant in redefining what it means to grow old and questions opera's aesthetic focus on vocal beauty, purity, and perfection.

CARLO LANFOSSI is research fellow (Ricercatore RTDA) at the University of Milan, Italy. His research focuses on opera historiography and hauntology, at the intersection of psychoanalysis and performance studies. He is currently working on a digital project cofinanced by the European Union (FSE-REACT-EU, PON Research and Innovation, 2014–20) on the libretto collection of the Archivio Storico Ricordi in Milan. He has written on topics such as ghosting in baroque opera, the operatic pasticcio as listening inscription, the soundscape of nineteenth-century Milan, and the history of Italian musicology.

JASON LEDDINGTON is associate professor of philosophy at Bucknell University. He writes on perception (mainly on hearing and sound) and issues in aesthetics and philosophy of art (mainly on magic and other arts of impossibility, but also on music).

JANIS MCKAY is vice dean of the College of Fine Arts at the University of Nevada, Las Vegas. She performs as principal bassoonist of the Las Vegas Philharmonic, contrabassoonist of the Reno Philharmonic, and principal bassoonist of the Classical Music Festival in Austria. McKay has taught numerous undergraduate and graduate courses in music history and bassoon. She published in the *New Grove Dictionary of American Music* and authored *Played Out on the Strip: The Rise and Fall of Las Vegas Casino Bands* (2016).

SAM MURRAY is a lecturer in music business and arts management at Middlesex University in London, with a teaching focus on entrepreneurship, events management, and arts policy and finance. His PhD thesis was "Ethnography of the Music Scene in Portland, Oregon," with a particular focus on music policy making. He also explored the hermeneutics of the scene, interpreting the language and layers of meaning used throughout the city.

LOUIS NIEBUR is associate professor of musicology at the University of Nevada, Reno. His most recent book, *Menergy: San Francisco's Gay Disco Sound* (2022), tells the story of the queer dance-music labels that arose in San Francisco in the wake of the "death" of disco in 1979.

LYNDA PAUL is assistant director of Undergraduate Writing and Tutoring and the Academic Strategies Program at Yale University, where she also teaches in multiple departments across the arts and humanities. She holds degrees from the Eastman School of Music, the University of Rochester, the University of Chicago, the Yale School of Drama, and Yale's Graduate School of Arts and Sciences, where she received distinction on her PhD in music history/ethnomusicology.

ARIANNE JOHNSON QUINN is the Head of Manuscripts and College of Music Archivist, Florida State University. She has also worked as digital archivist and research associate for the Noël Coward Archive Trust. Her research explores the British and American musical in London's West End from 1920 to 1960.

MICHAEL M. REINHARD is a lecturer at Rutgers University, New Brunswick, and NEH Postdoctoral Fellow at Montclair State. Currently, he is developing his research monograph, *The Diva's Public: Celebrity, Media Activism, and the New Cultural Citizenship*, to explore new logics of mediated citizenship and social activism in contemporary media. His work has appeared in *Velvet Light Trap*, *Intersectional Feminist Readings of Comics* (Routledge, 2021), and *Feminist Media Studies*. Dr. Reinhard's upcoming research will be featured in *Television & New Media*, *The Films of Susan Seidelman*, and *The Oxford Handbook of American Documentary*.

LAURA RISK is assistant professor of music and culture in the Department of Arts, Culture, and Media at the University of Toronto, Scarborough, with a graduate cross-appointment at the Faculty of Music, University of Toronto. She has published in *Ethnomusicology*, *Critical Studies in Improvisation*, and *MUSICultures*. In 2020 she wrote a cover story on Ginger Smock for *Strings Magazine*.

CASSAUNDRA RODRIGUEZ is an assistant professor of sociology at the University of Nevada, Las Vegas. She specializes in Latinx sociology, immigration, family, race, and gender. She is currently collecting data for her second book project, *Viva Mariachi! Student Musicians Crafting Culture, Educational Resilience, and Resistance in Las Vegas*.

ARREANNA ROSTOSKY holds a PhD in musicology from UCLA. Her research interests include theater sound design, projection mapping, theme-park entertainment, and contemporary Broadway musicals. Arreanna is an avid fan of Sondheim, megamusicals, and Disney shows, all of which she wrote about in her dissertation, "Reconsidering the 'Golden Age' Narrative for the American Musical in the New Millennium."

BRIAN F. WRIGHT is assistant professor of music history at the University of North Texas. He is a former research assistant for the Rock & Roll Hall of Fame Library and Archive. His research primarily focuses on the history of the electric bass in American popular music, exploring issues such as authenticity, social stigma, amateur music making, race, gender, and popular music historiography.

Index

Music in American Life

Only a Miner: Studies in Recorded Coal-Mining Songs *Archie Green*
Great Day Coming: Folk Music and the American Left *R. Serge Denisoff*
John Philip Sousa: A Descriptive Catalog of His Works *Paul E. Bierley*
The Hell-Bound Train: A Cowboy Songbook *Glenn Ohrlin*
Oh, Didn't He Ramble: The Life Story of Lee Collins, as Told to Mary Collins *Edited by Frank J. Gillis and John W. Miner*
American Labor Songs of the Nineteenth Century *Philip S. Foner*
Stars of Country Music: Uncle Dave Macon to Johnny Rodriguez *Edited by Bill C. Malone and Judith McCulloh*
Git Along, Little Dogies: Songs and Songmakers of the American West *John I. White*
A Texas-Mexican *Cancionero*: Folksongs of the Lower Border *Américo Paredes*
San Antonio Rose: The Life and Music of Bob Wills *Charles R. Townsend*
Early Downhome Blues: A Musical and Cultural Analysis *Jeff Todd Titon*
An Ives Celebration: Papers and Panels of the Charles Ives Centennial Festival-Conference *Edited by H. Wiley Hitchcock and Vivian Perlis*
Sinful Tunes and Spirituals: Black Folk Music to the Civil War *Dena J. Epstein*
Joe Scott, the Woodsman-Songmaker *Edward D. Ives*
Jimmie Rodgers: The Life and Times of America's Blue Yodeler *Nolan Porterfield*
Early American Music Engraving and Printing: A History of Music Publishing in America from 1787 to 1825, with Commentary on Earlier and Later Practices *Richard J. Wolfe*
Sing a Sad Song: The Life of Hank Williams *Roger M. Williams*
Long Steel Rail: The Railroad in American Folksong *Norm Cohen*
Resources of American Music History: A Directory of Source Materials from Colonial Times to World War II *D. W. Krummel, Jean Geil, Doris J. Dyen, and Deane L. Root*
Tenement Songs: The Popular Music of the Jewish Immigrants *Mark Slobin*
Ozark Folksongs *Vance Randolph; edited and abridged by Norm Cohen*
Oscar Sonneck and American Music *Edited by William Lichtenwanger*
Bluegrass Breakdown: The Making of the Old Southern Sound *Robert Cantwell*
Bluegrass: A History *Neil V. Rosenberg*
Music at the White House: A History of the American Spirit *Elise K. Kirk*
Red River Blues: The Blues Tradition in the Southeast *Bruce Bastin*
Good Friends and Bad Enemies: Robert Winslow Gordon and the Study of American Folksong *Debora Kodish*
Fiddlin' Georgia Crazy: Fiddlin' John Carson, His Real World, and the World of His Songs *Gene Wiggins*
America's Music: From the Pilgrims to the Present (rev. 3d ed.) *Gilbert Chase*
Secular Music in Colonial Annapolis: The Tuesday Club, 1745–56 *John Barry Talley*
Bibliographical Handbook of American Music *D. W. Krummel*

Goin' to Kansas City *Nathan W. Pearson Jr.*
"Susanna," "Jeanie," and "The Old Folks at Home": The Songs of Stephen C. Foster from His Time to Ours (2d ed.) *William W. Austin*
Songprints: The Musical Experience of Five Shoshone Women *Judith Vander*
"Happy in the Service of the Lord": Afro-American Gospel Quartets in Memphis *Kip Lornell*
Paul Hindemith in the United States *Luther Noss*
"My Song Is My Weapon": People's Songs, American Communism, and the Politics of Culture, 1930–50 *Robbie Lieberman*
Chosen Voices: The Story of the American Cantorate *Mark Slobin*
Theodore Thomas: America's Conductor and Builder of Orchestras, 1835–1905 *Ezra Schabas*
"The Whorehouse Bells Were Ringing" and Other Songs Cowboys Sing *Collected and Edited by Guy Logsdon*
Crazeology: The Autobiography of a Chicago Jazzman *Bud Freeman, as Told to Robert Wolf*
Discoursing Sweet Music: Brass Bands and Community Life in Turn-of-the-Century Pennsylvania *Kenneth Kreitner*
Mormonism and Music: A History *Michael Hicks*
Voices of the Jazz Age: Profiles of Eight Vintage Jazzmen *Chip Deffaa*
Pickin' on Peachtree: A History of Country Music in Atlanta, Georgia *Wayne W. Daniel*
Bitter Music: Collected Journals, Essays, Introductions, and Librettos *Harry Partch; edited by Thomas McGeary*
Ethnic Music on Records: A Discography of Ethnic Recordings Produced in the United States, 1893 to 1942 *Richard K. Spottswood*
Downhome Blues Lyrics: An Anthology from the Post–World War II Era *Jeff Todd Titon*
Ellington: The Early Years *Mark Tucker*
Chicago Soul *Robert Pruter*
That Half-Barbaric Twang: The Banjo in American Popular Culture *Karen Linn*
Hot Man: The Life of Art Hodes *Art Hodes and Chadwick Hansen*
The Erotic Muse: American Bawdy Songs (2d ed.) *Ed Cray*
Barrio Rhythm: Mexican American Music in Los Angeles *Steven Loza*
The Creation of Jazz: Music, Race, and Culture in Urban America *Burton W. Peretti*
Charles Martin Loeffler: A Life Apart in Music *Ellen Knight*
Club Date Musicians: Playing the New York Party Circuit *Bruce A. MacLeod*
Opera on the Road: Traveling Opera Troupes in the United States, 1825–60 *Katherine K. Preston*
The Stonemans: An Appalachian Family and the Music That Shaped Their Lives *Ivan M. Tribe*
Transforming Tradition: Folk Music Revivals Examined *Edited by Neil V. Rosenberg*
The Crooked Stovepipe: Athapaskan Fiddle Music and Square Dancing in Northeast Alaska and Northwest Canada *Craig Mishler*

Traveling the High Way Home: Ralph Stanley and the World of Traditional Bluegrass Music *John Wright*
Carl Ruggles: Composer, Painter, and Storyteller *Marilyn Ziffrin*
Never without a Song: The Years and Songs of Jennie Devlin, 1865–1952 *Katharine D. Newman*
The Hank Snow Story *Hank Snow, with Jack Ownbey and Bob Burris*
Milton Brown and the Founding of Western Swing *Cary Ginell, with special assistance from Roy Lee Brown*
Santiago de Murcia's "Códice Saldívar No. 4": A Treasury of Secular Guitar Music from Baroque Mexico *Craig H. Russell*
The Sound of the Dove: Singing in Appalachian Primitive Baptist Churches *Beverly Bush Patterson*
Heartland Excursions: Ethnomusicological Reflections on Schools of Music *Bruno Nettl*
Doowop: The Chicago Scene *Robert Pruter*
Blue Rhythms: Six Lives in Rhythm and Blues *Chip Deffaa*
Shoshone Ghost Dance Religion: Poetry Songs and Great Basin Context *Judith Vander*
Go Cat Go! Rockabilly Music and Its Makers *Craig Morrison*
'Twas Only an Irishman's Dream: The Image of Ireland and the Irish in American Popular Song Lyrics, 1800–1920 *William H. A. Williams*
Democracy at the Opera: Music, Theater, and Culture in New York City, 1815–60 *Karen Ahlquist*
Fred Waring and the Pennsylvanians *Virginia Waring*
Woody, Cisco, and Me: Seamen Three in the Merchant Marine *Jim Longhi*
Behind the Burnt Cork Mask: Early Blackface Minstrelsy and Antebellum American Popular Culture *William J. Mahar*
Going to Cincinnati: A History of the Blues in the Queen City *Steven C. Tracy*
Pistol Packin' Mama: Aunt Molly Jackson and the Politics of Folksong *Shelly Romalis*
Sixties Rock: Garage, Psychedelic, and Other Satisfactions *Michael Hicks*
The Late Great Johnny Ace and the Transition from R&B to Rock 'n' Roll *James M. Salem*
Tito Puente and the Making of Latin Music *Steven Loza*
Juilliard: A History *Andrea Olmstead*
Understanding Charles Seeger, Pioneer in American Musicology *Edited by Bell Yung and Helen Rees*
Mountains of Music: West Virginia Traditional Music from *Goldenseal* *Edited by John Lilly*
Alice Tully: An Intimate Portrait *Albert Fuller*
A Blues Life *Henry Townsend, as told to Bill Greensmith*
Long Steel Rail: The Railroad in American Folksong (2d ed.) *Norm Cohen*
The Golden Age of Gospel *Text by Horace Clarence Boyer; photography by Lloyd Yearwood*

Aaron Copland: The Life and Work of an Uncommon Man *Howard Pollack*
Louis Moreau Gottschalk *S. Frederick Starr*
Race, Rock, and Elvis *Michael T. Bertrand*
Theremin: Ether Music and Espionage *Albert Glinsky*
Poetry and Violence: The Ballad Tradition of Mexico's Costa Chica *John H. McDowell*
The Bill Monroe Reader *Edited by Tom Ewing*
Music in Lubavitcher Life *Ellen Koskoff*
Zarzuela: Spanish Operetta, American Stage *Janet L. Sturman*
Bluegrass Odyssey: A Documentary in Pictures and Words, 1966–86 *Carl Fleischhauer and Neil V. Rosenberg*
That Old-Time Rock & Roll: A Chronicle of an Era, 1954–63 *Richard Aquila*
Labor's Troubadour *Joe Glazer*
American Opera *Elise K. Kirk*
Don't Get above Your Raisin': Country Music and the Southern Working Class *Bill C. Malone*
John Alden Carpenter: A Chicago Composer *Howard Pollack*
Heartbeat of the People: Music and Dance of the Northern Pow-wow *Tara Browner*
My Lord, What a Morning: An Autobiography *Marian Anderson*
Marian Anderson: A Singer's Journey *Allan Keiler*
Charles Ives Remembered: An Oral History *Vivian Perlis*
Henry Cowell, Bohemian *Michael Hicks*
Rap Music and Street Consciousness *Cheryl L. Keyes*
Louis Prima *Garry Boulard*
Marian McPartland's Jazz World: All in Good Time *Marian McPartland*
Robert Johnson: Lost and Found *Barry Lee Pearson and Bill McCulloch*
Bound for America: Three British Composers *Nicholas Temperley*
Lost Sounds: Blacks and the Birth of the Recording Industry, 1890–1919 *Tim Brooks*
Burn, Baby! BURN! The Autobiography of Magnificent Montague *Magnificent Montague with Bob Baker*
Way Up North in Dixie: A Black Family's Claim to the Confederate Anthem *Howard L. Sacks and Judith Rose Sacks*
The Bluegrass Reader *Edited by Thomas Goldsmith*
Colin McPhee: Composer in Two Worlds *Carol J. Oja*
Robert Johnson, Mythmaking, and Contemporary American Culture *Patricia R. Schroeder*
Composing a World: Lou Harrison, Musical Wayfarer *Leta E. Miller and Fredric Lieberman*
Fritz Reiner, Maestro and Martinet *Kenneth Morgan*
That Toddlin' Town: Chicago's White Dance Bands and Orchestras, 1900–1950 *Charles A. Sengstock Jr.*
Dewey and Elvis: The Life and Times of a Rock 'n' Roll Deejay *Louis Cantor*
Come Hither to Go Yonder: Playing Bluegrass with Bill Monroe *Bob Black*
Chicago Blues: Portraits and Stories *David Whiteis*

The Incredible Band of John Philip Sousa *Paul E. Bierley*
"Maximum Clarity" and Other Writings on Music *Ben Johnston, edited by Bob Gilmore*
Staging Tradition: John Lair and Sarah Gertrude Knott *Michael Ann Williams*
Homegrown Music: Discovering Bluegrass *Stephanie P. Ledgin*
Tales of a Theatrical Guru *Danny Newman*
The Music of Bill Monroe *Neil V. Rosenberg and Charles K. Wolfe*
Pressing On: The Roni Stoneman Story *Roni Stoneman, as told to Ellen Wright*
Together Let Us Sweetly Live *Jonathan C. David, with photographs by Richard Holloway*
Live Fast, Love Hard: The Faron Young Story *Diane Diekman*
Air Castle of the South: WSM Radio and the Making of Music City *Craig P. Havighurst*
Traveling Home: Sacred Harp Singing and American Pluralism *Kiri Miller*
Where Did Our Love Go? The Rise and Fall of the Motown Sound *Nelson George*
Lonesome Cowgirls and Honky-Tonk Angels: The Women of Barn Dance Radio *Kristine M. McCusker*
California Polyphony: Ethnic Voices, Musical Crossroads *Mina Yang*
The Never-Ending Revival: Rounder Records and the Folk Alliance *Michael F. Scully*
Sing It Pretty: A Memoir *Bess Lomax Hawes*
Working Girl Blues: The Life and Music of Hazel Dickens *Hazel Dickens and Bill C. Malone*
Charles Ives Reconsidered *Gayle Sherwood Magee*
The Hayloft Gang: The Story of the National Barn Dance *Edited by Chad Berry*
Country Music Humorists and Comedians *Loyal Jones*
Record Makers and Breakers: Voices of the Independent Rock 'n' Roll Pioneers *John Broven*
Music of the First Nations: Tradition and Innovation in Native North America *Edited by Tara Browner*
Cafe Society: The Wrong Place for the Right People *Barney Josephson, with Terry Trilling-Josephson*
George Gershwin: An Intimate Portrait *Walter Rimler*
Life Flows On in Endless Song: Folk Songs and American History *Robert V. Wells*
I Feel a Song Coming On: The Life of Jimmy McHugh *Alyn Shipton*
King of the Queen City: The Story of King Records *Jon Hartley Fox*
Long Lost Blues: Popular Blues in America, 1850–1920 *Peter C. Muir*
Hard Luck Blues: Roots Music Photographs from the Great Depression *Rich Remsberg*
Restless Giant: The Life and Times of Jean Aberbach and Hill and Range Songs *Bar Biszick-Lockwood*
Champagne Charlie and Pretty Jemima: Variety Theater in the Nineteenth Century *Gillian M. Rodger*
Sacred Steel: Inside an African American Steel Guitar Tradition *Robert L. Stone*

Gone to the Country: The New Lost City Ramblers and the Folk Music Revival
Ray Allen
The Makers of the Sacred Harp *David Warren Steel with Richard H. Hulan*
Woody Guthrie, American Radical *Will Kaufman*
George Szell: A Life of Music *Michael Charry*
Bean Blossom: The Brown County Jamboree and Bill Monroe's Bluegrass Festivals
Thomas A. Adler
Crowe on the Banjo: The Music Life of J. D. Crowe *Marty Godbey*
Twentieth Century Drifter: The Life of Marty Robbins *Diane Diekman*
Henry Mancini: Reinventing Film Music *John Caps*
The Beautiful Music All Around Us: Field Recordings and the American Experience
Stephen Wade
Then Sings My Soul: The Culture of Southern Gospel Music *Douglas Harrison*
The Accordion in the Americas: Klezmer, Polka, Tango, Zydeco, and More!
Edited by Helena Simonett
Bluegrass Bluesman: A Memoir *Josh Graves, edited by Fred Bartenstein*
One Woman in a Hundred: Edna Phillips and the Philadelphia Orchestra
Mary Sue Welsh
The Great Orchestrator: Arthur Judson and American Arts Management
James M. Doering
Charles Ives in the Mirror: American Histories of an Iconic Composer
David C. Paul
Southern Soul-Blues *David Whiteis*
Sweet Air: Modernism, Regionalism, and American Popular Song
Edward P. Comentale
Pretty Good for a Girl: Women in Bluegrass *Murphy Hicks Henry*
Sweet Dreams: The World of Patsy Cline *Warren R. Hofstra*
William Sidney Mount and the Creolization of American Culture
Christopher J. Smith
Bird: The Life and Music of Charlie Parker *Chuck Haddix*
Making the March King: John Philip Sousa's Washington Years, 1854–1893
Patrick Warfield
In It for the Long Run *Jim Rooney*
Pioneers of the Blues Revival *Steve Cushing*
Roots of the Revival: American and British Folk Music in the 1950s
Ronald D. Cohen and Rachel Clare Donaldson
Blues All Day Long: The Jimmy Rogers Story *Wayne Everett Goins*
Yankee Twang: Country and Western Music in New England *Clifford R. Murphy*
The Music of the Stanley Brothers *Gary B. Reid*
Hawaiian Music in Motion: Mariners, Missionaries, and Minstrels
James Revell Carr
Sounds of the New Deal: The Federal Music Project in the West *Peter Gough*
The Mormon Tabernacle Choir: A Biography *Michael Hicks*

The Man That Got Away: The Life and Songs of Harold Arlen *Walter Rimler*
A City Called Heaven: Chicago and the Birth of Gospel Music *Robert M. Marovich*
Blues Unlimited: Essential Interviews from the Original Blues Magazine
Edited by Bill Greensmith, Mike Rowe, and Mark Camarigg
Hoedowns, Reels, and Frolics: Roots and Branches of Southern Appalachian Dance
Phil Jamison
Fannie Bloomfield-Zeisler: The Life and Times of a Piano Virtuoso
Beth Abelson Macleod
Cybersonic Arts: Adventures in American New Music *Gordon Mumma, edited with commentary by Michelle Fillion*
The Magic of Beverly Sills *Nancy Guy*
Waiting for Buddy Guy *Alan Harper*
Harry T. Burleigh: From the Spiritual to the Harlem Renaissance *Jean E. Snyder*
Music in the Age of Anxiety: American Music in the Fifties *James Wierzbicki*
Jazzing: New York City's Unseen Scene *Thomas H. Greenland*
A Cole Porter Companion *Edited by Don M. Randel, Matthew Shaftel, and Susan Forscher Weiss*
Foggy Mountain Troubadour: The Life and Music of Curly Seckler *Penny Parsons*
Blue Rhythm Fantasy: Big Band Jazz Arranging in the Swing Era *John Wriggle*
Bill Clifton: America's Bluegrass Ambassador to the World *Bill C. Malone*
Chinatown Opera Theater in North America *Nancy Yunhwa Rao*
The Elocutionists: Women, Music, and the Spoken Word *Marian Wilson Kimber*
May Irwin: Singing, Shouting, and the Shadow of Minstrelsy *Sharon Ammen*
Peggy Seeger: A Life of Music, Love, and Politics *Jean R. Freedman*
Charles Ives's *Concord*: Essays after a Sonata *Kyle Gann*
Don't Give Your Heart to a Rambler: My Life with Jimmy Martin, the King of Bluegrass *Barbara Martin Stephens*
Libby Larsen: Composing an American Life *Denise Von Glahn*
George Szell's Reign: Behind the Scenes with the Cleveland Orchestra
Marcia Hansen Kraus
Just One of the Boys: Female-to-Male Cross-Dressing on the American Variety Stage
Gillian M. Rodger
Spirituals and the Birth of a Black Entertainment Industry *Sandra Jean Graham*
Right to the Juke Joint: A Personal History of American Music *Patrick B. Mullen*
Bluegrass Generation: A Memoir *Neil V. Rosenberg*
Pioneers of the Blues Revival, Expanded Second Edition *Steve Cushing*
Banjo Roots and Branches *Edited by Robert Winans*
Bill Monroe: The Life and Music of the Blue Grass Man *Tom Ewing*
Dixie Dewdrop: The Uncle Dave Macon Story *Michael D. Doubler*
Los Romeros: Royal Family of the Spanish Guitar *Walter Aaron Clark*
Transforming Women's Education: Liberal Arts and Music in Female Seminaries
Jewel A. Smith
Rethinking American Music *Edited by Tara Browner and Thomas L. Riis*

Leonard Bernstein and the Language of Jazz *Katherine Baber*
Dancing Revolution: Bodies, Space, and Sound in American Cultural History *Christopher J. Smith*
Peggy Glanville-Hicks: Composer and Critic *Suzanne Robinson*
Mormons, Musical Theater, and Belonging in America *Jake Johnson*
Blues Legacy: Tradition and Innovation in Chicago *David Whiteis*
Blues Before Sunrise 2: Interviews from the Chicago Scene *Steve Cushing*
The Cashaway Psalmody: Transatlantic Religion and Music in Colonial Carolina *Stephen A. Marini*
Earl Scruggs and Foggy Mountain Breakdown: The Making of an American Classic *Thomas Goldsmith*
A Guru's Journey: Pandit Chitresh Das and Indian Classical Dance in Diaspora *Sarah Morelli*
Unsettled Scores: Politics, Hollywood, and the Film Music of Aaron Copland and Hanns Eisler *Sally Bick*
Hillbilly Maidens, Okies, and Cowgirls: Women's Country Music, 1930–1960 *Stephanie Vander Wel*
Always the Queen: The Denise LaSalle Story *Denise LaSalle with David Whiteis*
Artful Noise: Percussion Literature in the Twentieth Century *Thomas Siwe*
The Heart of a Woman: The Life and Music of Florence B. Price *Rae Linda Brown, edited by Guthrie P. Ramsey Jr.*
When Sunday Comes: Gospel Music in the Soul and Hip-Hop Eras *Claudrena N. Harold*
The Lady Swings: Memoirs of a Jazz Drummer *Dottie Dodgion and Wayne Enstice*
Industrial Strength Bluegrass: Southwestern Ohio's Musical Legacy *Edited by Fred Bartenstein and Curtis W. Ellison*
Soul on Soul: The Life and Music of Mary Lou Williams *Tammy L. Kernodle*
Unbinding Gentility: Women Making Music in the Nineteenth-Century South *Candace Bailey*
Punks in Peoria: Making a Scene in the American Heartland *Jonathan Wright and Dawson Barrett*
Homer Rodeheaver and the Rise of the Gospel Music Industry *Kevin Mungons and Douglas Yeo*
Americanaland: Where Country & Western Met Rock 'n' Roll *John Milward, with Portraits by Margie Greve*
Listening to Bob Dylan *Larry Starr*
Lying in the Middle: Musical Theater and Belief at the Heart of America *Jake Johnson*
The Sounds of Place: Music and the American Cultural Landscape *Denise Von Glahn*
Peace Be Still: How James Cleveland and the Angelic Choir Created a Gospel Classic *Robert M. Marovich*
Politics as Sound: The Washington, DC, Hardcore Scene, 1978–1983 *Shayna L. Maskell*

Tania León's Stride: A Polyrhythmic Life *Alejandro L. Madrid*
Elliott Carter Speaks: Unpublished Lectures *Edited by Laura Emmery*
Interviews with American Composers: Barney Childs in Conversation
Edited by Virginia Anderson
Queer Country *Shana Goldin-Perschbacher*
On the Bus with Bill Monroe: My Five-Year Ride with the Father of Blue Grass
Mark Hembree
Mandolin Man: The Bluegrass Life of Roland White *Bob Black*
Music and Mystique in Muscle Shoals *Christopher M. Reali*
Buddy Emmons: Steel Guitar Icon *Steve Fishell*
Music in Black American Life, 1600–1945: A University of Illinois Press Anthology
Compiled by Laurie Matheson
Music in Black American Life, 1945–2020: A University of Illinois Press Anthology
Compiled by Laurie Matheson
Ballad Hunting with Max Hunter: Stories of an Ozark Folksong Collector
Sarah Jane Nelson
Play Like a Man: My Life in Poster Children *Rose Marshack*
Samuel Barber: His Life and Legacy *Howard Pollack*
Aaron Copland in Latin America: Music and Cultural Politics *Carol A. Hess*
Stringbean: The Life and Murder of a Country Music Legend *Taylor Hagood*
Danzón Days: Age, Race, and Romance in Mexico *Hettie Malcomson*
Flaco's Legacy: The Globalization of Conjunto *Erin E. Bauer*
Circle of Winners: How the Guggenheim Foundation Composition Awards
Shaped American Music Culture *Denise Von Glahn*
The Propaganda of Freedom: JFK, Shostakovich, Stravinsky, and the Cultural
Cold War *Joseph Horowitz*
The Possibility Machine: Music and Myth in Las Vegas *Edited by Jake Johnson*

The University of Illinois Press
is a founding member of the
Association of University Presses.

University of Illinois Press
1325 South Oak Street
Champaign, IL 61820-6903
www.press.uillinois.edu